Japanese/Korean Linguistics
Volume 23

T0366964

Japanese/Korean Linguistics

Volume 23

edited by
**Michael Kenstowicz, Theodore Levin,
& Ryo Masuda**

*Published for the
Stanford Linguistics
Association by*

CSLI
PUBLICATIONS
Center for the Study of
Language and Information
Stanford, California

Copyright © 2016
CSLI Publications
Center for the Study of Language and Information
Leland Stanford Junior University
Printed in the United States
20 19 18 17 16   1 2 3 4 5

Library of Congress Cataloging-in-Publication Data

Conference on Japanese/Korean Linguistics (1st : 1989 :
University of Southern California)
    Japanese/Korean Linguistics / edited by Hajime Hoji.

    Volume 23 / edited by Michael Kenstowicz, Theodore Levin,
and Ryo Masuda

       p.   cm.

    Includes bibliographical references and index.
    ISBN-13: 978-1-57586-840-0
    ISBN-13: 978-1-57586-752-6 (pbk.)
  1. Japanese language—Congresses. 2. Korean
language—Congresses. 3. Japanese language—Grammar,
Comparative—Korean—Congresses. 4. Korean
language—Grammar, Comparative—Japanese—Congresses.
5. Linguistics—Congresses. I. Hoji, Hajime. II. Stanford Linguistics
Association. III. Center for the Study of Language and Information
(U.S.) IV. Title.
PL503.C6 1989
495.6–dc20   90-2550

CIP

∞ The acid-free paper used in this book meets the minimum requirements
of the American National Standard for Information Sciences—Permanence
of Paper for Printed Library Materials, ANSI Z39.48-1984.

CSLI was founded in 1983 by researchers from Stanford University, SRI
International, and Xerox PARC to further the research and development of
integrated theories of language, information, and computation. CSLI headquarters
and CSLI Publications are located on the campus of Stanford University.

CSLI Publications reports new developments in the study of language,
information, and computation. Please visit our web site at
http://cslipublications.stanford.edu/
for comments on this and other titles, as well as for changes
and corrections by the author and publisher.

Contents

III   Semantics   165

Acknowledgments

The 23rd Japanese/Korean Linguistics Conference was held October 11–13, 2013 at the Massachusetts Institute of Technology (MIT) in Cambridge, Mass. Nineteen papers and fifteen posters were selected by blind referee and we are pleased to have most of them appear in this proceedings volume. Submissions from the poster session appear in a supplementary online website, and their abstracts appear at the end of this physical volume. Additionally, invited talks were given by Yoonjung Kang (University of Toronto), Hideki Kishimoto (Kobe University), Junko Shimoyama (McGill University), and James Hye Suk Yoon (University of Illinois, Urbana-Champaign), all of whom also contributed a manuscript.

The editors of this volume are part of a larger Organizing Committee of the conference, which includes Prof. Shigeru Miyagawa and graduate students Michael Yoshitaka Erlewine, Michelle Fullwood, Isaac Gould, Yusuke Imanishi, Junya Nomura, Ayaka Sugawara, Wataru Uegaki, and Suyeon Yun. We thank Mary Grenham, administrative officer for the MIT Department of Linguistics and Philosophy, for ensuring that the conference ran smoothly.

The Japanese/Korean Linguistics conference continues to be supported by a large community of linguists who took time out from their busy schedules to review abstracts and offer useful feedback. We are very thankful for their assistance.

We are grateful for the financial support of the following groups at MIT: the Department of Linguistics and Philosophy, the Department of Foreign Languages and Literatures, and the School of Humanities, Arts and Social Sciences.

Finally, we appreciate the support by the editorial staff at CSLI who assisted in the production of this volume.

MICHAEL KENSTOWICZ
THEODORE LEVIN
RYO MASUDA
Massachusetts Institute of Technology

Part I

Phonology

A Corpus-Based Study of Positional Variation in Seoul Korean Vowels[1]

YOONJUNG KANG
University of Toronto Scarborough

[1]The research reported in the paper is part of a larger project on a corpus-based study of Korean phonetics and phonology funded by the SSHRC Partnership Development Grant (#890-2012-25). The author gratefully acknowledges the contribution of the collaborators, Tae-Jin Yoon and Sungwoo Han, and the partner institution, *the National Institute of the Korean Language*. The automatic alignment of the corpus was conducted by Tae-Jin Yoon and the *Praat* scripts used in the acoustic measurements were written by Tae-Jin Yoon and the author. The author thanks Matt Hunt Gardner for proofreading the paper as well as for helpful comments, and the research assistants, Yaruna Cooblal, Sohyun Hong, Roobika Karunananthan, Julianna So, Shawna-Kaye Tucker, and Cindy Yee, for conducting a manual check of the alignments in a subset of the corpus data. The paper benefited from valuable feedback from the Phonology-Phonetics Reading Group at the University of Toronto and the audience at *the 23rd Japanese Korean Linguistics Conference* at MIT, especially, Adam Albright, Elan Dresher, Edward Flemming, Chris Harvey, Michael Kenstowicz, Alexei Kochetov, Jen Smith, Donca Steriade, and Suyeon Yun.

Japanese/Korean Linguistics 23.
Edited by Michael Kenstowicz, Theodore Levin and Ryo Masuda.
Copyright © 2016, CSLI Publications

1   Introduction

It is a well-established observation that certain positions—stressed as opposed to unstressed syllables, initial as opposed to non-initial syllables,
roots as opposed to affixes, and onsets as opposed to codas—have a privileged status phonologically and the phonological patterns found in these
positions can differ from the patterns found in other positions (Beckman
1998, Steriade 2001, Crosswhite 2004, Smith 2002, Barnes 2006, Walker
2011, etc.). For vowels in particular, such privileged status is manifested in
the form of resistance to deletion or contrast neutralization, which affect
vowels in other positions, as well as a propensity to act as a trigger of harmony.

There are two general lines of explanation for such positional effects.
One line of explanation is that the special status is due to the phonetic properties of the position. For example, stressed vowels tend to allow contrasts
that are reduced or neutralized in unstressed vowels. This asymmetry can be
explained in large part by the longer duration of stressed vowels, which
allows more complete and unreduced realization of the underlying vowel
quality (Lindblom 1963, Lehiste 1970, Flemming 2004, 2005, Barnes 2006,
Giavazzi 2010). Another line of explanation attributes positional prominence to certain positions' psycholinguistic prominence. For example, it is
argued that word-initial segments or segments in a root resist phonological
contrast neutralization due to the importance of these positions in lexical
access and retrieval (Beckman 1998, Smith 2002).

While the phonetics of stress-conditioned asymmetry in vowel realization is relatively well understood, far less is known about the phonetics of
the word-initial syllable effect on vowel realization. We know that segments
in the initial position of various prosodic domains are subject to domain-
initial strengthening in terms of duration and articulatory strength (Fougeron 2001, Cho and Keating 2001), but these effects are mainly limited to
segments in absolute initial position, not to all segments in the initial syllable. Studies that specifically examine the phonetics of vowels in word-
initial syllables are very limited. Barnes (2006) found that in Turkish, vowels in initial syllables are longer than those in non-initial syllables, but the
effect size was small. Johnson and Martin (2003) found that in Creek, vowels in word-initial syllables are realized with a more peripheral quality than
vowels in final syllables; however, it is unclear whether this finding of
positional asymmetry can be attributed to a special property of word-initial
syllables or of word-final syllables.

Korean vowels exhibit a number of phonological properties of initial
syllable prominence, as will be illustrated in Section 2. The goal of the current paper is to provide a detailed case study of the word-initial syllable

effects on the phonetic realization of Korean vowels. Specifically, I will examine if the spectral realization of vowels in initial as opposed to non-initial syllables differs such that vowels in initial syllables are realized with more peripheral vowel quality and that these vowels exhibit clearer contrasts than those in non-initial position. I will also examine if spectral differences in vowel realization (if found) are byproducts of differences in duration between these positions—i.e. whether the longer duration of vowels in word-initial syllables results indirectly in their more peripheral realization—or whether spectral differences in vowel realization instead cannot be attributed to differences in vowel duration. The latter outcome would provide evidence that positional difference is due to an inherent difference in the phonetic target of the vowel quality, not to a physical restriction of articulation.

The paper is organized as follows. Section 2 presents phonological evidence of initial syllable prominence effects in Korean vowels. Section 3 introduces the corpus data for phonetic analysis and the analysis methods. Section 4 provides an overview of the vowel system and age-dependent variation uncovered in the data. Section 5 examines the effect of duration on vowel quality and Section 6 examines the positional effect on vowel quality. Section 7 concludes the paper.

2   Korean Vowels and Initial Syllable Prominence

Korean vowels exhibit a number of word initial syllable prominence effects. The first type of prominence effect is that contrast reduction, in certain synchronic alternations and diachronic sound changes, is blocked in word-initial position. The second type of prominence effect is that vowels in word-initial syllables are robust triggers of harmony while those in non-initial positions may be neutral with respect to vowel harmony. I review the relevant Korean facts below.

Vowel length is contrastive in Korean as illustrated by the minimal pairs listed in (1a), but this contrast is limited to word-initial syllables only because underlying long vowels shorten when they occur in non-initial syllables, as shown in (1b) (Han 1964, Sohn 1991).

(1)   a.   Vowel length contrast in word-initial syllables

/nun/	'eye'	/nu:n/	'snow'
/pɛ/	'pear'	/pɛ:/	'double'
/pɑm/	'night'	/pɑ:m/	'chestnut'
/il/	'one'	/i:l/	'work'
/tsʌk-ta/	'to write'	/tsʌ:k-ta/	'not plenty'

b. Vowel shortening in non-initial syllables
/**nu:n**-s'ʌlmɛ/ [nu:ns'ulmɛ] 'toboggan'
/tsʰʌs-**nu:n**/ [tsʰʌnnun] 'first snow'
/**so:k**-satsʌŋ/ [so:ks'ɑdzʌŋ] 'behind story'
/mɑim-**so:k**/ [mɑims'ok] 'one's mind'
/**pʌ:llita**/ [pʌ:llida] 'open, spread'
/t'ʌ-**pʌ:llita**/ [t'ʌbʌllida] 'brag'

The Middle Korean vowel /ɔ/ underwent a two-stage merger process whereby the merger in non-initial syllables preceded the merger in initial syllables. First, /ɔ/ merged with /i/ in non-initial syllables in the 15th-16th century, as illustrated in (2a), and then with /ɑ/ in initial syllable a few centuries later, as shown in (2b). The positional asymmetry is retained in the speech of older speakers of the Jeju dialect among whom /ɔ/ is retained in word-initial position, as shown in (2c). (Lee 1972, Lee and Ramsey 2011, Ko 2012).

(2) a. /ɔ/-/i/ merger: non-initial syllables (15th-16th century)
         /hanɔl/   > /hanil/   'sky'
         /nɑkɔnɑj/ > /nɑkine/ 'wanderer'
         /talɔ-/   > /tali-/   'different'
     b. /ɔ/-/ɑ/ merger: initial syllables (18th century)
         /pɔlɑm/   > /pɑlɑm/   'wind'
         /tɔl/   > /tɑl/   'moon'
         /hɔ-/   > /hɑ-/   'do'
     c. Older speakers of Jeju dialect: /ɔ/ retained in word-initial syllables
         /nɔmɔl/   > /nɔmʌl/   'vegetables'

In many dialects of Korean—the central, southern, and Jeju dialects specifically—the front mid vowel /e/ and the front low vowel /ɛ/ are undergoing a merger similar to the diachronic /ɔ/ merger. The merger in initial syllables lags behind the merger in non-initial syllables. As a result, some speakers and dialects show an intermediate pattern where the /e/-/ɛ/ merger is complete in non-initial syllables while the contrast is retained in initial syllables (Jung 2002, The Dialectology Society 2001).

The initial syllable also shows a privileged status in vowel harmony. In ideophone vowel harmony, 'dark' (D) vowels /e, ʌ, u/ and 'light' (L) vowels /ɛ, ɑ, o/ do not co-occur in a word, as shown in (3a). High vowels /i, i/ show dual patterns: when they occur in word-initial syllables they trigger dark vowel harmony, as shown in (3b); however, when they occur in non-initial position they are 'neutral' (N) and occur with both dark and light vowels, as shown in (3c) (Kim-Renaud 1976, Cho 1994, Larsen and Heinz 2012).

(3)   a. Ideophone vowel harmony
        /ʌluk tʌluk/ ~ /ɑlok tɑlok/
         D D D D   L L L L
    b. Dark /ɨ, i/ in initial position
        /k'ɨcʌk k'ɨcʌk/ ~ */k'ɨcɑk k'ɨcɑk/
         D D D D   D L   D L
        /k'icʌk k'icʌk/ ~ */k'icɑk k'icɑk/
         D D D D   D L   D L
    c. Neutral /ɨ, i/ in non-initial position
        /tɑlkɨlɑk/ ~ /tʌkɨkʌk/
         L **N** L   D **N** D
        /nɑmsil nɑmsil/ ~ /nʌmsil nʌmsil/
         L **N** L **N**   D **N** D **N**

Such positional asymmetry is also attested in verb suffix harmony. In Standard Korean, the last stem vowel determines the initial vowel of a group of vowel-initial suffixes. Dark stem vowels /i, ɨ, u, e, ɛ, ʌ/ take the [-ʌ] allomorph while light stem vowels /o, ɑ/ take the [-ɑ] allomorph, as shown in (4). There is a fair amount of variation, however, especially for /ɑ/ stems, such that /ɑ/ stems optionally take the disharmonic [-ʌ] allomorph (Kim-Renaud 1976, H. Kang 2012). On the other hand, /o/ stems tend to take the [-ɑ] allomorph more consistently. The only case where /o/ stems optionally allow a disharmonic [-ʌ] allomorph is when the /o/ occurs in the non-initial syllable of p-irregular verbs, as shown in (5b). In contrast, monosyllabic p-irregular verbs with stem vowel /o/ do not allow a disharmonic allomorph, as shown in (5a) (Kim 2000). In other words, /o/ in a word-initial syllable always triggers harmony while /o/ in a non-initial syllable may not.

(4)   a. Dark stem vowel: [-ʌ]
          /mʌk-ʌ/ 'eat'
           D D
    b. Light stem vowel /o/: [-ɑ]
          /cop-ɑ/ 'narrow'
           L L
    c. Light stem vowel /ɑ/: [-ɑ] ~ [-ʌ]
          /cɑp-ɑ/ ~ /cɑp-ʌ/ 'hold'
           L L   L D

(5)   a. Monosyllabic p-irregular /o/ stem: [-ɑ]

            /tow-ɑ/, */tow-ʌ/   'help'

            L L   L D

    b. Polysyllabic p-irregular /o/ stem: [-ɑ] ~ [-ʌ]

            /sɛlow-ɑ/ ~ /sɛlow-ʌ/ 'new'

              L L   L D

This section summarized the phonological evidence of a word-initial prominence for vowels in Korean. In the rest of the paper, I will examine if and how this positional effect is manifested in the phonetic realization of Korean vowels.

3   Data and Analysis

The data for this study come from *The Reading-Style Speech Corpus of Standard Korean* (The National Institute of the Korean Language 2005), which contains read speech of 60 male and 60 female speakers of Korean residing in the Seoul metropolitan area. The age of the speakers ranged from 19 to 71 at the time of recording in 2003. The distribution of the speakers by gender and year of birth is given in Table 1.

Table 1. Age and gender of speakers in the NIKL Corpus

	1930s	1940s	1950s	1960s	1970s	1980s	Total
Male	4	12	4	8	27	5	60
Female	2	10	25	3	11	9	60

The speech material consists of well-known short stories and essays. Table 2 provides the number of instances of each vowel in the portion of the text material that was read by all of the speakers in the NIKL corpus.

Table 2. Vowel distribution in the read text analyzed for the current study in the NIKL Corpus

a (ㅏ)	ɛ (ㅐ)	e (ㅔ)	ʌ (ㅓ)	ɨ (ㅡ)	i (ㅣ)	o (ㅗ)	u (ㅜ)	Total
2540	421	427	1224	1555	1683	1165	724	9739

The counts in Table 2 represent the number of vowel tokens produced by a single speaker, thus the grand total of vowel tokens for all speakers is well over 1 million. The acoustic analysis of these vowel tokens was aided by the forced alignment system for Korean developed by Tae-Jin Yoon (Yoon and Kang 2012, Yoon, this volume). The automatic aligner takes a sound file and its Korean transcription as input and automatically segments the sound file into component words and phones. The formant measurements (F1 and F2) were extracted using a Linear Predictive Coding (PLC) method, as implemented in *Praat*'s 'To Formant (burg)' function. To minimize the influence of local formant tracking errors, the average of the measurements from the mid 20% of the vowel duration was used. To improve the accuracy of the formant measurements, the formants for each vowel token were measured with twenty-six different formant ceiling settings, varying from 4,000 Hz to 6,500 Hz by 100 Hz increments. For each vowel type for each speaker, the formant ceiling that yielded the minimum variance in formant values was chosen as optimal (Escudero et al. 2009).[2]

In order to compare formant values across speakers, the format values were normalized using the Labov method (Labov et al., 2006) as implemented in the *vowels* package (Kendall and Thomas 2012) for *R* (R Development Core Team 2011). The Labov method recalibrates formant values based on the by-speaker grand mean of F1 and F2. All formant values in the following discussion refer to values as normalized by the Labov method.

For each vowel token, in addition to F1 and F2 values, duration (ms) and f0 (Hz) at the vowel midpoint were also measured. Tokens where f0 could not be detected were discarded as many of them were either completely devoiced or involved errors in the automatic alignment. The automatic aligner analyzes the input in 10 ms frames and assigns each frame a segment label; therefore, the resolution for duration measurements is 10 ms. In the analyses provided below, only vowels with a duration of less than 200 ms were included. Extreme values are often due to alignment errors or are mostly limited to utterance or phrase final position.

Contextual information, including position within a word (initial, medial, or final), preceding and following segments, and position within a phrase (see Yoon this volume for related discussion) was also recorded for each vowel token. Each vowel token was also coded for its morphological category (root or affix), and underlying vowel length (based on *the Great Standard Korean dictionary*)[3]. Because long vowels only occur in word-initial syllables, and to avoid confounding a vowel-length effect and a positional effect, only phonologically short vowels were included in the analysis. Also, as Korean is a predominantly suffixing language, to avoid the confounding of a morphological effect (root vs. affix) and a positional effect, only roots were included in the analysis.

---

[2]Variance was calculated using the following formula: variance(20*log(F1)) + variance(20*log(F2)). See Kang (2013) for more details on the formant measurement method.
[3] Available online at http://korean.go.kr/.

4   Age and Gender-Based Variation

This section provides an overview of the Korean short vowel system based on the analysis of NIKL corpus data. The graphs in Figure 1 show the by-speaker mean formant values for each vowel for female speakers (left panel) and for male speakers (right panel). The phonetic symbols in the graphs represent the grand mean for that vowel for the respective gender group. It is notable that the two non-high front vowels, /e/ and /ɛ/, are practically identical. When the data are partitioned by age and gender, the contrast appears to be marginally retained by older male speakers (born before 1962, the mean year of birth of all speakers). Figure 2 summarizes the mean F1 values of the two vowels as produced by older male speakers in word-initial, word-medial, and word-final syllables. This group retains the /e/-/ɛ/ contrast in word-initial position only and merges the two vowels in non-initial position as noted in previous studies (Jung 2002) and discussed above.

**Figure 1. By-speaker mean formant values
(Hz, normalized)**

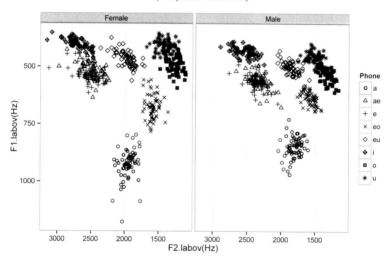

Figure 2. Positional neutralization of the /e/-/ɛ/ contrast in older male speakers

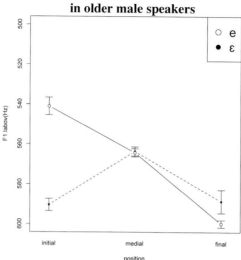

A number of age-dependent trends were also observed. Figure 3 shows four plots of by-speaker mean formant values by speaker year of birth. The four vowels, /i, u, ɛ, o/ in Figure 3 all showed a significant age effect. Separate trend lines are provided for male and female speakers. Solid trend lines indicate a statistically significant correlation between the particular formant measurement (on the y-axis) and year of birth (on the x-axis). For the purpose of this study, these age-dependent trends will be interpreted as indications of sound changes in progress (cf. Bailey et al. 1991). For dashed lines, there is a not a significant correlation between the relevant formant measurement and speaker year of birth.

Figure 3. Age-dependent trends in vowel realization

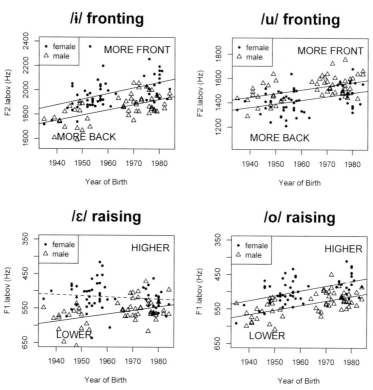

The bottom left panel of Figure 3 ('/ɛ/ raising') shows that for male speakers there is a significant age-dependent trend of F1 lowering (equivalent to tongue body raising), with younger men producing /ɛ/ higher than older men. This is another illustration of the /e/-/ɛ/ merger discussed above. For female speakers, on the other hand, there is not a significant correlation between /ɛ/ height and age. Also, females' /ɛ/ pronunciations are generally higher than the males. This suggests that the merger of /ɛ/ and /e/ is complete among women but that this change is still making its way through the male speakers and is nearing its completion.

The top two graphs in Figure 3 show that the high vowels /i/ and /u/ are realized with a higher F2 (equivalent to a more front vowel quality) among younger speakers, while the bottom right panel shows that among younger speakers the back round vowel /o/ is realized with a more raised vowel quality. When these trends are taken together, the three vowels /i, u, o/ seem to be involved in a chain shift-like change. Figure 4 schematically summarizes the changes that the Seoul Korean vowel system appears to be undergoing, based on the NIKL data.

Figure 4. Seoul Korean Vowel Shift

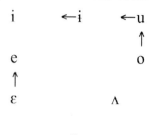

5   Duration and Vowel Quality

This section presents an examination of the effect of vowel duration on vowel quality. Figure 5 plots the mean F1 values of vowels by their duration (ms). The general trend is that at shorter durations F1 values are lower, indicating that vowels are raised. This trend is most pronounced for the low vowel /ɑ/, but also noticeable for the mid vowels /e, ɛ, o, ʌ/. For the high vowels /i, u/, the F1 values remain stable across different durations. The high vowel /ɨ/, which is a phonologically high vowel but is realized with an F1 value similar to that of mid vowels /o, ɛ, e/, shows a raising trend similar to mid vowels, particularly at durations below 100 ms, where over 95 percent of the /ɨ/ tokens are found. In other words, the pattern of reduction seems to depend on phonetic height, not phonological height. At shorter durations, the vertical vowel space (high-low) is compressed, but this is due to the raising of low and mid vowels and not due to the lowering of high vowels. This pattern of vertical contraction of vowel space is also consistent with the duration-conditioned reduction effect found in unstressed vowels (Flemming 2004, 2005).

Figure 6 shows mean F2 values of vowels by their duration (ms). The general trend is that at shorter durations, the vowel space is contracted along the horizontal (front-back) dimension. Front vowels are less front and back vowels are less back at shorter durations, as indicated by their F2 values. Conversely, central vowels show little difference in mean F2 values between shorter and longer durations.

Figure 5. Duration (ms) and F1 (Hz, normalized)

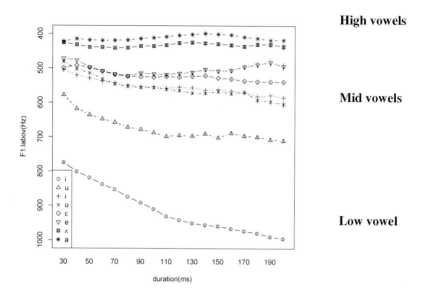

High vowels

Mid vowels

Low vowel

Figure 6. Duration (ms) and F2 (Hz, normalized)

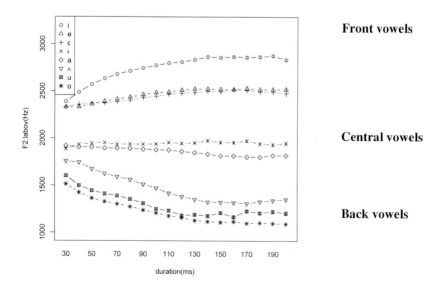

Front vowels

Central vowels

Back vowels

To summarize, there is an observably strong correlation between phonetic duration and vowel realization in Korean. When vowels are shorter, they tend to be raised and also centralized.

6   Position and Vowel Quality

This section examines how position within a word affects the realization of vowels. Figures 7 and 8 summarize the mean F1 and F2 values of each vowel by vowel duration and by position within a word. The crucial observation in the graphs presented in Figures 7 and 8 is how vowel realization differs depending on whether the vowel occurs in a word-initial (filled circle), word-medial (blank circle), or word-final syllable (square). The vowels in monosyllabic words were excluded as it is ambiguous whether their characteristics are due to their word-initial or word-final position. Similarly, vowels in word-initial syllables that are also IP (Intonational Phrase)-initial were also excluded. IP-initial syllables occur at the beginning of an utterance or are preceded by a silent pause; this position itself may influence vowel quality. Once monosyllabic and IP-initial vowel tokens have been excluded, what remains are non-initial (medial or final) vowel tokens and word-initial vowels tokens whose quality is, in theory, not affected by other positional effects. When duration is controlled, any difference observed between these remaining word-initial and non-initial vowel tokens should be the result of differences in positional prominence.

Figure 7 shows that the F1 values for high vowels /i, ɨ, u/ are lower in word-initial syllables compared to word-medial or final syllables, indicating that high vowels are produced with a higher tongue body position in word-initial syllables. This contrast is most noticeable in durations below 100 ms because high vowels tend to be shorter and the data above 100 ms are sparse.

The low vowel /ɑ/, on the other hand, exhibits higher F1 values in word-initial syllables, indicating a lower tongue body in this position compared to when in non-initial syllables. In other words, the vertical vowel space is more compressed in non-initial syllables compared to initial syllables and this compression is achieved by the lowering of high vowels and the raising of low vowels.

The mid vowels show a split pattern; the front mid vowels /e, ɛ/ do not show any clear position effect while the back mid vowel /o/ patterns like a high vowel—F1 values for /o/ are lower in initial position, indicating a higher tongue body position. This difference in mid-vowel patterning could be explained by the /o/ vowel's raising as part of a change in progress (see Figure 3) that leads in initial syllable position. Another way to interpret the result is that the underlying phoneme /o/ is raising diachronically and initial syllables more faithfully realize underlying targets phonetically compared to non-initial syllables. The mid back non-round vowel /ʌ/ patterns similarly to /ɑ/ and is produced with higher F1 values in initial versus medial syllables.

Figure 7. Position in word and F1 (Hz, normalized)

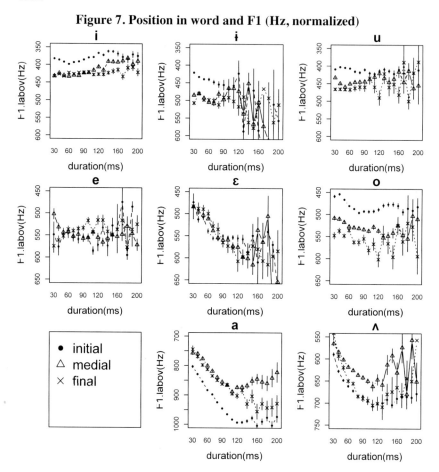

The positional effects on F2 realization of vowels are summarized in Figure 8. Overall, vowels in initial syllables have more peripheral realizations than in non-initial syllables—i.e., front vowels are more front and back vowels are more back in initial syllables than in non-initial syllables—but the positional effect on F2 is less consistent than the effect on F1. The front vowels /i, e, ɛ/ generally show a more front realization in word-initial syllables but the effect is not consistent. The back vowels /o, ʌ/ show a more back realization in word-initial syllables than in non-initial syllables. The back high vowel /u/, on the other hand, shows a more front realization in initial syllables, especially at shorter durations. This somewhat unexpected pattern for /u/ may be related to the fact the /u/ is fronting as part of a chain shift change in progress, as mentioned in Section 5. The central vowels /a, ɨ/ show a fronting tendency in word-initial syllables. Low vowel /ɑ/ is more front in initial syllables but the effect size is small. The high central vowel /ɨ/ shows a more front realization in initial compared to non-initial syllables and this may also be related to the fact that /ɨ/ is fronting as part of a change in progress.

Figure 8. Position in word and F2 (Hz, normalized)

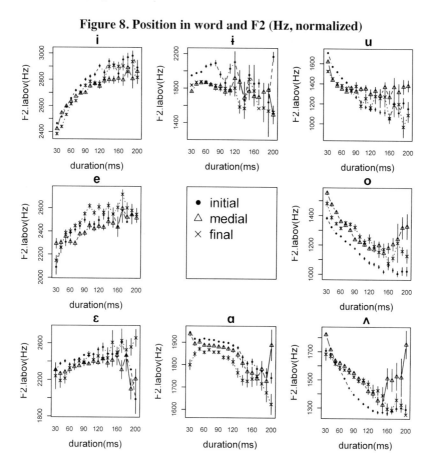

To summarize, the vowel space is more expanded and the vowel targets are more peripheral in word-initial syllables than in non-initial syllables, both along the vertical (F1) and the horizontal (F2) dimensions. This positional effect is not an epiphenomenon of a durational difference, as this contrast holds even when tokens of identical duration are compared. Also, this positional effect cannot be attributed to a morphological effect (i.e. root

versus suffix asymmetry) because the data included in this analysis consisted of only root vowels.

Position-conditioned variation is similar to the duration-conditioned variation discussed in Section 5 in that in the stronger context (initial syllables
or longer durations), the vowel space is expanded and the contrasts amongst
the vowels are more distinctive than in the weaker context (non-initial syllables or shorter durations). At the same time, the position effect and the
duration effect differ in crucial ways. First of all, the vertical space reduction in weaker position is achieved by both high vowel lowering and low
vowel raising in non-initial syllables, while the duration-conditioned reduction is due to raising of non-high vowels and does not involve lowering of
high vowels. This difference in reduction patterns is schematically summarized in Figure 9. The larger triangles represent the vowel space in the
stronger contexts (initial syllables or longer durations) and the smaller triangles represent the vowel space in the weaker contexts (non-initial syllables or shorter durations).

**Figure 9. Schematic representation of duration- and position-based
vowel space reduction**

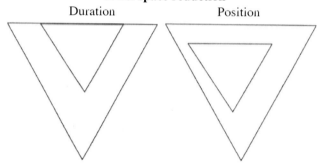

Another difference between duration-based and position-based vowel
variation is that position-based variation interacts with a chain shift change
in progress such that word-initial syllables tend to show the vowel quality
that is more advanced in the direction of the sound change than non-initial
syllable; /i/ and /u/, which are fronting diachronically, are realized as more
front in word-initial syllables than in non-initial syllables, while /o/, which
is raising diachronically, is realized as more raised in word-initial syllables
than in non-initial syllables.

This difference can be interpreted as an indication of the different
mechanisms underlying the variation. While the duration-based reduction is
due to articulatory undershoot of the vowel target, the position-based reduction is speaker-controlled. In word-initial syllables, the vowel targets are
more peripheral overall and also interact with the direction of sound change.

7 Discussion

This paper examined the positional effect on vowel realization in Korean. It demonstrated that vowels in word-initial syllables show a privileged phonological patterning—they tend to resist neutralization and they are more robust triggers of harmony compared with vowels in non-initial syllables. This special status in phonological patterning is also mirrored in their phonetic realization—vowels tend to have a more peripheral target in word-initial compared to non-initial syllables, and in the case of those vowels involved in a chain shift-like sound change, the vowel targets for word-initial syllables are more advanced in the direction of change compared to the targets for non-initial syllables.

These findings are consistent with a number of different views of the relationship between phonetics and phonology in regards to initial syllable prominence. One of these views is that these types of phonological patterns arose from diachronic phonologicalization of phonetic tendencies (Barnes 2002). An alternative view is that these phonological patterns directly refer to phonetic tendencies in synchronic grammar in the form of phonetically grounded grammatical constraints (Hayes et al. 2004). A third view is that these phonological and phonetic patterns are both expressions of the psycholinguistic prominence of word-initial syllable position, and that the phonetic and the phonological patterns need not be directly related to one another (Smith 2002).

What the findings show is that, at least in Korean, there is a substantial word-initial syllable effect on the phonetic realization of vowels that cannot be explained by morphological effects or durational effects; after controlling for morphological condition and duration, the position effects are clearly observable and the pattern of position-conditioned vowel variation differs from that of duration-conditioned vowel variation.

The current study has a number of limitations. A number of contextual factors that are known to affect realization of vowels—e.g. the features of the preceding and following consonants and vowels—were not taken into account. A statistical model that includes these contextual factors is expected to account for more of the variance currently unaccounted for and also to test some alternative explanations for the observed pattern. For example, word-initial syllables are inherently different from word-medial syllables in that the vowels in word-initial syllables are subject to co-articulatory influence of only one adjacent vowel, i.e. the vowel of the second syllable, while the vowels in word-medial position are affected by vowels on both sides. A future study will examine if the peripherality of vowel targets in word-initial syllables persists even when the co-articulatory effects are factored out.

Also, a more careful examination of the word position effect in relation to phrasal position may prove insightful. In the current study, in order to examine the possibility of a word-initial syllable position effect on its own, tokens of vowels in IP-initial syllables were excluded. However, the word-initial syllable effect may have arisen from the overgeneralization of a phrase-initial (Intonational Phrase or Accentual Phrase) position effect. Yoon (this volume) shows that vowels in phrase-initial syllables are subject to more substantial lengthening than vowels in word-initial, phrase-medial syllables; therefore, it is plausible that the longer duration of vowels in phrase-initial syllables could have given rise to more peripheral vowel quality realizations as part of the general durational effects on vowel articulation. As IP-initial syllables are always word-initial, learners may attribute the peripheral vowel quality of IP-initial or AP-initial syllables to a property of word-initial syllables in general, which subsequently results in the pattern observed in the above data. Martin (2011) and Myers and Padgett (2014) present evidence for such transfers or 'leaks' of generalization across different prosodic domains. This alternative explanation of the word position effect entails that word position effect is actually an indirect consequence of a duration effect.

The current study and its future developments aim to contribute to our understanding of word position effects in phonology by examining their phonetic underpinnings using Korean vowels as a case study. The tentative finding is that vowels in word-initial syllables do differ in their spectral realization compared to vowels in non-initial syllables, and that the difference cannot be ascribed to articulatory undershoot due to shorter durations or as resulting from differences in morphological status. A more complete model of vowel realization that takes into account the co-articulatory influence of surrounding consonants and vowels as well as phrasal position will help to determine whether the apparent word position effect can be attributed to more general articulatory constraints or if the position effect is instead speaker-controlled and requires distinct underlying vowel targets, resulting in variations that are not attributable to articulatory restrictions of surface phonetic realizations.

References

Bailey, Guy, Tom Wikle, Jan Tillery & Lori Sand (1991). The apparent time construct. *Language Variation and Change, 3*, 241–264.

Barnes, J. 2006. *Strength and Weakness at the Interface: Positional Neutralization in Phonetics and Phonology.* Berlin: Mouton de Gruyter.

Beckman, J. N. 1998. *Positional Faithfulness.* Doctoral dissertation, University of Massachusetts, Amherst.

Cho, M. H. 1994. *Vowel Harmony in Korean: a Grounded Phonology Approach.* Doctoral dissertation, Indiana University.

Cho, T. and P. Keating. 2001. Articulatory and Acoustic Studies of Domain-Initial Strengthening in Korean. *Journal of Phonetics* 29:155-90.

Crosswhite, K. 2004. Vowel Reduction. *Phonetically-Based Phonology*, eds. B. Hayes et al., 313-45. Cambridge: Cambridge University Press.

Escudero, P., P. Boersma, A. S. Rauber, and R. A. H. Bion. 2009. A Cross-Dialect Acoustic Description of Vowels: Brazilian and European Portuguese. *Journal of the Acoustical Society of America* 126: 1379-93.

Flemming, E. 2004. Contrast and Perceptual Distinctiveness. *Phonetically-Based Phonology.* eds. B. Hayes, R. Kirchner, and D. Steriade, 232-76. Cambridge: Cambridge University Press.

Flemming, E. 2005. A Phonetically-Based Model of Phonological Vowel Reduction. Ms, MIT.

Fougeron, C. 2001. Articulatory Properties of Initial Segments in Several Prosodic Constituents in French. *Journal of Phonetics* 29:109-36.

Giavazzi, M. 2010. *The Phonetics of Metrical Prominence and its Consequences for Segmental Phonology.* Doctoral dissertation, MIT.

Han, M. S. 1964. *Studies in the Phonology of Asian Languages II: Duration of Korean vowels.* University of Southern California, Los Angeles: Acoustic Phonetics Research Laboratory.

Hayes, B., R. Kirchner, and D. Steriade. 2004. *Phonetically-Based Phonology.* Cambridge: Cambridge University Press.

Hong, Y. 1991. *A Sociolinguistic Study of Seoul Korean: with a Special Section on Language Divergence between North and South Korea.* Seoul: The Research Center for Peace and Unification of Korea.

Johnson, K. and J. B. Martin. 2001. Acoustic Vowel Reduction in Creek: Effects of Distinctive Length and Position in the Word. *Phonetica* 58:81-102.

Jung, M. S. 2002. Sound change of language used in broadcasting [방송 언어에 나타난 말소리의 사적 변천]. *Kwukehak* [국어학] 39:221–49.

Kang, H. 2012. *Diachrony in Synchrony: Korean Vowel Harmony in Verbal Conjugation.* Doctoral dissertation, Stony Brook University.

Kang, Y. 2013. A Progress Report on the Vowel Analysis of the *Reading Style Speech Corpus of Seoul Korean* [서울말 낭독체 발화 말뭉치의 모음자료 연구 경과 보고]. *Presentation at the Workshop on Dialects of Korean.* The National Institute of the Korean Language.

Kendall, T. and E. R. Thomas. 2012. *Vowels* package.

Kim, J. K. 2000. Quantity Sensitivity and Feature Sensitivity of Vowels: a Constraint-Based Approach to Korean Vowel Phonology. Doctoral dissertation, Indiana University.

Kim-Renaud, Y.-K. 1976. Semantic Features in Phonology: Evidence from Vowel Harmony in Korean. *CLS* 12:397–412.

Ko, S. 2012. Tongue Root Harmony and Vowel Contrast in Northeast Asian Languages. Doctoral dissertation, Cornell University.

Labov, W., S. Ash, and C. Boberg. 2006. *The Atlas of North American English: Phonology, Phonetics, and Sound Change. A Multimedia Reference Tool.* Berlin: Mouton de Gruyter.

Larsen, D. and J. Heinz. 2012. Neutral Vowels in Sound Symbolic Vowel Harmony in Korean. *Phonology* 29:434-64.

Lee, K.-M. 1972. *A Study of the History of Korean Phonemes* [국어 음운사 연구]. Seoul: Hankwuk Mwunhwa Yenkwuso.

Lee, K.-M. and S. R. Ramsey. 2011. *A History of the Korean Language.* Cambridge: Cambridge University Press.

Lehiste, I. 1970. *Suprasegmentals.* Cambridge, MA: MIT Press.

Lindblom, B. 1963. Spectrographic Study of Vowel Reduction. *Journal of Acoustical Society of America* 35:1773-81.

Martin, A. 2011. Grammars Leak: Modeling how Phonotactic Generalizations Interact within the Grammar. *Language* 87:751-70.

Myers, S. and J. Padgett. 2014. Domain Generalization in Artificial Language Learning. Ms., UT Austin and UC Santa Cruz.

R Development Core Team. 2011. *R: A Language and Environment for Statistical Computing.* Vienna, Austria: R Foundation for Statistical Computing. < http://www.r-project.org/>

Smith, L. J. 2002. *Phonological Augmentation in Prominent Positions.* PhD dissertation, University of Massachusetts, Amherst.

Sohn, H.-N. 1991. *The Korean Language.* Cambridge: Cambridge University Press.

Steriade, D. 2001. Directional Asymmetries in Place Assimilation: a Perceptual Account. *The Role of Speech Perception in Phonology.* eds. E. Hume and K. Johnson, 219–50. San Diego: Academic Press.

The Dialectology Society [방언 연구회]. 2001. *The Dialect Dictionary* [방언학 사전]. Seoul: Thayhaksa.

The National Institute of the Korean Language. (2005). *A Speech Corpus of Reading-Style Standard Korean* [DVDs]. Seoul, Korea: The National Institute of the Korean Language.

Walker, R. 2011. *Vowel Patterns in Language.* Cambridge: Cambridge University Press.

Yoon, T.-J. this volume. A Corpus-based Study on the Layered Duration in Standard Korean.

Yoon, T.-J. and Y. Kang 2012. A Forced-Alignment-Based Study of Declarative Sentence-Ending 'da' in Korean. *The Proceedings of 2012 Speech Prosody.*

Wh Prosody is Not Focus Prosody in Fukuoka Japanese

JENNIFER L. SMITH
University of North Carolina, Chapel Hill

1 Introduction

One fundamental question concerning the syntax-phonology interface is the extent to which syntactic information is available to the phonology. Influential in this discussion has been the special intonational contour that occurs in Tokyo Japanese *wh* questions. This paper presents quantitative evidence from the Fukuoka dialect of Japanese that demonstrates, more strongly than the Tokyo pattern does, that the phonology of pitch accent and prosodic phrasing is sensitive to *wh* constructions.

In a *wh* construction in Tokyo Japanese, the *wh* element has a particularly high pitch, and the domain following the *wh* element has a reduced pitch range with low overall pitch. Crucially, this special prosody at least tends to correlate with the scope of the *wh* element (Deguchi & Kitagawa 2002; Ishihara 2002; but see also Hirotani 2012).

Japanese/Korean Linguistics 23.
Edited by Michael Kenstowicz, Theodore Levin and Ryo Masuda.
Copyright © 2016, CSLI Publications

The Tokyo pattern does not, however, prove conclusively that the phonological grammar is directly sensitive to syntactic [+wh] features. Phonologically, Tokyo *wh* prosody is argued to be an instance of focus prosody (Deguchi & Kitagawa 2002; Ishihara 2002; though see Hwang 2011 for evidence that there may be more to Tokyo *wh* prosody than focus alone). The phonological grammar is known to have access to focus features cross-linguistically (Jackendoff 1972; Truckenbrodt 1995; Selkirk 2002), so if Tokyo Japanese *wh* prosody is subsumed by focus prosody, then it does not present novel implications for the syntax-prosody interface.

According to descriptions by Kubo (1989, 2005, 2010), Fukuoka Japanese, like Tokyo, has special *wh* prosody that tends to correlate with *wh* scope. Crucially, however, the surface realization is different. Fukuoka *wh* prosody involves the deletion of all pitch accents from the *wh* element to the end of the *wh* scope domain, creating a large, unaccented phrase, which surfaces with a high flat tone (for quantitative evidence supporting this description, see Igarashi 2007; Smith 2013). Moreover, Igarashi (2007) and Kubo (2010) present initial evidence that this high flat contour is *not* characteristic of Fukuoka focus prosody. If this is indeed the case, then some mechanism distinct from focus prosody is needed to account for Fukuoka *wh* prosody.

This paper makes two contributions. First, it provides a systematic empirical investigation of Fukuoka focus and *wh* prosody and confirms that the two are distinct. Second, it implements a simplified methodology for diagnosing and comparing pitch accent that does not require accent location to be specified in advance; this methodology has potential applications for further research on pitch accent and intonation across varieties of Japanese.

2 Fukuoka Japanese Pitch Accent and Intonation

Many Japanese dialects have lexical pitch accents; a word can be accented (realized with an abrupt fall in pitch) or unaccented, as exemplified in (1).

In Tokyo Japanese (Pierrehumbert & Beckman 1988; Venditti 2005), a pitch accent is represented as a /H*+L/ tone melody. An unaccented word has a high, gradually decreasing pitch, as in (1)(b), because of a phrasal H tone. The 'initial lowering' seen in (1)(a–b) is due to a L boundary tone.

(1) Tokyo examples

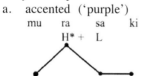
a. accented ('purple')
mu   ra   sa   ki
H* +   L

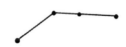
b. unaccented ('pink/peach color')
mo   mo   i   ro

Fukuoka Japanese is much like Tokyo in having a contrast between accented and unaccented words, a /H*+L/ pitch accent, a H phrase tone, and initial lowering (Kubo 1989, 2005). The accentedness or accent location of a particular lexical item may differ between the two, as in Tokyo [tábeta] vs. Fukuoka [tabéta] 'ate'. Another difference is that verbs and adjectives receive a default accent in Fukuoka, but may be unaccented in Tokyo.

Where Fukuoka prosody differs markedly from Tokyo is in the prosody of *wh* constructions, which undergo a process of accent deletion, resulting in a high flat contour resembling that in (1)(b) (Kubo 1989, 2005; Igarashi 2007; Smith 2013). The *wh* word itself surfaces as unaccented, and all material from the *wh* word to the end of its semantic/syntactic scope likewise surfaces as unaccented (except that one default accent is inserted at the end of the *wh* scope domain in the case of an embedded question).

The empirical goal of this paper is to determine whether *wh* prosody is an instance of focus prosody in Fukuoka as it is in Tokyo. In particular, does Fukuoka focus prosody cause accent deletion? The next section presents the methodology by which focus prosody and *wh* prosody are to be compared.

3   A Quantitative Diagnostic for Accentedness

Since accent in Japanese is realized as a pitch fall, a quantitative investigation of accent must compare changes in pitch. The measure of pitch change implemented here is a value to be called the *min/max f0 ratio*.[1] This value is determined as follows for each target noun. First, the maximum pitch in the noun, or *max f0*, is measured. Next, the minimum pitch from the max f0 to the end of the noun (plus case particle) is measured; this is the *min f0* value. From these two values, the min/max f0 ratio is calculated.

If a noun is unaccented, it has no abrupt pitch drop, though there may be gradual declination (Ladd 1984); the min and max f0 values are similar, so the min/max f0 ratio is close to 1.0. But if a noun is accented, then it does have a large pitch drop. In this case, the min f0 value is considerably lower than the max f0 value, so the min/max f0 ratio is less than 1.0.

For a noun in a neutral context, where neither a *wh* element nor a focused element precedes, lexical accent status should surface unchanged; accented nouns should have a low min/max f0 ratio, and unaccented nouns should have a min/max f0 ratio near 1.0. In the post-*wh* context, we expect accent deletion (Kubo 1989; Igarashi 2007; Smith 2013), so both (lexically)

---

[1]A ratio is used, rather than a difference, for purposes of normalization. Different speakers have different pitch ranges, so a 20 Hz change might be relatively large or small depending on the speaker, but a min/max f0 ratio of 0.8 gives an indication of the magnitude of the pitch change regardless of the level of the starting pitch.

accented and unaccented nouns should have similar max/min f0 ratios, near 1.0. The question of interest here is: Does the post-focus context show the same pattern as the post-*wh* context, or are the two distinct?

4 Experiment: Design and Procedure

4.1 Materials

Matched sets of sentences were constructed in order to place target nouns (nouns for which the min/max f0 ratio would be measured) in three contexts: *neutral* (2)(a), following neither a *wh* item nor a focus item, to serve as a baseline; *post-wh* (2)(b), following a *wh* item, where accent deletion is expected (Kubo 1989, 2005); and *post-focus* (2)(c), the context of interest.

(2) Representative utterances in three contexts; target nouns in **bold**

   a. | Yoneyama-ga | doyoobi **aniyome-o** yonda tte siran'yatta.
      | Yoneyama-NOM | Sat. s.in.law-ACC called C didn't.know
      '(I) didn't know Yoneyama called (my) sister-in-law on Saturday.'

   b. | dare-ga | doyoobi **aniyome-o** yonda ka siran'yatta.
      | who-NOM | Sat. s.in.law-ACC called C didn't.know
      '(I) didn't know who called (my) sister-in-law on Saturday.'

   c. | YONEYAMA-GA | doyoobi **aniyome-o** yonda tte siran'yatta.
      | Yoneyama-NOM | Sat. s.in.law-ACC called C didn't.know
      '(I) didn't know YONEYAMA called (my) sis.-in-law on Saturday.'

Each target noun consists of four light syllables and is followed by a case particle, either *-o* ACCUSATIVE or *-ni* DATIVE/LOCATIVE. Nouns were chosen with the intention that half would be accented and half would be unaccented. This was generally the case, but there were a small number of differences in lexical accentedness for certain speakers; see (3) below.

4.2 Participants

The utterances examined in this study were produced by seven female speakers of Fukuoka Japanese (the seven speakers who produced Fukuoka prosody in at least 50% of the *wh* utterances analyzed in Smith 2013).

participant	age	place of origin	participant	age	place of origin
s05	20	Fukuoka city	s10	21	Fukutsu city
s07	20	Fukuoka city	s11	21	Hisayama town
s08	21	Oogori city	s12	22	Fukuoka city
s09	20	Oogori city			

Table 1: Participant information

4.3 Elicitation Procedure

Sentences were elicited via written prompts. Each sentence was presented with a written scenario designed to create a discourse context with the desired information-structure properties; speakers were asked to produce each target sentence as they would utter it if they were a participant in the scenario described. Focus was elicited using scenarios in which the speaker was correcting someone's mistaken assumption. Each participant produced each sentence twice; when possible, if a speech error occurred, an additional repetition was solicited. Participants were recorded at Kyushu University, Fukuoka, in a sound-attenuated room, with a Marantz PMD-660 digital recorder (44.1 kHz) and a Radio Shack 33-3012 head-mounted microphone.

5   Results

5.1 Neutral Context and Accent Classification of Target Nouns

Analysis of the neutral-context items, in which target nouns were produced in neither a post-*wh* nor a post-focus context, confirms that the min/max f0 ratio measure successfully distinguishes accented from unaccented nouns.

Each repetition of each target noun was analyzed for min/max f0 ratio, max f0, and accentedness. The min/max f0 ratio and max f0 value were determined as described above. As for accentedness, the eight target nouns were selected in consultation with a native speaker such that four would be accented and four unaccented. However, participants actually varied a little with respect to the accentedness of the target nouns. Therefore, accentedness was reexamined post hoc separately for each speaker, as follows.

(3) Accentedness for each noun, by speaker (● accented, ○ unaccented)

		intended	s08	s10	s12	s05	s11	s07	s09
onigiri	'rice ball'	●	●	●	●	●	●	●	●
amaguri	'chestnut'	●	●	●	●	●	●	●	●
aomusi	'caterpillar'	●	●	●	●	●	●	●	○
aniyome	'sister-in-law'	●	●	●	●	●	●	○	○
mararia	'malaria'	○	○	○	○	●	○	○	○
yamamori	'full plate'	○	○	○	○	○	●	○	○
yamaimo	'yam'	○	○	○	○	○	○	○	○
muraoka	(name)	○	○	○	○	○	○	○	○

Since each noun appeared in two sentences, and each sentence had two repetitions, there were four min/max f0 ratio values for every target noun. If three or four of the four productions of any noun fell within the range of values corresponding to the other accent class for that speaker, then the noun was reclassified into the other accent class for that speaker. The results are shown in (3). (See min/max f0 ratio plots by noun for each speaker at <www.unc.edu/~jlsmith/home/pdf/smith2013_jk23-handout_long.pdf>.)

The data for each speaker are plotted in (4) and (5). Each point is one repetition of one target noun. Nouns are classified as accented (●) or unaccented (○) for each speaker as in (3). The horizontal axis shows the max f0 value, with higher values to the right. The vertical axis shows the min/max f0 ratio. A ratio of 1.0 (top of plot) indicates no pitch drop, while the larger the pitch drop in a given target noun, the lower the point appears in the plot.

Regression lines are plotted separately for the unaccented (- - -) and accented (—) points in each plot. If unaccented nouns are realized with little or no pitch drop (as expected), they will have a min/max f0 ratio near 1.0 regardless of the max f0 value, so the slope of the regression line is expected to be near horizontal. For accented nouns, on the other hand, the higher the max f0 value, the more range available for a pitch drop, so it is possible that the regression line might slope down to the right.

A linear-regression analysis was performed to determine whether the min/max f0 ratio is affected by accentedness, by max f0, or by an interaction between the two; see Table 2. For all speakers, the min/max f0 ratio for accented (●) items is different from that for unaccented (○) items (there is a main effect of accentedness).

	accentedness		acc * max f0	
s05	$p<0.0001$	**	$p<0.0001$	**
s09	$p<0.0001$	**	$p=0.0494$	*
s12	$p<0.0001$	**	$p=0.038$	*
s10	$p<0.0001$	**	$p=0.0761$	.
s11	$p<0.0001$	**	$p=0.0563$	.
s07	$p<0.0001$	**	$p=0.604$	n.s.
s08	$p=0.001$	**	$p=0.4834$	n.s.

Table 2: Results of linear-regression analysis for neutral context

For most speakers, shown in (4), the way that max f0 affects the ratio — the slope of the line — is different for accented (●) vs. unaccented (○) items; there is a significant (s05, s09, s12) or marginal (s10, s11) interaction.

(4)   Speakers with an interaction: accentedness * max f0

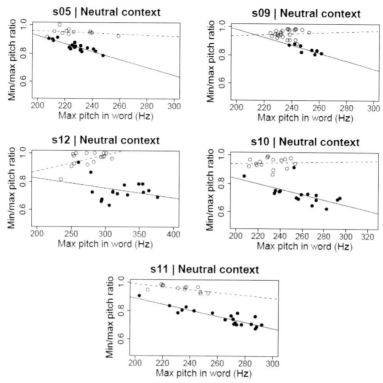

For the other two speakers (s07, s08), shown in (5), the way that max f0 affects the min/max f0 ratio is not significantly different for accented (●) and unaccented (○) items—the slopes of the lines are not distinct (no inter-action), although the min/max f0 ratio itself is still different for accented and unaccented items (main effect of accentedness).

(5)   Speakers with only a main effect of accentedness

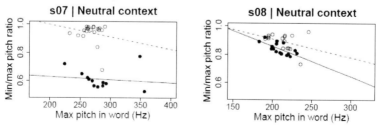

5.2 Post-Focus Context

An analysis of target nouns in the post-focus context shows that there is no pattern of accent deletion in this context. Just as for the neutral context, each repetition of each target noun was analyzed for min/max f0 ratio, max f0, and accentedness (according to (3), which reflects speakers' productions in the neutral context). A linear-regression analysis was carried out to see whether the min/max f0 ratio for nouns in the post-focus context is affected by accentedness, by max f0, or by an interaction between the two (Table 3).

If accent deletion does occur in the post-focus context, there should be no difference in the min/max f0 ratio between unaccented (○) and lexically accented (●) nouns. Contrary to this prediction, however, there is a main effect of accentedness on the min/max f0 ratio for all seven speakers. Thus, accented and unaccented target nouns do differ in amount of pitch fall, indicating that there is no accent deletion in this context.

	accentedness		acc * max f0	
s05	p=0.0005	**	p=0.0792	.
s07	p=0.0083	**	p=0.249	n.s.
s08	p=0.0004	**	p=0.2944	n.s.
s09	p<0.0001	**	p=0.2408	n.s.
s10	p=0.0011	**	p=0.7935	n.s.
s11	p<0.0001	**	p=0.133	n.s.
s12	p=0.0151	**	p=0.2365	n.s.

Table 3: Results of linear-regression analysis for post-focus context[2]

Although the linear-regression analysis shows that no speakers treat unaccented and accented nouns identically in the post-focus context, there are nevertheless some differences among speakers in this context. For three speakers (s05, s09, s12), in (6), unaccented (○) target nouns have a min/max f0 ratio near 1.0. This is the expected pattern, since a ratio near 1.0 means very little pitch fall.

---

[2]The lack of an interaction, beyond a marginal one for s05, shows that the effect of max f0 on the min/max f0 ratio is not different for unaccented vs. accented nouns. See also (6)–(8).

(6) Speakers with an unaccented (○) ratio near 1.0

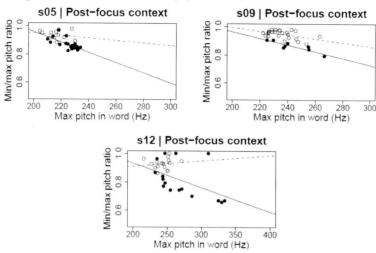

However, for another three speakers (s08, s10, s11), in (7), the min/max f0 ratio for unaccented (○) nouns is lower than the expected 1.0. If anything, these speakers are realizing some unaccented nouns with an accent in the post-focus context—but this is not accent *deletion*.

(7) Speakers with an unaccented (○) ratio lower than 1.0

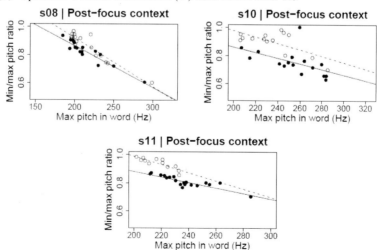

Data from the final speaker (s07) are shown in (8). Here, six out of twelve *accented* (●) nouns have ratios near 1.0, the value that is expected for *unaccented* nouns. It might therefore seem as though this speaker does realize lexically accented nouns in the post-focus context with accent deletion in some cases, despite an overall significant difference in min/max f0 ratio (pitch fall) for the two classes of nouns even for this speaker.

(8) Speaker with ratio for six accented (●) nouns near 1.0

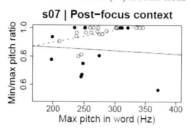

However, an inspection of these six items reveals that little or no pitch drop is measured after the max f0 within the noun because there is a H tone on the postnominal particle. This phrase-final H tone resembles one realization of focus in Tokyo Japanese (the 'prominence-lending rise'; Maeda & Venditti 1998). In fact, a similar phrase-final H appears in many of the *focused* nouns in the Fukuoka utterances recorded for this study. Thus, s07 seems to have produced six target nouns in the post-focus context as though they too were focused (even though this pattern was not encouraged by the discourse context). What is relevant for the present discussion is that these accented target nouns with a ratio near 1.0 do not indicate accent *deletion*.

In summary, none of the speakers in this study show evidence of a pattern of accent deletion in the post-focus context.

5.3 Post-*wh* Context

The preceding discussion shows that there is no evidence for accent deletion in the post-focus context. But for this result to serve as evidence that Fukuoka *wh* prosody is distinct from focus prosody, it must also be confirmed that the methodology used above to examine accentedness in the post-focus context *does* find accent deletion in the post-*wh* context.

Indeed, the results for the post-*wh* context, presented in this section, show that Fukuoka *wh* prosody is, overall, distinct from focus prosody. However, in analyzing the post-*wh* items, it is not possible to do exactly the same statistical comparison as for the neutral and post-focus contexts, for two reasons. First, target nouns that were produced with four repetitions in the neutral and post-focus contexts were only produced with two repetitions in the post-*wh* context (this is because there were additional, different target nouns elicited in the post-*wh* context; unfortunately, except for speaker s12, speaker-specific accentedness information as in (3) is not available for these nouns, so they cannot be included in the statistical analysis for the post-*wh* context). Consequently, even if no significant difference is found between the min/max f0 ratios for unaccented and accented nouns in the post-*wh* context, reduced statistical power due to the smaller data set becomes an alternative explanation for any such lack of statistical significance.

The second complication is that even Fukuoka-typical speakers sometimes produce non-Fukuoka-like *wh* utterances (seen also in Igarashi 2007), perhaps because they are code-switching with the normative Tokyo dialect. Such speakers may have significantly different means or regression-line slopes for accented and unaccented items, but only because a few examples produced with non-Fukuoka prosody are outliers that distort the measures for the accented items. This effect is shown in (9) for speaker s12.[3]

(9) The effect of non-Fukuoka *wh* productions on the statistical analysis

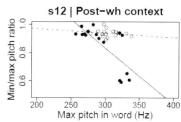 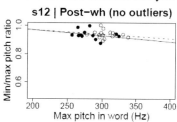

The four accented (●) points at lower right in (9)(a) are from utterances in which s12 did not conform to her usual clear pattern of accent deletion. When these points are included, a linear-regression analysis shows a significant main effect of accentedness ($p=0.0006$) and a significant interaction between accent and max f0 ($p=0.0170$), indicating that accented and unaccented target nouns behave differently in the post-*wh* context. However, when these points are excluded, as in (9)(b), there is neither a main effect of accent ($p=0.425$) nor an interaction ($p=0.864$). In other words, the apparent difference between accented and unaccented target nouns for speaker s12 in the post-*wh* context is entirely due to those four outliers.

Results of the linear-regression analysis for target nouns in the post-*wh* context for the remaining six speakers are shown in Table 4. For most

---

[3]The plots in (9) show two repetitions of *sixteen* target nouns (the eight nouns in (3) plus the eight additional nouns recorded only in the post-*wh* context), because for speaker s12, accentedness judgments for all sixteen nouns were collected.

speakers, there is no significant effect of accentedness and no interaction, which is indeed what we would expect in this context if *wh* prosody involves accent deletion.

	accentedness		acc * max f0	
s05	*p*=0.743	n.s.	*p*=0.148	n.s.
s07	*p*=0.196	n.s.	*p*=0.291	n.s.
s08	*p*=0.1817	n.s.	*p*=0.0556	.
s09	*p*=0.0152	*	*p*=0.2438	n.s.
s10	*p*=0.0295	*	*p*=0.0087	**
s11	*p*=0.432	n.s.	*p*=0.171	n.s.

Table 4: Results of linear-regression analysis for post-*wh* context

As shown above, this linear-regression analysis cannot be directly compared to the post-focus analysis. However, visual inspection of the post-*wh* plots in (9) and (10) confirms that for all speakers, the post-*wh* pattern does appear to involve accent deletion, exceptional non-Fukuoka-like utterances aside (see also Smith 2013).

(10) Target nouns in the post-*wh* context

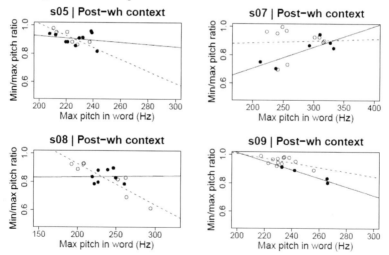

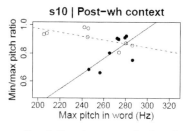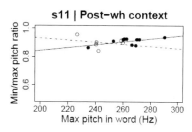

Crucially, the post-*wh* plots in (9) and (10) are very different from the post-focus plots in (6)–(8), where accented and unaccented points form distinct clusters. Thus, *wh* prosody is not an instance of focus prosody in Fukuoka Japanese.

6   Conclusions and Implications

The results of this study show that *wh* prosody is distinct from focus prosody in Fukuoka Japanese. This finding has implications for the syntax-phonology interface: If *wh* constructions influence phonological structure directly and not via focus phonology, then [+wh] features are relevant for the phonological grammar. This finding has potential connections with Richards's (2010) proposal that typological patterns of *wh* movement and *wh* prosody are related, as well as with Kuroda's (2013) discussion of "Rising Prosody" in Tokyo indeterminate constructions. A similar prosodic system is also found in South Kyeongsang Korean (Kubo 2005; Hwang 2011).

Methodologically, the min/max f0 ratio successfully differentiates accented and unaccented words. This method must be employed with care when comparing words of very different lengths or in very different positions in the utterance, because declination (Ladd 1984) could systematically lower minimum pitch or pitch range in longer words or later in an utterance. Still, pitch fall caused by declination will likely be smaller than pitch fall caused by accent in most contexts. Useful next steps would be to calibrate this method against accentedness judgments by native speakers, and to test its usefulness in additional varieties of Japanese and other pitch-accent languages.

Acknowledgments

Thanks above all to the experiment participants and to Tomoyuki Kubo, without whom this project would not have been possible. Thanks also to Yoshi Kitagawa, Satoshi Tomioka, Elliott Moreton, Yosuke Igarashi, the P-Side Research Group at UNC, and the J/K 23 audience for discussion and comments; to Noriyuki Ikeda, Yui Izumo, Naomi Matsunaga, Go Mizumoto, Tsutomu Sakamoto, Kumiko Sato, Maki Takahashi, and Daichi Yasunaga for assistance with experiment design and preparation; to Chris Wiesen of the Odum Institute at UNC for statistics consultation and support; to Shigeto Kawahara for his list of Japanese words with sonorant consonants; and to Mietta Lennes for making Praat scripts available. Additional research support was provided by the Kyushu University Linguistics Department and the UNC Carolina Asia Center.

References

Deguchi, M., and Y. Kitagawa. 2002. Prosody and *Wh*-Questions. *NELS* 32: 73–92.

Hayata, T. 1985. *Hakata hougen no akusento • keitairon* [The accent and morphology of the Hakata dialect]. Fukuoka: Kyushu University Press.

Hirotani, M. 2012. Prosodic Phrasing of Wh-Questions in Tokyo Japanese. *Prosody Matters*, ed. T. Borowsky et al., 446–486. London: Equinox.

Hwang, H. 2011. Distinct Types of Focus and *Wh*-Question Intonation. *ICPhS* 17: 922–925.

Igarashi, Y. 2007. Pitch Accent Deletion and Pitch Range Compression in Fukuoka Japanese. *21st General Meeting of the Phonetic Society of Japan*.

Ishihara, S. 2002. Invisible but Audible Wh-Scope Marking: Wh-Constructions and Deaccenting in Japanese. *WCCFL* 21: 180–193.

Ishihara, S. 2007. Major Phrase, Focus Intonation, Multiple Spell-Out. *Linguistic Review* 24: 137–167.

Jackendoff, R. 1972. *Semantic Interpretation in Generative Grammar*. Cambridge, Mass.: MIT Press.

Kubo, T. 1989. Hukuoka-si hougen no, dare • nani tou no gimonsi o hukumu bun no pitti pataan [The pitch patterns of sentences containing WH-words in the Fukuoka City dialect]. *Kokugogaku* 156: 1–12.

Kubo, T. 2005. Phonology-Syntax Interfaces in Busan Korean and Fukuoka Japanese. *Cross-Linguistic Studies on Tonal Phenomena IV*, ed. S. Kaji, 195–209. Tokyo: ILCAA.

Kubo, T. 2010. Hukuoka hougen ni okeru dousi • keiyousi to gimonsi-gimonbun no akusento ni kansuru oboegaki [Accent in verbs, adjectives, and WH-questions of the Fukuoka dialect]. *Bungaku kenkyuu* 107: 157–183.

Kuroda, S. 2013. Prosody and the Syntax of Indeterminates. *Lingua* 124: 74–95.

Ladd, D. 1984. Declination: A Review and Some Hypotheses. *Phonology* 1: 53–74.

Maeda, K., and J. Venditti. 1998. Phonetic Investigation of Boundary Pitch Movements in Japanese. *ICSLP-98*: paper 0800.

Pierrehumbert, J., and M. Beckman. 1988. *Japanese Tone Structure*. Cambridge, Mass.: MIT Press.

Richards, N. 2010. *Uttering Trees*. Cambridge, Mass.: MIT Press.

Selkirk, E. 2002. Contrastive FOCUS vs. Presentational Focus: Prosodic Evidence from Right Node Raising in English. *Speech Prosody 2002*, ed. B. Bel and I. Marlin, 643-646. Aix-en-Provence: Université de Provence.

Smith, J. 2011. [+wh] Complementizers Drive Phonological Phrasing in Fukuoka Japanese. *NLLT* 29: 545–559.

Smith, J. 2013. Fukuoka Japanese *Wh* Prosody in Production and Perception. *Lingua* 124: 96–130.

Truckenbrodt, H. 1995. Phonological Phrases: Their Relation to Syntax, Focus and Prominence. Doctoral dissertation, MIT.

Venditti, J. 2005. The J_ToBI Model of Japanese Intonation. *Prosodic Typology*, ed. S. Jun, 172–200. Oxford: Oxford University Press.

A Corpus-based Study on the Layered Duration in Standard Korean

Tae-Jin Yoon
Cheongju University

1 Introduction

This paper uses a large-scale spoken corpus of Standard Korean and investigates duration adjustments of vowels observed at the vicinity of word boundary with the phrase-medial duration serving as reference. Research in spoken language has shown that "a potential set of cues lie in the fact that an individual speech sound can be produced differently in different structural contexts, even though its abstract lexical representation is presumably the same" (Turk & Shattuck-Hufnagel 2000). Thus, cues for linguistically organized framework can be found in these contextually determined variant phonetic characteristics. Perhaps the most well-known cases of lengthening induced by linguistically structured boundaries are domain-initial strengthening (Fougeron & Keating 1997; Cho & Keating 2001) and domain-final lengthening (Oller 1973; Beckman & Edwards 1990; Edwards, Backman, & Fletcher 1991; Fletcher 2010). Together, these two effects of lengthening conspire to increase the distance between

Japanese/Korean Linguistics 23.
Edited by Michael Kenstowicz, Theodore Levin and Ryo Masuda.
Copyright © 2016, CSLI Publications

adjacent vowel onsets when they are separated by a boundary (Port 2003; Fletcher 2010). While phrase-final lengthening is well documented, it is more difficult to find convincing evidence for other boundary-related lengthening such as word-final lengthening in non-phrase-final position (Turk and Shattuck-Hufnagel 2000; Kim 2004) and non-consonantal phrase-initial lengthening. By citing Turk & Shattuck-Hufnagel (2000), Kim (2004) notes that many previous studies have failed to distinguish between phrase-final lengthening and word-final lengthening. It is plausible to assume that the domain of phrase-final position (either in syntactic terms or in terms of prosodic hierarchy) is broader than that of word-final position, and therefore it is also plausible to assume that the phrase-final lengthening will be greater in its magnitude than word-final lengthening, if the duration signals linguistically-organized structures. Word-final duration in turn may be lengthened more than word-medial duration.

Convincing evidence is more difficult to find in cases of non-consonantal phrase-initial lengthening. For example, Fougeron (1998) found no evidence of lengthening for the vowel following a phrase-initial consonant in French. Likewise, Byrd (2000) and Cho & Keating (2001) found no consistent evidence of lengthening beyond the phrase-initial consonant in English and Korean. Given the lack of evidence of initial-lengthening on non-initial vowel, it is expected that in the case of the consonant-initial words of the form #CV..., final lengthening is greater in its magnitude than initial lengthening, and there will be no difference between phrase-initial lengthening and word-initial lengthening regardless of the scope of the lengthening domain. However, an expectation is yet to be made with regard to the comparison of lengthening in phrase-initial position and in word-initial position.

The other problem with regard to lengthening concerns with the distinction between the domain effect and the position effect. It is observed that there seems to be a conflict between the domain effect and the position effect, in that greater domains are signaled by longer duration, and finality is also signaled by longer duration. Thus, it is not known whether phrase-initial lengthening will be greater than word-final lengthening, because the phrase-initial position is greater in its domain than the word-final position. But word-final lengthening will be greater than phrase-initial position, because finality is more than often signaled by longer duration.

This paper reexamines the position-induced lengthening effects of a post-consonantal vowel with a large-corpus of spoken Korean, and tests the relative effect of lengthening with regard to the position and the domain. Previous studies have used a limited set of carefully constructed sentences, and this raises a question whether the findings from the controlled stimuli can be replicated in a large-scale corpus of naturally produced speech.

2   A speech-corpus of reading-style Standard Korean

The data used for this study was drawn from "A Speech Corpus of Reading-Style Standard Korean," created around 2003 and distributed by the National Institute of the Korean Language (NIKL: http://korean.go.kr) in 2007. Throughout the paper, I will refer to the corpus as the NIKL corpus. Speakers are from Seoul and its neighboring Gyeonggi area. Ten male speakers in the 20's were selected from the corpus. Each speaker read 930 sentence types from 19 different well-known fairy tales, short stories and essays for more than an hour in a sound-treated booth. Table 1 lists the names of the 19 reading materials, the number of sentences (of various length) for each script, and the total time it took for a male speaker to read the reading scripts.

Table 1. List of script name, sentence number, and duration (in min)

	Name	Sent. Num.	Dur. (in min)
1.	요람기	51	5.37min
2.	소나기	87	4.00min
3.	아름다움에 대하여	69	5.20min
4.	방망이를 깎던 노인	62	4.59min
5.	문학의 세계와 삶의 세계	47	5.35min
6.	독서와 인생	54	4.92min
7.	수난 이대	62	5.29min
8.	메밀꽃 필 무렵	94	7.10min
9.	토끼와 자라	60	3.09min
10.	선녀와 나무꾼	73	4.92min
11.	호랑이와 곶감	42	2.67min
12.	해님 달님	28	2.07min
13.	그리운 시내가	36	4.61min
14.	광화문 지하도 아주머니	27	2.47min
15.	막 지은 밥	17	1.77min
16	눈 오던 날	35	2.46min
17.	숭늉의 지혜	19	1.58min
18.	까만 눈동자들 앞에서	27	3.43min
19.	내 고향 개울 물에서	40	2.72min
	Total	930	73.61min

The following (1) is an excerpt from a reading material of 'yoramgi,' ("the childhood") written in the Korean writing script, Hangul. The leading number indicates the sentence number of the script.

(1) An excerpt from the NIKL Corpus
   1. 기차도 전기도 없었다.
   2. 라디오도 영화도 몰랐다.
   3. 그래도 소년은 마을 아이들과 함께 마냥 즐겁기만 했다.
   4. 봄이면 뻐꾸기 울음과 함께 진달래가 지천으로 피고, 가을이면
     단풍과 감이 풍성하게 익는, 물 맑고 바람 시원한 산간
     마을이었다.

3   Korean forced-alignment system

Even though the NIKL corpus is not spontaneous per se, speakers who participated in the construction of the NIKL corpus read the script as natural as possible, ensuring enough inter- and intra-speaker variation. The sheer amount of speech data is challenging for manual transcription. In order to overcome the challenge, I developed a forced-alignment system for the NIKL corpus following the procedures in the HTK book (Young et al. 2010). HTK stands for Hidden Markov Model Toolkit, and is a bundle of computer programs that are designed to build automatic speech recognition. Forced alignment refers to an automatic alignment of the phonemes in an utterance by constraining the search in a phonetic recognizer to the known sequence of phonemes (Cole & Hasegawa-Johnson 2012; Hosom 2000; Rapp 1995). Phone and word sequences in the speech files are force-aligned using a custom-made automatic phone alignment system based on Unicode and the Hidden Markov Model (HMM, cf. Young et al. 2010). The Hidden Markov Model (HMM) is currently the most dominant method for automatic speech recognition.

A typical HMM system works by dividing the speech into short frames, where each frame corresponds to a state in a state sequence. As for short frames of speech signals, short-term spectral-domain features with a window length of 16ms are computed from the input speech. The delta and delta-delta values of these features are also computed in order to capture some of the dynamics of the speech signal. These features are computed at short, regularly-spaced frames (10ms per frame), and are modified to emphasize the perceptually-relevant aspects of the speech signal called MFCC (Mel-Frequency Cepstral Coefficients). In sum, 39 features from each 10ms frame were extracted and used for the development of the forced-alignment system.

Each state is marked by a phonetic symbol in Korean and is associated with phonetic likelihoods. That is, the phonetic symbols can be thought of as the most likely phonetic observation that will occur in that state. And states are connected by unidirectional links. A series of connected states forms a word, and word-ending states are connected to word-beginning states in order to create a continuous-speech recognizer (Hosom 2000).

Note that the word-like unit in the current system is called *eojeol,* which is a space-delimited orthographic words in Korean, and which roughly corresponds to an Accentual Phrase (Yoon 2005). In many cases, *eojeol* consists of a lexeme and particles are grammatical markers (e.g., *gicado* 'train-too'). And there are about 55,000 *eojeol's* or words in the NIKL corpus. Phonetic-based recognition is performed on each frame, and the most likely word-level path through the state sequence is computed using a Viterbi search. Viterbi search is a dynamic programming algorithm that finds the single most-likely path through a sequence of states, based on each state's occupation probabilities and transition probabilities. The output of the Viterbi search contains not only the most likely word sequence, but also the times at which each state is occupied. As Rapp (1995) noted, because "the task of phoneme alignment can be considered as simplified speech recognition, it is natural to adopt a successful paradigm of automatic speech recognition, namely, HMMs, for alignment." Therefore, HMM-based speech recognizers can be used to obtain phoneme alignment using a process called forced alignment. In forced alignment, the HMM is used to recognize the input speech with the Viterbi search constrained to only the correct sequence of phonemes together with their time information.

In cases where the words are known but the phoneme sequence is not, a dictionary can be used in combination with pronunciation rules to generate a phoneme sequence for each word (see Fosler-Lussier (2003) for ways of building up pronunciation models for speech recognition). These sequences can then be concatenated together, with optional pause between words, to arrive at a phoneme sequence for the entire utterance. In such a case, the HMM-based alignment system trains as its required component acoustic models for each phoneme based on a pronunciation dictionary. One challenge in building a forced-alignment system for languages such as Korean is the lack of an easily available pronunciation dictionary with which to build an accurate acoustic model. A mismatch between a word and its phone sequence is a major source of performance degradation. Thus, a pronunciation dictionary was constructed based on Unicode for Korean, and it was used to build acoustic models for each phone with HTK (Hidden Markov Toolkit; Young et al. 2010).

A technical problem encountered in using HTK is the limitation of the HTK in dealing with CJK (Chinese, Japanese, Korea) encoding systems. Thus, converting the Korean encoding system to computer-readable encoding, i.e., a Romanized encoding system, was the first step that we did in building the Korean forced-alignment system. Each sentence in the script is Romanized following the Unicode convention.[1] For example, sentences as in (1) are Romanized as those in (2). That is, each word in the sentences in (1) are converted to a syllable-delimited Romanized word in (2). In (2), the underscore (_) is used for the syllable-boundary mark, instead of the conventional period to distinguish from punctuation at the end of each sentence.

(2) Syllable-delimited romanized words
    1. gi_ca_do jeon_gi_do eobs_eoss_da.
    2. ra_di_o_do yeong_hwa_do mol_rass_da.
    3. geu_rae_do so_nyeon_eun ma_eul a_i_deul_gwa ham_gge
       ma_nyang jeul_geob_gi_man haess_da.
    4. bom_i_myeon bbeo_ggu_gi ul_eum_gwa ham_gge jin_dal_rae_ga
       ji_ceon_eu_ro pi_go, ga_eul_i_myeon dan_pung_gwa gam_i
       pung_seong_ha_ge ig_neun, mul malg_go ba_ram si_weon_han
       san_gan_ ma_eul_i_eoss_da.

We adopted a knowledge-based approach to generate the dictionary based on the syllable-delimited words as in (2): information about pronunciation variation was extracted from the phonological rules of Korean. The phonological rules include, among others, place and nasal assimilation across syllables, coda neutralization, and post-obstruent tensification (Ahn 1998; Sohn 1999). No exhaustive implementation of the phonological rules has been made. Some phonological rules (obligatory or optional) deteriorated the output of the forced-alignment. When such cases occurred, the rules were excluded from the implementation. At the moment, no systematic investigation of the role of phonological rules is made, leaving it for future research. Due to the lack of morphological information, certain rules that operate across morpheme-boundaries were not implemented. Acoustic models were trained for each phone, using the NIKL corpus. Thus, the pronunciation dictionary contains phoneme sequences for entries like eoboessda (없었다, 'did not exist') as in (3), in which the coda [ss] underwent tensification together with the stem-final obstruent [d]:

(3) EOBSEOSSDA   eo b s eo dd a

Figure 1 illustrates a forced-aligned waveform. The utterance is 'sonyeoneun gaeulgaesso' (the boy-NOM brook-LOC; the boy by the brook).

---

[1] For the character mapping between Korean characters and corresponding Romanized characters, see http://www.unicode.org/charts/PDF/U1100.pdf

The words are time-aligned on the second tier, and the time-aligned phone sequences are on the first tier, below the corresponding waveform.

Figure 1. An example of waveform with the forced-aligned word and phone intervals.

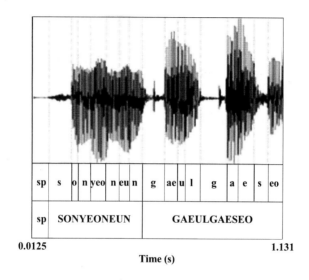

4   Position-based feature extraction

With the phone- and word-aligned data, it is now possible to investigate phonetic and phonological variation both within and across speakers. The current result is based on data drawn from 10 male speakers in their 20's. In order to test the duration adjustment of a post-consonantal vowel in various positions, I decided to examine the duration of /a/ whose preceding consonant is either /k/ or /t/. All instances of /ka/ and /ta/ were visually examined and corrected, if needed, and then extracted from the phone-aligned data.

The selection of /ka/ and /ta/ is based on the fact that the distribution of these two forms are highly frequent in the corpus due in part to their use in Korean as postpositional grammatical markers. In the NIKL corpus, /ta/ and /ka/ are among the six most frequent syllable types. Table 2 lists the top 6 most frequent syllable types in the NIKL Corpus. For comparison, the distribution of syllable type from other corpora is also listed.

Table 2: frequency of the top 6 syllable types in corpora.[2]

Rank	Syllable	NIKL Corpus		Sejong Corpus	Newspaper
1	이 ([i])	1092	4.44%	3.19%	3.26%
2	**다 ([ta])**	**919**	**3.74%**	**2.45%**	**2.78%**
3	는 ([neun])	689	2.80%	2.16%	2.05%
4	을 ([eul])	578	2.35%	1.74%	1.76%
5	고 ([ko])	536	2.18%	1.46%	1.51%
6	**가 ([ka])**	**517**	**2.10%**	**1.42%**	**1.37%**

The frequent occurrence of the syllable types, together with the relative ease for separating the types from other syllables in the words and the identity of the target vowel, let us examine the phonetic properties of the target /a/ from different locations within a phrase, as exemplified in (4), where instances of /ka/ are observed word- and phrase-finally, word- and phrase-initially, and word-medially. The decision between phrase-boundary and word-boundary is made based on the presence or absence of a silent pause at the vicinity of the target syllable.

(4) Chulswu-**ka**   han**ka**unde   iss-neun   **ka**gu-lul   sa-ss-ta.
    Chulswu-NOM in the middle being-ADN furniture-ACC buy-PAST-DECL
    'Chulswu bought a piece of furniture which was located in the middle.'

In addition, as predicate final language, Korean has /ka/ and /ta/ as its grammatical markers. For example, /ka/ and /ta/, respectively, serve as a nominative marker and a declarative sentence ender in (4). Thus, it is possible to examine the phonetic properties of these morphological morphemes of /ka/ and /ta/ in the context of phrase structure. The position in which these syllables occur in a phrase, in turn, highly correlates with the positions in a prosodic hierarchy. As mentioned in Section 2.1, the word-like unit in Korean is *eojeol*, and it roughly corresponds to an AP (Accentual Phrase). The presence of a silent pause is important in the formation of an IP, such that an IP is accompanied by phrase final lengthening and is either preceded or followed by the presence of a silent pause. The nominative marker /ka/ may form a right-edge of either an AP if it is followed by no silent pause or a right edge of an IP (Intonational Phrase) if a silent pause follows (Jun 1993; Jun 1996; Jun 2005).

---

[2] The frequency of the syllable types for Sejong corpus and Newspaper corpus is obtained from the site: http://nlp.kookmin.ac.kr/cgi-bin/hit_syl_freq.cgi

5   Results

Duration measurements were taken at the syllable nucleus of /ta/ and /ka/, respectively and were classified into one of five positions: phrase-final (pf), word final (wf), phrase-initial (pi), word-initial (wi), and word-medial (wm) position. Figure (2) is a flow chart that illustrates how the instances of /ta/ and /ka/ are classified into one of the five positional categories. It is noted that depending on the speaker's rendition of the reading material, the same words in the same sentence may be classified differently. For example, there are possibilities that some words may be word-final for some speaker and phrase-final for other speakers.

Figure 2: Flow chart for feature extraction

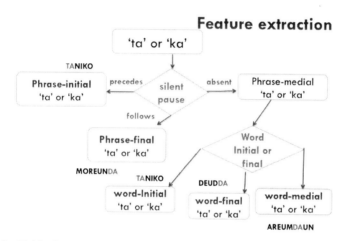

In Table 3, I present the total number of tokens under the five different positions summed up from 10 male speakers in their 20's.

Table 3: Total number of tokens under the five different positions

context	'ta'	'ka'
word-initial	342	773
word-medial	599	1301
word-final	98	706
phrase-initial	44	111
phrase-final	1116	120
Total	2247	3011

An error-bar graph is presented in Figure 3. The figure illustrates the mean and standard error of syllabic nucleus duration at the five different positions.

Figure 3: (a) Vowel duration of /ka/ and /ta/ as measured at five different positions; (b) vowel duration of /ka/ and /ta/ of the shaded positions in figure 3(a).

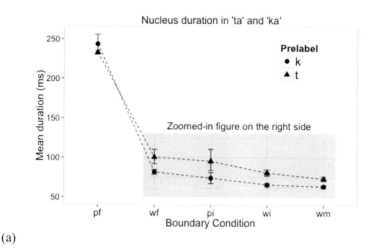

(a)

(b)

The shaded area in Figure 3(a) is zoomed-in and shown again in Figure 3(b) for clarity. As evident in the figure, positional effects of lengthening are most evident in phrase-final position. The duration at word-final and phrase-initial is longer than the duration of word-medial and word-initial tokens. Given the longer duration of word-final vowels than that of word-initial vowels, it appears that the positional effect is stronger than the domain effect.

As for statistical tests, a series of planned contrast tests are conducted to test the effect of lengthening of /ka/ and /ta/ in different positions within a phrase. Results of the planned contrast tests are in Tables 4 to 7. In Table 4 and Table 5, the vowel duration in /ta/ and /ka/ is lengthened significantly longer when they occur in a position other than the word-medial position.

Table 4: Planned contrasts test: Treatment contrast with word-medial 'ta' as the baseline level.

	Estimate	Std. Error	t value	Pr(>|t|)
(Intercept)	73.295	2.326	31.509	< 2e-16 ***
pf vs. wm	162.736	2.728	59.652	< 2e-16 ***
pi vs. wm	22.089	8.127	2.718	0.00662 **
wf vs. wm	27.113	5.435	4.989	6.59e-07 ***
wi vs. wm	8.488	3.511	2.418	0.01570 *

Table 5: Planned contrasts test: Treatment contrast with word-medial 'ka' as the baseline level.

	Estimate	Std. Error	t value	Pr(>|t|)
(Intercept)	64.409	1.152	55.896	< 2e-16 ***
pf vs. wm	180.591	3.812	47.379	< 2e-16 ***
pi vs. wm	9.645	3.950	2.442	0.0147 *
wf vs. wm	17.390	1.890	9.202	< 2e-16 ***
wi vs. wm	2.978	1.838	1.620	0.1053

The effect of final position seems to be much stronger than that of domain, suggesting that even the word-final duration may be longer than the phrase-initial duration. However, Table 6 and Table 7 illustrate that the word-final lengthening and phrase-initial lengthening do not show any statistically significant difference.

Table 6: Planned contrasts test: Treatment contrast with word-final 'ta' as the baseline level.

	Estimate	Std. Error	t value	Pr(>|t|)
(Intercept)	100.408	4.912	20.441	< 2e-16 ***
pf vs. wf	135.623	5.115	26.517	<2e-16 ***
pi vs. wf	-5.024	9.206	-0.546	0.585361
wf vs. wf	-18.625	5.572	-3.343	0.000844 ***
wi vs. wf	-27.113	5.435	-4.989	6.59e-07 ***

Table 7: Planned contrasts test: Treatment contrast with word-final 'ka' as the baseline level.

	Estimate	Std. Error	t value	Pr(>|t|)
(Intercept)	81.799	1.498	54.609	< 2e-16 ***
pf vs. wf	163.201	3.930	41.528	<2e-16 ***
pi vs. wf	-7.745	4.064	-1.906	0.0568
wf vs. wf	-14.412	2.072	-6.956	4.32e-12 ***
wi vs. wf	-17.390	1.890	-9.20	<2e-16 ***

6   Discussions and Conclusion

Results support that the phonetic manifestation of the utterance boundary is conditioned by the linguistically organized structure. Both initial and final lengthening effects are observed when they are compared to word-medial position. It is also suggested that final position induces much longer durational adjustment than initial position. The failure of earlier studies to find the effect of phrase-initial lengthening may be due to the greater variation in that position. The findings observed in the study are a reading style by male speakers, which warrants detailed phonetic analyses for more speakers of different gender and more speaking styles as well as speaker-dependent variations. This is made possible with the custom-made forced alignment at hand.

One puzzling question that is interesting to see is why there is a systematic difference in post-consonantal vowels under different preceding consonants. As shown in Figure 3, the vowel duration of /a/ when it is not in phrase-final position but in other positions is greater when the preceding consonant is alveolar /t/ than when the preceding consonant is velar /k/. A possibility is that total duration of VOT plus the following vowel is consistent. The VOT of alveolar stops is short and that of velar stops is long. The post-alveolar vowel is longer than the post-velar vowel in order to keep the combined duration consistent. Since the measurement of the VOT values for the stops at various positions requires manual labeling of the stop consonant at present, I will leave this question for future research till an automatic VOT measurements are available for the NIKL corpus.

The other remaining question is the source of variability of phrase-initial post-consonantal vowel duration. "Phrase-initial" in this paper is defined purely in terms of syntax and the presence of a silent pause rather than prosodic annotation. Thus, the phrase-initial position in the paper can either be an Accentual Phrase (AP) Initial position or an Intonational-Phrase (IP) initial position in prosodic terms. The confounding effect of AP and IP may have contributed to the variability of the phrase-initial vowel duration. There may be a possibility that the phrase-initial lengthening may differ from word-final lengthening if AP-induced lengthening and IP-induced lengthening are distinguished. Since prosodic annotation requires time-consuming manual annotation, the question is also left for future research.

The paper examined boundary-related phenomena from naturally produced large-scale Korean corpus, and obtained results that were different from the results drawn from laboratory setting (cf. Crystal & House 1988). Experiments with laboratory speech are nice because they are revealing of regular underlying patterns that otherwise remain obscure due to the extreme variability of speech. Whether and how these regularities show up in real speech depends on many factors. As Nooteboom (1997) asserts, "a first reassurance we need is whether similar temporal regularities can be demonstrated for real words and phrases," and whether such regularities can be shown to be part of what language users implicitly know about the way words and phrases in their language should sound. Further research is needed to find out reasons of the disparity between the result taken from a laboratory setting and the outcome of large-scale corpus study. This result takes us a step further toward solving the long-standing enigma of how abstract linguistic form is communicated through the medium of the speech waveform. Significant patterning relations may be encoded at a certain degree of abstraction from the physical data, but must have a regular manifestation in the speech signal if they are to be successfully conveyed from speaker to hearer.

References

Ahn, S.-C. (1998). *An Introduction to Korean Phonology*. Seoul: Hanshin Publishing Co.

Beckman, M. E., & Edwards, J. (1990). Lengthenings and shortenings and the nature of prosodic constituency. In J. Kingston & M. E. Beckman (Eds.), *Papers in laboratory phonology I: between the grammar and physics of speech*, 152-178. Cambridge: Cambridge University Press.

Byrd, D. (2000). Articulatory Vowel Lengthening and Coordination at Phrasal Junctures. *Phonetica, 57*, 3-16.

Cho, T., & Keating, P. A. (2001). Articulatory and acoustic studies on domain-initial strengthening in Korean. *Journal of Phonetics, 29*, 155-190.

Cole, J., & Hasegawa-Johnson, M. (2012). Corpus phonology with speech resources. In A. Cohn, C. Fougeron & M. K. Huffman (Eds.), *Handbook of Laboratory Phonology* (pp. 431-440). Oxford, UK: Oxford University Press.

Crystal, T. H., & House, A. S. (1988). Segmental durations in connected-speech signals: Current results. *Journal of Acoustical Society of America, 83*, 1553-1573.

Edwards, J. R., Backman, M. E., & Fletcher, J. (1991). The articulatory kinematics of final lengthening. *Journal of Acoustical Society of America, 89*, 369-382.

Fletcher, J. (2010). The Prosody of Timing: Timing and Rhythm. In W. Hardcastle, J. Laver & F. E. Gibbon (Eds.), *The Handbook of Phonetic Sciences* (Second edition ed., pp. 523-602). Oxford: Wiley-Blackwell.

Fosler-Lussier, E. (2003). A Tutorial on Pronunciation Modeling for Large Vocabulary Speech Recognition. *Text- and Speech-Triggered Information Access, 2705*, 38-77.

Fougeron, C. (1998). *Variations Articulatoires en Début de Constituants Prosodiques de Différents Niveaux en Français.* : Université Paris III-Sorbonne Nouvelle.

Fougeron, C., & Keating, P. A. (1997). Articulatory strengthening at edges of prosodic domains. *Journal of the Acoustical Society of America, 101*, 3728-3740.

Hosom, J.-P. 2000. *Automatic Time Alignment of Phonemes Using Acoustic-Phonetic Information.* Doctoral Dissertation. Oregon Graduate Institute of Science and Technology, Oregon.

Jun, S.-A. (1993). *The Phonetics and Phonology of Korean Prosody.* Unpublished Ph. D. dissertation, The Ohio State University, Columbia, Ohio.

Jun, S.-A. (1996). The Accentual Phrase in the Korean prosodic hierarchy. *Phonology, 15*, 189-226.

Jun, S.-A. (2005). Korean Intonational Phonology and Prosodic Transcription. In S.-A. Jun (Ed.), *Prosodic Typology: The Phonology of Intonation and Phrasing* (pp. 201-229). Oxford: Oxford University Press.

Kim, S. (2004). *The Role of Prosodic Phrasing in Korean Word Segmentation.* Doctoral Dissertation, UCLA.

Nooteboom, S. (1997). The prosody of speech: melody and rhythm. In W. Hardcastle & J. Laver (Eds.), *The Handbook of Phonetic Sciences* (pp. 640-673). Oxford: Basil Blackwell Limited.

Oller, D. K. (1973). The effect of position in utterance on speech segment duration in English. *Journal of the Acoustical Society of America, 54*, 1235-1247.

Port, R. (2003). Meter and speech. *Journal of Phonetics, 31*, 599-611.

Rapp, S. (1995). Automatic phonemic transcription and linguistic annotation from known text with Hidden Markov Models: An aligner for German. In *Proceedings of ELSNET Goes East and IMACS Workshop.* Moscow, Russia.

Sohn, H.-M. (1999). *The Korean Language.* Cambridge: Cambridge University Press.

Turk, A. E., & Shattuck-Hufnagel, S. (2000). Word-boundary-related duration patterns in English. *Journal of Phonetics, 28*, 397-440.

Yoon, K. (2005). *Building a prosodically sensitive diphone database for Korean Text-To-Speech synthesis system.* The Ohio State University.

Young, S., Evermann, G., Gales, M., Hain, T., Kershaw, D., Liu, X. A., Moore, G., Odell, J., Ollason, D., Povey, D., Valtchev, V., & Woodland, P. (2006). *The HTK Book.*

Part II

Syntax

An Experimental Investigation of Island Effects in Korean[1]

BOYOUNG KIM AND GRANT GOODALL
University of California, San Diego

1   Introduction

Finding the source of island phenomena continues to be a central concern in linguistic theory, and *wh*-in-situ languages have an important role to play. Whether these languages display island effects or not, despite their apparent lack of overt *wh*-movement, can potentially tell us a lot about the nature of islands. Unfortunately, though, the facts are still not as clear as one would like. Some have argued for the presence of island effects (e.g. Lee 1982, Han 1992, Hong 2004 for Korean; Nishigauchi 1990, Watanabe 1992 for Japanese), while others have argued against it (e.g. Suh 1987, Choi 2006, Hwang 2007 for Korean; Ishihara 2002, Sprouse et al. 2011 for Japanese).

---

[1] We thank the audience of the 23rd Japanese/Korean Linguistics Conference, especially Marcel den Dikken, Hyun Kyung Hwang, Shigeru Miyagawa, Jennifer L Smith, Satoshi Tomioka, and James Hye Suk Yoon.

Japanese/Korean Linguistics 23.
Edited by Michael Kenstowicz, Theodore Levin and Ryo Masuda.

This situation points to the need for formal acceptability experiments to determine exactly what the facts are. Such experiments involve, at a minimum, carefully designed stimuli being presented to subjects, who indicate their sense of acceptability for each sentence through a numerical response. This approach has been very successfully applied to *wh*-movement languages (e.g. Sprouse and Hornstein 2013), but languages like Korean raise difficult methodological concerns, as the techniques developed for other languages cannot be straightforwardly transferred to Korean. The main reason for this is that Korean *wh*-questions allow for ambiguities with respect to the interpretation and scope of the *wh*-word. First, bare *wh*-words in Korean may be interpreted as such (i.e. as true *wh*-words) or as existential pronouns. Even if one reading is disallowed, the other is typically not, with the result that all questions with *wh*-words thus appear to be fully acceptable. Furthermore, in *wh*-island contexts, even if the *wh*-word is interpreted as such, its scope may be either inside or outside the island domain; the *wh*-in-situ nature of Korean means that this is not indicated overtly. As a result, most *wh*-questions are at least two-ways ambiguous in Korean, which means that in an experiment, we cannot be sure how subjects are interpreting the stimuli. This makes meaningful evaluations of the results very difficult, and an experimental approach to the acceptability of islands in Korean has thus been virtually impossible.

In the present study, we attempt to provide a solution to this problem. We show that it is possible to probe island effects in Korean experimentally, despite the difficulties, and that interesting results obtain when we do. What makes our experimental approach possible is that we present subjects with question-answer pairs, rather than simply questions, and we ask subjects to judge the acceptability of the answer, rather than the question. This differs substantially from standard acceptability experiments with *wh*-movement languages, but as we show below, it allows us to get judgments on specific interpretations of *wh*-questions. We use this procedure in four experiments, probing both *wh*-island (*whether*-island) and adjunct island effects in Korean.

2 Experiments

In the following sections, we report on four formal acceptability experiments that test for the existence of island effects in Korean. Experiments 1 and 2 investigate *wh*-island and adjunct island effects, respectively, with canonically ordered embedded clauses. Experiments 3 and 4 attempt to replicate Experiments 1 and 2 with scrambled embedded clauses.

2.1 Experiment 1: Canonical *Wh*-islands (*whether*-islands) in Korean

2.1.1 Participants

Forty-eight native speakers of Korean who were residing in Korea at the time of testing (M: 28 years old, range: 20-34) participated in this experiment online. Their first and dominant language was Korean, and they had no training in linguistics. Their participation was voluntary.

2.1.2 Stimuli

Stimuli consisted of question-answer pairs, preceded by a context. All question sentences were biclausal. They differed as to the location of the *wh*-word (matrix vs. embedded clause) and the structure of the embedded clause (declarative (non-island) vs. interrogative (island)). Answers were either "*wh*-answers" or "yes/no answers". "*Wh*-answers" were appropriate for a direct *wh*-question interpretation of the preceding question, while "yes/no answers" were appropriate for a yes/no question interpretation. The latter case arises when the *wh*-word is interpreted as an existential pronoun or as a true *wh*-word with scope over only the embedded clause (yielding an indirect question).

There were thus three factors (Location of *wh*-word, Structure of embedded clause, Answer type), with a total of eight conditions. Sample stimuli are provided in (1)-(8). In (1)-(2), the *wh*-word is in the matrix clause and the embedded clause is declarative, while in (3)-(4), the embedded clause is interrogative. In (5)-(6), the *wh*-word is in an embedded clause that is declarative, while in (7)-(8), the embedded clause is interrogative.

(1) Q: **Nwukwu**-ka [Obama-ka Mary-ul manna-ss-ta-**ko**] tul-ess-**ni**?
     who -Nom   -Nom   -Acc meet-Past-Decl-that hear-Past-Q
     'Who heard that Obama met Mary?' or
     'Did somebody hear that Obama met Mary?'
   A: WH-ANSWER: Hillary-ka 'Hillary'

(2) Q: Same as (1).
   A: YES-NO ANSWER: Ney, tul-ess-eyo 'Yes, heard'

(3) Q: **Nwukwu**-ka [Obama-ka Mary-ul manna-ss-nun-**ci**] tul-ess-**ni**?
     who -Nom   -Nom   -Acc meet-Past-Adn-Q hear-Past-Q
     'Who heard whether Obama met Mary?' or
     'Did somebody hear whether Obama met Mary?'
   A: WH-ANSWER: Hillary-ka 'Hillary'

(4) Q: Same as (3).
   A: YES-NO ANSWER: Ney, tul-ess-eyo 'Yes, heard'

(5) Q: Mary-nun [Obama-ka **nwukwu**-ul manna-ss-ta-**ko**]   tul-ess-**ni**?
       -Top   -Nom who   -Acc meet-Past-Decl-that hear-Past-Q
       'Who did Mary hear that Obama met?' or
       'Did Mary hear that Obama met somebody?'
   A: WH-ANSWER: Hillary-lul 'Hillary'

(6) Q: Same as (5).
   A: YES-NO ANSWER: Ney, tul-ess-eyo 'Yes, heard'

(7) Q: Mary-nun [Obama-ka **nwukwu**-ul manna-ss-nun-**ci**] tul-ess-**ni**?
       -Top   -Nom who   -Acc meet-Past-Adn-Q   hear-Past-Q
       'Who did Mary hear whether Obama met?' or
       'Did Mary hear who Obama met?'
   A: WH-ANSWER: Hillary-lul 'Hillary'

(8) Q: Same as (7).
   A: YES-NO ANSWER: Ney, tul-ess-eyo 'Yes, heard'

All question-answer pairs were preceded by a context consisting of a situation (e.g. "at the White House") and a list of people involved in the situation (e.g. "Mary, Obama, Hillary"). These contexts were designed to make the *wh*-answer pragmatically plausible, even when this interpretation of the question would violate an island.

40 sets of experimental sentences were distributed using a Latin Square design among eight lists consisting of five tokens of each of the eight conditions. Each list included 63 fillers, for an experimental/filler ratio of 1:1.5. All lists were randomized.

In 30 of the 40 sets, the matrix verb was matched across all conditions in the set. In the remaining 10 sets, however, one verb is used with declarative complements and another verb with interrogative complements (e.g. *sayngkakhata* 'think' with declaratives and *kungkumhata* 'wonder' with interrogatives). This was due to the limited number of verbs (e.g. *tutta* 'hear') that can take both declarative and interrogative complements. The *wh*-word *nwukwu* 'who' is used in all stimuli.

2.1.3   Method

The experiments were conducted online. Subjects were instructed to rate the acceptability of the answer as a first response to the question, using a 7-point scale (with 1 "very bad" and 7 "very good").

상황: 미국 백악관 방문
등장인물: 오바마, 매리, 힐러리
Q: **누가 오바마가 매리를 만났다고 들었니?**
A: 힐러리가

FIGURE 1. An Example of the Experiment Presentation in Experiment 1

2.1.4　Analysis

Acceptability scores from each participant were z-score transformed prior to analysis. The z-score results were separated by answer type, and separate repeated measures ANOVAs were run for each answer type, with Location of *wh*-word (matrix vs. embedded) and Structure of embedded clause (non-island 'declarative' vs. island "interrogative") as within-subjects variables, and either 'subject' (F1) or 'item' (F2) as a random factor.

2.1.5　Results

The results are plotted in Figure 2. The left graph represents the acceptability of *wh*-answers and the right graph shows that of yes/no answers.

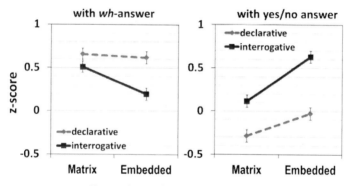

FIGURE 2. Results of Experiment 1

For *wh*-answers, there were main effects for both Location (F1 (1, 47) = 10.17, p = .003, F2 (1, 39) = 15.22, p < .0001) and Structure (F1 (1, 47) = 29.83, p < .0001, F2 (1, 39) = 28.12, p < .0001), as well as a significant interaction between these two factors (F1 (1, 47) = 16.17, p < .0001, F2 (1, 39) = 7.13, p = .011).

The pattern is similar with yes/no answers. There were main effects for Location (F1 (1, 47) = 33.64, p < .0001, F2 (1, 39) = 39.21, p < .0001), and Structure (F1 (1, 47) = 76.08, p < .0001, F2 (1, 39) = 61.83, p < .0001). The interaction of Location and Structure was significant in the subjects analysis and close to significant in the items analysis (F1 (1, 47) = 5.04, p = .03, F2 (1, 39) = 3.89, p = .056).

These results suggest a very clear *wh*-island effect in Korean. The interactions with both *wh*-answers and yes/no answers seem to be driven by the condition in which the *wh*-word is within an embedded interrogative clause. In this case, the *wh*-answer is strongly dispreferred and the yes/no answer is strongly preferred, thus suggesting that the *wh*-word is not able to scope out of the embedded interrogative clause.

2.2 Experiment 2: Canonical Adjunct-islands in Korean

2.2.1 Participants, Method, and Analysis

The participants, method, and analysis of the results were the same as in Experiment 1.

2.2.2 Stimuli

The basic design of the experiment is the same as in Experiment 1, consisting of a total of 8 conditions, reflecting three factors: Location of *wh*-word (matrix vs. embedded) x Structure of embedded clause (complement (non-island) vs. adjunct (island)) x Answer type (*wh*-answer vs. yes/no-answer). What distinguishes this experiment from the previous one is that here, we are contrasting embedded complement clauses with embedded adjunct clauses.

All 8 conditions in this experiment were lexically matched except for the matrix verb, which had to differ between declarative and adjunct conditions for selectional reasons (e.g. *tutta* 'hear' in declarative conditions vs. *natanata* 'appear' in adjunct conditions).

As in Experiment 1, 40 sets of experimental sentences were distributed using a Latin Square design among eight lists consisting of five tokens of each of the eight conditions. Each list included 63 fillers, for an experimental/filler ratio of 1:1.5. All lists were randomized. The *wh*-word *nwukwu* 'who' is used in all stimuli. Sample stimuli with adjunct clauses are provided in (9)-(12). Stimuli with complement clauses were seen earlier in (1)-(2) and (5)-(6).

(9) Q: **Nwukwu**-ka [Obama-ka Mary-ul manna-ss-ul-**ttay**]   natana-ss-**ni**?
    who -Nom   -Nom   -Acc meet-Past-Adn-when appear-Past-Q
    'Who appeared when Obama met Mary?' or
    'Did somebody appear when Obama met Mary?'
    A: WH-ANSWER: Hillary-ka 'Hillary'

(10) Q: Same as (9).
     A: YES-NO ANSWER: Ney, natana-ss-eyo 'Yes, appeared'

(11) Q: Mary-nun [Obama-ka **nwukwu**-ul manna-ss-ul-**ttay**] natana-ss-**ni**?
       -Top   -Nom who -Acc meet-Past-Adn-when appear-Past-Q
    'Who did Mary appear when Obama met?' or
    'Did Mary appear when Obama met somebody?'
    A: WH-ANSWER: Hillary-lul 'Hillary'

(12) Q: Same as (11).
    A: YES-NO ANSWER: Ney, natana-ss-eyo 'Yes, appeared'

2.2.3 Results

In Figure 3, the first graph shows the results with the *wh*-answer, and the second graph displays the results with the yes/no answer.

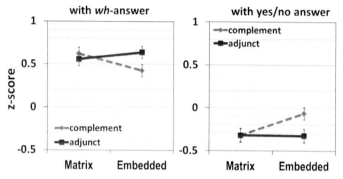

FIGURE 3. Results of Experiment 2

The results reveal a main effect of Structure with yes/no answers (F1 (1, 47) = 8.52, p = .005, F2 (1, 39) = 8.25, p = .007), but not with *wh*-answers (F1 (1, 47) = .79, p = .38, F2 (1, 39) = .62, p = .44). No significant main effect of Location was observed with either answer type, but there was a largely significant interaction of Structure and Location with both types of answers (with *wh*-answer: F1 (1, 47) = 12.05, p = .001, F2 (1, 39) = 4.54, p = .039; with yes/no answer by subject-analysis: F1 (1, 47) = 6.31, p = .016, F2 (1, 39) = 3.04, p = .089). However, the direction of the interaction was the opposite of what one would expect for a classic island effect: the condition in which the *wh*-word is located within an adjunct clause was rated the highest out of the four conditions with *wh*-answers, and the lowest with yes/no answers. There is thus no sign of an adjunct island effect.

2.3 Interim Summary

In Experiments 1 and 2 with canonically ordered embedded interrogative and adjunct clauses, we found *wh*-island effects, but no adjunct island effects in Korean.

In Experiments 3 and 4, we attempt to replicate these results with a different group of participants and different types of stimuli. The embedded clauses in these experiments are scrambled to a sentence-initial position. Since this is a natural position for embedded clauses in Korean, and the preferred position for adjunct clauses, it is possible that this will allow for a fairer test for the presence of island effects.

2.4 Experiment 3: Scrambled *Wh*-islands (*whether*-island) in Korean

2.4.1 Participants

Another 48 native speakers of Korean who were residing in Korea participated in this experiment online (M: 26 years old, range: 20-37). Their first and dominant language was Korean, and they had no training in linguistics. Their participation in this study was voluntary.

2.4.2 Stimuli, Method, and Analysis

The stimuli differed from those in Experiment 1 only by the location of the embedded clauses: the embedded clauses in this experiment were sentence-initial, whereas those in Experiment 1 were in their canonical (center-embedded) position. There were 8 experimental conditions reflecting 3 factors, just as in Experiment 1: (i) Location of *wh*-word (matrix clause vs. embedded clause), (ii) Structure of embedded clause (declarative vs. interrogative), and (iii) Answer type (*wh*-answer vs. yes/no-answer). Sample stimuli with embedded interrogative clauses are provided in (13)-(16). The methods and analysis of results were the same as in Experiment 1.

(13) Q: [Obama-ka Mary-ul manna-ss-nun-**ci**] nwukwu-ka tul-ess-**ni**?
        -Nom   -Acc meet-Past-Adn-Q who -Nom hear-Past-Q
    'Who heard whether Obama met Mary?' or
    'Did somebody hear whether Obama met Mary?'
    A: WH-ANSWER: Hillary-ka 'Hillary'

(14) Q: Same as in (13).
    A: YES-NO ANSWER: Ney, tul-ess-eyo 'Yes, heard.'

(15) Q: [Obama-ka **nwukwu**-ul manna-ss-nun-**ci**] Mary-ka tul-ess-**ni**?
        -Nom who -Acc meet-Past-Adn-Q   -Nom hear-Past-Q
    'Who did Mary hear whether Obama met?' or
    'Did Mary hear who Obama met?'
    A: WH-ANSWER: Hillary-lul 'Hillary'

(16) Q: Same as in (15).
    A: YES-NO ANSWER: Ney, tul-ess-eyo 'Yes, heard.'

2.4.3   Results

The results, presented in Figure 4, reveal main effects of Location (with *wh*-answers ($F1$ (1, 47) = 183.01, p < .0001, F2 (1, 39) = 260.41, p < .0001); with yes/no answers ($F1$ (1, 47) = 85.11, p < .0001, F2 (1, 39) = 167.63, p < .0001), and Structure (with *wh*-answers ($F1$ (1, 47) = 48.57, p < .0001, F2 (1, 39) = 63.24, p < .0001); with yes/no answers ($F1$ (1, 47) = 28.67, p < .0001, F2 (1, 39) = 29.80, p < .0001), as well as a significant interaction of Location and Structure (with *wh*-answers, F1 (1, 47) = 42.46, p < .0001, F2 (1, 39) = 42.15, p < .0001; with yes/no answers, F1 (1, 47) = 6.12, p = .017, F2 (1, 39) = 5.86, p = .02).

The significant interaction between Location and Structure suggests a strong *wh*-island effect in Korean. When the *wh*-word is within an embedded interrogative clause, acceptability drops for the *wh*-answer and rises for the yes/no answer, as we would expect if the *wh*-word is unable to take scope out of that clause.

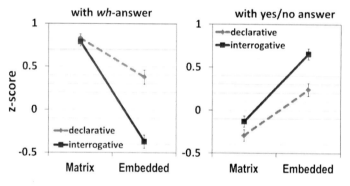

FIGURE 4. Results of Experiment 3

2.5   Experiment 4: Scrambled Adjunct-islands in Korean

2.5.1   Participants

The participants in this experiment were the same as in Experiment 3.

2.5.2   Stimuli, Method, and Analysis

The stimuli in this experiment were the same as those in Experiment 2, but with sentence-initial embedded clauses. There was a total of 3 factors with 8 conditions: Location of *wh*-word (matrix clause vs. embedded clause) x Structure of embedded clause (complement vs. adjunct) x Answer type (*wh*-answer vs. yes/no-answer). Sample stimuli with adjunct clauses are presented in (17)-(20). The method and analysis were identical to Experiment 2.

(17) Q:[Obama-ka Mary-ul manna-ss-ul-**ttay**]   **nwukwu**-ka natana-ss-**ni**?
         -Nom   -Acc meet-Past-Adn-when who -Nom appear-Past-Q
      'Who appeared when Obama met Mary?' or
      'Did somebody appear when Obama met Mary?'
      A: WH-ANSWER: Hillary-ka 'Hillary'

(18) Q: Same as in (17).
      A: YES-NO ANSWER: Ney, natana-ss-eyo 'Yes, appeared'

(19) Q: [Obama-ka **nwukwu**-ul manna-ss-ul-**ttay**]   Mary-ka natana-ss-**ni**?
         -Nom who   -Acc meet-Past-Adn-when   -Nom appear-Past-Q
      'Who did Mary appear when Obama met?' or
      'Did Mary appear when Obama met somebody?'
      A: WH-ANSWER: Hillary-lul 'Hillary'

(20) Q: Same as in (19).
      A: YES-NO ANSWER: Ney, natana-ss-eyo 'Yes, appeared'

2.5.3   Results

As plotted in Figure 5, we found a significant main effect of Location with both *wh*-answers ($F1$ $(1, 47) = 35.02$, $p < .0001$, $F2$ $(1, 39) = 40.09$, $p < .0001$) and yes/no answers ($F1$ $(1, 47) = 39.79$, $p < .0001$, $F2$ $(1, 39) = 47.91$, $p < .0001$). Neither a main effect of Structure nor an interaction between Location and Structure was significant with either answer-type.

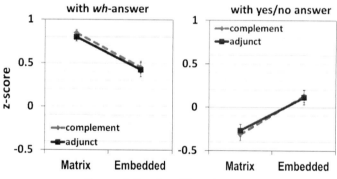

FIGURE 5. Results of Experiment 4

The results here provide further support for the conclusion reached in Experiment 2 that there is no adjunct island effect in Korean. The lack of an interaction between Location and Structure suggests that there is no restriction on *wh*-words in adjunct clauses taking wide scope, i.e. that there is no adjunct island.

3   Discussion

As we have now seen, it does seem feasible to explore the possible existence of island effects in Korean experimentally. We did this here by presenting question-answer pairs as stimuli and then measuring the acceptability not of the *wh*-question itself (which would not yield useful results in Korean), but of the answer, given a particular context. This yielded an interesting and reasonable pattern of results, suggesting that the method is valid.

As we have also seen, there appears to be a robust island effect with interrogative clauses in Korean, though not with adjunct clauses, with both canonically ordered and scrambled sentences. At a very basic level, these results show that island effects may in principle arise even without overt *wh*-movement and support claims that island effects exist in languages like Korean and Japanese (e.g. Lee 1982, Han 1992, Hong 2004 for Korean; Nishigauchi 1990, Watanabe 1992 for Japanese).

If *wh*-islands exist in Korean, however, it then becomes mysterious why adjunct islands do not. A possible answer may lie in the indeterminate nature of *wh*-words in Korean (Kuroda 1965), which as we have seen, can be used as either true *wh*-words or indefinites. *Wh*-expressions in Korean (and Japanese) have been argued to be variable expressions that require appropriate operators to bind them, such as existential or question particles (e.g. Kim 1989, Nishigauchi 1990, Aoun and Li 1993, 2003, Cole and Hermon 1998, Kim 2000, Hong 2004, Choi 2009). For a *wh*-word to be interpreted as a true *wh*-word, it must thus be bound by a (clause-final) question marker. Since interrogative clauses have such markers and adjunct clauses do not, this is likely the source of the asymmetry between *wh*-islands and adjunct non-islands in Korean. The local question marker in interrogative clauses would appear to be preventing the *wh*-word from taking scope outside of such clauses. In clauses without question markers, such as embedded declarative or adjunct clauses, the *wh*-word will not be prevented from taking scope outside of the clause. This could then be what is behind the contrast between the *wh*-island effects seen in Experiments 1 and 3, and the lack of adjunct island effects seen in Experiments 2 and 4.

If an analysis like this is on the right track, it then remains to ask why *wh*-words show this locality effect. That is, what forces the *wh*-word to be bound by the local question marker (in the embedded clause), rather than by a more distant one (in the matrix clause), when both are available? There are various proposals, but we consider two possibilities here. One is that proposed by Shimoyama (2006) for Japanese. Adopting Hamblin's (1973) semantics for *wh*-phrases as set of alternatives, Shimoyama claims that indeterminate phrases (e.g. *wh*-phrases) in Japanese create infinite sets of individuals, and this set creation expands until the first relevant operator (e.g. a question marker) takes the sets of alternatives and generates singleton sets. This absorption by the first question marker inside the interrogative clause makes the sets of alternatives no longer accessible by higher particles, creating the *wh*-island effect. On the other hand, adjunct clauses lack such an operator inside the clause and thus allow a long-distance association between the indeterminate phrase and the matrix particle, therefore yielding no island violation.

Another possible approach is to analyze the relation between the *wh*-word and the question marker in processing terms, given that these two elements have been argued to form a dependency in *wh*-in-situ languages that is similar to the more familiar filler-gap dependency in *wh*-movement languages, (e.g. Miyamoto and Takahashi 2002, Aoshima et al. 2004, Ueno and Kluender 2009, Sprouse et al. 2011). In these terms, when the processor encounters a *wh*-word, it anticipates a scope marker (i.e. question particle) so that it may complete the *wh*-scope dependency as soon as possible, in a way similar to the Active Filler strategy in *wh*-movement languages, in which the processor begins searching for a gap as soon as the *wh*-word is encountered (e.g. Crain and Fodor 1985, Stowe 1986, Frazier and Clifton 1989). As a result, the parser prefers to associate the *wh* phrase with the closest scope marker. In interrogative clauses, the question particle located at the end of the clause is the closest target, and thus the search is complete when this is encountered, resulting in the *wh*-island effect seen in Experiments 1 and 3. In adjunct clauses, on the other hand, there is no such question marker and the scope marker search continues until it is resolved outside of the adjunct clause. This leads to the lack of an island effect with adjunct clauses, as seen in Experiments 2 and 4.

One question that arises with regard to our results is whether they would change if we manipulated the prosody of the *wh*-island stimuli, since some researchers have claimed that island effects in *wh*-in-situ languages like Japanese may disappear with a certain kind of prosody (e.g. Ishihara 2002, Kitagawa 2005). It has been argued, for instance, that in (Tokyo) Japanese both matrix and subordinate *wh*-scope interpretations are possible in potentially ambiguous *wh*-interrogative clauses (e.g. *wh*-island constructions in this study), by using two distinct types of prosody, each of which induces either matrix or embedded *wh*-scope.

Since the experiments in this study were conducted with written stimuli only, it is possible that our results would be different if participants heard auditory stimuli with prosody that favored a *wh*-island-violating interpretation (i.e. matrix scope for a *wh*-word in an embedded interrogative clause). Even so, it is not obvious that the evidence for a *wh*-island in Korean would be overturned in this case. It has been reported, for instance, that the relationship between prosody and *wh*-scope varies significantly among speakers (e.g. in Korean, Jun and Oh. 1996; in Japanese, Kitagawa and Hirose 2012), and even in cases where the stimuli are accompanied by a prosody favoring matrix scope, embedded scope is still more readily available and preferred over matrix scope, (e.g. Hirose and Kitagawa 2010).

In addition, it is not yet clear how much improvement in the acceptability of the matrix scope reading we might get by supplying an appropriate prosody in Korean. Impressionistically, however, it appears that although a certain prosodic contour may reduce *wh*-island effects, it does not eliminate them (cf. Hwang 2007). In this regard, the prosodic effect in Korean may be similar to the effect of D-linking on island violations in *wh*-movement languages: these generally improve with D-linked *wh*-phrases, but not to the point where the effect of the island is eliminated (e.g. Kluender 1998, Hofmeister et al. 2010, Goodall 2013).

Another question concerns the effects of the matrix verbs in our stimuli. As pointed out by Satoshi Tomioka (p.c.), some of these could be factive verbs, and in that case, we could be capturing more an effect of factive islands (e.g. Rooryck 1992, Szabolcsi and Zwarts 1993) than of *wh*-islands. This is indeed a possibility, since factive verbs were used in some of the stimuli in Experiments 1 and 3 (e.g. *tutta* 'hear'). However, it seems unlikely that this is driving the effect, because in 30 of the 40 sets of stimuli in Experiments 1 and 3, the same matrix verbs were used across all 8 conditions. If we were witnessing pure factive island effects, we would expect to see these in both embedded declaratives and embedded interrogatives, with no significant interaction between Location and Structure. These are not the results that we obtained, however.

4 Conclusion

The four experiments in this study show a robust island effect with interrogative clauses, but not with adjunct clauses in Korean, thus potentially helping to resolve a longstanding debate in the literature about the status of island effects in Korean.[2] This was made possible by an experimental approach that was able to avoid some of the inherent difficulties in doing formal acceptability studies of *wh*-questions in Korean.

References

Aoshima, S., C. Phillips, & A. Weinberg. 2004. Processing filler-gap dependencies in a head-final language. *Journal of Memory and Language*, 51, 23-54.

---

[2] This is part of a larger study comparing island behavior in two populations of Korean speakers: native speakers residing in Korea and bilingual speakers raised and living in the U.S. For further details, see Kim and Goodall, in press.

Aoun, J., & A. Li. 1993. Wh-elements in situ: Syntax or LF? *Linguistic Inquiry*, 24, 199-238.

Aoun, J., & A. Li. 2003. Essays on the Representational and Derivational Nature of Grammar. The Diversity of Wh-Constructions. Cambridge, Mass. MIT Press.

Choi, M. H. 2009. The acquisition of wh-in-situ constructions in second language acquisition. Doctoral dissertation, Georgetown University.

Choi, Y. S. 2006. Asymmetry of Locality: A Minimalist View. *Korean Linguistics*, 13(1), 115-129.

Cole, P., & G. Hermon. 1998. The typology of wh-movement: wh-questions in Malay. *Syntax*, 1, 221-258.

Crain, S., & J. D. Fodor. 1985. How can grammars help parsers. *Natural language parsing: Psycholinguistic, computational, and theoretical perspectives*, 94-128.

Frazier, L., & C. Clifton Jr. 1989. Successive cyclicity in the grammar and the parser. *Language and cognitive processes*, 4(2), 93-126.

Goodall, G. 2013. New evidence on D-linking. Paper presented at CUNY Conference on Human Sentence Processing.

Hamblin, C. L. 1973. Questions in Montague English. *Foundations of language*, 10(1), 41-53.

Han, H. S. 1992. Notes on reflexive movement. *Journal of East Asian Linguistics*, 1(2), 215-218.

Hirose, Y., & Y. Kitagawa. 2010. Production–perception asymmetry in Wh-scope marking. *Processing and Producing Head-final Structures*, 93–110. Springer Netherlands.

Hofmeister, P., & I. A. Sag. 2010. Cognitive constraints and island effects. *Language*, 86(2), 366-415.

Hong, S. H. 2004. On the lack of syntactic effects in Korean wh-Questions. *The Linguistic Association of Korea Journal*, 12(3), 43-57

Hwang, H. J. 2007. Wh-phrase questions and prosody in Korean. In *The Proceedings of the 17th Japanese/Korean Linguistic Conference*. UCLA. Los Angeles, CA.

Ishihara, S. 2002. Invisible but Audible Wh-scope Marking: Wh-constructions and Deaccenting in Japanese. *WCCCFL*, 21, 180-193.

Jun, S-A., & M. Oh. 1996. A Prosodic Analysis of Three Types of Wh-Phrases in Korean. *Language and Speech*, 39(1), 37-61

Kim, A.-R. 2000. Korean Wh-phrases Void of Operator. *Japanese/Korean Linguistics*, 9, 311-324.

Kim, B, & G. Goodall. In press. Islands and non-islands in heritage Korean. In *Proceedings of the 38th annual Boston University conference on language development*. Somerville, MA: Cascadilla Press.

Kim, S.-W. 1989. Wh-Phrases in Korean and Japanese are QPs. *MIT Working Papers in Linguistics*, 11, 119-138.

Kitagawa, Y. 2005. Prosody, syntax and pragmatics of Wh-questions in Japanese. *English Linguistics*, 22(2), 302–346.

Kitagawa, Y., & Y. Hirose. 2012. Appeals to prosody in Japanese Wh-interrogatives-Speakers' versus listeners' strategies. *Lingua*, 122(6), 608–641.

Kluender, R. 1998. On the distinction between strong and weak islands: A processing perspective. *Syntax and Semantics*, 241-280.

Kuroda, S.-Y. 1965. Generative Grammatical Studies in the Japanese Language. Doctoral dissertation, MIT.

Lee, H.-S. 1982. Asymmetry in island constraints in Korean. Unpublished manuscript, University of California, Los Angeles.

Miyamoto, E.T., & S. Takahashi. 2002. The processing of Wh-phrases and interrogative complementizers in Japanese. *Japanese/Korean Linguistics*, 10, 62–75.

Nishigauchi, T. 1990. Quantification in the theory of grammar. Dordrecht: Kluwer Academic Publishers.

Rooryck, J. 1992. Negative and Factive Islands Revisited. *Journal of Linguistics*, 28, 343–373.

Shimoyama, J. 2006. Indeterminate phrase quantification in Japanese. *Natural Language Semantics*, 14(2), 139-173.

Sprouse, J., S. Fukuda, H. Ono, & R. Kluender. 2011. Reverse Island Effects and the Backward Search for a Licensor in Multiple Wh-Questions. *Syntax*, 14(2), 179-203.

Sprouse, J., & N. Hornstein. 2013. Experimental syntax and island effects. Cambridge University Press.

Stowe, L.A. 1986. Parsing WH-constructions: evidence for on-line gap location. *Language and cognitive processes*, 1(3), 227–245.

Suh, C.-M. 1987. A Study of the Interrogative Sentences in Korean (in Korean). Top Press.

Szabolcsi, A. & F. Zwarts. 1993. Weak Islands and an Algebraic Semantics for Scope Taking. *Natural Language Semantics*, 1, 235–284.

Tsai, W.-T. 1994. On Economizing the Theory of A-Bar Dependencies. Doctoral dissertation, MIT.

Ueno, M., & R. Kluender. 2009. On the processing of Japanese wh-questions: An ERP study. *Brain Research*, 1290, 63-90.

Watanabe, A. 1992. Subjacency and S-structure movement of wh-in-situ. *Journal of East Asian Linguistics*, 1, 255-292.

Idioms in Korean and Japanese: A phase based account[*]

KYUMIN KIM
University of Ottawa

1 Introduction

In recent studies on idioms (Harley and Stone to appear, Kim to appear), it has been suggested that a phase (Chomsky 2000) may be a boundary that delimits idiomatic expressions. Chomsky proposes that syntactic derivations undergo semantic and phonological interpretation in incremental chunks or *phases*. Once a phase is complete, the complement of the phase (i.e., the domain) is sent for phonological (PF) or *semantic* (LF) interpretation. Those recent studies on idioms have hypothesized that if syntactic computation is interpreted cyclically in phases, it is predicted that there should be a strict boundary restricting idiomatic interpretations. For instance, idiomatic

[*] I wish to thank to the audiences of JK 23 and WAFL9 for valuable comments, Shigeru Miyagawa and Ted Levin for discussion on idioms in Japanese passives, and the editors of this proceedings. I wish to thank Eugenia Suh and Sarah Clarke for help. This research is supported by the Social Science and Humanities Research Council of Canada (SSHRC). Of course, all errors are my responsibility.

Japanese/Korean Linguistics 23.
Edited by Michael Kenstowicz, Theodore Levin and Ryo Masuda.

interpretations would depend on the context no larger than a phase, as a phase is the maximum boundary that can be semantically interpreted at a *single* time. Harley and Stone (to appear) have shown that this is the case with the agent-introducing phase head Voice. Kim (to appear) has shown that this prediction is true with another phase head, ApplH, in the Double Object Construction (DOC) in Korean and Japanese. Moreover, Kim has shown that this may be a cross-linguistic pattern.

In this paper, I expand on these approaches to idioms, by showing how a phase-based account of idioms interacts with passivization. As mentioned above, the domain of a phase is sent for both PF and LF interpretations once the phase is complete. As a consequence, it has been suggested that the domain of the phase is not accessible to further operations, e.g., A-movement. However, an EPP feature can be available on a phase head, and this can allow an element in the domain to undergo A-movement. Thus, under the phase-based account, it is predicted that the direct object of an idiomatic expression in the domain could undergo a type of A-movement, e.g., passivization, as EPP on the phase head, Voice or ApplH, is available. Contrary to this prediction, however, I show that passivization is not always possible with the direct object of idioms. I propose that this is because a phase head may be a part of idiomatic expressions.[1] In this paper, I provide evidence from Korean and Japanese showing that the phase head is absent from passivized idioms, yielding ungrammaticality.

This paper is organized as follows. Section 2 presents a phase-based account for the distribution of idioms in Korean and Japanese in Kim (to appear). Section 3 provides evidence that a phase head, ApplH, can be part of an idiomatic expression. Section 4 discusses the predictions of the phase based account for passivization of idioms, and shows that the evidence in section 3 plays an important role in accounting for the ungramaticality of passivization. This section also discusses passivization of the direct object in idioms of simple transitives in Korean and Japanese, and provides potential evidence that Voice in simple transitives may constitute a part of the idiomatic menaing as ApplH does. Section 5 concludes the paper.

2 Phase and the distribution of idioms in Korean and Japanese

It has recently been proposed that a phase head (above the VP domain) can be a boundary for idiomatic expressions, as schematically represented in (1) (Kim to appear).

---

[1] A similar idea has been suggested by Stone (2009) for English transitives, which is discussed in section 4.2.

(1) [X ↓ [$_{VP}$ V ZP]] where X is a phase head

a phase boundary for idiomatic expressions

Evidence for (1) comes from a cross-linguistic pattern that seems to suggest that an external argument, either the agent (of Voice) or non-agentive argument (of e.g. ApplH) that merges *outside* VP (i.e., the spell-out domain) does not easily constitute an idiomatic expression. For instance, Kim (to appear) observes that across languages an agent in a simple transitive or an indirect object in Double Object Construction (DOC) tends to be excluded from idiomatic expressions.[2] On the other hand, material inside the domain of a phase, i.e., VP, can be part of idiomatic expressions (for instance, ApplLP or PP that appear inside VP). Given this contrast, Kim argues that a phase head above the domain of VP, such as Voice or ApplH, can be a boundary for idiomatic interpretations. In order to be interpreted as an idiom, each part of the idiomatic expression must be accessed in the domain of the phase, namely inside the VP, which is sent for PF and LF interpretations. After spell-out, the material in the domain will not interfere with the elements outside the VP, which exactly predicts the exclusion of those elements from the idiomatic expressions.

In what follows, I discuss some core evidence and arguments presented in Kim as evidence that either ApplH or Voice head delimit idiomatic expressions. Evidence for ApplH comes from DOC and Postpositional Dative (PD) constructions in Korean and Japanese, and evidence for Voice comes from simple transitives. The following represent the structures for the complement of DOC and simple transitives assumed for both languages.

(2) a. ... [$_{ApplHP}$ DP [$_{ApplH'}$ [ApplH [$_{VP}$ DP V]]]]   DOC

b. [$_{VoiceP}$ DP [$_{Voice'}$ [Voice [$_{VP}$ DP V]]]]   simple transitive

In DOC (2a), the complement of DOC has ApplHP, where an indirect object is introduced in the specifier of ApplH, and the VP is the complement of ApplH (e.g., Bruening 2010, Miyagawa and Tsujiok 2004). In a simple transitive (2b), Voice introduces an agent and takes a VP complement. The claim that ApplH and Voice are phase heads (see (1)) predicts that their specifiers (an indirect object or an agent) are excluded from idiomatic expressions. This is shown to be borne out by data from Korean and Japanese. For instance, Korean DOC (3) has an idiomatic expression that consists of

---

[2] More generally, it has been proposed that material outside the VP domain seems to be excluded from idiomatic expression (Kim to appear). For instance, in Blackfoot (Algonquian), a functional p that merges outside VP is excluded from idioms, in contrast to a lexical P that merges insided VP.

the verb and the direct object, and importantly, as predicted by (1), the indirect object in the specifier of ApplH is excluded from the idiomatic expression.

(3) nwuna-un   (sopung kacako maku) [$_{\text{ApplHP}}$ tongsayng-lul
    elder sister-TOPIC picnic   go   a lot   brother-ACC
    [$_{\text{VP}}$ palam-ul   neh]]-ess-ta
      wind-ACC   put.into-PAST-DEC
    'Elder sister instigated her brother to go on a picnic.'

The data from simple transitives also support the prediction, as Korean (4) and Japanese (5) idioms illustrate:

(4) a. Swuni-ka   miyeykkuk-lul   mek-ess-ta
      Suni-NOM   seaweed soup-ACC   eat-PAST-DEC
      'Suni failed the exam.'

    b. Minswu-ka   (cikcang-eyse) os-lul   pes-ess-ta
      Minsu-NOM   (work-at)   cloth-ACC   take.off-PAST-DEC
      'Minsu resigned.'   (Kim, to appear)

(5) a. me o tukeru [eye ACC attach] 'pay attention'
    b. keri o tukeru [end ACC attach] 'put an end to' (Kishimoto, to appear)

In contrast, however, an element in the domain of a phase is predicted to belong to idiomatic expressions. For instance, in both Korean and Japanese, the core structure of PD is as shown in (6) (Bruening 2010, Miyagwa and Tsujiok 2004). Kim shows that in both languges a PP that merges in the VP domain as in (6) can belong to an idiomatic expression. As examplified in (7), P in Korean (7a), and in Japanese (7b) constitue a part of idioms. In Korean (7a), PP *kasum-ey* 'on chest' forms an idiom together with the object (*kal* 'knife') and the verb (*pum* 'bear') meaning 'harbored resentment.' The Japanese idiom in (7b) shows a similar pattern in that the PP 'in hometown' is a part of the idiom 'return in glory' with the verb and object. Although the PP in Japanese can be marked with *-ni*, the marker is postpositional, as it can alternate with the postposition *-e*.

(6) [$_{\text{VoiceP}}$ DP [$_{\text{Voice'}}$ [Voice [$_{\text{VP}}$ PP [$_{\text{V'}}$ [DP V]]]]]]

(7) a. Swuni-ka   [$_{\text{VP}}$ [$_{\text{PP}}$ kasum-ey]   [kal-lul   pum]]-ess-ta.
      Suni-NOM   chest-P   knife-ACC   bear-PAST-DEC
      'Suni harbored resentment.'   (Kim to appear)

b. kokyoo-ni/-e   nisiki-o kazar-u
   hometown-DAT/-P   silk-ACC decorate-PRES
   'return in glory'   (Miyagawa and Tsujioka 2004)

In the following sections, I explore the interaction of idioms and passivization, assuming the phase-based account for the distribution of idioms in Korean and Japanese (1) proposed in Kim (to appear). As data that involve morphologically overt ApplH reveal, the phase head ApplH can be a part of idiomatic expressions. I discuss the consequences of this for the passivization of direct objects in ditransitives, and suggest a similar approach to the passivization of direct objects in simple transitives.

3   ApplH constitutes a part of an idiomatic expression

In Korean, there are other types of clauses that bear ApplHP, in addition to DOC. For instance, consider the adversity clause in (8). In (8a), the nominative DP subject 'Suni' is adversely affected by the event complement phrase, 'Minsu's taking away money'. The dative DP 'Minsu' is the one who performs the event. Importantly, the dative DP is not a full-fledged agent in that it is not compatible with an agent oriented adverb and thus is introduced by ApplH rather than by Voice. (Kim 2012a, b) This is illustrated with a partial structure of an adversity clause (8b). In (8b), ApplH is realized by the adversity morpheme -I whose allomorphs are -i, -hi, -li, and -ki.[3]

(8) a. Swuni-ka [$_{\text{ApplHP}}$ Minswu-eykey(-lul) ton-lul   *ilpule
       Suni-NOM   Minsu-DAT-(ACC)   money-ACC   on purpose
       ppay-ki]-ess-ta
       take away-I-PAST-DEC
       'Suni$_1$ had$_{\text{exp}}$ [Minsu take away her$_1$ money *on purpose].'

   b. [$_{\text{ApplHP}}$ [**DP-DAT** [$_{\text{VP}}$ theme V] ApplH]]]   (Kim 2012b)
                                          -I

Interestingly, the specifier of ApplH in an adversity clause is also excluded from idiomatic expressions (9), like ApplH in DOC. In (9), the idiom consists of the verb 'catch' and the object 'neck' and its meaning is '(something) is revealed' (Naver Online Dictionary). In (9), for example, Suni's mistake was revealed by Minsu. Crucially, the dative DP is excluded from the idiomatic expression.

---

[3] A dative DP in an adversity clause as in (8) can be marked with accusative, like a goal in DOC, which supports the ApplHP account for an adversity clause. Thanks to John Whitman for bringing this issue to my attention.

(9) Swuni-ka   (caki-uy silswuhan-kes-lul)
  Suni-NOM   (self-GEN mistake-do-NOMINAL-ACC)
  [$_{ApplP}$ **Minswu-eykey** [$_{VP}$ telmi-lul   cap]-hi]-ess-ta
     Minsu-DAT   neck-ACC catch-I-PAST-DEC
  'Suni's mistake was revealed by Minsu
  (regarding the mistake that she did).'
  (Lit. 'Suni was caught by her neck by Minsu.')

The adversity clause thus provides more support to Kim's proposal discussed in section 2 that in Korean the ApplH, can be a phase head that delimits an idiomatic expression. A new contribution of this data is that the ApplH seems to form a part of an idiomatic expression. The idiom in (9) includes the adversity morpheme -I that is realized under ApplH. If this is true, then the idiomatic meaning cannot be retained without the morpheme. This is borne out by the data. The same V-Obj idiom in the adversity clause (9) without the ApplH (i.e., without the applicative morpheme -I) does not have the same idiomatic interpretation, as shown in (10) (Naver Online Dictionary). The sentence (10) is a simple transitive, and thus the ApplH is not present in the sentence. However, the same verb and object unit in (10) does not have the idiomatic meaning as in (9) with the ApplH, but a different one: 'have someone under one's control'. This difference suggests that the ApplH contributes to the meaning of idiomatic expressions, and is therefore part of the idiom.

(10) Minswu-ka   Swuni-uy [telmi-lul   cap]-ass-ta
   Minsu-NOM Suni-GEN   neck-ACC catch-PAST-DEC
   *'Minsu caught Suni (regarding the mistake that she made).'
    'Minsu had Suni under his control.'

Thus, the ApplH as a phase head can delimit idiomatic expressions as argued in Kim (to appear), but can also be a part of the idiomatic expressions as the contrast between (9) and (10) suggests. The fact that the ApplH can belong to the idiomatic interpretation will play an important role in the availability of passivization of idioms, as discussed in the following section: the absence of the ApplH will result in the ungrammaticality of passivization of a direct object in idioms. In section 4.2, I will show that morphologically overt Voice in simple transitives patterns with morphologically overt ApplH with respect to passivization.

4   Passivization and idioms

As discussed in section 2, the phase-based account (1) of idioms suggests that the phase head, ApplH, delimits idiomatic expressions. As the boundary is a phase head, it is expected that the head bears an EPP feature, as suggested in

Chomsky (2000). An EPP feature on a phase head allows a direct object (DO) to undergo A-movement, e.g., passivization, as illustrated in (11) (McGinnis 2001). By contrast, a non-phase head such as ApplL does not bear an EPP feature; as a result, passivization of the direct object of ApplL is not allowed. As Voice is also a phase head, it bears an EPP feature that allows its object to undergo passivization.

(11)

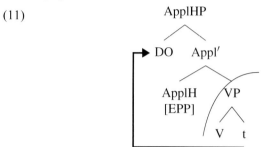

Thus, the proposed account for delimiting idiomatic interpretations (1) in Kim (to appear) has consequences for the passivization of idioms. The delimiting head is a phase head, and this predicts that the object in the idiomatic phrases can undergo passivization.

However, the prediction is not borne out: the direct object in DOC cannot undergo passivization and retain its idiomatic meaning (see (16)).[4] I argue that this is because the ApplH is part of the idiom, as concluded in section 3, not because the ApplH is not a phase head. Regarding the variability of passivization of idioms in simple transitives in Korean and Japanese (see section 4.2), I show that the phase head Voice, like the ApplH, may be part of an idiomatic expression in some cases, and this also could affect the availability of passivization.

4.1 Idioms and passivization in Korean and Japanese

Among the passives in both Korean and Japanese, there are morphologically marked passives whose subject position is theta-marked. In Korean, morphological passives are marked with the same homophonous morpheme as morphological causatives (see Kim 2012 and references therein). In Japanese, they are direct and indirect passives (Kuroda 1979, 1992). As has been discussed in the literature (e.g., Hoshi 1999, Park and Whitman 2003), idioms lose their idiomatic meanings after these types of passivization. Thus, I only consider passives whose subject position is not theta marked, similar to English verbal passivization. In Korean, it is *ci*-passivization where the

---

[4] An indirect object seems to undergo passivization in both langauges. The main concern of this paper is whether a direct object of an idomatic expression in the domain can undergo passivization.

morpheme *(e) ci-* is realized on the verb in passivization. An example of *ci-*passivization is illustrated in (12).

(12) chayksang-i Swuni-ey uyhay mantul-e.ci-ess-ta
     desk-NOM   Suni-by   make-PASS-PAST-DEC
     'A desk was made by Suni.'

In Japanese, it is *niyotte* passive:

(13) John-ga   Mary-ni yotte   nagur-are-ta
     John-NOM   Mary-by   hit-PASS-PAST
     'John was hit by Mary.'

In both Korean and Japanese DOCs, as shown in section 2, an indirect object does not belong to idiomatic expressions. As discussed in section 2, Kim (to appear) accounts for this distribution of idioms in terms of phases: indirect objects merge in the specifier of a phase head, ApplH, which excludes them from idiomatic expressions.

Regarding passivization, then, an accusative marked direct object in the VP domain in Korean or Japanese DOC is predicted to be able to undergo passivization. This is because ApplH is a phase head that can bear EPP, as discussed earlier (see (11)). In Japanese, it seems that there are no idioms consisting of an indirect object and idiomatic VP (Hideki Kishimoto p.c.). Thus, the prediction cannot be tested for this language, and it is not clear whether the ApplH can belong to idiomatic expressions like Korean. For these reasons, I discuss how direct objects in VP idioms in Korean DOC interact with passivization.

It has been observed that *ci*-passivization of ditransitives is possible only if a direct object is nominative marked (Whitman and Park 2003). Consider the examples in (14).

(14) a. Wuywenhoy-ka   Chelswu- lul   sang-ul   cwu-ess-ta.
       committee-NOM   Chelswu-ACC   prize-ACC give-PAST-DEC
       'The committee gave Chelswu a prize.'

     b. Sang **i**   wuywenhoy-ey uyhay Chelswu-eykey/*-**ul**
       prize-NOM   committee-by   Chelswu-DAT/ACC
       cwue-ci-essta.
       give-PASS-PAST-DEC
       'Chelswu was given a prize by the committee.'

The sentence (14a) is a DOC and the verb is 'give'. In (14b), the direct object, *sang* 'the prize' undergoes passivization, and the sentence is grammatical only if the goal 'Chelswu' is marked with dative. When it is marked with accusative, the sentence is ungrammatical. Thus, a simple generalization regarding ci-passivization is that passivization is not possible with accusative marking (Kang 1986).

Taking this generalization as one piece of evidence, Park and Whitman (2003) proposed the following structure as a source structure of ci-passivization of the direct object (see Park and Whitman 2003 for further details).[5] The structure (15) captures the generalization that a direct object can undergo ci-passivization when the goal is not accusative-marked, as in (14b). The goal in the structure (15) is always a dative-marked PP.

(15)

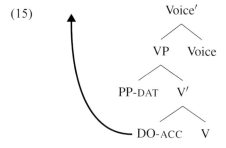

Equipped with this approach (15) to the passivization, let us consider the passivization of direct objects that are part of idioms in Korean DOC. The passivization of DOC (3) is shown in (16) below:

(16) *palam-i   [tongsayng-eykey [_{VP} neh-eci]]-ess-ta
     wind-NOM   brother-DAT   put.into-PASS-PAST-DEC
     *'Brother was instigated.' (Lit. 'Wind was put into her brother')

As illustrated in (16), the direct object *palam* 'wind' cannot undergo passivization. The ungrammaticality is not expected under Kim's approach discussed in section 2: a direct object in idiomatic expressions can move out of the domain of a phase head, ApplH, as EPP on the phase head, ApplH, is available.[6] However, as discussed in section 3, if ApplH can belong to idiomatic expressions, this may capture the ungrammaticality. The source structure of ci-passivization of the direct object does not have ApplHP in (15). In other words, ApplH that forms a part of an idiomatic meaning is absent in the source structure of the passivization. As a result, the idiomatic meaning cannot be available in (16), yielding an ungrammatical result. At the same time, the literal meaning of passivization is still possible, as ApplH is not

---

[5] The source structure (15) is modified in accordance with the assumption in this paper; e.g. Voice head, instead of v.

[6] Direct objects of idiomatic DOCs do not undergo passivization, and Bruening (2010) shows that in English, ApplH is part of idiomatic expressions. Therefore, the passivization of English DOC idioms may be accounted for by the present proposal.

required for this. Thus, the non-availability of passivization with idioms is not because EPP is absent on the phase head, ApplH, but because the head that constitutes the part of the idiomatic meaning is not present in the source structure of passivization. This absence yields infelicity.

4.2 Passivization and idioms in simple transitive of Korean and Japanese

I turn to the passivization of idioms in simple transitives, and suggest that the same type of explanation proposed for ditransitives in the previous section may be possible. As in ditransitives, there are numerous verb-object idioms in simple transitives in Korean as shown in section 2, and in (17). (Naver Online Dictionary, Ko 2005).

(17) a. Swuni-ka (cek-eykey) mulup-lul   kkulh-ess-ta
       Suni-NOM   (enemy-P)   knee-ACC   kneel down-PASS-DEC
       'Suni gave in.'

    b. Swuni-ka   katak-ul   cap-ass-ta
       Suni-NOM   thread-ACC   catch-PAST-DEC
       'Suni understood (a problem).'/ 'Suni got it.'

As suggested in Kim (to appear), agents are excluded from these idioms because Voice, which introduces those agents, is a phase head that delimits idiomatic interpretations. Moreover, those idioms are predicted to undergo passivization, as Voice can bear an EPP feature.

This prediction is partly true in that some idioms in the literature are reported to undergo passivization. An example is illustrated in (18).

(18) Cwuuy-ka   Chelswu-ey uhay(e)   kiwulye-ci-ess-ta.
     attention-NOM Chelswu-BY   devote-PASS-PAST-DEC
     'Attention was devoted by Chelswu.'

However, there are also ungrammatical examples of passivization of idioms. The idioms in (17) cannot undergo passivization, as shown in (19):

(19) a. *(cek-eykey) Swuni-ey uhay mulup-i
        (enemy-P)   Suni-BY   knee-NOM
        kkulh-eci- ess-ta
        kneel.down-PASS-PAST-DEC
        *'Suni was given in.'/ 'Swuni's knee was knelt down.'

    b.*Swuni-ey uhay katak-i   cap-a ci-ess-ta
       Suni-BY   thread-NOM   catch-PASS-PAST-DEC
       'A problem was understood by Suni.'

In Japanese, we can observe a similar pattern. It has long been observed that a direct object of idioms can undergo *niyotte* passivization as shown in (20) (Kuroda 1979, Hoshi 1999). The verb-object idiom in (20a) can undergo passivization without losing its idiomatic meaning, as in (20b).

(20) a. John-ga   tyuui-o   harat-ta
      John-NOM   heed-ACC   pay-PAST
      'John paid heed.'

      b. tyuui-ga John-ni yotte   haraw-are-ta
        heed-NOM John-to owing   pay-PASS-PST
        'Heed was paid by John.'

In fact, with some idioms, the direct object such as in (21a) can undergo *niyotte* passivization as in (21b) and its idiomatic meaning is retained (Kishimoto to appear).

(21) a. Ken-ga   giron-ni   mizu-o   sasi-ta
      Ken-NOM discussion-DAT   water-ACC   pour-PAST
      'Ken interrupted the discussion.'

      b. (Ken-ni yotte) giron-ni   mizu-ga   sas-are-ta
        Ken by   discussion-DAT water-NOM   pour-PASS-PAST
        'The discussion was interrupted (by Ken).'

However, there is another set of idioms that do not allow *niyotte* passivization, as shown in (22), and the idioms in (23) belong to this type.

(22) *Ken-ni yotte   mitikusa-ga   kuw-are-ta
      Ken-by   weed.on.road-NOM   eat-PASS-PAST
      'The weeds on the road were eaten.'

(23) a. abura-o uru [oil acc sell] 'idle away one's time.'
      b. taka-o kukuru [amount acc bind] 'think too lightly.'
                                 (Kishimoto to appear)

The variable behavior of passivization in Korean and Japanese is in parallel to verb-object idioms in English simple transitives, as illustrated in (24) and (25) (e.g., Katz and Postal 1964 among many others). The idiom in (24a) can undergo passivization keeping its idiomatic meaning as in (24b). On the other hand, the idiom in (25a) cannot undergo passivization as in (25b).

(24) a. Spill the beans.   'divulge a secret'
      b. The beans were spilled.

(25) a. kick the bucket.   'die'
     b. *The bucket was kicked.

Regarding the variability of idiom passivization in English, it has been suggested that the grammaticality of passivization (25b) may be because the Voice head that introduces an agent in (25a) belongs to the idiomatic interpretation (Stone 2009).[7] When passivization takes place, as in (25b), only a passive Voice is present. That is, passivization causes the loss of agentive Voice, which is a part of the idiom. In contrast, the passivization shown in (24b) is grammatical, as Voice head in (24a) is not part of the idiomatic interpretation.

Although this account is not expressed in terms of phase, the core idea is similar to the proposal for passivization of a direct object in DOC: a crucial factor for passivizability is whether a phase head, an external argument introducing head, belongs to an idiomatic interpretation. I propose that this factor plays a crucial role in the passivization of simple transitives. Like ApplH, the Voice head in simple transitives may be a part of the idiomatic meaning in some idioms, and this results in the loss of idiomatic interpretation in passives in both Korean (19) and Japanese (22).[8] On the other hand, with grammatical passives as in Korean (18) or Japanese (20b) and (21b), the Voice head is not part of the idiom; as a result, its absence does not affect the grammaticality of passivization. Thus, it appears that a phase head, either ApplH or Voice, is flexible in being able to be part of some idioms, but not all.

There is morphological evidence in Korean that suggests that Voice as well can be a part of an idiomatic expression, like ApplH. Transitives in Korean can be derived by morphological causativization. For instance, in (26a), the verb 'fly' is an intransitive verb, and it can be transitivized by suffixing the causative morpheme as in (26b).

(26) a. pihayngki-ka   nal-ass-ta
      airplane-NOM   fly-PASS-DEC
      'An airplane flew.'

     b. Swuni-ka   pihayngki-lul   nal-li-ess-ta
      Suni-NOM   airplane-ACC   fly-CAUS-PAST-DEC
      'Swuni flew an airplane.'

The transitivized verb can form an idiomatic meaning, as in (27a) below, when it merges with the direct object 'strong fast ball' that consists of *tol*

---

[7] In Stone (2009), a relevant external argument introducing head is flavors of little v, e.g. v_{DO}
[8] I do not pursue the question of what makes Voice part of some idioms but not others.

'stone' and *cikku* 'fast ball'. This is a common Korean idiom that means 'say straightforwardly (something negative)'. The idiom consists of the VP and the causative morpheme under Voice. Importantly, the meaning is lost if the causative morpheme is not present (27b). These data suggest that the Voice phase head in a simple transitive can be part of an idiomatic expression like the ApplH.[9]

(27) a. Swuni-ka (Minswu-eykey) tolcikku-lul   nal-li-ess-ta
     Suni-NOM (Minsu-P)   very fast ball-ACC fly-CAUS-PAST-DEC
     'Suni said something negative straightforwardly (to Minsu).'

    b. *tolcciku-ka   nal-ass-ta
      very fast ball-NOM fly-PAST-DEC
      '?? A very fast ball flew.'/
      *'Something negative is said straightforwardly.'

Thus, I conclude for now that the variable behavior of availability of passivization of idioms may depend on whether the phase Voice head can belong to the idiomatic interpretation.

5 Conclusion

In this paper, I provided evidence from Korean and Japanese that a phase head can be flexible in that it can belong to idiomatic expressions. Morphological evidence is provided from Korean. The consequence of the proposed account is that an idiom cannot be passivized if the phase head is part of the idiom, as its absence affects the idiomatic interpretation. This indicates that the non-availability of passivization is not because a given head is not a phase head and thus lacks an EPP feature. The proposed account suggests that a phase head can be a part of LF interpretation, and as such, it can play a role in A-movement, e.g., passivization, resulting in non-interpretable idioms.

References

Bruening, B. 2010. Ditransitive Asymmetries and a Theory of Idiom Formation. *Linguistic Inquiry* 41: 519–62.

Chomsky, N. 2000. Minimalist Inquiries: The Framework. *Step by step: Essays on Minimalist Syntax in Honor of Howard Lasnik*, eds. R. Martin, D. Michaels, and J. Uriagereka. 89–155. Cambridge, MA: MIT Press.

Harley, H., and M. Stone. In press. The 'No Agent Idioms' Hypothesis. *Proceedings of OnLi (On Linguistic Interfaces)*. Oxford: Oxford University Press.

---

[9] The passivization of (27a) is grammatical when the causative morpheme appears, but ungrammatical without it, which suggests that a phase head is present in the passivization.

Hoshi, H. 1999. Passives. *The handbook of Japanese linguistics*, N. Tsujimura, ed., 191-235. USA: Blackwell.

Katz, J. J., and P. Postal. 1964. *An Integrated Theory of Linguistic Descriptions*. Cambridge, MA: MIT Press.

Kang, Y.-S. 1986. Korean Syntax and Universal Grammar. Doctoral dissertation, Harvard University.

Ko, K.-J. 2005. A Study on Ergativity in Korean. Doctoral dissertation. Korea University, Korea.

Kim, K. To appear. Phase and Idioms. *MIT Working Papers in Linguistics: Proceedings of 9th Workshop on Altaic Formal Linguistics (WAFL 9)*.

Kim, K. 2012a. External Argument-Introducing Heads: Voice and Appl. *The end of Argument Structure?*, Syntax and Semantics, eds., Cuervo, M.C. and Y. Roberge. Bingley, 132–54. UK: Emerald.

Kim, K. 2012b. Affectees in Subject Position and Applicative Theory. *Canadian Journal of Linguistics*, 57: 77–107.

Kishimoto, H. to appear. Idioms. *Handbook of Japanese Word Formation and Lexicon*, eds., T. Kageyama and H. Kishimoto. Mouton: de Gruyter.

Kishimoto, H. 2008. Ditransitive Idioms and Argument Structure. *Journal of East Asian Linguistics*. 17: 141–79.

Kuroda, S.Y. 1979. On Japanese passives. *Exploration in Linguistics: Papers in Honor of Kazuko Inoue*, eds. G. Bedell, E. Kobayashi, and M. Mraki, 305–47. Tokyo: Kenkyusha.

Marantz, A. 1984. *On the Nature of Grammatical Relations*. Cambridge : MIT Press.

McGinnis, M. 2001. Variation in the Phase Structure of Applicatives. *Variations Yearbook 1*: 101–42.

Miyagawa, S., and T. Tsujioka. 2004. Argument Structure and Ditransitive Verbs in Japanese. *Journal of East Asian Linguistics* 13:1–38.

Park, S.-D., and J. Whitman. 2003. Direct Movement Passives in Korean and Japanese. *Proceedings of Japanese/Korean Linguistics* 12: 307–321.

Pylkkänen, L. 2008. *Argument Introducers*. Cambridge: MIT press.

Stone, M. 2009. Idioms and Domains of Interpretation. Arizona Linguistics Circle 3. Tucson, Arizona.

Suffer as a Not-at-issue Meaning: Evidence from the Affected Experiencer Construction in Korean*

LAN KIM
Queens College, City University of New York

1 Introduction

In this paper, I examine the affected experiencer construction (henceforth, the AEC) in Korean that is marked on a verb with the passive morphemes -*i/hi/li/ki* (e.g., Yeon 1991; Chung 1993; Kim, K. 1994; Park 1994; Yeon 2000; Oshima 2006). (1) illustrates an example of the AEC.

* I am very thankful to Satoshi Tomioka and Benjamin Bruening for their invaluable comments and suggestions. I would also like to thank the audience at the conference, in particular Marcel den Dikken, Kyumin Kim, Ji Young Shim, and James H. Yoon for their comments and discussions on this topic, and SySeL members at UD. Due to space limitations, I was not able to incorporate all of their suggestions in the present paper. My special thanks go to Jane Chandlee for her help throughout the writing of the paper. All errors are my own.
¹ The allomorphy of the four types of passive suffix is conditioned by the stem-final sound.

Japanese/Korean Linguistics 23.
Edited by Michael Kenstowicz, Theodore Levin and Ryo Masuda.

(1) Chelswu-ka   Yuna-eykey ilum-ul   cek-hi-ess-ta.
     Chelswu-Nom Yuna-Dat   name-Acc   write.down-Pss-Pst-Dec
     'Chelswu's name was written down by Yuna.'

(1) denotes an event in which Chelswu (the nominative argument) had his name (the accusative argument) written down by Yuna (the dative argument), by which Chelswu was adversely affected; the event mattered to Chelswu in a way that had an adverse effect on him.

What is interesting is that this negative meaning, in an intuitive sense, adds some content to an utterance but in a way independent of the main assertion the speaker intends to make. As shown in (2), an ordinary passive sentence in Korean, which is formed with the same passive suffixes, lacks an adversative meaning.

(2) Chelswu-ka   sey   salam-ulo wancenhi   pakkw-i-ess-ta.
     Chelswu-Nom new   person-to completely   change-Pss-Pst-Dec
     'Chelswu was completely changed to a new person (by someone).'

Given the contrast between (1) and (2), two questions arise: (a) what does the adversative meaning contribute to the semantics, and (b) how is this meaning encoded in the strucutre of the AEC? Despite its distinct meaning, the semantic contribution of the AEC has received relatively less attention in the previous literature. In this paper, I answer these questions by proposing a lexical decomposition anlaysis of the AEC, based on the idea that a sentence may involve two tiers of meaning in the semantics, the at-issue meaning (i.e., its main assertion) and the not-at-issue meaning (e.g., Karttunen 1973; Karttunen and Peters 1979; Potts 2005; Roberts et al. 2009; Simons et al. 2010, Bosse et al. 2012). Specifically, I demonstrate that the adversative meaning associated with the AEC is a not-at-issue meaning, like an implicature. Also, I show that the AEC is a passive sentence, and its active counterpart is the subtype of Tomioka and Sim's (2007) double object construction (henceforth, DOC), in which the possessor is animate. The semantic parallelism between the AEC and the DOC indicates that the AEC is derivationally related to the DOC. In this analysis, the passive morphemes are a phonological realization of the Passive head that is associated with the two tiers of meaning in the semantics.

The remainder of this paper is organized as follows. In Section 2, I describe the meaning of the AEC. Section 3 establishes that the AEC is derivationally related to the subtype of Tomioka and Sim's (2007) DOC and demonstrates that the adversative meaning associated with the AEC is a not-at-issue meaning, like an implicature. In Section 4, I provide my own proposal. Consequences and remaining issues follow in Section 5. Section 6 provides concluding remarks.

2   Meaning of the AEC

This section describes the meaning of the AEC and shows that (a) the nominative argument is an affected experiencer and (b) the possession relation that is established between the nominative and the accusative arguments is encoded as a material part-whole relation.

2.1   Adversative Implication

As introduced in Section 1, the nominative argument in the AEC is an affected experiencer. One piece of evidence illustrating this is the fact that the nominative argument must be animate and sentient. Park (1994) takes this animacy requirement as an indication that the nominative argument is an affected entity.

(3)   Yejin/*chayksang-i   Chelswu-eykey   tali-lul   cap-hi-ess-ta.
      Yejin/desk-Nom   Chelswu-Dat   leg-Acc   grab-Pss-Pst-Dec
      'Yejin's leg/The leg of the desk was grabbed by Chelswu.' (Modified
      from Yeon 1991)

In (3), the nominative argument *Yejin* is animate and receives an affected experiencer role: Yejin suffered from Chelswu grabbing her leg. By contrast, (3) with *chayksang* 'desk' is ungrammatical because an inanimate NP is not an entity that can be understood to suffer.

Next, the experience is always negative. For example, (3) with *Yejin* cannot mean that Yejin was positively affected or not affected at all by the event of Chelswu grabbing her leg.

Note that the effect of the experience need not be physical; the experiencer can also be understood to be psychologically affected. As illustrated in (1) above, for instance, the event of Yuna writing down Chelswu's name does not have any physical effect on Chelswu. Rather, Chelswu is understood to feel displeased as a result of the event.

2.2   Possession Meaning

In addition to the adversative meaning, the AEC involves a possession relation between the nominative argument (the possessor) and the accusative argument (the possessee). I interpret this possession meaning as coming from a material part-whole relation.

First, the AEC often involves an inalienable possession relation, such as body parts, shoes, and clothing, as illustrated in (4) (e.g., Yeon 1991; Chung 1993; Kim, K. 1994; Park 1994; Yeon 2000; Oshima 2006).

(4) a. Julie-ka   Chelswu-eykey   meli-lul   cap-hi-ess-ta.
       Julie-Nom Chelswu-Dat   hair-Acc   grab-Pss-Pst-Dec
       'Julie's hair was grabbed by Chelswu.'
   b. Yuna-ka   Chelswu-eykey   sinpal-ul   palp-hi-ess-ta.
       Yuna-Nom Chelswu-Dat   shoes-Acc   step.on-Pss-Pst-Dec
       'Yuna's shoes were stepped on by Chelswu.'

Note also that (4a) is acceptable even when some other possessor is explicitly spelled out. One can say *Mina-uy meli-lul* 'Mina-Gen hair-Acc', where Mina's hair is understood as attached to Julie (i.e., Mina's hair has been transplanted to Julie and is now a part of Julie in some sense). However, the AEC is infelicitous if the accusative argument is understood to be a detached part of the nominative argument. (4a) cannot be used in the context of a salon, where Chelswu grabbed Julie's hair when it was on the floor.

     In addition, a sentence like (5), which is from Yeon (1991), is reported to be grammatical to the extent that the general (the nominative argument) is assumed to be riding on the horse (the accusative argument) (Kim, K. 1994), i.e., when the horse bridle is understood to be metaphorically part of the general.

(5) cangkwun-i   pwuha-eykey   mal.koppi-lul   cap-hi-ess-ta.
     general-Nom   subordinate-Dat horse.bridle-Acc   hold-Pss-Pst-Dec
     'The horse bridle of the general was held by his subordinate.'

     Thus, I take the possession relation to be a part-whole relation: the nominative argument encodes the whole of a part-whole relation with the accusative argument, and there is often a semantic extension from this core. Later in Section 3 I will show that this part-whole relation in the AEC in fact comes from its active counterpart, namely the DOC.

3   *Suffer* as a Not-at-Issue Meaning

I shall demonstrate that the adversative meaning associated with the AEC is a not-at-issue meaning, like an implicature. To motivate this, I first establish that the AEC is a passive sentence, and its active counterpart is a particular type of the DOC, namely the subtype of Tomioka and Sim's (2007) DOC in which the possessor is animate. Next, I demonstrate that the adversative meaning belongs to an implicature.

3.1   The AEC as a Passive Sentence

To begin with, there is disagreement in the literature on whether the AEC is derivationally related to the DOC (e.g., Washio 1993; Shim 2008; among others). An example of the AEC is given in (6a), and its corresponding DOC is given in (6b).

(6) a. Julie-ka   Chelswu-eykey meli-lul   cap-hi-ess-ta.
       Julie-Nom Chelswu-Dat   hair-Acc   grab-Pss-Pst-Dec
       'Julie's hair was grabbed by Chelswu.'
   b. Chelswu-ka   Julie-lul meli-lul cap-ass-ta.
       Chelswu-Nom Julie-Acc hair-Acc grab-Pst-Dec
       'Chelswu grabbed Julie's hair.'

One main reason for this controversy is that there are differet types of DOCs in Korean, and they look superficially similar to each other because they have the same case marking on the object.[3] This fact often leads researchers to reject the derivational approach. In particular, given that in Korean the passive morphemes are homophonous with some of the causative morphemes[4], much work on the AEC has in fact focused on the question of whether passives are derived from causatives. For example, Shim (2008) shows that the AEC is a causative sentence with an experiencer interpretation.

Contrary to the literature, however, I contend that once we clarify what kind of DOCs we are dealing with in connection with the AEC, it is possible to establish an argument in favor of the derivational approach. Specifically, I suggest that the AEC is derivationally related to the DOC, namely the subtype of Tomioka and Sim's (2007) DOC in which the possessor consists of an animate entity. The semantic parallelism between the AEC and the DOC constitutes one piece of evidence for this claim. Another is the evidence that the AEC qualifies as a passive sentence.

I start with the evidence that the AEC qualifies as a passive sentence. As illustrated in (7), when the dative argument is missing, it is interpreted as an existential quantifier, a clear diagnostic for passives (Bach 1980, Keenan 1980, 1985, Bhatt and Pancheva 2006, Bruening 2013, and Bruening and Tran ms.).

---

[3] See Sim (2005), which provides a detailed discussion of DOCs in Korean in which seemingly similar DOCs are in fact classified as distinct constructions that encode different semantic relations between the two objects.
[4] There are seven causative suffixes in Korean: *-i, -hi,-li,-ki, -wu, -kwu,* and *–chwu.*

(7) motun haksayng-i Chelswu-ka   ilum-ul   cek-hi-ki-lul
    every student-Nom Chelswu-Nom name-Acc write.down-Pss-Nml-Acc
    pala-n-ta.
    hope-Pres-Dec
    'All the students hope that Chelswu's name is written down.'
    a. 'All the students hope that Cheswu's name is written down by
       someone.'
    b. *'All the students$_1$ hope that Cheswu's name is written down by
       them$_1$.'

Next, the semantic parallelism between the AEC and the DOC shows
that the AEC is derivationally related to the DOC. Specifically, Tomioka
and Sim's (2007) DOC, like the AEC, involves a material part-whole
relation[5], and there is often a semantic extension from this core. Consider
(8), in which (8a) and (8b) are the DOCs that correspond to the AECs in (3)
and (5), respectively.

(8) a. Chelswu-ka   Yejin-ul   tali-lul cap-ass-ta.
       Chelswu-Nom   Yejin-Acc   leg-Acc grab-Pst-Dec
       'Chelswu grabbed Yejin's leg.'
    b. pwuha-ka   cangkwun-ul   mal.koppi-lul   cap-ass-ta.
       subordinate-Nom   general-Acc   horse.bridle-Acc hold-Pst-Dec
       'The subordinate held the horse bridle of the general.'

Like the AEC discussed in Section 2, the DOC in (8a) is felicitious insofar
as Yejin and the leg stand in a part-whole relation: the leg is an attached
part of Yejin (Tomioka and Sim 2007). Similarly, (8b) is acceptable when
the horse bridle is understood metaphorically to be part of the general.
    Note, however, that the possessor in the DOC, unlike in the AEC, can
be inanimate, as shown in (9).

(9) Chelswu-ka   sap-ul   calwu-lul   cap-ass-ta.
     Chelswu-Nom   shovel-Acc   handle-Acc   grab-Pst-Dec
     'Chelswu grabbed the handle of the shovel.' (Tomioka and Sim 2007)

Related to this fact, the DOC under consideration, unlike the AEC, lacks an
adversative meaning. As shown in (10), in which the preceding clause
describes the reason why Mina looks prettier, only the DOC in (10a), and
not the AEC in (10b), is a possible continuation of the clause.

---

[5] According to Tomioka and Sim (2007), the material part-whole relation is established
between the two events "affect" and lexical verb instead of two entities.

(10) Mina-ka   te   yeppe poi-nun   iyu-nun
     Mina-Nom more   pretty look-Adn reason-Top
     'The reason why Mina looks prettier is...
     a. Julie-ka   Mina-lul   meli-lul cal-lass-ki ttaymwun-i-ta.
       Julie-Nom Mina-Acc hair-Acc cut-Pst-Nml because-Cop-Dec
       ...because Julie cut Mina's hair.'
     b. #Mina-ka   Julie-eykey meli-lul cal-li-ess-ki   ttaymwun-i-ta.
       Mina-Nom Julie-Dat   hair-Acc cut-Pss-Pst-Nml because-Cop-Dec
       ...because Mina's hair was cut by Julie.'

Taken together, the examples in (9) and (10) show, as discussed in Section 2, that an animacy requirement is tied to the interpretation of the possessor as being affected (see also Park 1994). In the DOC, both animate and inanimate entities are allowed, indicating that the adversative meaning is not necessarily part of the meaning, which is confirmed in (10). In the AEC, by contrast, only animate entities are allowed, which suggests that the adversative meaning is necessarily part of the meaning. Therefore, I conclude that the AEC is a passive sentence and its active counterpart is the subtype of Tomioka and Sim's (2007) DOC in which the possessor is animate. Then the questions that immediately arise are: What does the adversative meaning contribute in the AEC and why is this meaning missing in the corresponding DOC? In what follows, I demonstrate that the adversative meaning is a not-at-ssue meaning, like an implicature, which explains straightforwardly why it is present only in the AEC.

3.2   *Suffer* as a Not-at-Issue Meaning

Crucial to my argument is that, as discussed in the literature (Karttunen 1973, Chierchia and McConnell-Ginet 1990, Potts 2005, inter alia), elements of a not-at-issue meaning project past various semantic operators such as yes/no questions, negation, and conditionals (the standard presupposition holes). One example illustrating this is given in (11), in which the content of a non-restrictive relative clause projects past yes/no questions.

(11) A: Did Chris adopt Tommy, the smartest cat in NYC?
     B: No

Turning to Korean, the adversative meaning associated with the AEC escapes the scope of the various semantic operators, which leads us to the conclusion that the adversative meaning is a not-at-issue meaning, like an implicature.

First, the adversative meaning projects past yes/no questions.

(12) A: Julie-ka   Chelswu-eykey   meli-lul   cap-hi-ess-ni?
     Julie-Nom Chelswu-Dat   hair-Acc   grab-Pss-Pst-Q
     'Was Julie's hair grabbed by Chelswu?'
   B: ani.
     Neg
     'No.'

In (12), answering the question using *ani* 'no' implies that Chelswu's name was not written down by Yuna. *Ani* 'no' cannot be used to indicate that Chelswu's name was written down by Yuna, but he was not adversely affected by it. For this meaning to be conveyed, a more elaborate answer needs to be added.

Second, the adversative meaning does not add a condition to a conditional, as shown in (13).

(13) Julie-ka   Chelswu-eykey meli-lul   cap-hi-n-ta-myen
     Julie-Nom   Chelswu-Dat   hair-Acc   grab-Pss-Pres-Dec-if
     nay-ka   ne-hantey   o.sip   pwul-ul   cwu-kess-ta.
     I-Nom   you-Dat   five.ten dollar-Acc   give-Fut-Dec
     'If Julie's hair is grabbed by Chelswu, I will give you fifty dollars.'

In (13), the condition under which the listener gets fifty dollars is that Julie's hair is grabbed by Chelswu; whether or not Julie suffers from the event is irrelevant for the condition under which the listener is given money.

Futhermore, the adversative meaning is not presupposed, nor is it conversationally implicated. It is widely noted that not all elements of a not-at-issue meaning are presuppositional in the classical sense. For example, Chierchia and McConnelle-Ginet (1990) do not class the content of the non-relative clause in (11) as presuppositional, because it does not convey old information, the standard property of presupposition. More recently, Potts (2005) and Roberts et al. (2009) discuss various elements of a not-at-issue meaning that project but do not behave like presuppositions. One such example is given in (14), which illustrates that a presupposition, unlike other elements of a not-at-issue meaning, does not always project.

(14) a. If Eddie has a dog, then his dog is a ferocious man-eater.
      b. *If Armstrong did win the 2003 Tour, then Lance Armstrong, the
         2003 Tour winner, is training.   (Potts 2005)

In (14a), the presupposition triggered by *his dog*, unlike the content of the appositive in (14b), does not project; the antecedent of the conditional entails the presupposition of the consequent clause.

Turning to Korean, the adversative meaning associated with the AEC does not behave like a presupposition. Consider (15).

(15) *manyak   Chelswu-ka   anh cohun yenghyang-ul patu-myen
       if   Chelswu-Nom   Neg good effect-Acc   receive-if
      Chelswu-ka   sensayngnim-kkey   meli-lul   kkakk-i-ess-ta.
      Chelswu-Nom teacher-Dat.Hon   hair-Acc cut-Pss-Pst-Dec
      'If Chelswu was adversely affected, Chelswu's hair was cut by the
      teacher.'

(15) is infelicitous because the adversative meaning implicated in the consequent clause is entailed by the antecedent of the conditional introduced by *manyak* 'if'. This illustrates that the adversative meaning associated with the AEC, unlike a presupposition, projects.

Furthermore, the adversative meaning does not belong to Potts' (2005) conventional implicature. For example, when the AEC is embedded under a propositional attitude verb, the adversative meaning can be attributed to the higher subject of the main clause other than the speaker.

Finally, the adversative meaning associated with the AEC is not a conversational implicature (e.g., Grice 1969). As shown in (16), it is difficult to cancel the adversative meaning, indicating that this meaning is not context-dependent.

(16) a. Yuna-ka   Thim-eykey pal.swuken-ulo elkwul-ul
        Yuna-Nom Tim-Dat   foot.towel-Ins face-Acc
        takk-i-ess-ta.
        wash-Pss-Pst-Dec
        'Yuna's face was washed by Tim with a foot towel.'
      b. #haciman kuke-n   Yuna-eykey   cohun   il-i-ess-ta.
         but   that-Top Yuna-Dat   good   thing-Cop-Pst-Dec
         'But that was a good thing for Yuna.'

Therefore, I draw the conclusion that the adversative meaning associated with the AEC belongs to the not-at-issue meaning, like an implicature.

4   A Lexical Decomposition Analysis of the AEC

I assume, following the basic idea of event semantics and a lexical decomposition approach, that events are grammatical objects that represent the meaning and structure of a linguistic unit like a verb (Parsons 1990, building on work in Davidson 1967). Further, the external argument is not an argument of the verb but is introduced by a syntactic head, Voice, above the lexical VP (Kratzer 1996). In addition, advocating the idea, as mentioned earlier, that a sentence may involve two tiers of meaning in the semantics, an at-issue meaning and a not-at-issue meaning like an implicature or presupposition (e.g., Karttunen 1973; Karttunen and Peters 1979; Potts 2005; Simons et al. 2010), I posit that a syntactic head may be related to both tiers of meaning (e.g., Bosse 2011, Bosse et al. 2012, Bruening and Tran ms., Kim forthcoming).

Based on these assumptions, I propose that two types of syntactic heads, *PW* (*Part-Whole*) and *Pass* (*Passive*), are responsible for the meaning of the AEC in Korean and that the adversative meaning is introduced by the *Pass* head, which is a phonological realization of the passive morphemes.

First, as represented in (17) the *PW* head denotes the material part-whole relation between the possessor and the possessee; $x \blacktriangleleft y$ means that x is a material part of y.

(17) Semantics of *PW* (*Part-Whole*)

$[\![PW]\!] = \lambda f_{<e, st>}. \lambda x. \lambda y. \lambda e. f(x)(e) \mathbin{\&} x \blacktriangleleft y$ at $\tau(e)$ (Based on Bosse 2011)

Next, the *Pass* head is associated with two dimensions of meaning, the main assertion on the at-issue tier and the adversative meaning on the not-at-issue tier; the not-at-issue meaning is represented after the colon, as in (18).

(18) Semantics of *Pass* (*Passive*)

a. $[\![Passive]\!] = \lambda f_{<st>}. \lambda x. \lambda e. f(e). Agent(e,x): \lambda z. \exists e'(Suffer(e') \mathbin{\&} Exp(e',z)) \mathbin{\&} RESULT(e')(e)$

b. $[\![Passive]\!] = \lambda f_{<st>}. \exists x. \lambda e. f(e). Agent(e,x): \lambda z. \exists e'(Suffer(e') \mathbin{\&} Exp(e',z)) \mathbin{\&} RESULT(e')(e)$

Notice that contingent upon the presence of the dative argument, the semantic denotation of the *Pass* head is either (18a) or (18b). If the dative argument is present, the denotation of the *Pass* head is (18a), in which *Pass* introduces the external argument (adjoined to Spec of PassP). If the dative argument is absent, the external argument is existentially closed, as in (18b).

Putting these arguments together, I propose the structure in (19a), with the semantic interpretation in (19b), in which the meaning of the AEC is computed compositionally.

(19) Chelswu-ka   Yuna-eykey   ilum-ul   cek-hi-ess-ta.
Chelswu-Nom Yuna-Dat   name-Acc   write.down-Pss-Pst-Dec
'Chelswu's name was written down by Yuna.'   Repeated from (1)

a. Structure

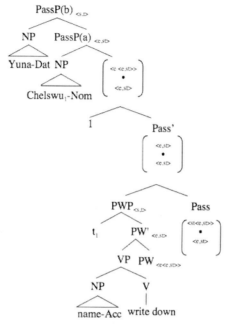

b. ⟦PassiveP(b)⟧ = λe. write.down(e) & Agent(e,Yuna) &
Theme(e,name) & name ◀Chelswu at τ(e):∃e'(Suffer(e') &
Exp(e',Chelswu)) & RESULT(e')(e)

First, VP is formed by V and the accusative argument *ilum* 'name' but is not
computed semantically. Instead, the verb moves to PW, and they build a
complex predicate [V+PWP], which takes *ilum* 'name' as its complement.
This denotes that *ilum* 'name' is the material part of the referent of the
whole of the part-whole relation as well as the theme of the writing-down
event. The nominative argument *Chelswu* is generated in Spec-PWP, where
it is identified as the whole of the part-whole relation with the accusative
argument *ilum* 'name', and combines with *ilum* 'name'. Recall from Section
3 that the AEC is derivationally related to the DOC, and the part-whole
relation in the AEC comes from the corresponding DOC. Next, the whole of
the part-whole relation *Chelswu* moves to Spec-PassP(a) in passivization,
where it is associated with the adversative meaning, the meaning that is on
the not-at-issue tier. I assume that an at-issue meaning and a not-at-issue
meaning are computed on separate tiers. In this way, the adversative
meaning does not obtain until *Chelswu* arrives in the Spec-PassP(a) through

passivization. The interpretation based on the semantic composition is expressed in (19b), such that the sentence is a set of eventualities such that Yuna is the agent in e, the name is the theme in e, the name is the material part of Chelswu in e, and there is an e' such that Chelswu suffered in e', and e' is the result of e.

5   Consequences and Remaining Issues

One important consequence of the current work is that contrary to Potts' (2005) prediction, a single lexical item can make semantic contributions to both tiers of meaning. This observation is not new to this paper. A growing number of studies (e.g., Kubota and Uegaki 2009; McCready 2010; Bruening et al. 2012; Kim and Tomioka ms.) have shown that some elements of meaning can contribute both at-issue and not-at-issue meanings simultaneously. In the present study, I have compensated for Potts' (2005) empirical inadequacy with a proposal in the framework of lexical decomposition based on event semantics.

Second, I have discussed that the passive morphemes in Korean are a phonological realization of the *Pass* head that is associated with the two tiers of meaning in the semantics. If this analysis is on the right track, it follows that the passive morphemes in Korean are ambiguous as to which tier(s) of meaning they are associated with, as illustrated in (20a) for the AEC and (20b) for an ordinary passive.

(20)   a. $[\![Passive]\!] = \lambda f_{<s\,t>}. \lambda x. \lambda e. f(e). Agent(e,x): \lambda z. \exists e'(Suffer(e')$ &
   $Exp(e',z))$ & $RESULT(e')(e)$ Repeated from (20a)
   b. $[\![Passive]\!] = \lambda f_{<s\,t>}. \lambda x. \lambda e. f(e). Agent(e,x)$

As mentioned in Section 1, an ordinary passive sentence, unlike the AEC, lacks the adversative meaning, which indicates that the *Pass* head contributes only an at-issue meaning, as represented in (20b). Left unanswered at this time is the question: why are the passive morphemes ambiguous in Korean? Also, note that unlike in Korean, an adversative meaning is (arguably) missing in Japanese passives, both the possessive passive which involves the part-whole relation and the indirect passive without the part-whole relation. As shown so far, however, the adversative meaning is necessarily part of the meaning of the AEC in Korean, which also involves the part-whole relation. Why, then, is the adversative meaning obtained when a sentence involving the part-whole relation is passivized in Korean, but not in Japanese? I leave these questions for future work.

6 Conclusion

Establishing that the AEC is derivationally related to the subtype of Tomioka and Sim's (2007) DOC based on the semantic parallelism between the AEC and the DOC, I have demonstrated that the adversative meaning associated with the AEC is a not-at-issue meaning, like an implicature, and is independent of the truth-conditional meaning of a sentence. Also, adopting a lexical decomposition approach, I have suggested that there are two types of syntactic heads, *PW* and *Pass*, that are responsible for the meaning of the AEC and the adversative meaning is introduced by the *Pass* head: the *Pass* head is associated with two dimensions of meaning, and it is a phonological realization of the passive morphemes. The current analysis of the AEC straightforwardly explains the obligatorily presence of the adversative meaning in the AEC, and not in the corresponding DOC. Also, it provides empirical evidence for the recent observation that in many East Asian languages, the adversative meaning may belong to an implicature or a presupposition (see Bruening and Tran, ms. and Kim, forthcoming).

References

Bach, E. 1980. In Defense of Passive. *Linguistics and Philosophy* 3: 297–341.

Bhatt, R. and R, Pancheva. 2006. Implicit Arguments. *The Blackwell Companion to Syntax* 2. 558– 588. eds. Martin Everaert and Henk van Riemsdijk. Oxford: Blackwell.

Bosse, S. 2011. The Syntax and Semantics of Applicative Arguments in German and English. Doctoral dissertation, University of Delaware.

Bosse, S., B. Bruening and M. Yamada. 2012. Affected Experiencers. *Natural Language and Linguistic Theory* 30: 1185–1230.

Bruening, Benjamin. 2013. By-phrases in Passives and Nominals. *Syntax* 16.1: 1–41.

Bruening, B., and T. Tran. Manuscript. Chinese-Type "Passives": A Vietnamese Perspective. University of Delaware.

Chierchia, G. and S. McConnell-Ginet. 1990. *Meaning and Grammar: An Introduction to Semantics*. MIT Press.

Chung, T. 1993. The Affected Construction in Korean and Japanese. *Japanese/Korean Linguistics* 3. 154–170. ed. S. Choi. CSLI, Stanford.

Davidson, D. 1967. The Logical Form of Action Sentences. *The Logic of Decision and Action*. 81–95. ed. N. Reschler. University of Pittsburgh Press.

Karttunen, L. 1973. Presuppositions of Compound Sentences. *Linguistic Inquiry* 4: 167–193.

Karttunen, L., and P. Stanley. 1979. Conventional Implicature. *Syntax and Semantics* 11: Presupposition. 1–56. ed. Choon-Kyu Oh and David A. Dinneen. New York: Academic Press.

Keenan, E. L. 1980. Passive is Phrasal (not Sentential or Lexical). *Lexical Grammar*. 181–214. eds. Teun Hoekstra, Harry van der Hulst, and Michael Moortgat, Dordrecht: Foris.

Keenan, E. L. 1985. Passive in the World's Languages. *Language Typology and Syntactic Description 1: Clause Structure*. 243–281. ed. Timothy Shopen. Cambridge: Cambridge University Press.

Kim, K. 1994. Adversity and Retained Object Passive Constructions. *Japanese/Korean Linguistics* 4. 331–346. ed. N. Akatsuka. CSLI, Stanford.

Kim, L. Forthcoming. Projective Meanings of Thai Passive-type Constructions, and Implications for East Asian (Chinese *bei*) Passive Constructions. *Proceedings of the 37th Penn Linguistics Conference*.

Kratzer, A. 1996. Severing the External Argument from its Verb. *Phrase Structure and the Lexicon*. 109–137. eds. J. Rooryck and L. Zaring, The Netherlands, Dordrecht: Kluwer Academic Publishers.

Oshima, D. 2006. Adversity and Korean/Japanese Passives: Constructional Analogy. *Journal of East Asian Linguistics* 15 (2): 137–166.

Park, J.-W. 1994. Morphological Causatives in Korean: Problems in Grammatical Polysemy and Constructional Relations, Doctoral dissertation, University of California, Berkeley.

Parsons, T. 1990. *Events in the Semantics of English. A Study in Subatomic Semantics*. Cambridge: MIT press.

Potts, C. 2005. *The Logic of Conventional Implicatures*. Oxford: Oxford University Press.

Roberts, C., S. Mandy, B. David and T. Judith. 2009. Presupposition, Conventional Implicature, and Beyond: A Unified Account. *Proceedings of Workshop on New Directions in the Theory of Presupposition*.

Shim, J. Y. 2008. Unifying Korean -i/hi/li/ki Constructions. *Minimalist explorations of the syntax-lexicon interface*. 221-241. Hankook: Seoul.

Sim, C. 2005. To Make a Case for All: Syntactic Structure, Semantic Interpretation and Case Morphology, Doctoral dissertation. University of Delaware.

Tomioka, S. and C. Sim. 2007. The Event Semantic Root of Inalienable Possession. Manuscript. University of Delaware; Gyeongin National University of Education.

Washio, R. 1993. When Causatives Mean Passive: A Cross-linguistic Perspective. *Journal of East Asian Linguistics* 2: 45–90.

Yeon, J.-H. 1991. The Korean Causative-Passive Correlation Revisited. *Language research* 27: 337–358.

Yeon, J.-H. 2000. When Causatives Meet Passives in Korean. *SOAS Working Papers in Linguistics* 10: 249–268.

Another Look at Negative Polarity Items in Japanese*

HIDEKI KISHIMOTO
Kobe University

1   Introduction

The main objective of this paper is to show that the syntactic behavior of negative polarity items (NPIs) allows us to assess the structural organization of clauses in Japanese. NPIs fall into two types. One type of NPI, which is referred to as 'argument NPI', is licensed with reference to its overt constituent position (i.e. this type of NPI is licensed in a position in which it appears after A-movement, if it applies) and the other, which is referred to as 'floating NPI', can be licensed in its underlying theta-marking position (the position before A-movement takes place). In this paper, by looking at how the scope of these NPIs extends in a clause, I argue that in Japanese, sub-

---

* This is a revised version of the paper presented at the 23rd Japanese/Korean Linguistics Conference (October 2013, MIT). I would like to thank the audience, in particular, Shigeru Miyagawa, Norvin Richards, Daiko Takahashi, James Yoon, Marcel den Dikken, Junko Shimoyama, Takeo Kurafuji, Hideaki Yamashita, Hiromu Sakai, Hitatsugu Kitahara, Yusuke Imanishi, Sayaka Goto, and Michael Yoshitaka Erlewine for helpful comments and suggestions.

Japanese/Korean Linguistics 23.
Edited by Michael Kenstowicz, Theodore Levin and Ryo Masuda.
Copyright © 2016, CSLI Publications

jects are moved into Spec-TP via A-movement when they are marked with nominative or dative case, but not when they receive oblique marking. The syntactic behavior of NPIs also illustrates that negative *nai* is raised to T when it is associated with a verbal predicate, but not an adjectival predicate.

2   Negative Polarity and Negative Scope

Japanese has several different kinds of NPIs, such as *dare-mo* 'anyone', *Ken-sika* 'Ken-only', and *amari* 'very'. NPIs are licensed under the scope of negation, and hence occur only in negative contexts.

(1) a. {Ken-sika/Dare-mo/Amari ooku-no   gakusei-ga}   ko-nakat-ta.
       Ken-only/anyone-Q/very   many-GEN student-NOM come-NEG-PST
       '{Only Ken/No one/Not very many students} came.'
    b. *{Ken-sika/Dare-mo/Amari ooku-no   gakusei-ga}   ki-ta.
        Ken-only/anyone-Q/very   many-GEN student-NOM come-PST
        '{Only Ken/Anyone/Very many students} came.'

In Japanese, no subject-object asymmetry is observed in NPI licensing. In simple clauses, NPIs are legitimate regardless of whether they appear in subject or object position.

(2) a. {Ken-sika/Dare-mo/Amari ooku-no   gakusei-ga}   hon-o
       Ken-only/anyone-Q/very   many-GEN student-NOM book-ACC
       yoma-nakat-ta.
       read-NEG-PST
       '{Only Ken/No one/Not very many students} read books.'
    b. Ken-ga   {hon-sika/nani-mo/amari   ooku-no   hon-o}
       Ken-NOM book-only/anything-Q/very many-GEN book-ACC
       yoma-nakat-ta.
       read-NEG-PST
       'Ken read {only books/nothing/not very many books}.'

In contrast, English displays a subject-object asymmetry with regard to NPI licensing, as seen in (3).

(3) a. John did not read any book.
    b. *Anyone did not read the book.

Since negative scope does not extend over TP in English, an NPI cannot appear in subject position, even though it is allowed to occur in object position. The difference in the behavior of NPIs between Japanese and English raises the question of why Japanese does not show a subject-object asymmetry in NPI licensing.

In the discussion that follows, I suggest that the head raising of a negative head provides a key to understanding the issue on the difference in the syntactic behavior of NPIs. I claim that in Japanese, Neg-head raising applies to verbal clauses, so that no subject-object asymmetry is observed for (2) with regard to the licensing of NPIs. More specifically, I argue that negative scope extends over TP if Neg-head raising is instantiated, as in (4).

(4) [$_{FinP}$ [$_{TP}$ SBJ [$_{NegP}$ [$_{vP}$ [$_{vP}$ OBJ V]v] ~~Neg~~] ~~Neg-T~~]] Neg-T-Fin]

I assume that FinP, which determines the finiteness of a clause, is projected over TP (Rizzi 1997, 2004), and that in Japanese, the T-head, which marks finiteness, is head-raised to Fin. On this premise, we can state that when the Neg-head is raised to T, the complex head including Neg and T formed by virtue of Neg-head raising undergoes raising to Fin, as represented in (4). In (4), negative scope extends over TP, because the complex head comprised of Neg and T takes TP as its c-command domain. If Neg-head raising does not take place, negative scope extends over NegP, but not TP. Since Neg-head raising is not implemented in the English sentences in (3), a subject-object asymmetry is observed in NPI licensing.[1]

The present proposal is in line with the Neg-head raising analysis advanced in Kishimoto (2007, 2008), in the sense that Neg-head raising is held responsible for the clause-wide negative scope in Japanese. In the literature, there is another line of research, which attempts to account for the absence of a subject-object asymmetry by assuming that in Japanese, unlike English, subjects stay in vP-internal position.

(5) [$_{FinP}$ [$_{TP}$ [$_{NegP}$ [$_{vP}$ **SBJ** OBJ V-v] Neg] T] Fin]

In this analysis, no subject-object asymmetry in NPI licensing obtains in Japanese, because a subject NPI is located in a structural position low enough to be licensed by a negative head in NegP (via either Spec-head agreement (Aoyagi and Ishii 1994, Watanabe 2004) or c-command (Kato 1994)). Attractive as this analysis looks at first blush, there is good reason to believe that the presence or absence of a subject-object asymmetry in NPI licensing can be attributed to a difference in the position of a Neg-head.

It is in fact easy to confirm empirically that nominative subjects in Japanese undergo raising to TP, just as subjects in English, and that Neg-head

---

[1] In English, an NPI can appear in subject position when *not* resides in a higher position than TP, e.g. the NPI *anyone* is licensed in a sentence like *What didn't anyone see?*.

raising makes it possible for its negative scope to extend over TP. I will turn to this discussion in the next section.

3 Two Types of NPIs

In Japanese, NPIs, which need to be licensed under the scope of negation, are divided into two classes. One class of NPIs ('argument-type') includes expressions that occur with *sika* 'only' and *amari* 'very', and they are licensed if they fall under negative scope in their surface position. *Wh*-NPIs such as *nani-mo* 'anything' and *dare-mo* 'anyone' are included in the other class of NPIs ('floating-type'). They behave like floating numeral quantifiers, and can be licensed in underlying theta-marking position.

In simple clauses, the behavioral differences between the two classes of NPIs are not easily detected, mainly because negative scope extends over TP. Nevertheless, the relevant differences show up in raising constructions where the thematic subject of the main verb is raised to the matrix Spec-TP from within vP in the lower clause. The two classes of NPIs provide evidence that nominative subjects undergo raising to TP.

3.1 Raising Construction

In this section, I will look at the raising construction constructed from the aspectual verb *iru* 'be'. In (6), the main verb *yomu* 'read' in the *te*-form is embedded under the aspectual verb *iru* 'be'.

(6) Ken-ga   hon-o   yon-de ir-u.
    Ken-NOM book-ACC read   be-PRS
    'Ken is reading books.'

The aspectual construction with the verb *iru* can be assumed to have a biclausal structure. Given that -*te* attached to the main verb is a non-finite tense marker (Kishimoto 2012), the configuration (7) can be posited for the aspectual construction in (6) if the subject is raised to the matrix Spec-TP.

(7) [$_{FinP}$ [$_{TP}$ SBJ [$_{FinP}$ [$_{TP}$ ~~SBJ~~ [$_{vP}$ ~~SBJ~~ [$_{vP}$ OBJ V]v] T]Fin]T]Fin]

One particularly interesting feature of this aspectual construction is that the negator *nai* 'not' can appear in two different syntactic positions. As shown in (8), the negative *nai* may either precede or follow the aspectual verb (but must follow the main verb).

(8) a. Mari-ga   hon-o   yon-de i-na-i.
       Mari-NOM book-ACC read   be-NEG-PRS
       'Mari is not reading the book.'   V-BE-NEG

b. Mari-ga   hon-o   yoma-nai-de ir-u.
   Mari-NOM book-ACC   read-NEG   be-PRS
   'Mari is not reading the book.'   V-NEG-BE

The aspectual construction is one species of raising construction, where the subject located in the matrix Spec-TP originates from within the embedded clause. The examples in (9) show that inanimate subjects and clausal idioms can be embedded under the verb *iru*, which suggests that the aspectual construction under investigation should involve raising.

(9) a. Sora-ga   mada {hare-te i-na-i/hare-nai-de   i-ru}.
       sky-NOM still   clear   be-NEG-PRS/clear-NEG be-PRS
       'The sky has not been clear yet.'
    b. Kono mise-de-wa   mada kankodori-ga {nai-te i-na-i/naka-
       this shop-at-TOP   still cuckoo-NOM   sing   be-NEG-PRS/sing-
       nai-de i-ru}.
       NEG   be-PRS
       'There are still many customers at this shop.'

Importantly, the grammatical status of the examples in (9) remains the same regardless of whether the negative *nai* precedes or follows the aspectual verb. This fact suggests that the two variants of the aspectual construction in (8) have raising structures.[2]

The extent in which negative scope extends in the aspectual construction differs depending on whether the negator precedes or follows the aspectual verb. It turns out that this property of the raising construction is instrumental in confirming the presence of subject raising in Japanese. By way of illustrating this point, I will make crucial use of an NPI like *amari ooku* 'very many', which is licensed in surface position by falling under negative scope.[3] (The NPI *amari ooku* has the property that when it is licensed under the scope of negation, negation is interpreted as taking scope over *ooku* 'many', obtaining the meaning of 'not many').

First of all, note that the predicate-internal subject hypothesis makes two subject positions available in a simple clause—one is Spec-vP, where a sub-

---

[2] The aspectual verb *iru* does not impose any selectional restriction on the subject, which is characteristic of raising verbs, and thus, any type of subject is allowed in the two variants of the aspectual construction as long as it satisfies the selectional requirement of the main verb.

[3] *Amari* can be combined with other adjectival expressions, such as *amari kasikoi hito* 'very smart people'. Even in this case, *amari* serves as an NPI, as (i) illustrates.

(i) Amari kasikoi hito-ga   koko-ni {i-nakat-ta/*i-ta}.
    very   smart   people-NOM here-in   be-NEG-PST/be-PST
    '(Not) very smart people are here.'

ject receives its theta role from the verb, and the other, Spec-TP. The raising
construction allows us to assess whether subjects in Japanese undergo subject raising from Spec-vP to Spec-TP or remain in Spec-vP without movement. To illustrate this point, let us consider how expressions modified by
amari ooku-no 'very (many)' behave in the aspectual construction. First, a
subject-object asymmetry in NPI licensing is observed when the negator is
embedded under *iru*, as shown by the contrast in acceptability between
(10a) and (10b).

(10) a. *<u>Amari ooku-no hito-ga</u>   hon-o   yoma-nai-de i-ru.
       very   many-GEN man -NOM book-ACC read-NEG   be-PRS
       'Very many people have not been reading books.'
   b. John-ga <u>amari ooku-no hon-o</u>   yoma-nai-de i-ru.
       John-NOM very   many-GEN book-ACC read-NEG   be-PRS
       'John has not been reading very many books.'

Second, if the negative *nai* is placed after the aspectual verb *iru*, no subject-
object asymmetry arises in NPI licensing.

(11) a. <u>Amari ooku-no hito-ga</u>   hon-o   yon-de i-na-i.
       very   many-GEN man -NOM book-ACC read   be-NEG-PRS
       'Not very many any people have been reading books.'
   b. John-ga <u>amari ooku-no hon-o</u>   yon-de i-na-i.
       John-NOM very   many-GEN book-ACC read   be-NEG-PRS
       'John has not been reading very many books.'

It is also worthy of remark that all types of nominative subjects, including
the nominative subjects of unergative, unaccusative and passive predicates,
fall outside the scope of negation when *nai* precedes the aspectual verb *iru*.

(12) *<u>Amari ooku-no hito-ga</u>   {hasira-nai-de i-ru/taore-nai-de i-ru/
       very   many-GEN man-NOM run-NEG   be-PRS/fall-NEG be-PRS/
       nagur-are-nai-de i-ru}.
       hit-PASS-NEG   be-PRS
       'Very many people have not been {running/falling down/beaten}.'

The facts fall out if nominative subjects undergo raising to Spec-TP. The
behavioral difference of the NPI observed in (10) and (11) can be attributed
to the fact that the negative *nai* resides in the embedded clause when it precedes the aspectual verb, but that *nai* resides in the main clause when it follows the aspectual verb *iru*, as illustrated in (13).

(13) a. [$_{FinP}$ [$_{TP}$ SBJ [$_{vP}$ [$_{FinP}$ [$_{TP}$ [$_{NegP}$ [$_{vP}$ OBJ V-v]]]**NEG-T-Fin**]Be]]T-Fin]

    b. [$_{FinP}$[$_{TP}$ SBJ [$_{NegP}$ [$_{vP}$ [$_{FinP}$ [$_{TP}$ [$_{vP}$ OBJ V-v]]T-Fin]Be]]] **NEG-T-Fin**]

In (10), where *nai* precedes the aspectual verb, the negative *na* is raised to the embedded Fin, but not any further, and thus, its scope extends only over the embedded clause. The subject-object asymmetry observed in (10) suggests that the subject, but not the object, is extracted from within the embedded clause, i.e. the subject is moved to Spec-TP from within embedded vP. In (11), where *nai* follows the aspectual verb *iru*, the scope of *nai* extends over the main clause, because *nai* resides in the matrix Fin. In this case, the subject as well as the object of the main verb falls under the scope of negation, even if the subject undergoes raising to the matrix TP. Note that this behavior of the NPI *amari ooku* is not expected if the subjects remain within vP without subject raising to TP.

It is important to see at this point that not all NPIs behave this way. With NPIs like *dare-mo* 'anyone' and *nani-mo* 'anything', no subject-object asymmetry is observed even when *nai* precedes the aspectual verb *iru*.

(14) a. Mada <u>dare-mo</u>   hon-o   yoma-nai-de i-ru.
       yet   anyone-Q book-ACC read-NEG   be-PRS
       'No one has been reading books yet.'

    b. John-ga   mada <u>nani-mo</u>   yoma-nai-de i-ru.
       John-NOM yet   anything-Q read-NEG   be-PRS
       'John has not been reading anything yet.'

It is beyond doubt that the NPIs in (14) are licensed by *nai*. This is verified by the fact that the affirmative counterparts without a negator *nai* are unacceptable, as exemplified in (15).

(15) *Mada <u>dare-mo</u>   hon-o   yon-de i-ru.
      yet   anyone-Q book-ACC read   be-PRS
      'Anyone has been reading books yet.'

Moreover, the examples in (16), where *amari ooku-no hito* in (12) is replaced by *dare-mo*, are acceptable.

(16) Mada <u>dare-mo</u> {hasira-nai-de i-ru/taore-nai-de i-ru/
     yet   anyone-Q   run-NEG   be-PRS/fall-NEG be-PRS/
     nagur-are-nai-de i-ru}.
     hit-PASS-NEG   be-PRS
     'No one has been {running/falling down/beaten} yet.'

The behavior of the NPI *dare-mo* in (14a) and (16) looks puzzling at first sight, but the fact falls out naturally if it is licensed in embedded vP-internal position, behaving like a floating numeral quantifier, as depicted in (17).

(17) [$_{FinP}$ [$_{TP}$ SBJ [$_{vP}$ [$_{FinP}$ [$_{TP}$ [$_{NegP}$ [$_{vP}$ ~~SBJ~~ **dare-mo** OBJ V-v]][**NEG**-T-Fin] Be]]] T-Fin]

In (17), the thematic subject of the main verb is first merged with the embedded vP (to receive a theta role) and is moved to the matrix Spec-TP. If the NPI *dare-mo* is placed in the embedded vP position thanks to the presence of a copy of the subject, this NPI can be licensed by the negator appearing in the embedded Fin. This analysis is reasonable, since this type of NPI does behave like a floating numeral quantifier, as observed by Kawashima and Kitahara (1992).

(18) Mada (gakusei-ga) {dare-mo/hito-ri-mo} hon-o yoma-nai-de
    yet   student-NOM anyone-Q/single-CL-Q book-ACC read-NEG
    i-ru.
    be-PRS
    'No student has been reading books yet.'

Example (18) shows that an argument (i.e. the thematic subject) can occur with a simple *wh*-NPI like *dare-mo*, just like *hito-ri-mo*. As argued by Miyagawa (1989) and others, floating numeral quantifiers can be placed in theta-marking position where their associated hosts are first merged (to receive theta roles). If *dare-mo* can be positioned in vP-internal position, as in (17), the acceptability of (14a) and (16) is naturally expected.

The present view gains support from the fact that a genitive-marked NPI like *dare-no* gives rise to the same subject-object asymmetry as does the NPI *amari ooku-no* 'very many'.

(19) a. *Mada dare-no tomodati-mo hon-o yoma-nai-de i-ru.
       yet anyone-GEN friend-Q   book-ACC read-NEG   be-PRS
       'No one's friend has been reading books yet.'
   b. Mada Ken-wa dare-no hon-mo yoma-nai-de i-ru.
       yet Ken-TOP anyone-GEN book-Q   read-NEG   be-PRS
       'Ken has not been reading anyone's book yet.'

The data suggest that the NPI *dare-no tomodai-mo* 'anyone's friend' should belong to the argument-type, unlike simple *wh*-NPIs like *dare-mo* and *nani-mo*. In fact, (20) illustrates that the NPI *dare-no tomodai-mo* does not behave like a floating numeral quantifier.

(20) Mada (*gakusei-ga) <u>dare-no   tomodati-mo</u> hon-o   yon-de
      yet   student-NOM anyone-GEN friend-Q   book-ACC read
      i-na-i.
      be-NEG-PRS
      'No one's friend (among students) has been reading books yet.'

If the subject NPI *dare-no tomodai-mo* in (19a) is construed only as an argument, it must be raised to the matrix Spec-TP. This gives rise to the contrast in acceptability in (19). This fact in turn suggests that (14a) and (16) are acceptable, because *dare-mo* is a floating NPI, which is allowed to appear in the vP-internal subject position.[4]

3.2   Control Construction

Let us now turn to the discussion of control constructions, which show syntactic behavior distinct from what is observed for the raising construction owing to the fact that their subjects are not merged in the embedded clause. In this section, I will look at the type of control construction (21) where the main verb in the *te*-form is combined with *oku* 'put'.

(21) John-ga   hon-o   yon-de   oi-ta.
      John-NOM book-ACC read   put-PST
      'John read the books.'

Example (21) represents a case of control construction, where the subject is selected by *oku*, i.e. the thematic subject is placed in the matrix clause, and PRO appears in the complement clause, as (22) illustrates.

(22) [$_{FinP}$ [$_{TP}$ [$_{vP}$ SBJ [$_{FinP}$ [$_{TP}$ PRO [$_{vP}$ V-v]]T-FIN]PUT]]T-FIN]

In this type of control construction, negative *nai* can either precede or follow the auxiliary verb *oku*, as shown in (23).

---

[4] *Wh*-NPIs falling into the floating class generally do not have overt case marking, but they can be marked with dative case. In fact, the example (i) shows that the dative-marked NPI *dare-ni-mo* behaves like a floating numeral quantifier, just like non-case-marked NPIs *dare-mo* and *nani-mo*.

    (i) Gakusei-ni-wa   dare-ni-mo   hon-ga   hituyoo-de naka-ta.
       student-DAT-TOP anyone-DAT-Q book-NOM necessary   NEG-PST
       'No students needed books.'

Note that this type of NPI behaves as a negative concord item (see Watanabe 1994; Miyagawa, Nishioka, and Zeijlstra 2013).

(23) a. Kare-ga   sono koto-o   hanasi-te oka-nakat-ta.
      he-NOM   that   fact-ACC   talk   put-NEG-PST
      'He did not talk about that matter.'
    b. Kare-ga   sono koto-o   hanasa-nai-de oi-ta.
       he-NOM   that   fact-ACC   talk-NEG   put-PST
       'He did not talk about that matter.'

The fact that neither inanimate subjects nor clausal idioms can be embedded under *oku*, as in (24), shows that the verb *oku* takes a control complement.

(24) a. *Sora-ga {hare-te oka-nakat-ta/hare-nai-de oi-ta}.
       sky-NOM clear   put-NEG-PST/clear-NEG put-PST
       'The sky was not cleared.'
    b. *Kono mise-de-wa   kankodori-ga {nai-te oka-nakat-ta/
       this   shop-at-TOP cuckoo-NOM   sing   put-NEG-PST/
       naka-nai-de oi-ta}.
       sing-NEG   put-PST
       'There were many customers at this shop.'

Importantly, the verb *oku* 'put' takes a control complement, irrespective of whether *nai* follows or precedes *oku*.

In control constructions, NPIs display behavior distinct from what they show in raising constructions. First, both argument and floating NPIs are allowed to appear in subject position when the upper verb *oku* is negated.[5]

(25) a. <u>Amari ooku-no   hito-ga</u>   maemotte   kyookasyo-o kat-te
       very many-GEN man-NOM in.advance textbook-ACC buy
       oka-nakat-ta yooda.
       put-NEG-PST seem
       'It seems that not very many people bought textbooks in advance.'
    b. <u>Dare-mo</u>   kyookasyo-o maemotte   kat-te   oka-nakat-ta.
       anyone-Q   textbook-ACC in.advance buy   put-NEG-PST
       'No one bought a textbook in advance.'

The acceptability of the sentences in (25) is naturally expected, since the negative *nai,* which follows *oku,* resides in the matrix Fin, as (26) illustrates.

---

[5] The control construction makes an assertion about the subject's intentional action. When *amari ooku-no* modifies the subject, the sentence asserts the proportion of intentions held by a large number of people. Since it is hard to imagine a situation where the speaker is familiar with all of their intentions, the sentence often sounds pragmatically odd if it is simply asserted. This oddity can be avoided if the clause occurs with a modal like *yooda* 'seem', which signifies the speaker's conjecture, as in (25a).

(26) [FinP [TP [NegP [vP **NPI** [FinP [TP PRO [vP V-v]]]T-FIN]PUT]]**NEG-T-FIN**]

If Neg-head raising takes place, as in (26), its scope extends over the matrix TP, with the result that both argument and floating NPIs in the main clause are licensed.

More interesting is the fact that when the negator precedes the verb *oku*, NPIs in subject position are not licensed, regardless of whether they belong to the argument type (i.e. thematic subjects) or the floating type.

(27) a. *<u>Amari ooku-no hito-ga</u>   konkai   maemotte kyookasyo-o
      very   many-GEN man-NOM this.time in.advance textbook-ACC
      kawa-nai-de   oi-ta   yooda.
      buy-NEG   put-PST seem
      'It seems that very many people did not buy textbooks in advance this time.'
  b. *<u>Dare-mo</u>   kyookasyo-o   maemotte kawa-nai-de oi-ta.
      anyone-Q textbook-ACC in.advance buy-NEG   put-PST
      'Anyone did not buy a textbook in advance.'

These NPIs are licensed when they appear in object position, as in (28).

(28) a. Karera-wa konkai   <u>amari ooku-no mono-o</u>   kawa-nai-de
      they-TOP   this.time very   many-GEN thing-ACC buy-NEG
      oi-ta   yooda.
      put-PST seem
      'It seems that they did not buy very many things this time.'
  b. Ken-wa konkai   <u>nani-mo</u>   kawa-nai-de oi-ta.
      Ken-TOP this.time anything-Q buy-NEG   put-PST
      'Ken did not buy anything this time.'

Notably, both argument and floating NPIs are not licensed when they appear in subject position. The facts fall into place if the floating NPI *dare-mo*, as well as the argument NPI *amari ooku-no hito*, cannot be associated with PRO, i.e. if it can be associated only with the subject, which has been moved from the matrix Spec-vP to the matrix Spec-TP.

(29) [FinP [TP **NPI**[vP **NPI**[FinP[TP PRO[NegP [vP V-v]]]**NEG-T-FIN**]PUT]]T-FIN]

In the control construction where the negator precedes the verb *oku* 'put', NPIs associated with the subject can only appear in the matrix clause, since the subject is not originated from within the embedded clause, as illustrated in (29). Both argument and floating NPIs in subject position fall outside the scope of negation, and hence are not licensed in the control construction.

The results are the same irrespective of whether the NPIs appear in the matrix Spec-TP or in the matrix Spec-vP.

The present proposal draws on the assumption that a floating NPI, which behaves like a floating numeral quantifier, cannot be associated with PRO. One piece of evidence in favor of this view may be adduced from the object control construction (30).

(30) Sensei-ga   gakusei$_i$-o   (san-nin) [asita   PRO$_i$ (*san-nin)
     teacher-NOM student-ACC three-CL   tomorrow   three-CL
     soko-ni iku yoo-ni] settoku-si-ta.
     there   go COMP   persuade-PST
     'The teacher persuaded (three) students to go there tomorrow.'

In (30), the floating numeral quantifier *san-nin* 'three' can be linked to the object, specifying the number of the students, when they are contiguous in the main clause. This interpretation is not available when the floating numeral quantifier appears in the embedded clause.[6] This fact shows that controlled PRO does not serve as a host for a floating numeral quantifier launched off the object, which suggests that PRO cannot be a host for a floating NPI.

In this section, it has been shown that NPIs are divided into two types. A subject-object asymmetry found with regard to the licensing of argument NPIs in the raising construction where *nai* 'not' precedes the aspectual verb *iru* 'be' comes from the fact that the negator takes scope only over the embedded TP. The data pertaining to NPIs provide empirical evidence that nominative subjects undergo raising to TP in Japanese, just like English.

4   Subjects with Various Markings

In Japanese, while subjects most typically bear nominative case, other types of case marking are also possible. This section shows that the possibility of subject raising differs depending on whether subjects receive oblique mark-

---

[6] In (30), when the floating quantifier is located in the embedded clause, it does not specify the number of the students, but invokes an irrelevant interpretation where three people, possibly out of the students being persuaded, will go there. The embedded clause can be scrambled to the sentence front when control is involved.

(i) [Asita   PRO$_i$ (*san-nin) soko-ni iku yoo-ni] sensei-ga   gakusei$_i$-o
    tomorrow   three-CL   there   go   COMP   teacher-NOM student-ACC
    (san-nin) settoku-si-ta.
    three-CL persuade-PST
    (lit.) 'To go there tomorrow, the teacher persuaded (three) students.'

The scrambled sentence in (i) makes it easier to see whether the floating numeral quantifier *san-nin* appears in the matrix or embedded clause. With regard to the possibility of floating numeral quantifiers, the same distribution that is observed in (30) is found in (i).

ing or not, and that oblique subjects, unlike nominative and dative subjects, are not susceptible to subject raising.

Let us begin by observing that in Japanese, subjects are most typically marked with nominative case, but that they can bear other types of case marking, as shown in (31) (Inoue 1998, Kishimoto 2005, 2010).

(31) a. Gakusei-ga   ronbun-o   kai-ta.
        student-NOM paper-ACC write-PST
        'The student wrote a paper.'
     b. Mari-ni   sore-ga   mie-ta.
        Mari-DAT that-NOM see-PST
        'Mari saw that.'
     c. Watasi-kara sono koto-o   hanasi-ta.
        I-from   that fact-ACC speak-PST
        'I talked about that matter.'
     d. Kodomo-tati-de atumat-ta.
        child-PL-with   gather-PST
        'The children gathered.'

The subject is marked with nominative case in (31a), and dative case in (31b). In (31c), the subject bears ablative *kara* 'from', since it is thematically conceived as a source, as well as an agent. In (31d), the subject is assigned *de* 'with', for it is an agent argument that refers to a group of people (Kishimoto 2005, Takubo 2010).

The underlined arguments bearing different markings in (31) all count as subjects syntactically. This can be confirmed by the fact that they can be the antecedents of subject-oriented *zibun*.

(32) a. Ken$_i$-ga   zibun$_i$-no ronbun-o   kai-ta.
        Ken-NOM self-GEN   paper-ACC write-PST
        'Ken wrote his own paper.'
     b. Mari$_i$-ni   zibun$_i$-no ie-ga   mie-ta.
        Mari-DAT self-GEN house-NOM see-PST
        'Mari saw her own house.'
     c. Ken$_i$-kara-wa   zibun$_i$-no koto-o   hanasa-nakat-ta.
        Ken-from-TOP self-GEN fact-ACC speak-NEG-PST
        'Ken did not talk about his own matter.'
     d. Kodomo-tati$_i$-de zibun$_i$-no nimotu-o   hakon-da.
        child-PL-with   self-GEN luggage-ACC carry-PST
        'The children carried their own luggage.'

Subject honorification provides another type of corroboration for the adequacy of the present view. The examples in (33) show that the underlined arguments in (31) can be targeted for subject honorification.

(33) a. Sensei-ga   ronbun-o   o-kaki-ni-nat-ta.
       teacher-NOM paper-ACC write-HON-PST
       'The teacher wrote a paper.'

    b. Sensei-ni   sore-ga   o-mie-ni-nat-ta.
       teacher-DAT that-NOM   see-HON-PST
       'The teacher saw that.'

    c. Sensei-kara   sono koto-o   o-hanasi-ni-nar-u.
       teacher-from that fact-ACC speak-HON-PRS
       'The teacher talked about that matter.'

    d. Sensei-tati-de   o-atumari-ni-nat-ta.
       teacher-PL-with gather-HON-PST
       'The teachers got together.'

Since both subject honorification and reflexivization have subject orientation, it is safe to state that the underlined arguments (with various case markings) in (31) all serve as subjects.

As discussed previously, since nominative subjects undergo raising to the matrix Spec-TP, a subject-object asymmetry in the licensing of the NPI *amari ooku-no* is observed for the clauses in (34), where the negator precedes the aspectual verb *iru*.

(34) a. *Amari ooku-no   hito-ga   ronbun-o   kaka-nai-de i-ta.
       very many-GEN man-NOM paper-ACC write-NEG   be-PST
       'Very many people have not been writing papers.'

    b. Ken-wa   amari ooku-no   ronbun-o   kaka-nai-de i-ta.
       Ken-NOM very many-GEN paper-ACC write-NEG   be-PST
       'Ken has not been writing very many papers.'

Similarly, in the dative-subject constructions in (35), the nominative object, but not the dative subject, can include the NPI *amari ooku-no*.

(35) a. *Amari ooku-no   hito-ni   mada sore-ga   mie-naid-de i-ru.
       very many-GEN man-DAT yet   that-NOM see-NEG   be-PRS
       'Very many people have not been able to see that yet.'

    b. Ken-ni-wa   mada amari ooku-no   mono-ga mie-nai-de i-ru.
       Ken-DAT-TOP yet   very   many-GEN thing-NOM see-NEG   be-PRS
       'Ken has not been able to see very many things yet.'

In contrast, the NPI *amari ooku-no* modifying *kara*-marked and *de*-marked subjects are licensed in the *nai-de iru* construction.

(36) a. <u>Amari ooku-no   hito-kara</u>   kare-ni hanasikake-nai-de i-ta.
       very   many-GEN man-from he-to   speak-NEG   be-PST
       'Not very many people have been talking to him.'
   b. <u>Amari ooku-no   hito(-tati)-de</u>   atumara-nai-de i-ta.
       very   many-GEN man-PL-with   gather-NEG   be-PST
       'Not very many people have been gathering.'

These data suggest that oblique subjects (which are marked either *kara* 'from' or *de* 'with') do not undergo A-movement to Spec-TP, while dative and nominative subjects do.

The difference in the possibility of subject raising can be attributed to the nature of tense. To understand this point, observe that the nominative-subject and dative-subject constructions are constrained by the nominative-case constraint (Shibatani 1978). The nominative-case constraint is trivially satisfied in nominative-subject constructions, which include nominative subjects. Dative-subject constructions also need to include a nominative argument by virtue of the nominative-case constraint, as illustrated in (37a).

(37) a. Sensei-ni   sore-ga/*-o   mie-na-i.
       teacher-DAT that-NOM/-ACC see-NEG-PRS
       'The teacher cannot see that.'
   b. Watasi-tati-kara/-de   sono koto-o   hanas-u.
       I-PL-from/-with   that fact-ACC speak-PRS
       'We will talk about that fact.'

In contrast, the *de*-marked and *kara*-marked subject constructions are exempt from the nominative-case constraint; (37b) is acceptable despite the fact that the clause does not contain any nominative argument.

The crucial difference that distinguishes between the dative/nominative-subject and oblique-subject constructions lies in the requirement of a nominative argument, whose case feature is valued by tense (Chomsky 2000, 2001, 2008). Since subject raising is instantiated in a clause constrained by the nominative-case requirement, I propose that when tense carries the uninterpretable case feature [+Nom], i.e. when T values the case on a nominative argument, an EPP feature is assigned to T. Under this proposal, subject raising is instantiated in (31a) and (31b), but not in (31c) and (31d). If the possibility of subject raising is conditioned by the property of tense, we can provide a ready account for the contrast in acceptability observed between

(34a) and (35a) on the one hand, and (36a) and (36b), on the other hand, with regard to the licensing of NPIs in subject position.

5 Subject-Object Asymmetry in Simple Clauses

Thus far, it has been seen that in the *nai-de iru* construction where the negator precedes the aspectual verb *iru*, a subject-object asymmetry arises with regard to the licensing of NPIs such as *amari ooku-no*, which belongs to the argument type. This asymmetry is due to the fact that the negator embedded in the subordinate clause extends its scope over the embedded TP, but does not take scope over the matrix TP. On the other hand, in simple clauses, the subject-object asymmetry in NPI licensing usually does not obtain, because the negative head takes scope over the entire clause.

Under the present view, when the negative *nai* counts as a category that undergoes head raising to T, it takes clause wide scope. The present analysis leads to the prediction that if negative *nai* does not undergo Neg-head raising, a subject-object asymmetry in the licensing of argument NPIs will be observed even in simple causes. This prediction is in fact borne out. One case confirming the correctness of the prediction is found in a clause headed by the negated predicate *ira-nai* 'not need'. As seen in (38), a clause headed by *iru* 'need' displays a subject-object asymmetry in NPI licensing.

(38) a. *<u>Amari ooku-no   hito-ni/-ga</u>   yosyuu-ga   ira-na-i.
　　　 very many-GEN man-DAT/-NOM preparation-NOM need-NEG-PRS
　　　 'Very many people do not need preparation for lessons.'
　　 b. Kare-ni/-ga   <u>amari ooku-no   yosyuu-ga</u>   ira-na-i.
　　　 he-DAT/-NOM very   many-GEN preparation-NOM need-NEG-PRS
　　　 'He does not need very much preparation for lessons.'

When NPIs like *dare-mo* and *nani-mo*, which serve as floating modifiers to the subject of the verb, are used instead of the NPI *amari ooku-no*, no subject-object asymmetry arises, as illustrated in (39).

(39) a. <u>Dare-mo</u>   yosyuu-ga   ira-na-i.
　　　 anyone-Q preparation-NOM need-NEG-PRS
　　　 'No one needs preparation for lessons.'
　　 b. Kare-ni/-ga (yosyuu-mo)   <u>nani-mo</u>   ira-na-i.
　　　 he-DAT/-NOM preparation-Q anything-Q need-NEG-PRS
　　　 'He does not need anything (even preparation for lessons).'

Crucially, in the clause headed by *iru* 'need', the scope of *nai* does not extend over TP. Accordingly, the NPI *amari ooku-no gakusei* appearing in the subject position in (38a) is not licensed.[7]

The presence of a subject-object asymmetry in the licensing of argument NPIs, and its absence in the licensing of floating NPIs can be taken as an indication that the subject of *iru* 'need' undergoes raising to Spec-TP. If this is the case, the failure of *nai* to license the NPI in subject position in (38a) should result from the absence of Neg-head raising, as depicted in (40).

(40) [$_{FinP}$ [$_{TP}$ SBJ [$_{NegP}$ [~~SBJ~~ (dare-mo) V-v]Neg] ~~T~~]T-FIN]

In (38a), the argument NPI *amari ooku-no hito* in subject position is not licensed because the scope of negation does not extend over TP. In contrast, the floating NPI *dare-mo* in (39a) is licensed under the scope of negation, since it can appear with a copy of the subject in vP-internal position. Note that the existence of subject raising to Spec-TP in the clause with the predicate *iru* 'need' is naturally expected, since the clause has a nominative argument whose case feature is valued by T.

The reason why Neg-head raising is not instantiated in the clause headed by *iru* 'need' is that the negator *nai* is a lexical predicate. As discussed by Kishimoto (2008), a grammatical negator, but not a lexical negator, undergoes Neg-head raising. The lexical adjectival status of *nai* can be confirmed by considering whether it can be embedded under *omou* 'think'.

(41) Ken-wa [kono hon-o ira-naku] omot-ta.
Ken-TOP this book-ACC need-NEG think-PST
'Ken thought this book unnecessary.'

---

[7] The grammatical relation of the dative argument of *iru* 'need' differs depending on how it is interpreted. The dative argument counts as a non-subject when it specifies a goal (rather than an experiencer). In such a case, *ni* can be replaced by the complex preposition *ni-taisite* 'for', and the NPI *amari ooku-no* included in the dative DP is licensed by the negator *nai*, as in (i).

    (i) <u>Amari ooku-no gakusei{-ni/-ni-taisite}</u> obentoo-ga ira-na-i.
       very many-GEN student-DAT/-for lunch.box-NOM need-NEG-PRS
       'Lunch boxes are not necessary for very many students.'

The ambivalence of the *ni*-marked argument is resolved when subject honorification is used. When subject honorification is anchored to the dative argument, it must be construed as a subject, and thus, the dative argument cannot comprise the NPI *amari ooku-no*.

    (ii) *<u>Amari ooku-no sensei-ni</u> obentoo-ga o-iri-ni-nara-na-i.
       very many-GEN teacher-DAT lunch.box-NOM need-HON-NEG-PRS
       'Very many teachers do not need books.'

The data confirm that in the dative-subject construction headed by *iru* 'need', the dative subject undergoes subject raising to Spec-TP, while *nai* stays in place without Neg-head raising.

Example (42) shows that the embedded predicate can be an adjective or a nominal adjective.

(42) Ken-wa [Mari-o   kawaiku/sinsetu-ni] omot-ta.
     Ken-TOP Mari-ACC   cute/kind   think-PST
     'Ken thought Mari cute/kind.'

In contrast, a grammatical negator associated with a verbal predicate, even if it inflects like an adjective, is not licensed in this syntactic context.

(43) *Ken-wa [eigo-o   wakara-naku]   omot-ta.
     Ken-TOP English-ACC understand-NEG think-PST
     'Ken thought English not understandable.'

In (41), the embedded predicate has a sequence where the verb is embedded under negative *nai*. Since *omou* can take an adjectival clause as its complement, the negator *nai* in *ira-nai* 'do not need' must be a lexical adjective, which does not undergo Neg-head raising. Thus, the negative *nai* appearing with *iru* 'need' does not take scope over TP. Note that *nai* projects scope whether it is categorized as a lexical or grammatical negator. This is because the negative *nai*, regardless of its categorization, has the semantic function of reversing the polarity of a proposition (Kishimoto 2008).

There are other cases where a negative head does not extend over TP due to the absence of Neg-head raising. Broadly speaking, negative *nai* associated with adjectives and nominal adjectives does not take scope over TP.[8] (44) illustrates that *nai* associated with an intransitive adjective like *isogasii* 'busy' does not license an argument NPI in subject position.

(44) *Kyoo-wa <u>amari ooku-no   hito-ga</u>   isogasiku na-i.
     today-TOP very   many-GEN person-NOM busy   NEG-PRS
     'Very many people are not busy today.'

When a floating NPI appears in subject position instead, it is licensed under the scope of negation.

(45) Kyoo-wa <u>dare-mo</u> isogasiku na-i.
     today-TOP anyone-Q busy   NEG-PRS
     'No one is busy today.'

---

[8] Adjectival predicates are generally associated with lexical negative *nai*, but it appears that a grammatical negator *nai* is associated with adjectives possessing verbal case properties, such as *suki-da* 'like' and *hosii* 'want'. For reasons of space, I will not go into this discussion.

In (46), which involves the transitive adjective *sinsetu-da* 'kind', a subject-complement (or object) asymmetry is observed in NPI licensing.

(46) a. *<u>Amari ooku-no hito-ga</u>   kodomo-ni sinsetu-de nakat-ta.
     very   many-GEN person-NOM child-DAT kind   NEG-PST
     'Very many people were not kind to children.'
   b. Kare-wa <u>amari ooku-no   hito-ni</u>   sinsetu-de nakat-ta.
     he-TOP   very   many-GEN man-DAT kind   NEG-PST
     'He was not kind to very many people.

Again, a floating NPI like *dare-mo* appearing in subject position is licensed by the negated adjective *sinsetu-de nai*, as shown in (47).

(47) <u>Dare-mo</u>   kodomo-ni   sinsetu-de nakat-ta.
    anyone-Q   child-DAT   kind   NEG-PST
    'No one was kind to children.'

The fact that an argument NPI in subject position cannot be licensed under the scope of negation follows straightforwardly, if the subject is raised to Spec-TP, whereas the negative *nai* does not undergo Neg-raising.

In essence, ordinary verbs are associated with a grammatical negator undergoing Neg-raising. By contrast, the negator associated with the verb *iru* 'need' is a lexical negator and hence does not undergo Neg-raising. Since Neg-raising is not implemented in the clause headed by *iru*, a subject-object symmetry is observed with regard to the licensing of argument NPIs. The negator *nai* appearing in adjectival clauses shows the same property as the negator appearing with *iru*, in that it does not take scope over TP.

6   Conclusion

In this paper, it has been shown that NPIs in Japanese are divided into two types—the argument-type, which is licensed with reference to its surface A-position (i.e. the position in which it appears after A-movement) and the floating-type, which can be licensed in theta-marking position (i.e. the position where an argument appears before A-movement). On the basis of data pertaining to these two types of NPIs, it has been argued that in Japanese, subjects are moved into Spec-TP via A-movement when they are marked with nominative or dative case, but not when they receive oblique marking, and further, that when negative *nai* does not undergo Neg-raising, a subject-object asymmetry with regard to the licensing of argument NPIs arises even in simple clauses.

References

Aoyagi, H., and T. Ishii. 1994 On NPI Licensing in Japanese. *Japanese/Korean Linguistics* 4, ed. N.Akatsuka 295-311. Stanford: CSLI.

Chomsky, N. 2000. Minimalist Inquiries: The Framework. In *Step by Step: Essays on Minimalist Syntax in Honor of Howard Lasnik*, ed. R. Martin, D. Michaels, and J. Uriagereka, 89-155. Cambridge, MA: MIT Press.

Chomsky, N. 2001. Derivation by Phase. In *Ken Hale: A Life in Language*, ed. M. Kenstowicz, 1-52. Cambridge, MA: MIT Press.

Chomsky, N. 2008. On Phases. In *Foundational Issues in Linguistic Theory: Essays in Honor of Jean-Roger Vergnaud*, ed. R. Freidin, C. Otero, and M.-L. Zubizarreta, 133-166. Cambridge, MA: MIT Press.

Inoue, K. 1998. Sentences without Nominative Subjects in Japanese. *Grant-in-Aid for COE Research Report (2A): Researching and Verifying an Advanced Theory of Human Language*, 1-34. Chiba: Kanda University of International Studies.

Kato, Y. 1994. Negative Polarity and Movement. *Formal Approaches to Japanese Linguistics 1, MIT Working Papers in Linguistics* 24, ed. M. Koizumi and H. Ura, 101-120. Cambridge, MA: MIT Working Papers in Linguistics.

Kawashima, R., and H. Kitahara 1992. Licensing of Negative Polarity Items and Checking Theory. *FLSM III: Papers from the Third Annual Meeting of the Formal Linguistics Society of Midamerica*, 139-154. Indiana: IULC.

Kishimoto, H. 2005. *Toogo Koozoo-to Bunpoo Kankei*. Tokyo: Kurosio.

Kishimoto, H. 2007. Negative Scope and Head Raising in Japanese. *Lingua* 117: 247-288.

Kishimoto, H. 2008. On the Variability of Negative Scope in Japanese. *Journal of Linguistics* 44: 379-435.

Kishimoto, H. 2012. Subject Honorification and the Position of Subjects in Japanese. *Journal of East Asian Linguistics* 21: 1-41.

Miyagawa, S. 1989. *Syntax and Semantics 22: Structure and Case Marking in Japanese*. San Diego: Academic Press.

Miyagawa, S., N. Nishioka, and H. Zeijlstra. 2013. Negative Dependencies in Japanese. *Proceedings of the 8th Workshop on Formal Altaic Linguistics* ed. Umut Ögze, 231-244. Cambridge, MA: MIT Working Papers in Linguistics.

Rizzi, L. 1997. The Fine Structure of the Left Periphery. *Elements of Grammar: Handbook of Generative Syntax*, ed. L. Haegeman, 281-337. Dordrecht: Kluwer.

Rizzi, L. 2004. On the Cartography of Syntactic Structures. *The Structure of CP and IP: The Cartography of Syntactic Structures: Volume 2*. ed. L. Rizzi, 3-15, Oxford: Oxford University Press.

Shibatani, M. 1978. *Nihongo-no Bunseki*. Tokyo: Taishukan.

Takubo, Y. 2010. *Nihongo-no Koozoo*. Tokyo: Kurosio.

Watanabe, A. 2004. The Genesis of Negative Concord: Syntax and Morphology of Negative Doubling. *Linguistic Inquiry* 35: 559-612.

NP-Ellipsis in the Nagasaki Dialect of Japanese*

MASAKO MAEDA AND DAIKO TAKAHASHI
Kyushu Institute of Technology and *Tohoku University*

1 Introduction

In this article we consider reduced nominal phrases in the Nagasaki dialect of Japanese (hereafter, Nagasaki Japanese or just NJ), which is one of the dialects spoken on the islands of Kyushu. We argue that they involve ellipsis despite the fact that they apparently contain a pro-form.

Before going to Nagasaki Japanese, let us consider the examples from Standard Japanese (SJ) below:

---

* This paper was read at the 23rd Japanese/Korean Linguistics conference held at MIT in October, 2013. Some material used here was also presented at the Syntax Workshop held at the Center for Linguistics, Nanzan University in August, 2013. For their comments and questions we are grateful to the participants of those meetings, especially to Željko Bošković, Marcel den Dikken, Tomohiro Fujii, Shigeru Miyagawa, Yoichi Miyamoto, Keiko Murasugi, Mamoru Saito, and Koji Sugisaki. We also thank our NJ informants, Ayumi Kumabe, Yudai Kumabe and Yoshimitsu Nakashima for their generous help. Needless to say, we are solely responsible for any remaining inadequacy. The names of the authors are alphabetically ordered.

Japanese/Korean Linguistics 23.
Edited by Michael Kenstowicz, Theodore Levin and Ryo Masuda.

(1) a. Haruna-no   kenkyuu-nitaisuru   taido-wa   ii   ga,
         Haruna-GEN   research-toward   attitude- TOP   good   though
         'Though Haruna's attitude toward research is good,'
     b. Mariko-no   kenkyuu-nitaisuru   taido-wa   yoku-nai.
         Mariko- GEN   research-toward   attitude- TOP   good-not
         'Mariko's attitude toward research is not good.'
     c. Mariko-no-wa   yoku-nai.
         Mariko- GEN- TOP   good-not
         'Mariko's is not good.'

Example (1a) corresponds to *Though Haruna's attitude toward research is good*, which may be followed either by (1b) or by (1c). In (1b) the part corresponding to *attitude toward research* is repeatedly used. On the other hand, (1c) avoids the repetition and the relevant portion is missing. So SJ allows this kind of reduction of nominal phrases.

There have been two lines of analysis proposed for the reduction in question in the literature. One is what we call the NP-ellipsis analysis and it is proposed by Saito and Murasugi (1990), among others (see Jackendoff (1971) and Lobeck (1995) for discussions about NP-ellipsis, previously known as N'-deletion, in English and other languages). According to this analysis, the reduced nominal phrase in (1c) is analyzed as in (2).

(2)   [DP Mariko-no   [D' [NP ~~kenkyuu-nitaisuru taido~~] D]
             Mariko-GEN   research-toward   attitude

The whole structure is DP, the remnant genitive phrase *Mariko-no* is located in its specifier position, and the NP part containing the head noun *attitude* and the internal argument *toward research* is elided (we indicate ellipsis by strike-through). Note that one important consequence of the NP-ellipsis analysis is that the nominal phrase in Japanese must be the projection of a functional head selecting NP as its complement. To see why, let us look at (3).

(3)   [NP Mariko-no   [N'/NP ~~kenkyuu-nitaisuru taido~~]]
             Mariko-GEN   research-toward   attitude

If the whole nominal phrase were an NP, as was standardly assumed until the early 1980s, it would be necessary to apply ellipsis to N' or the lower segment of NP depending on whether the remnant genitive phrase is in the specifier position or is adjoined to NP, and it should not be allowed because neither intermediate projections nor segments of adjunction can be targeted by transformations.

The other analysis of the reduction in question is what we may call the "pronoun plus haplology" analysis, which is proposed by Okutsu (1974) and has recently been revived by Li (2011) and Bae (2012). These researchers note that in SJ, the pro-form corresponding to the pronoun *one* in English is expressed as *no*, which happens to have the same phonetic form as the genitive marker (see also Kitagawa and Ross (1982)). Consider the following examples:

(4) a. Haruna-wa   akai   wanpiisu-o   katta.
      Haruna-TOP   red   one-piece.dress-ACC bought
      'Haruna bought a red one-piece dress.'
   b. Mariko-wa   aoi   **no**-o   katta.
      Mariko-TOP   blue   one-ACC bought
      'Mariko bought a blue one.'

Here (4a) is intended to be followed by (4b), where the nominal expression *wanpiisu* 'one-piece dress' in (4a) is replaced with the pro-form *no* 'one.' From (1) and (4b), we can know that it is isomorphic to the genitive marker. The pronoun plus haplology analysis assumes that the reduced nominal in (1c) has the underlying form indicated below:

(5)   [$_{NP}$ Mariko-no   ~~no~~]
         Mariko-GEN   one

In (5) the whole expression is headed by the pronoun *no*, which is deleted by haplology because we have a sequence of two phonetically identical expressions, namely the genitive marker *no* and the pronoun *no*. Just for convenience, we illustrate the analysis in such a way that the pronoun *no*, not the genitive marker *no*, is subject to deletion by haplology.

Recently Li (2011) and Bae (2012) have claimed that Japanese lacks D and hence DP (see Bošković (2008) and Fukui (1986), among others, for that issue). Accordingly, Japanese should not have NP-ellipsis, either, because NP-ellipsis must be licensed by D as indicated in (2). Therefore, they argue that reduced nominal phrases as in (1c) should not involve NP-ellipsis, but rather the pro-form. They point out that in the dialects of Japanese where the genitive marker and the pronoun have different phonetic forms, the pronoun does surface in their counterparts of (1c). Among the relevant dialects they mention is Nagasaki Japanese. We illustrate relevant facts in NJ below:

(6) a. Takuya-**n**   {keitai   /hahaoya   /taido   /aizyoo}
     Takuya-GEN   cell.phone /mother   /attitude /love
     'Takuya's {cell phone/mother/attitude/love}'
   b. Mariko-wa   aoka   **to**-ba   katta.
     Mariko-TOP   blue   one-ACC   bought
     'Mariko bought a blue one.'
(7)   Haruna-n   taido-wa   Mariko-**n**   **to**   yorimo   rippayatta.
     Haruna-GEN   attitude-TOP   Mariko-GEN   one   than   good
     'lit. Haruna's attitude was better than Mariko's one.'

First, (6a) shows that the genitive marker in NJ is *n*: irrespective of the type of head nouns, the possessor *Takuya* is accompanied by *n*. Second, (6b) is the NJ counterpart of (4b): notice that the pronoun corresponding to *one* in English is expressed as *to*. Of interest to us is (7), where the pronoun *to* is overtly expressed and follows *Mariko-n*: the sentence is literally translated as *Haruna's attitude was better than Mariko's one*. This fact is directly predicted by the pronoun plus haplology analysis, which just says that haplology is not operative so that the pronoun comes to the surface. On the other hand, the NP-ellipsis analysis would have difficulty accommodating (7) since it would not assume that the pro-form is involved in NP-ellipsis.

As far as we can see, however, Li (2011) and Bae (2012) merely point out the existence of cases like (7), and stop short of showing whether reduced nominal phrases like the ones in (1c) and (7) really do not involve ellipsis. In order to resolve the issue, we have undertaken to examine whether reduced nominals in NJ really do not involve ellipsis, and what follows is an interim report of our research on NJ. What we have so far discovered indicates that although they apparently employ the pro-form strategy, cases like (7) actually involve ellipsis.

2   Reduced Nominal Phrases in Nagasaki Japanese

In this section, we take a close look at reduced nominal phrases in NJ. When we began to undertake this research, we thought that the possibility of sloppy interpretation could provide us with a litmus test to determine whether ellipsis is involved or not. This was based on the contrast between (8a) and (8b).

(8) a. John loves his wife, and Bill loves her, too.
   b. John loves his wife, and Bill does, too.

(9) a. Bill loves John's wife.   <strict interpretation>
   b. Bill loves Bill's wife.   <sloppy interpretation>

In (8a), the second clause contains the pronoun *her*, which we take to be anaphorically dependent on the object of the first clause. The example is limited to the so-called strict interpretation in (9a). In contrast, in (8b), the second clause has VP-ellipsis, and as is well-known, it is ambiguous between the strict interpretation in (9a) and the sloppy interpretation in (9b). So the sloppy interpretation in (9b) is only available with ellipsis.

Bearing that in mind, let us consider the following data from NJ:

(10) a. Satuma-n   soko-n   tonosama-e-n   tyuusei-wa
        Satsuma-GEN   it-GEN   lord-to-GEN   loyalty-TOP
        rikaidekiru   batten,
        understandable though
        'Though Satsuma's loyalty to its lord is understandable,'
     b. Simabara-n   **to**-wa   rikaidekin.
        Shimabara-GEN one-TOP   not.understandable
        'lit. Shimabara's one is not understandable.'
(11) a. Shimabara's loyalty to Satsuma's lord is not understandable.
     b. Shimabara's loyalty to Shimabara's lord is not understandable.

In (10a) the pronoun *soko* 'it/there' is intended to be bound by the first genitive phrase *Satuma*. The sentence serves as the antecedent sentence for (10b), where the subject is a reduced nominal phrase consisting of the genitive phrase and the alleged pronoun *to*. In the context given, (10b) is ambiguous between the strict reading in (11a) and the sloppy reading in (11b). In particular, the possibility of the sloppy reading appears to suggest the involvement of ellipsis.

Things are not that simple, however. The reduced nominal phrase in English in (12), which is cited from Llombart-Huesca (2002), does permit sloppy interpretation, in spite of the fact that it contains the pro-form *one*.

(12)   I saw Janet's beautiful picture of her cat and Jack saw Julie's ugly
        one.

We do not think that the existence of cases like (12) immediately leads to the conclusion that reduced nominals in NJ should be analyzed as involving pronominalization (in fact, Llombart-Huesca (2002) argues on the basis of cases like (12) that the construction with the pro-form *one* actually involves ellipsis). That said, it at least obscures the picture. So it is preferable if we can find clearer evidence for ellipsis.

For that purpose, we may consider the possibility of extracting an element out of an elided constituent. Let us consider the schematic representations below:

(13) a. ... [$_{XP}$ α X β] ...
      b. ... β ... [$_{XP}$ α X $t_β$] ...
      c. ... β ... [$_{XP}$ ~~α X~~ $t_β$] ...

In (13a), XP contains some elements within it. Suppose XP is fated to be elided. But before ellipsis applies, some element internal to XP, say, β, may evacuate from XP by movement, as shown in (13b); in (13c), ellipsis applies to XP, but β survives and is overtly expressed in the dislocated position. This kind of phenomenon is attested in a number of elliptic constructions such as sluicing, pseudogapping, and so on. The possibility of extracting an element can be used to test the involvement of ellipsis, because it necessitates the existence of full-fledged internal structure prior to reduction.

In this connection, let us consider the following examples in NJ:

(14) a. Haruna-n   piano-n   toriatukai-wa   teineiya   kedo,
         Haruna-GEN   piano-GEN   handling-TOP   careful   though
         'Though Haruna's handling of the piano is careful,'
      b. Mariko-n   to-wa   sozatuya   ne.
         Mariko-GEN   one-TOP   rough   PART
         'lit. Mariko's one is rough.'
      c. Mariko-n   **furuuto-n**   to-wa   sozatuya   ne.
         Mariko-GEN   flute-GEN   one-TOP   rough   PART
         'lit. Mariko's one of the flute is rough.'

The subject in (14a) is headed by the noun corresponding to *handling*, which takes two arguments, *Haruna*, an external argument, and *piano*, an internal argument. (14a) can be followed either by (14b), which is literally like *Mariko's one is rough*, meaning Mariko's handling of the piano is rough, or by (14c), which is literally like *Mariko's one of the flute is rough*. Particularly important is (14c), where the internal argument of the missing noun, namely *the flute*, survives reduction.[1] For (14b), we assume that the phrasal constituent corresponding to *handling of the piano* is understood. In analyzing (14c), let us keep the assumption that a phrasal constituent is missing. Then we are led to assume that (14c) should be analyzed as indicated below:

(15)   [$_{DP}$ Mariko-GEN [$_{DP}$ flute-GEN [$_{D'}$ [... [$_{NP}$ t~~flute~~ ~~handling~~] to] D]]]

---

[1] Incidentally, this is observed for Standard Japanese by Kimura (1994). The English counterpart with the pronoun *one*, which results in ungrammaticality, is discussed by Jackendoff (1977).

The two remnant genitive phrases are in the edge positions of DP; especially the internal argument *flute-GEN* must be dislocated by movement, and moreover, to θ-mark it, the head noun must be present underlyingly; finally ellipsis applies to elide the phrase containing the noun and the trace (or copy) of the internal argument. Thus, (14c) is an indication that the internal structure of NP exists in the underlying form, which is nothing but what the NP-ellipsis analysis postulates.

Another argument for the existence of ellipsis in NJ comes from what we call "covert" extraction. Let us explain step by step, beginning with the following example in SJ:

(16)   Azia-no   ikka-koku-no   taitei-no   sosiki-kara-no
       Asia-GEN   one-country-GEN most-GEN   organization-from-GEN
       dattai-wa   mitomerareta.
       withdrawal-TOP   was.approved
       'One Asian country's withdrawal from most organizations was approved.'

In this example the subject nominal phrase contains two quantified phrases, *one Asian country* and *most organizations*. In (16), the former asymmetrically takes wide scope over the latter, which is natural in light of the widely accepted view that scope rigidity holds in multiply quantified structure in Japanese (Kuno (1973) and Kuroda (1971), among others): namely, when two quantifiers show up preserving the basic word order, the higher one asymmetrically takes wide scope over the lower one. Scope ambiguity can be obtained if we apply scrambling to the lower quantifier, as in (17), where we assume that the internal argument PP *from most organizations* is adjoined to DP by scrambling.

(17)   Taitei-no   sosiki-kara-no   azia-no   ikka-koku-no
       most-GEN   organization-from-GEN   Asia-GEN   one-country-GEN
       dattai-wa   mitomerareta.
       withdrawal-TOP   was.approved.
       'lit. From most organizations one Asian country's withdrawal was approved.'

Let us now combine (16) and (17) with NP-ellipsis. First, let us look at (18).

(18) a. Azia-no   ikka-koku-no   taitei-no   sosiki-kara-no
        Asia-GEN   one-country-GEN most-GEN   organization-from-GEN
        dattai-wa   mitomerareta   ga,
        withdrawal-TOP   was.approved   though
        'Though one Asian country's withdrawal from most organizations was approved,'

    b. yooroppa-no ikka-koku-no-wa   mitomerarenakatta.
       Europe-GEN   one-country-GEN-TOP was.not.approved
       'one European country's was not approved.'

(18a) has the same arrangement of the two quantifiers as (16) and is intended to be followed by the reduced sentence in (18b). According to Takahashi (2008b), both (18a) and (18b) have the scope interpretation in which *one* asymmetrically takes wide scope over *most*. This is natural because in (18a), the two quantifiers are arranged in conformity to the basic word order.

    Let us now turn our attention to (19).

(19) a. Taitei-no   sosiki-kara-no   azia-no   ikka-koku-no
       most-GEN   organization-from-GEN Asia-GEN   one-country-GEN
       dattai-wa   mitomerareta   ga,
       withdrawal-TOP   was.approved   though
       'lit. Though from most organizations one Asian country's
       withdrawal was approved,'
    b. yooroppa-no ikka-koku-no-wa   mitomerarenakatta.
       Europe-GEN   one-country-GEN-TOP was.not.approved
       'one European country's was not approved.'

While (19b) is the same as (18b), (19a) is slightly different from (18a) in that the internal PP argument *from most organizations* is scrambled to precede *one Asian country*. Very interestingly, Takahashi (2008b) observes that (19a-b) are ambiguous in a parallel fashion, just as Fox (2000) notes for VP-ellipsis in English. That is, when (19a) has the reading in which *most* takes wide scope, (19b) too has that scope interpretation; similarly, when (19a) has the reading in which *one* has wide scope, (19b) too has that scope interpretation.

    Below we illustrate Takahashi's (2008b) analysis of (19a-b) with the reading where *most* scopes out *one* (just for convenienece, we represent them with English words).

(20) a. [DP one Asian country's [NP withdrawal from most
       organizations]] ...
    a'. [DP one European country's [NP withdrawal from most
       organizations]] ...
    b. [DP from most organizations [DP one Asian country's
       [NP withdrawal *t*PP]]] ...
    b'. [DP from most organizations [DP one European country's
       [NP withdrawal *t*PP]]] ...

   c. [$_{DP}$ from most organizations [$_{DP}$ one Asian country's
      [$_{NP}$ withdrawal t_{PP}]]] ...
   c'. [$_{DP}$ ~~from most organizations~~ [$_{DP}$ one European country's
      [$_{NP}$ ~~withdrawal~~ t_{PP}]]] ...

(20a-a') show the underlying forms of (19a-b), respectively. (20b-b') are derived from (20a-a'), respectively, by applying scrambling to the internal PP arguments in a parallel fashion. Finally, two ellipsis operations apply to (20c') to derive the surface form of (19b): NP-ellipsis elides NP and what is called argument ellipsis elides the scrambled PP internal argument.[2] What is important in (20) is that in (20b') extraction takes place out of the ultimately elided NP, though the effect of the extraction too is ultimately made invisible by argument ellipsis.

    Bearing this in mind, let us consider (21), which is the NJ counterpart of (19).

(21) a. Taitei-no   sosiki-kara-n   azia-n   ikka-koku-n
          most-GEN organization-from-GEN Asia-GEN one-country-GEN
          dattai-wa   mitomerareta   kedo,
          withdrawal-TOP   was.approved   though
          'lit. Though from most organizations one Asian country's
          withdrawal was approved,'
    b. yooroppa-n ikka-koku-n   **to**-wa   mitomerarenyatta.
          Europe-GEN one-country-GEN one-TOP was.not.approved
          'lit. one European country's one was not approved.'

In (21a), which is comparable to (19a), the internal PP argument is scrambled. It is followed by (21b), where the subject nominal phrase is reduced and has the alleged pro-form *to*. Though we have the alleged pronoun, (21b) can have the reading where *most* takes wide scope, provided that the preceding sentence (21a) also has that reading. Given the analysis in (20), (21b) ought to involve "covert" extraction of the internal PP argument, which necessitates the NP structure to be present underlyingly.

    To sum up, it seems that NP-ellipsis is indeed available in NJ, where reduced nominal phrases in question are composed of genitive remnants and the alleged pro-form. Therefore, that such expressions exist in some dialects does not necessarily refute the NP-ellipsis analysis for Japanese.

---

[2] Argument ellipsis is assumed in the literature to be available in Japanese grammar. Because of space limitation, we do not go into argument ellipsis here and just assume it is available. Interested readers are referred to Takahashi (2008a) and the references therein.

3   An Analysis and Implications

If reduced nominals in NJ, which contain the alleged pro-form, actually involve ellipsis, how can we analyze them? Here we propose an analysis, pointing out one of its implications for SJ. But before getting to our analysis, let us note some further properties of the relevant construction in NJ. First of all, the alleged pro-form *to* never co-occurs with overt nouns, as shown below:

(22) a. *Haruna-n   taido-wa   Mariko-n   **taido**   **to**   yorimo
          Haruna-GEN   attitude-TOP   Mariko-GEN   attitude   one   than
          rippayatta.
          good
          'lit. Haruna's attitude was better than Mariko's attitude one.'
      b. *Haruna-n   taido-wa   Mariko-n   **to**   **taido**   yorimo
          Haruna-GEN   attitude-TOP   Mariko-GEN   one   attitude   than
          rippayatta.
          good
          'lit. Haruna's attitude was better than Mariko's one attitude.'

In (22a) the overt noun *taido* 'attitude' occurs and precedes *to*, whereas in (22b) it follows it. Both sentences are impossible.

Next, in (23), we consider the location of *to* relative to the number (#) and classifier heads.

(23) a. Haruna-wa [Murakami-n   hon   san-satu]-ba   katta.
          Haruna-TOP   Murakami-GEN   book   three-CL-ACC   bought
          'lit. Haruna bought Murakami's three books.'
      b. Mariko-wa   [Isaka-n   **to**   **ni-satu**]-ba   katta.
          Mariko-TOP   Isaka-GEN   one   two-CL-ACC   bought
          'lit. Mariko bought Isaka's two ones.'

In (23a), the object nominal phrase contains the noun *hon*, which is followed by the number/classifier expression *sansatu*. Here we simply assume that Japanese phrase structure is head-final, and hence in (23a), the noun should be structurally lower than the number/classifier heads. As shown in (23b), the head noun *book* can be replaced by the alleged pro-form *to*, without causing any word order change. This indicates that *to* is also lower than the number/classifier heads.

Given these, we propose the structures below ((see Cheng and Sybesma (1999) and Watanabe (2006) for analyses of nominal phrases containing # and classifier heads).

(24) a. [$_{DP}$ Isaka-n [$_{D'}$ [$_{\#P}$ [$_{CLP}$ [$_{nP}$ [$_{NP}$ hon$_N$] to$_n$] satu$_{CL}$] 2$_\#$] D]]
  b. [$_{DP}$ Mariko-n [$_{D'}$ [$_{nP}$ [$_{NP}$ taido$_N$] to$_n$] D]]

(24a) is the structure of the reduced nominal in (23b), where *to* co-occurs with the number and classifier elements. The topmost projection is DP and the genitive phrase is in its specifier position; below DP we have the projections of # and classifier: since the final form is the number followed by the classifier, that is *ni-satu* '2-CL,' we just assume either that the classifier head-moves to # or that they are morphologically merged: in either case, what is important is that below Classifier Phrase, we have *n*P and the alleged pro-form *to* is actually an *n* head, which in turn selects NP, whose head is *hon* 'book' in this case. To derive the ultimate form, we assume that NP must undergo ellipsis in this configuration.[3]

When there is no #/classifier head, we have the structure in (24b), which is the structure of the reduced nominal in (7) *Mariko's one*, meaning *Mariko's attitude*. Here too, the NP headed by the noun *taido* 'attitude' is the complement of the *n* head *to*. The NP must be elided to obtain the actual surface form.

To capture the obligatory ellipsis of the NP selected by *to*, we may assume that the *n* head *to* contains what Merchant (2001) calls the E(llipsis)-feature, which instructs PF not to pronounce its complement. Or it may simply be a realization of the E-feature for NP-ellipsis.

We may apply the basic idea to SJ, as shown below:

(25)   [$_{DP}$ Mariko-no [$_{D'}$ [$_{nP}$ [$_{NP}$ ~~taido$_N$~~] ~~no$_n$~~] D]]

Just as *to* in NJ is reanalyzed as an *n* head, its counterpart in SJ, namely the so-called pronoun *no*, may be regarded as an *n* head, which selects an NP complement and demands that it be deleted because it contains an E-feature. As indicated in (25), if NP is elided, the genitive marker on *Mariko* is immediately followed by the *n* head *no*. We can follow the previous literature and assume that somehow, SJ does not tolerate a sequence of two *no*'s and that haplology deletes one of them to derive the surface form of reduced nominals such as the one in (1c). This amounts to a hybrid analysis of the NP-ellipsis analysis and the haplology analysis. An obvious advantage is that we can draw attractive features from both analyses, though we leave a detailed examination of this possibility to our future research.

---

[3] When an element is extracted from NP, as discussed in the previous section, it evacuates NP before deletion applies. See Aelbrecht (2009) and Baltin (2012), among others, for recent discussions concerning extraction out of elided constituents.

4 Conclusion

To conclude, we provided some arguments that reduced nominal phrases with the alleged pronoun *to* in NJ actually involve NP-ellipsis. The mere presence of the alleged pro-form, therefore, does not suffice to deny the involvement of NP-ellipsis. In presenting our analysis, we suggested that the alleged pronoun is actually an *n* head with an E-feature for NP-ellipsis, whereby we can handle the fact that it never co-occurs with overt nouns. An important consequence is that the nominal phrase in Japanese cannot simply be NP: it must contain the projection of a functional head that licenses NP-ellipsis, though it is left open to identify exactly what category the functional head belongs to.

References

Aelbrecht, L. 2009. You Have the Right to Remain Silent: The Syntactic Licensing of Ellipsis. Doctoral dissertation, Catholic University of Brussels.

Bae, S.-H. 2012. NP Languages Do Not Have NP-ellipsis: Examination of Korean and Japanese. Ms. Harvard University.

Baltin, M. 2012. Deletion Versus Pro-Forms: An Overly Simple Dichotomy? *Natural Language and Linguistic Theory* 30: 381-423.

Bošković, Ž. 2008. What Will You Have, DP or NP? *Proceedings of the North East Linguistic Society* 37: 101-114. GLSA, University of Massachusetts.

Cheng, L. L.-S. and R. Sybesma. 1999. Bare and Not-So-Bare Nouns and the Structure of NP. *Linguistic Inquiry* 30: 509-542.

Fox, D. 2000. *Economy and Semantic Interpretation.* Cambridge, Mass.: MIT Press.

Fukui, N. 1986. A Theory of Category Projection and Its Applications. Doctoral dissertation. MIT.

Jackendoff, R. 1971. Gapping and Related Rules. *Linguistic Inquiry* 2: 21-35.

Jackendoff, R. 1977. *X'-Syntax: A Study of Phrase Structure.* Cambridge, Mass.: MIT Press.

Kimura, N. 1994. Multiple Specifiers and Long Distance Anaphora. *MIT Working Papers in Linguistics* 24: *Formal Approaches to Japanese Linguistics* 1: 159-178.

Kitagawa, C. and C. N. G. Ross. 1982. Prenominal Modification in Chinese and Japanese. *Linguistic Analysis* 9: 19-53.

Kuno, S. 1973. *The Structure of the Japanese Language.* Cambridge, Mass.: MIT Press.

Kuroda, S.-Y. 1971. Remarks on the Notion of Subject with Reference to Words like Also, Even, or Only: part II. *Annual Bulletin*, vol. 4, 127-152. Research Institute of Logopedics and Phoniatrics, Tokyo University.

Li, A. 2011. Missing NPs: Licensing and Structures. Talk given at Harvard University.

Llombart-Huesca, A. 2002. Anaphoric *One* and NP-Ellipsis. *Studia Linguistica* 56: 58-89.

Lobeck, A. 1995. *Ellipsis: Functional Heads, Licensing, and Identification.* Oxford University Press.

Merchant, J. 2001. *The Syntax of Silence: Sluicing, Islands, and the Theory of Ellipsis.* Oxford: Oxford University Press.

Okutsu, K. 1974. *Seisei Nihon Bunpooron: Meisiku-no Koozoo* [Generative grammar of Japanese: noun phrase structure]. Tokyo: Taishukan.

Saito, M. and K. Murasugi. 1990. N'-Deletion in Japanese: A Preliminary Study. *Japanese/Korean Linguistics* 1: 258-301.

Takahashi, D. 2008a. Noun Phrase Ellipsis. In S. Miyagawa and M. Saito eds. *The Oxford Handbook of Japanese Linguistics*: 394-422. Oxford: Oxford University Press.

Takahashi, D. 2008b. Scope Interaction in DPs with NP-Deletion in Japanese. In Y. Kaneko, A. Kikuchi, Y. Ogawa, E. Shima, and D. Takahashi eds. *The State of the Art in Linguistic Research: the Interface of Form and Meaning*, 397-407. Tokyo: Kaitakusya.

Watanabe, A. 2006. Functional Projections of Nominals in Japanese: Syntax of Classifiers. *Natural Language and Linguistic Theory* 24: 241-306.

Why Japanese and Korean Differ in the Behavior of Genitive Subjects*

HIDEKI MAKI
Gifu University

MEGUMI HASEBE
Shinshu University

LINA BAO
Osaka University

MICHAEL SEVIER

LING-YUN FAN
Gifu University

SHOGO TOKUGAWA

1 Introduction

Harada (1971) originally discussed a nominative/genitive case marker alternation phenomenon in Japanese, called the *ga/no* conversion, as illustrated in (1).

(1) a.   kinoo   John-ga   katta   hon
             yesterday John-NOM   bought   book
             'the book John bought yesterday'

     b.   kinoo   John-no   katta   hon
             yesterday John-GEN   bought   book
             'the book John bought yesterday'   (J)

* An earlier version of this paper was presented at the 23rd Japanese/Korean Linguistics Conference held at Massachusetts Institute of Technology on October 13, 2013. We would like to thank the audience of the conference, Duk-Ho An, Amanullah Bhutto, Sukhwa Choi, Jessica Dunton, Yin-Ji Jin, Jeong-Seok Kim, Jaklin Kornfilt, Masako Maeda, Shigeru Miyagawa, Hisashi Morimoto, Sikder Murshed, Fumikazu Niinuma, Keun-Won Sohn, Daiko Takahashi, Yukiko Ueda, Jeong-Hee Yoo, and especially, the editors of this volume, Michael Kenstowicz, Theodore Levin, and Ryo Masuda for their valuable comments. All errors are our own.

Japanese/Korean Linguistics 23.
Edited by Michael Kenstowicz, Theodore Levin and Ryo Masuda.
Copyright © 2016, CSLI Publications

However, Japanese and Korean show a crucial difference in the behavior of genitive subjects, namely, while Japanese allows the conversion, Korean does not, as shown in (2), which is from Sohn (1997).[1]

(2) a.   ecey   John-i   san   chayk
            yesterday John-NOM   bought   book
            'the book John bought yesterday'

     b.   ?*   ecey   John-uy   san   chayk
            yesterday John-GEN   bought   book
            'the book John bought yesterday'   (K)
            (Sohn (1997) slightly edited)

Yet, possessor nominals are marked genitive both in Japanese and Korean, as shown in (3a) and (3b), respectively.

(3) a.   John-no   hon
            John-GEN   book
            'John's book'   (J)

     b.   John-uy   chayk
            John-GEN   book
            'John's book'   (K)

Also, in some fixed expressions, a genitive subject is allowed in Korean, if it is not preceded by anything, as shown in (4a) and (4b).

(4) a.   na-uy   sal-deon   kohyang
            I-GEN   lived   hometown
            'the hometown where I lived'
            (Lee Won Soo (1911-1981))

     b.   na-uy   saranghanun   nara
            I-GEN   love   mother.land
            'the mother land I love'   (K)
            (Kim Kwang Seop (1905-1977))

(4a) is from the song *My hometown's spring* by Lee Won Soo (1911-1981), and (4b) is the title of the song *The mother land I love* by Kim Kwang Seop (1905-1977). These expressions are frozen expressions, and are not created productively. The research question to be addressed in this paper is then what factor is involved in the difference between the two languages. In this paper, we point out a correlation between genitive subjects and NP-deletion in the two languages, and then argue that Korean genitive case marker contains an invisible affix, while Japanese genitive case marker does not, and that this variation is responsible for the difference between the two languages.

---

[1] Sohn (1997) was published as Sohn (2004).

The organization of this paper is as follows. Section 2 reviews the data with genitive subjects in Japanese and Korean as the background to the subsequent sections. Section 3 provides the NP-deletion data in the two languages, and points out a correlation between genitive subjects and NP-deletion. Section 4 discusses what factor is involved in the correlation, and examines whether it is observed in other languages as well. Finally, Section 5 concludes this paper.

2   Background

As the background to the subsequent sections, this section reviews the data with genitive subjects in Japanese and Korean.

2.1   Japanese

First, let us consider genitive subject data in Japanese. As shown in (1b) in Section 1, genitive subjects are allowed in Japanese. Note that in (1b), the subject is preceded by an adverb, which guarantees that it is within the relative clause in overt syntax.

(1) b. kinoo   John-no   katta   hon
         yesterday John-GEN   bought   book
         'the book John bought yesterday'   (J)

In (1b), the predicate in the relative clause is a transitive verb *katta* 'bought.' Hasebe et al. (2014) point out, on the basis of a statistical study, that genitive subjects in Japanese are the most favored in the configuration where the predicate in the relative clause is an adjective, as shown in examples such as (5b).

(5) a. [Doyoobi-ni   tamago-ga   yasui]   mise-wa   kono
         Saturday-on   egg-NOM   cheap   store-TOP   this
         mise   desu.
         store   be
         'The store where eggs are cheap on Saturdays is this store.'
     b. [Doyoobi-ni   tamago-no   yasui]   mise-wa   kono
         Saturday-on   egg-GEN   cheap   store-TOP   this
         mise   desu.
         store   be   (J)
         'The store where eggs are cheap on Saturdays is this store.'

In this paper, we use the structure in (5b) in discussing genitive subjects in Japanese, as the grammaticality status of (5b) with genitive subject is not controversial at all.

Note here that genitive subjects are not allowed in independent clauses, as shown in (6).

(6) a.   Sono   mise-de-wa   doyoobi-ni   tamago-ga   yasui.
          that   stor-at-TOP   Saturday-on   egg-NOM   cheap
          'Eggs are cheap on Saturdays at that store.'

    b. * Sono   mise-de-wa   doyoobi-ni   tamago-no   yasui.
          that   stor-at-TOP   Saturday-on   egg-GEN   cheap
          'Eggs are cheap on Saturdays at that store.'   (J)

Therefore, some condition should be imposed on it.

There are three approaches to formalizing such a condition: Miyagawa's (1993)/Maki and Uchibori's (2008) D-licensing approach, (ii) Watanabe's (1996)/Hiraiwa's (2001) C-licensing approach, and (iii) Miyagawa's (2012) *v*-licensing approach. The D-licensing approach and the C-licensing approach license the genitive subject *tamago-no* 'egg-GEN' in (5b) because the nominal head *mise* 'store,' which is a complex of D and N, agrees with it, and because the adnominal form of the predicate *yasui* 'cheap' agrees with it, respectively. The *v*-licensing approach proposed by Miyagawa (2012) licenses genitive subjects in examples such as (7).

(7)   John-wa [ame-ga/-no   yam-u]   made   ofisu-ni
       John-TOP rain-NOM/-GEN   stop-PRES   until   office-at
       ita.
       was
       'John was at his office until it stopped raining.'   (J)

In (7), the tense of the predicate in the relative clause is determined by the tense of the predicate in the matrix clause, and the predicate in the relative clause is unaccusative. Miyagawa (2012) calls this type of genitive as a genitive of dependent tense (GDT), and argues that the genitive subject *ame-no* 'rain-GEN' is licensed by *v*. Note that it is also licensed by the adnominal form of the predicate *yam-u* 'stop-PRES' under the C-licensing approach proposed by Hiraiwa (2001).

In this paper, only for purposes of exposition, we assume the condition in (8), following Hiraiwa (2001).

(8)   *Condition on Genitive Subject Licensing in Japanese*
    A genitive subject must be in a local relationship with the adnominal form of a predicate.

2.2   Korean

Second, let us consider genitive subject data in Korean. As shown in (2b) in Section 1, genitive subjects are not allowed in Korean.

(2) b. ?* ecey   John-uy   san   chayk
           yesterday   John-GEN   bought   book
           'the book John bought yesterday'   (K)
           (Sohn (1997) slightly edited)

The Korean counterpart of the Japanese example in (5b) with an adjective in the relative clause is not well-formed, either, when the subject is genitive, as shown in (9b).

(9) a.   [Thoyoil-eye kyelan-i   ssan]   sangcem-un   i
              Saturday-on   egg-NOM   cheap   store-TOP   this
              sangcem ita.
              store   be
              'The store where eggs are cheap on Saturdays is this store.'

     b. *   [Thoyoil-eye kyelan-uy   ssan]   sangcem-un   i
              Saturday-on   egg-GEN   cheap   store-TOP   this
              sangcem ita.
              store   be   (K)
              'The store where eggs are cheap on Saturdays is this store.'
              (personal communication with Jeong-Seok Kim)

Furthermore, a genitive of dependent tense is not allowed, either, as shown in (10).

(10)   John-un [bi-ga/*-uy   kunki-l] *(ttay) kkaci
         John-TOP rain-NOM/-GEN   stop-ADN time   until
         samusil-ey   issoeta.
         office-at   was
         'John was at his office until it stopped raining.'   (K)

Note that Maki et al. (2006) conducted a statistical study, and report that genitive subjects are consistently worse than nominative subjects in relative clauses in Korean.[2]

---

[2] Maki et al. (2006) conducted a statistical analysis of the distribution of genitive subjects in Korean using the structures in (i) and (ii).

(i)   a.   [NP-NOM V] N
       b.   [NP-GEN V] N

(ii)   a.   [AdvP NP-NOM V] N
       b.   [AdvP NP-GEN V] N

The participants were asked to indicate the grammaticality of each of the examples on the scale ranging from 1 (= totally ungrammatical) to 5 (= perfectly grammatical). Maki et al. (2006) then

3 Data

Having established the relevant background in the above section, let us now consider the NP-Deletion data in Japanese and Korean. It seems that the two phenomena (genitive subject licensing and NP-Deletion) have been investigated independently in the literature, and the correlation between the two phenomena has not been pointed out. Saito and Murasugi (1990) originally point out that NP-Deletion is possible in Japanese. The data in (11) is from Saito, Lin, and Murasugi (2008).

(11) [Taroo-no taido]-wa yoi ga, [Hanako-no
 Taro-GEN attitude-TOP good though Hanako-GEN
~~taido~~]-wa yokunai.
attitude-TOP not.good
'Though Taro's attitude is good, Hanako's isn't.' (J)
(Saito, Lin, and Murasugi (2008))

On the other hand, NP-Deletion is not possible in Korean. The data in (12) is from An (2012).

(12) * [John-uy thayto]-nun coh-ciman, [Mary-uy
 John-GEN attitude-TOP good-though Mary-GEN
~~thayto~~]-nun cohci ahnta.
attitude-TOP good not
'Though John's attitude is good, Mary's isn't.' (K)
(An (2012))

However, An (2012) points out that NP-Deletion in (12) involves another factor: the sequence of case markers/particles is not allowed in Korean, as shown in (13). Therefore, (12) does not genuinely show the impossibility of NP-Deletion in Korean.

---

conducted a repeated measure of 2x2 ANOVA (Case Type x Adverb Type) on the ratings (1 to 5). The results are shown in (iii).

(iii) The Descriptive Statistics

Structure	Case Type	Adverb Type	Observations	Average Scores (SD)
(ia)	Nom	0	275	3.74 (.88)
(ib)	Gen	0	275	1.89 (.90)
(iia)	Nom	1	275	3.81 (.87)
(iib)	Gen	1	275	1.89 (.91)

They found statistically significant differences between structures (ia) and (ib) ($p<.001$) and between structures (iia) and (iib) ($p<.001$), which shows a significant effect on Case marker: in each pair in (i) and (ii), the rating was far higher for sentences with nominative subjects than sentences with genitive subjects, whether or not the subjects are preceded by an adverb.

(13) a.   *   Mary-ka/-lul/-uy/-nun
                Mary-NOM/-ACC/-GEN/-TOP

    b.   Mary-ka/-lul/-uy
                Mary-NOM/-ACC/-GEN

    c.   Mary-nun
                Mary-TOP   (K)
                (An (2012) slightly edited)

Avoiding this problem, we found that NP-Deletion is actually impossible in Korean based on examples such as (14), where the genitive case marker is not followed by any other case marker.

(14) a.   Nuku-uy thayto-ga   cohci   ansumni ka?
                who-GEN attitude-NOM   good   not.be   Q
                'Whose attitude is not good?'

    b.   John-uy   [NP thayto/*e]   imnida.
                John-GEN   attitude   be
                'John's (attitude) is.'   (K)

Note here that the corresponding Japanese examples are fine, as shown in (15).

(15) a.   Dare-no taido-ga   yoku   nai desu ka?
                who-GEN attitude-NOM   good   not   be   Q
                'Whose attitude is not good?'

    b.   John-no   [NP taido/e]   desu.
                John-GEN   attitude   be
                'John's (attitude) is.'   (J)

Therefore, there seems to be a correlation between the fact that genitive subjects are allowed in the language and the fact that NP-deletion is also allowed in the same language.

Note here that English allows NP-deletion, as shown in (16), while it does not allow genitive subjects, as shown in (17).

(16) a.   I can tolerate the undergraduates' reliance on the faculty, but I cannot tolerate [DP the graduate students' [NP reliance on the faculty]].

    b.   I can tolerate the undergraduates' reliance on the faculty, but I cannot tolerate [DP the graduate students' [NP e]].   (E)
                (Maki and Niinuma (2011))

(17) a.   I know the book which John read.
    b.   *   I know the book which John's read.   (E)

Therefore, the correlation is actually not bidirectional, but a unidirectional relation, as shown in (18).[3]

(18)   Relation Between Genitive Subjects and NP-Deletion
        If a language allows genitive subjects, it also allows NP-deletion.

4   Discussion

The Korean data in the above section show two things. First, genitive subjects in Korean are not allowed at all, which indicates that no approach to genitive subject licensing is available in Korean. Second, NP-Deletion is totally unavailable in Korean. We therefore claim that the unavailability of (i) genitive subjects and (ii) NP-Deletion suggests that it is not directly due to the structural properties of the phenomena, but due to the morphological property of the genitive case marker, and that these two facts should receive a uniform account. To be specific, we propose that the genitive case marker is affix-like in Korean, while it is not in Japanese, as stated in (19).

(19)   Korean genitive case marker contains an invisible affix that must attach to the head noun in overt syntax. Japanese genitive case marker does not contain such an affix.

With this proposal, let us consider the relevant Korean data shown above. First, the examples in (9b) and (14b), reproduced as (20) and (21), respectively, receive a uniform account under the proposal.

(20) * [Thoyoil-eye   kyelan-**uy**   ssan]   sangcem-un   i
        Saturday-on   egg-GEN   cheap   store-TOP   this
        sangcem ita.
        store   be
        'The store where eggs are cheap on Saturdays is this store.'   (K)

(21) * John-**uy** [NP *e*]   imnida.
        John-GEN   be
        'John's.'   (K)

In (20), the invisible affix adjoins to N across another head V (or V+I), as shown in (22).

---

[3] There may be another unidirectional relation between genitive subjects and NP-deletion, as shown in (i).

(i)   Relation Between Genitive Subjects and NP-Deletion
       If a language disallows NP-deletion, it also disallows genitive subjects.

We will not examine the validity of (i) in this paper for space limitations.

(22)   [$_{IP}$ ADV John-GEN…V I]$_{IP}$ N
          |_____*____↑

In (21), the affix cannot adjoin to N in overt syntax, if N had already been elided, as shown in (23).

(23)   [$_{DP}$ John-GEN [$_{NP}$ ø] D]
          |__*__↑

Alternatively, if N were elided after the affix attaches to it in overt syntax, the affix cannot survive at the LF representation, which would cause the situation in which the stranded NP/DP to which the genitive case marker has been attached cannot be properly interpreted.

On the other hand, in (3b) and (4a), the affix can adjoin to N without crossing any intervening head, as shown in (24) and (25). We assume with Sohn (1997) that the NP marked genitive is in DP SPEC in overt syntax in these examples.

(3) b.   John-uy   chayk
              John-GEN   book
              'John's book'   (K)
(4) a.   na-uy   salten   kohayng
              I-GEN   lived   hometown
              'the hometown where I lived'   (K)
              (Lee Won Soo (1911-1981))

(24)   [$_{DP}$ John-GEN [$_{NP}$ book] D]
          |_____↑

(25)   [$_{DP}$ I-GEN [$_{AP/IP}$…] [$_{NP}$ hometown] D]
          |_____↑

Thus, the invisible affix movement hypothesis provides an account for the relation between genitive subjects and NP-deletion in the given language. The relation between genitive subjects and NP-deletion in Japanese and Korean is summarized in (26).

(26)   The Relation Between Genitive Subjects and NP-Deletion in
          Japanese and Korean

	Japanese	Korean
Genitive Subjects	√	*
NP-Deletion	√	*

Before investigating whether the relation between genitive subjects and NP-deletion as observed in Japanese and Korean holds in other languages as well, let us consider whether another factor may enter into the relation. The potential factor is the *pro*-form meaning 'one.' Japanese has a *pro*-form *no* 'one,' which is identical to the genitive case marker *no*, as shown in (27a), but Korean does not have such a *pro*-form, as shown in (27b).

(27) a.   akai-no/-mono
             red-one/-thing
             'red one/thing'   (J)

     b.   ppalkan*-uy/-ke(s)
             red-one/-thing
             'red one/thing'   (K)

The *pro*-form *no* in Japanese seems somehow morphologically related to the genitive case marker *no*. However, Korean does not have such a *pro*-form, which then must be represented as *ke(s)* 'thing.' It may be the case then that in Korean, the morphological change from the genitive case marker to the *pro*-form was unsuccessful, which might be due to the invisible affix on the genitive case marker in the language. Then, the relation seems to hold in Japanese and Korean among the three factors, namely, genitive subjects, NP-deletion, and *pro*-forms, as shown in (28).

(28)   The Relation among Genitive Subjects, NP-Deletion, and *Pro*-Forms in Japanese and Korean

	Japanese	Korean
Genitive Subjects	√	*
NP-Deletion	√	*
Pro-Forms	√	*

However, the hypothesis that the *pro*-form in Japanese is somehow morphologically related to the genitive case marker does not seem correct, given the Toyama variety of Japanese, for instance. This is because in the Toyama variety of Japanese, the genitive case marker is realized as *no*, but the *pro*-form is realized as *ga*, which is not morphologically related to *no* at all. Consider the examples in (29)-(31) from Murasugi (1991).

(29) a.   siroi   ga
             white   one
             'the one which is white'
     b.   John-no   ga
             John-gen   one
             'the one which is John's'   (TJ)

(30) a.   siroi   no
    white   one
    'the one which is white'

  b.   John   no
    John   one
    'the one which is John's'   (J)

(31) a.   Taroo-no   katta   ga
    Taro-GEN   bought one
    'the one that Taro bought'

  b.   botan-no   toreteiru ga
    button-GEN   detached one
    'the one without a button'   (TJ)
    (Murasugi (1991: 74))

The examples in (29) show that the *pro*-form in the Toyama variety of Japanese is *ga*, and those in (30) show the corresponding examples in standard Japanese, where the *pro*-form is *no*. The examples in (31) show that the genitive subject is possible in the Toyama variety of Japanese, where the genitive case marker is realized as *no*, just as in standard Japanese. These data suggest that it seems incorrect to hypothesize that the *pro*-form in a variety of Japanese is morphologically related to the genitive case marker in the same variety. Therefore, it seems safe to conclude that the relation is restricted to the two factors, namely, genitive subjects and NP-deletion in the given language.[4]

Let us now investigate whether the relation between genitive subjects and NP-deletion as observed in Japanese and Korean holds in other languages as well. First, let us consider the data in Mongolian, another Altaic language. Maki et al. (2010) report that Mongolian allows genitive subjects, as shown in (32).

(32)   öčügedür Baүatur-ø/-un   qudaldun-abu-үsan /*-čai
    yesterday Bagatur-NOM/-GEN buy-take-PAST.ADN/-PAST.CON
    nom
    book
    'the book which Bagatur bought yesterday'   (M)

---

[4] Note that Murasugi (1991: 71, footnote 35) states that the distributions of *no* and *ga* in the Toyama variety of Japanese are quite similar to those of Korean *uy* and *kes*: *uy* functions as the genitive case marker, and what corresponds to the *pro*-form *ga* in the Toyama variety of Japanese is *kes*.

In (32), the predicate in the relative clause must be in the adnominal form, whether or not the subject is genitive or nominative. Let us then examine whether Mongolian allows NP-deletion. Consider the examples in (33).

(33) a. Ken-nü obur-ø maɣu boi?
who-GEN attitude bad Q
'Whose attitude is bad?'

b. Baɣatur-un [NP obur/*e*].
Baɣatur-GEN attitude
'Baɣatur's (attitude).' (M)

(33b) shows that the NP *obur* 'attitude' can be elided. Therefore, the relation between genitive subjects and NP-deletion holds in Mongolian as well. (34) summarizes the relation between genitive subjects and NP-deletion in Japanese, Mongolian, and Korean.

(34) The Relation Between Genitive Subjects and NP-Deletion in Japanese, Mongolian, and Korean

	Japanese	Mongolian	Korean
Genitive Subjects	√	√	*
NP-Deletion	√	√	*

Let us finally examine Urdu, a language from the non-Altaic language family. Urdu is a dialect of the Hindi-Urdu or Hindustani language, and belongs to the Indo-European family. It is the national language of Pakistan. Maki and Bhutto (2013) report that Urdu also allows genitive subjects, althhough there is no "genuine" ergative/genitive alternation. Urdu is an ergative language. Therefore, the subject of the sentence with a verb in past tense appears with the ergative case marker *ne*, as shown in (35).

(35) John-ne kal kitab kahreedi.
John-ERG yesterday book bought
'John bought a book yesterday.' (U)

(36) and (37) show that in a relative clause in Urdu, the subject can be marked genitive, not ergative.

(36) [Kal John-ki khareedi-hui] kitab buhut
yesterday John-GEN bought-PERF book very
dilchasp hai.
interesting be.PRES
'The book which John bought yesterday is very interesting.' (U)
(Maki and Bhutto (2013))

(37) *   [Kal   John-ne   khareedi-hui] kitab   buhut
         yesterday   John-ERG   bought-PERF   book   very
         dilchasp   hai.
         interesting   be.PRES
         'The book which John bought yesterday is very interesting.'   (U)

Therefore, genitive subjects are permitted in Urdu. Let us then examine whether Urdu allows NP-deletion. Consider the examples in (38).

(38) a.   Kis-ka   rawayya acha   hai?
          who-GEN.M   attitude good   be
          'Whose attitude is good?'   (U)

     b.   John-ka   [$_{NP}$ rawayya/e]   acha   hai.
          John-GEN.M   attitude   good   be
          'John's (attitude) is good.'   (U)
          (personal communication with Amanullah Bhutto)

(38b) shows that the NP *rawayya* 'attitude' can be elided. Therefore, the relation between genitive subjects and NP-deletion holds in Bengali as well. (39) summarizes the relation between genitive subjects and NP-deletion in Japanese, Mongolian, Bengali, Urdu, and Korean.

(39)   The Relation Between Genitive Subjects and NP-Deletion in
         Japanese, Mongolian, Urdu, and Korean

	Japanese	Mongolian	Urdu	Korean
Genitive Subjects	√	√	√	*
NP-Deletion	√	√	√	*

5   Conclusion

This paper pointed out a relation between genitive subjects and NP-deletion in Japanese and Korean, and discussed what factor would be involved in the relation. We proposed that Korean genitive case marker contains an invisible affix that must attach to the head noun in overt syntax, while Japanese genitive case marker does not contain such an affix. We then examined whether the relation would be general enough, and found that it was also observed in Mongolian and Urdu.

References

An, D. 2012. NP-Ellipsis, its Impostors, and Minor Argument Pronominalization in Korean. *Korean Journal of Linguistics* 37:345–356.

Harada, S.-I. 1971. Ga-No Conversion and Ideolectal Variations in Japanese. *Gengo Kenkyu* 60:25–38.

Hasebe, M., H. Maki, and T. Umezawa. 2014. Where the Nominative/Genitive Alternation Genuinely Takes Place in Modern Japanese. *English Linguistics* 31:149–160.

Hiraiwa, K. 2001. On Nominative-genitive Conversion. *MIT Working Papers in Linguistics 39: A Few from Building E39*, ed. E. Guerzoni and O. Matushansky, 66–125. Cambridge, MA.: MIT Working Papers in Linguistics.

Maki, H., L. Bao, Q. Wu, W. Bao, A. Uchibori, F. Niinuma, and K. Goto. 2010. The Nominative/Genitive Alternation in Modern Mongolian. *MIT Working Papers in Linguistics 61: Proceedings of the 6th Workshop on Altaic Formal Linguistics (WAFL6)*, ed. H. Maezawa and A. Yokogoshi, 229–245. Cambridge, MA.: MIT Working Papers in Linguistics.

Maki, H. and F. Niinuma. 2011. NP Deletion in English and Japanese. *JELS* 28 (Papers from the 28th Conference of the English Linguistic Society of Japan): 82–88.

Maki, H., K. Shin, and K. Tsubouchi. 2006. A Statistical Analysis of the Nominative/Genitive Alternation in Modern Korean: A Preliminary Study. *Proceedings of the 133rd Meeting of the Linguistic Society of Japan*, 71–76.

Maki, H. and A. Uchibori. 2008. *Ga/No* Conversion. *Handbook of Japanese Linguistics*, ed. S. Miyagawa and M. Saito, 192–216. Oxford: Oxford University Press.

Miyagawa, S. 1993. Case-Checking and Minimal Link Condition. *MIT Working Paper in Linguistics 19: Papers on Case and Agreement II*, ed. C. Phillips, 213–254. Cambridge, MA.: MIT Working Papers in Linguistics.

Miyagawa, S. 2012. Genitive of Dependent Tense in Japanese and Its Correlation with Genitive of Negation in Slavic. *Case, Argument Structure, and Word Order*, 146–168. New York: Routledge.

Murasugi, K. 1991. Noun phrases in Japanese and English: A study in Syntax, Learnability and Acquisition. Doctoral dissertation, University of Connecticut, Storrs.

Saito, M., T.-H. J. Lin, and K. Murasugi. 2008. N'-Ellipsis and the Structure of Noun Phrases in Chinese and Japanese. *Journal of East Asian Linguistics* 17:247–271.

Saito, M. and K. Murasugi. 1990. N'-Deletion in Japanese: A Preliminary Study. *Japanese/Korean Linguistics* 1:285–301.

Sohn, K. 1997. Some Notes on the So Called Nominative-genitive Conversion. *Proceedings of the Fourth Seoul International Conference on Linguistics*, 533–541.

Sohn, K. 2004. Nom-gen Conversion as a Spurious Phenomenon. *The Jungang Journal of English Language and Literature* 46: 183–202.

Watanabe, A. 1996. Nominative-genitive Conversion and Agreement in Japanese: A Cross-Linguistic Perspective. *Journal of East Asian Linguistics* 5:373–410.

Implications of Constraints on Null Constituents for Analyses of the Right Dislocation Construction

JAMES HYE SUK YOON
University of Illinois, Urbana-Champaign

1 Introduction*

The construction known most commonly as the Right Dislocation Construction (RD, hereafter) shown in (1) below has come into the

---

*This paper represents a portion of the materials presented at the Twenty-Third Japanese/Korean Linguistics Conference held at MIT in October, 2013. Earlier versions of some of the ideas discussed in this paper were presented at the Sixth Workshop in Altaic Formal Linguistics (Nagoya University, 2009), University of Chicago (2009), CUNY Graduate Center (2012), and at Dongguk University (2013). Special thanks go to Karlos Arregi, Marcel den Dikken, Chris Kennedy, Jonathan Macdonald, Jiyoung Shim, and Satoshi Tomioka for helpful comments, and to Wooseung Lee and Daeho Chung for discussion of related issues over the years. Finally, I would like to thank the organizers of J/K 23, in particular, Mike Kenstowicz, for the invitation that allowed me to share the ideas discussed here. Needless to say, this is still very much a work in progress.

Japanese/Korean Linguistics 23.
Edited by Michael Kenstowicz, Theodore Levin and Ryo Masuda.
Copyright © 2016, CSLI Publications

theoretical spotlight in recent years, due in part to the surge of interest in different types of elliptical constructions in natural languages.

(1) Cheli-ka   **pro/kyay-lul**   ecey   mannass-e,   **Tongswu-lul**
    C-nom   him-acc   yesterday   met-decl   T-acc
    'Cheli met him yesterday, namely, Tongswu.'

Before we proceed, it is useful to fix some terminology. We shall refer to the dislocated constituent (*Tongswu-lul*) as the **Appendix**, and the clause that precedes it as the **Host**. The gap or the overt constituent within the Host that is linked interpretively to the Appendix (*pro/kyay-lul*) shall be called the **Target**.

Most recent analyses of RD in Korean and Japanese are based on Tanaka (2001), which takes RD to be a bi-clausal, paratactic collocation of clauses, as shown in (2) below. In the input to RD, the second clause (=CP2, TP2) must be identical to the first, and the Appendix (=XP below) must be matched (that is, coindexed with) to a Target (=YP) within the Host clause.

(2) $[_{CP1} [_{TP1}... \begin{pmatrix} e_i \\ YP_i \end{pmatrix} ... V]_k]$ $[_{CP2} XP_i \ [_{TP2}... \quad t_i \quad ... \quad V]_k]$

RD arises when the Appendix undergoes leftward movement/Scrambling in the second clause and the remainder of the clause is deleted, under some algorithm that determines identity of the second clause with respect to the preceding one (cf. Merchant 2001 for a detailed analysis of Sluicing along these lines as well as a specific algorithm for computing identity that allows deletion).

This analysis differ substantially from earlier analyses which took RD to be derived by rightward movement/Scrambling of the Appendix from a within a single-rooted clause.

There is good evidence that RD consists of two separate root clauses. For example, there must be two rising intonational contours at the right edge of the Host clause and the Appendix when the Host is a Yes-No question. This clearly indicates the presence of two distinct clauses.

(3) a. __   ecey   Yenghi-lul   manna-ss-ni?↗   Cheli-ka?↗
            yesterday   Y-acc   meet-pst-Q   C-nom

     b. *__   ecey   Yenghi-lul   manna-ss-ni   Cheli-ka? ↗
            yesterday   Y-acc   meet-pst-Q   C-nom
         'Did Yenghi meet Cheli yesterday?'

Another salient property of RD is that it is restricted to root domains. Embedded RD is not possible (cf. 4a), but when an embedded constituent occurs at the root level as an Appendix, the structure is fine (cf. 4b).

(4) a. *Cheli-ka   [Yenghi-ka __   mannassta-ko **Tongswu-lul**]
        C-nom   Y-nom   met-comp   T-acc
        malhayss-e
        said-decl
        'Cheli said that Yenghi met him, namely, Tongswu.'

     b. Cheli-ka   [Yenghi-ka __   mannassta-ko]   malhayss-e,
         C-nom   Y-nom   met-comp   said-decl
         Tongswu-lul
         T-acc

Scrambling from an embedded clause is not similarly restricted, as it need not displace the moved constituent to the root domain (cf. 5a).

(5) a. Cheli-ka [**Tongswu-lul**   Yenghi-ka __   mannassta-ko]
         C-nom   T-acc   Y-nom   met-comp
         malhayss-e
         said-decl
         'Cheli said Yenghi met Tongswu.'

     b. **Tongswu-lul**   Cheli-ka   [Yenghi-ka __   mannassta-ko]
         T-acc   C-nom   Y-nom   met-comp
         malhayss-e
         said-decl

Since paratactic structures are concatenations of root clauses, the root-only restriction of RD, coupled with the prosodic evidence indicating multiple root clauses, favors the Tanaka-style analysis of RD.

Nonetheless, the idea that the Appendix results from deletion subsequent to movement has been the subject of intense scrutiny. This is because the movement derivation of the Appendix predicts that it should be constrained by properties of movement, in particular, movement locality. However, data that appear problematic for the movement derivation of the Appendix have been identified in earlier work (Yoon 2009, Lee 2009, *inter alia*). This paper focuses on the type of Appendices that have been claimed to be problematic for the dominant account of RD, and show that constraints on ellipsis, together with a particular understanding of Sprouting (based on Chung, Ladusaw and McCloskey (CLM) 2011), can provide an account of these Appendices within an approach that is largely similar to the dominant account of RDs.

2 Adnominal and Conjunct Appendices

The type of constituents that can occur as Appendices in RD include Left Branch constituents—such as demonstratives and relative clauses, as shown in (6a). We also find conjuncts occurring as Appendices, as seen (6b).

(6) a. na-nun [__ John]-ul mannass-e
     I-top J-acc met-decl
     wuli-thim-ey saylo haplyuha-n
     our-team-loc newly joined-rel
     'I met John, who recently joined our team.'

  b. Cheli-ka phathi-eyse [__ Yenghi]-lul mannasse-e,
     C-nom party-loc Y-acc met–decl
     Tongswu-hako
     T-conj
     'Cheli met Yenghi at the party, and Tongswu as well.'

Yoon (2009) and Lee (2009) rightly take these data to be problematic for the reigning analysis of RDs. The specific challenge is how an Appendix can be related to a position within an island (Left Branches and Coordinate Structures) if movement is responsible for its licensing in (6a,b).

A possible response to the insensitivity of adnominal/Left Branch and conjunct Appendices to movement locality might be to invoke the island-repairing power of ellipsis, an idea that is widely adopted in the literature. However, the generality of such an account is immediately compromised by the following fact. Though adnominal modifiers and demonstratives can occur as Appendices, nominal Heads (and their projections) modified by them cannot (Baker 2007, Sells 1999, Yoon 2009, and Lee 2009) (cf. 7a). And conjuncts that occur as Appendices are limited to non-final conjuncts (cf. 6b). A final conjunct cannot occur as Appendix with a non-final conjunct stranded in the Host clause (cf. 7b).

(7) a. *na-nun [wuli-thim-ey saylo haplyuha-n __]
     I-top our-team-loc newly joined-rel
     mannass-e **John-ul**
     met-decl J-acc
     'I met John, who recently joined our team.'

  b. *Cheli-ka phathi-eyse [Tongswu-hako __]
     Cheli-nom party-loc T-conj
     mannass-e, **Yenghi-lul**
     met-decl Y-acc
     'Cheli met Tongswu at the party, and Yenghi as well.'

Therefore, any account of (6a,b) that appeals to the island-repairing power of ellipsis must ensure that the power is curtailed so as to distinguish between the movements of Left Branches and nominal Head projections (6a vs. 7a) and between movements of non-final and final Conjuncts (6b vs. 7b) in their ability to amnesty island violations, even though the Complex NP Constraint and the Coordinate Structure Constraint (specifically, the Conjunct Condition) are violated in both cases.

A further indication that the island repair account is doomed to failure comes from the fact that islands cannot be seemingly repaired in other RDs. The following RDs show that Appendices cannot be related to a null Target contained within islands (Adjunct and Complex NP/Subject Island, respectively).

(8) a. *Cheli-ka   [Swuni-ka __   mannaki   ttaymwuney]
       C-nom   S-nom   meet   because
       hwa-ka   nass-tay,   **Tongswu-lul**
       anger-nom   came-I.hear T-acc
       '(I hear that) Cheli got upset because Swuni is going out with him (=Tongswu).'

    b. *[[Cheli-ka   __   mannanta]-nun   sasil]-i   wuli-lul
        C-nom   meet-rel   fact-nom   we-acc
        nollakay   hayss-e,   **Yenghi-lul**
        surprise   did-decl   Y-acc
        'The fact that Cheli is going out with her(=Yenghi) surprised us.'

Since we are unlikely to find a principled account that permits island repair in (6) but not in (7) or (8), we should look elsewhere for a possible explanation.

Our search for a solution will unfold in two stages. In the first stage, we shall look for the cause underlying the contrast between (6) and (7) (section 2.1). In the second, we seek to understand why islands can be apparently disregarded in (6), but not in (8) (section 3).

2.1 Illegitimate Ellipsis

Note that island violations are incurred by the movement of the Appendix in both (6) and (7) under the current account of RD. Therefore, island violations cannot be the culprit behind the difference in acceptability of (6) and (7).

We suspect that the real culprit is the **Target** within the Host clause. That is, while (6) has a legitimate null Target in the Host clause, (7) does not. The rationale behind this idea is that the contrast between (6) and (7) is reminiscent of what D-H Chung (2009, 2011) discovered about predicates and dependents in RD.

Chung found that predicates (and projections of predicates) cannot occur as Appendices in RDs while stranding the dependents (arguments and adjuncts) associated with the predicate (cf. 9b,c). By contrast, dependents can occur as Appendices without the accompanying predicate (cf. 9a).

(9) a. Cheli-nun   [nay-ka ___   cikcep   mannassta-ko]
        C-top   I-nom   in.person   met-comp
        sayngkakhay,   **Tongswu-lul**
        thinks   T-acc
        'Cheli thinks that I met him in person, namely, Tongswu.'

     b. *Cheli-nun   [nay-ka Tongswu-lul   cikcep   ___]
        C-top   I-nom   T-acc   in.person
        sayngkakhay,   **mannassta-ko**
        thinks   met-comp

     c. *Cheli-nun   [nay-ka ___]   sayngkakhay
        C-top   I-nom   thinks
        Tongswu-lul   **cikcep**   **mannassta-ko**
        T-acc   in.person   met-comp

D-H Chung (2009, 2011) proposed that the reason why predicates (and their projections) cannot occur in RD is because a verb and the attendant functional projections (that is, the sequence V-*v*-T-C that underlie the string *manna-ss-ta-ko* in 9b,c above) do not form a constituent in Korean, due to the lack of verb raising in syntax (Yoon 1994). If we assume that a null Target is licensed via ellipsis, since constituency is a pre-condition for ellipsis (or pro-formation), the RD's in (9b,c) are illegitimate because ellipsis has targeted a non-constituent string in the Host clause.

Confirmation that the ill-formedness of (9b,c) stems from the null Target comes from the fact that the sentences become well-formed when the Target is not null.[1]

---

[1] Now, if Chung is correct that the inflected verb string is not a constituent that can undergo ellipsis yielding a null Target in (9b,c), the same string should be impermissible as Appendix, since the Appendix is derived by movement, and movement, like ellipsis, is constrained by constituency. Thus, his account predicts that even when the Target has not undergone ellipsis, the resulting RD should still be bad, because a non-constituent string has undergone movement in the Appendix. However, (10a,b) is well-formed, falsifying this prediction.

In order to get out of this impasse, Chung hypothesizes that for (10a,b), the Target is the entire embedded CP within the Host clause. Correspondingly, the Appendix is also a

(10)a.   Cheli-nun   [nay-ka Tongswu-lul cikcep   **mannassta-ko]**
       C-top   I-nom T-acc   in.person met-comp
       sayngkakhay,   **mannassta-ko**   (cf. 9b)
       thinks   met-comp

    b.   Cheli-nun   [nay-ka **kulayssta-ko]**   sayngkakhay
       C-top   I-nom did.so-comp   thinks
       Tongswu-lul   **cikcep**   **mannassta-ko**   (cf. 9c)
       T-acc   in.person   met-comp

The idea we are pursuing is that the contrast between (6) and (7) also boils down to the difference between legitimate and illegitimate null Targets. That is, ellipsis yielding a null Target is allowed in (11a) (=6a) but not in (11b) (=7a).

(11)a. ^{ok}na-nun   [[~~wuli-thim-ey   saylo   haplyuha]-n~~ John]-ul
       I-top   our-team-loc   newly joined-rel   J-acc
       mannass-e, **wuli-thim-ey saylo   haplyuha-n**
       met-decl   our-team-loc newly joined-real

    b. *na-nun   [_{DP} [wuli-thim-ey   saylo   haplyuha]-n ~~John]-ul~~
       I-top   our-team-loc   newly joined-rel   J-acc
       mannass-e, **John-ul**
       met-decl   J-acc

What could be the reason why ellipsis fails to target the string *John-ul* in (11b) but not the string *wuli-thim-ey saylo haplyuha-n* in (11a)?

If we apply Chung's logic regarding the inability of predicate (projections) to occur as null Targets, we can hypothesize that since the case-marker (=*lul*) combines with the entire phrase (=DP) as indicated (cf. Yoon 1995, who argues that case-markers are enclitics/ad-phrasal suffixes), ellipsis of the case-marker plus the Head noun alone without its dependents effects a non-constituent substring. By contrast, the adnominal modifier is a

---

constituent CP containing empty categories that are coindexed with the matched constituents within the Target CP. That is, the structure of (10a) is as follows.

(i) Cheli-nun [_{CP} **nay-ka₁ Tongswu-lul₂ cikcep₃   mannassta-ko]** sayngkakhay,
                           TARGET
  [_{CP} **e₁ e₂ e₃ mannassta-ko]**
       APPENDIX

This alternative parse is not available for (9b), as one can tell, where only the string *mannassta-ko* is deleted (as Target) within the Host clause.

    There are a few questionable aspects of the analysis shown in (i), but we shall not address them here.

constituent that can undergo ellipsis without effecting the rest of the phrase in (11a).[2]

2.2 The Host Lacks Null Targets

If the preceding discussion is on the right track, the ill-formedness of (7) is attributable to the illegitimate ellipsis of the null Target string.[3]

---

[2] Alternatively, one might hypothesize that when a Head (Noun, in this case) undergoes deletion, all of its dependents must be affected as well. Such a constraint is appealed to in J-M Jo's (2013) analysis of the (Contrastive) Predicate Topic construction in Korean, though for overt pro-forms.

As we see below, the Predicate portion of the Predicate Topic construction can contain a copy of constituents (=*pap-ul*) that occur within the Topic constituent (cf. i). However, when the pro-verb *ha-* is employed, only the verb, but not its dependents, is permitted in the Predicate portion of the construction (cf. ii).

(i) Cheli-ka   pap-ul   mek-ki-nun   (pap-ul)   mek-ess-ta
    C-nom   meal-acc   eat-nml-top   (meal-acc) eat-pst-decl
    'As for eating his meal, Cheli did.'

(ii) Cheli-ka   pap-ul   mek-ki-nun   (*pap-ul)   hay-ss-ta
     C-nom   meal-acc   eat-nml-top   (*meal-acc)   do-pst-decl

J-M Jo (2013) proposes that the Predicate Topic construction with a reduplicated predicate (cf. i) and that with the pro-verb *ha-* (cf. ii) arise from the same underlying structure, where a vP occurs as both the Subject/Topic and the Predicate. Deletion of dependents applies freely within the Topic and the Predicate constituents (up to recoverability).

(iii) [$_{vP}$ Cheli-ka pap-ul mek]-ki-nun   [$_{vP}$ ~~Cheli-ka (pap-ul)~~ mek]-ess-ta   (= i)
         TOPIC   PREDICATE

(iv) [$_{vP}$ Cheli-ka pap-ul mek]-ki-nun   [$_{vP}$ ~~Cheli-ka pap-ul mek~~]-ess-ta   (= ii)
        TOPIC   → *ha*-replacement
                                                          PREDICATE

This accounts for the fact that the Predicate constituent can contain more than just the verb (a fatal problem for analyses that take the construction to involve reduplication of the verb alone, such as K-Y Choi 2001). However, the Predicate constituent cannot contain any stranded dependents (cf. ii) if, instead of the reduplicated verb, the pro-verb *ha-* is employed in the construction.

He takes this to imply that *ha-* replaces the entire Predicate constituent (=vP), and when it does so, the dependents of the verb that heads the Predicate constituent (*mek-*) cannot escape the replacement by the pro-form *ha-*. A constraint like this (extended to ellipsis yielding the null Target) will account for why, when the Head nominal (projection) is deleted, all of the dependents must be deleted as well.

Note also that this line of reasoning implies that Coordinate Structures in Korean are asymmetrical in Headedness. That is, the final Conjunct must count as the unique Head. This is not an unusual position to take about coordination in Head-final languages, as is well-known.

[3] Confirmation that the null Target is the culprit comes from the fact that when the Target is not null, the RD is well-formed. Cf.

(i) na-nun   [[wuli-thim-ey   saylo   haplyuha]-n   **ku salam**]-ul
    I-top   our-team-loc   newly   joined-rel   that person-acc
    mannass-e,   **John-ul**
    met-decl   J-acc

However, as noted earlier, the well-formedness of (6) is still without an explanation. This is so since locality is violated by the putative movement of the Appendix in (6). The Appendix in (6a), for example, would be derived as follows, where the movement violates the Left Branch Condition. But (12), without ellipsis of the clause from which the adnominal modifier has moved out, is ill-formed.

(12) [[wuli-thim-ey ... haplyuha-n]$_i$ [na-nun [$_{DP}$ t$_i$ [John]]-ul mannass-e

Recall that we cannot invoke repair by ellipsis in RDs in our answer since, as (8) shows, island violations in other RDs cannot be repaired. This is the first problem with (6)

The second problem with (6) is the following. The assumption we made that the Host clause of (6) contains a null Target that has undergone ellipsis (in the manner sketched in 11a above) is suspect. This is so because this assumption is at odds with the fact that adnominal modifiers cannot be licensed under ellipsis in other contexts. Consider the following

(13)

A: Cheli-nun   [[$_{RelC}$ **acwu   pissa**]-n   cha]-lul
    C-top   very   expensive-rel   car-acc
    kacko   iss-ta
    possess   is-decl
    'Cheli has a very expensive car.'

B: Yenghi-nun   kapang-ul   kacko   iss-ta
    Y-top   handbag-acc   possess is-decl
    =   (i) Yenghi has a handbag
    =/= (ii) Yenghi has a very expensive handbag

B': Yenghi-to   kacko   iss-ta
     Y-also   possess   is-decl
     = Yenghi has an expensive car too.

If adnominal modifiers could be licensed under ellipsis, (13B) should allow the interpretation indicated in B(ii), but it does not. (13B') on the other hand has an intepretation where the null Object NP includes the meaning of the modifier. If an adnominal modifier could be licensed under ellipsis (or as a null proform), the reading indicated in B(ii) should be possible. What this implies is that a null (deleted) adnominal modifier cannot be licensed by an anaphoric antecedent, unlike null Objects. Since the direction of licensing in RD is cataphoric, and cataphora is more restricted than anaphora, we have no reason to believe that ellipsis of an adnominal modifier Target can happen under cataphora.[4]

Therefore, in (6a), the Appendix must have been **Sprouted**, rather than moved (to use terminology from the literature on Sluicing). Thus, the proper analysis of (6a) is as follows, rather than as in (11a), where the Host clause does not contain a null adnominal modifier functioning as Target:

(14) na-nun John-ul mannass-e, [**wuli-thim-ey saylo haplyuha-n**]
 I-top J-acc met-decl our-team-loc newly joined-rel
 'I met John, who recently joined our team.'

Now, does the fact that the Appendices in (6a,b) are Sprouted (rather than moved) help with the problem of island violations incurred by the Appendix? Only if Sprouting is insensitive to islands in general.

Unfortunately, this is the exact opposite of the consensus on Sprouting in Sluicing. While non-Sprouting (or 'Merger' type, in the terminology of CLM 1995, 2011) Sluicing with indefinite Targets is known to repair islands, Sprouting-type Sluicing is generally assumed to be strictly island-sensitive (though see Kim and Kuno 2012 for exceptions). Consider the following.

(15)a. Bill met a person who speaks a Balkan language, but I don't remember which.

 b. Tony sent Mo a picture that he painted, but it's not clear why.

(15b), which instantiates a Sprouting-type Sluicing, does not allow *why* to modify the embedded verb *painted* that is within an island, while *which* in (15a), an example of a Merger-type Sluicing, can be related to the Target *a Balkan language* within an island.

In an update of their earlier work, CLM (2011) propose to capture the island-sensitive nature of Sprouting-type Sluicing by proposing that the mechanism behind Sprouting is none other than (the top-down/left-to-right version of) Internal Merge (movement), defined on the 're-used' copy of the Host clause. Since Sprouting is movement, it follows that it will be sensitive to islands.

3   Sprouting and Island Sensitivity

In the previous section we concluded that Adnominal and Conjunct Appendices in RD (cf. 6a,b) are Sprouted. But they can seemingly be related to positions within islands (specifically, to Left Branches and initial

---

[4] The same holds for (6b). (Initial) conjuncts cannot be licensed under ellipsis by anaphoric antecedents, which leads us to conclude that there is no Conjunct Target in (6b) that is licensed by the Appendix.

conjuncts in coordinate structures). In this they seem different from Sprouting in Sluicing. If the island-sensitivity of Sprouting in Sluicing owes to the fact that it is derived by top-down Internal Merge (as CLM 2011 argue), does it suggest that a non-movement mechanism is responsible for licensing Sprouting in RDs?

If that were the case, we expect that Sprouted Appendices in RDs to be insensitive to the presence of additional islands. However, this is not so.

(16) *[[nay-ka **cha-lul** sassta]-nun sasil]-i Yenghi-lul
    I-top car-acc bought-rel fact-nom Y-acc
    hwa-ka nakey hayssta, [**acwu pissa**]-n
    anger-nom cause did very expensive-rel
    Intended: 'The fact that I bought a very expensive car angered Yenghi.'

In (16) the Sprouted Appendix *acwu pissa-n* ('very expensive') cannot be construed as modifying *cha-lul* ('the car') contained within a Subject Island, to yield the intended interpretation. This suggests that locality still matters in the type of Sprouting involved in RD, but that somehow an adnominal Appendix is allowed to be interpretively connected to a nominal as long as no other islands intervene.

The key to resolving this problem lies in the realization that Sprouting/top-down Internal Merge in (6a) (and 14) does not reach **into** a Left Branch constituent (or a conjunct) or extract a Left Branch out of a DP (like bottom-up Internal Merge). Rather, a Left Branch modifier copy is **created** via adjunction to the modified phrase. By contrast, in (8) (and 16), Sprouting that creates/adjoins a Left Branch (of the DP *cha-lul*) must clearly reach into an island (Complex NP/Subject Island). We submit that this is why Sprouting in RD can seemingly disregard at most one island boundary.

Let's work out the details of this idea in terms of the mechanics of Sprouting proposed in CLM (2011). Assume first that the Appendix is base-generated/Sprouted in a Specifier position of a projection on the left periphery of a clause (indicated below as FP). (6a) then starts out as (17):

(17) Na-n John-ul mannass-e.
    [$_{FP}$ [wuli-thim … haplyuha-n] F [ ]]

F, as a left-peripheral Head, selects a clause. The empty Complement of F is then filled by a re-used copy of the Host clause, resulting in (18).[5]

> (18) Na-n John-ul mannass-e.
> [$_{FP}$ [wuli-thim ... haplyuha-n] F [na-n John-ul mannass-e]]

The next step is for the base-generated/Sprouted constituent in SpFP to initiate a Chain Formation (top-down Internal Merge) process with respect to a suitable constituent (i) that is within its c-command domain, (ii) is local/accessible to it, and (iii) meets conditions to count as its (lowest) Occurrence.[6] Specifically, the fact that the constituent in SpFP is marked as an adnominal modifier (as indicated by the ending –*n*) means that the lowest Occurrence (or Tail) of the Chain that is created by the top-down Internal Merge process must satisfy the following conditions.

> (19) The lowest Occurrence/Tail of [*wuli-thim-ey saylo haplyuha-n*]:
> → Must modify a nominal projection
> → Must be dominated by a nominal phrase

Since the DP *John-ul* is not separated from the constituent in SpFP (technically, the head F which Probes it) by any island/phase boundary (see 18), it is accessible to it.

Therefore lowest Copy of the modifier can be created through adjunction to this DP. This will result in the following structure, which will also yield the requisite interpretation for the Sprouted Chain:

> (20) [$_{FP}$ [wuli-thim ... haplyuha-n] F ....
> [na-n [$_{DP}$ [wuli-thim ... haplyuha-n] [$_{DP}$ John]]-ul mannass-e]]

By contrast, in (16), top-down Internal Merge initiated by the Sprouted adnominal modifier *acwu pissa-n* in SpFP must transgress an island

---

[5]This is the mechanism of LF-copying. In the representations, LF-copied material is indicated by outlining. Lack of outlining indicates the presence of both phonological and LF-features.

CLM (2011) are not specific about the nature of the copied material, but it seems they are assuming that it is an LF representation, that is, a structured P-marker with interpretable (LF) features (since the structure must supply an interpretation that is 're-used'), but not phonological features. The relevance of viewing the re-cycled material as consisting only of LF-interpretable features will become apparent shortly.

[6] I am adopting the analysis of Chain links due to Chomsky (2001), where links are defined as Occurrences, which are the structural contexts of a particular Copy in a Chain. In the case at hand, since the Sprouted Copy is an adnominal constituent, the lowest link/Copy/Occurrence must be sister to a nominal phrase and also be dominated by a nominal projection.

boundary (Subject Island), and that is why the creation of the Tail/lowest Occurrence at the DP *cha-lul* is not successful.

This analysis makes a prediction. Not all adnominal modifiers should be allowed as Appendices in RDs, but only those that can be adjoined to entire DPs. Such modifiers will of course be initial with respect to the modified phrase. Now, if an adnominal modifier is not the left-most constituent within a DP, then Sprouting/adjunction that creates a lower Copy of the modifier must reach **into** a DP, and in so doing, transgresses an island/DP boundary. In this case, it is predicted that the adnominal modifier should not be allowed as an Appendix. This prediction is borne out.

Though word order in DPs is quite flexible in Korean, the Possessor must precede the numeral modifier of the Noun in (21) below.

(21) a.   [Nay tongsayng   Cheli]-uy   [yele-myeng]-uy   chinkwutul
          My brother   C-gen   several-cl-gen   friends

   b.   *[Yele-myeng]-uy   [nay tongsayng   Cheli]-uy chinkwutul
         several-cl-gen   my brother   C-gen   friends
        'Several friends of my brother Cheli'

Of the two adnominal modifiers of the Head noun, only the Possessor can occur as Appendix in an RD, as shown below.

(22) a. ?Yenghi-nun yele-myeng-uy   chinkwutul-ul
          Y-top   several-cl-gen   friends-acc
          mannass-ta, **[nay tongsayng   Cheli]-uy**
          met-decl   my brother   C-gen
          'Yenghi met several of my brother Cheli's friends.'

   b. *Yenghi-nun nay tongsayng   Cheli-uy   chinkwutul-ul
        Y-top   my friend   C-gen   friends-acc
        mannass-ta, **[yele-myeng]-uy**
        met-decl   several-cl-gen

The reason for the ill-formedness of (22b) is that the lowest Copy of the Sprouted modifier *yele-myeng-uy* must be created inside the DP *Cheli-uy chinkwutul-i*, in a position lower than the Possessor, whereas in (22a), the Copy can be adjoined to the entire DP *yele-myeng-uy chinkwutul-i*.

The idea that apparent violations of locality can be allowed in Sprouting as long as the creation of the lowest Occurrence of the Sprouted XP is not inside an island seems to cut the pie in the right places, so far. However, there is a significant problem facing the analysis. This is because adnominal modifiers in apparent violation of movement locality are allowed only when they are fragments (i.e., as the Appendix in an RD in 23b or as a Fragment Answer in 23c). Adnominals cannot be extracted when the clausal source from which they have been moved remains intact (cf. 23a). In other words, though we have argued against the generality of island repair by ellipsis in RDs (because of facts like 8 and 16), it seems that there is a repair-like effect that is dependent on ellipsis of the clausal source from which the fragments have been putatively extracted.[7]

(23) a. *[acwu pissa]-n,   na-n [__ hwacangphum]-ul coahan-ta
        very expensive-rel I-top   cosmetics-acc   like-decl
        'I like very expensive cosmetics.'

   b. na-n hwacangphum-ul coahanta, [acwu   pissa]-n
       I-top cosmetics-acc   like   very   expensive-rel

   c. Q: Ne-n   etten   hwacangphum-ul   coaha-ni?
          You-top   which   cosmetics-acc   like-inter
          'What kind of cosmetics do you like?'

       A: **Acwu   pissa-n**
          Very   expensive-rel
          '(I like the) very expensive (kind).'

Specifically, if we assume that the adnominal fragments (in 23b, and possibly in 23c as well) are Sprouted and licensed via creation of a lower Copy (Tail) in the manner sketched earlier, what prevents a similar analysis of (23a)? That is, instead of being extracted out of the DP by bottom-up Internal Merge (a derivation that incurs an island violation), why can't the adnominal modifier be base-generated/Sprouted in the clause periphery and initiate a top-down Internal Merge process and create a lower Copy adjoined to the DP *hwacangphum-ul*? Since this operation does not intrude into the DP, no islands are transgressed and (23a) is predicted to be well-formed on this derivational option.

   Without attempting to resolve the issue fully, I will offer two tentative suggestions that may get us out of this impasse. One is to invoke some kind of priority ranking between regular, bottom-up application of Internal Merge/movement and the top-down application that is presumably at work in Sprouting, so that the former trumps the latter when both options are

---

[7] Of course, an alternative to pursue is to question whether the Appendix in RDs and Fragment Answers derive from a clausal source. If they don't, there's nothing to delete and no violations to repair. But then this alternative will have to explain the fact that these fragments do seem to be constrained by islands in other cases (cf. 8). We will not explore this alternative further.

possible. This reasoning assumes that Internal Merge normally works bottom-up, and that the top-down implementation is a Last Resort, employed when a fragment generated in a clause periphery needs to be accomodated with respect to the interpretation of a nearby clause.

The other is to capitalize on the fact that in the analysis of Sprouting derived from CLM (2011), the clause that is copied/re-used to provide the interpretation of the Sprouted constituent consists of only LF-interpretable features, not phonological features (cf. footnote 5). We take this to mean that the Copy of the Sprouted XP that is created within this re-used/copied clause also consists of LF-interpretable features only (cf. 20).

By contrast, let's assume that in (23a), the Copy of the adnominal XP that is created by Internal Merge (whether top-down or bottom-up) has both phonological and LF-interpretable features, because the P-marker into which it is being inserted (or from within which it moves) has both types of features. Because of linearization requirements of Chains (Nunes 1995), the phonological features of all but the highest Copy must be deleted. We have seen earlier that adnominal modifiers cannot undergo deletion, even when suitable antecedents exist (cf. 13). If this is true in general for such modifiers, deletion of the phonological features from the lowest Copy of the adnominal modifier will not be possible in (23a) as well. And this may be the reason why (23a) is ill-formed. (23a) is ill-formed if bottom-up Internal Merge applies because extraction takes place out of islands and because the phonological features of the lower Copy cannot be deleted. If, on the other hand, top-down Internal Merge applies and creates a lower Copy adjoined to the DP, no island boundaries are transgressed, but the phonological features of the lower Copy cannot be deleted, which leads to ungrammaticality.

This line of speculation predicts that when the phonological features of the lowest Copy have not undergone deletion, the structure should be fine. Indeed, it is, when a resumptive pro-form instead of a gap fills the adnominal position.

(24) **[acwu   pissa]-n,**   na-n **[kulen** hwacangphum]-ul coahan-ta
      very   expensive-rel I-top dem   cosmetics-acc   like-decl
      'I like very expensive cosmetics.'

4   Conclusion

The focus of this paper was an apparent challenge for the reigning analysis of RD coming from the fact that adnominal modifiers and initial conjuncts that cannot be extracted in non-elliptical contexts are allowed as Appendices in RDs, but not because islands are repaired under ellipsis in RDs in general. A further challenge came from the fact that while adnominal modifiers and initial conjuncts are possible as Appendices, head nominal projections modified by the adnominal constituents and final conjunct cannot.

The strategy adopted in the paper was to view the latter restriction as stemming from an illegitimate ellipsis taking place within the Host clause. Adoption of this answer in turn led us to the conclusion that adnominal and initial conjunct Appendices in well-formed RDs are Sprouted, rather than moved. A particular implementation of Sprouting under the updated LF-copying approach of CLM (2011) allowed us to make sense of the fact that while apparent Left Branch (and Conjunct Condition) violations are allowed in RDs, such violations become unacceptable when additional islands intervene.

While the conclusions we reached are tentative, they serve to highlight yet another area of the intricate interplay between ellipsis and locality in a construction that manifests 'syntax in silence' (Merchant 2001). They also point to LF-copying as a viable mechanism of modeling that silent syntax, at least in elliptical structures manifesting Sprouting.

References

Baker, B. 2007. Japanese Adnominal Postposing and an Argument Against Movement. Senior honors thesis, Ohio State University.

Choi, K-Y. 2001. The Echoed Verb Construction in Korean: Evidence for V-Raising. Paper presented at the 11th Japanese/Korean Linguistics Conference, UC Santa Barbara.

Chomsky, N. 2001. Derivation by Phase. *Ken Hale: A Life in Language*, ed. M. Kenstowicz, 1-53. Cambridge: MIT Press.

Chung, D-H. 2009. Do Not Target a Predicate: It's Not a Constituent! Paper presented at the 6th Workshop on Altaic Formal Linguistics, Nagoya University.

Chung, D-H. 2011. A Constituency-based Explanation of Syntactic Restrictions on Korean Predicates. *Linguistic Research* 28:393-207.

Chung, S., B. Ladusaw & J. McCloskey. 1995. Sluicing and Logical Form. *Natural Language Semantics* 3:239-282.

Chung, S., B. Ladusaw & J. McCloskey. 2011. Sluicing: Between Structure and Inference. *Representing Language: Essays In Honor of Judith Aissen*, eds. R. Gutierrez-Bravo, L. Mikkelsen, and E. Potsdam, 31-50. California Digital Library e-Scholarship Repository. Linguistic Research Center, Santa Cruz: University of California-Santa Cruz.

Jo, J-M. 2013. Predicate Contrastive Topic Constructions: Implications for Morpho-Syntax in Korean and Copy Theory of Movement. *Lingua* 131:80-111.

Kim, S-Y., and S. Kuno. 2012. A Note on Sluicing with Implicit Indefinite Correlates. *Natural Language Semantics* 21:315-332.

Lee, W-S. 2009. The Role of Case-marked Noun Phrases in Clause-Structure Building. Doctoral dissertation, University of Illinois, Urbana-Champaign.

Merchant, J. 2001. *The Syntax of Silence: Sluicing, Islands and the Theory of Ellipsis*. Oxford: Oxford University Press.

Nunes, J. 1995. The Copy Theory of Movement and Linearization of Chains in the Minimalist Program. Doctoral dissertation. University of Maryland, College Park.

Sells, P. 1999. Japanese Postposing Involves No Movement. Paper presented at the meeting of the Linguistic Society of Great Britain, Lancaster, UK.

Tanaka, H. 2001. Right Dislocation as Scrambling. *Journal of Linguistics* 37:551-579.

Yoon, J. 1994. Korean Verbal Inflection and Checking Theory. T*he Morphology-Syntax Connection*, Vol 22. MIT Working Papers in Linguistics, 251-270.

Yoon, J. 1995. Nominal, Verbal and Crosscategorial Affixation in Korean. *Journal of East Asian Linguistics* 4:325-356.

Yoon, J. 2009. The Architecture of Right Dislocation in Korean. Paper presented at the 6th Workshop on Altaic Formal Linguistics, Nagoya University.

Part III

Semantics

A Formal Analysis of Japanese V-*yuku* and its Grammaticalization*

FUMIHITO ARAI
Graduate School of Letters, Kobe Shoin Women's University

TOSHIO HIDAKA
Kyushu International University

1 Introduction

Grammaticalization, a historical process whereby lexical items or constructions come to serve grammatical functions, has been observed and analyzed empirically and cross-linguistically (Hopper and Traugott 2003, among others). Analyses from a syntactic perspective have been done as well (e.g., Roberts and Roussou 2003). Meanwhile, there seems to be a lack of formal-semantic analysis, which can be conducive to illustrate the process of grammaticalization.

This study addresses the grammaticalization process of a Japanese motion verb *yuku* 'go' in terms of Generative Lexicon (Pustejovsky 1995). We focus on V-*yuku* 'V-go', the infinitive form which is in the process of development from the full-verb *yuku* 'go' to V-*te-yuku* 'V-CON-go', the -*te* converb form, as in (1).[1]

* We express gratitude to Takao Gunji, Taisuke Nishigauchi, Michiko Bando and our colleagues at Kobe Shoin Women's University for their insightful comments and suggestions. We also thank the audience at the 23rd conference on Japanese/Korean Linguistics for their comments.

[1] Although *yuku* 'go' is usually pronounced as /iku/ instead of /yuku/ in the full-verb and -*te*

Japanese/Korean Linguistics 23.
Edited by Michael Kenstowicz, Theodore Levin and Ryo Masuda.
Copyright © 2016, CSLI Publications.

(1)   a. *yuku* 'go' (full verb)[2]

Taroo-ga   yukimiti-o   yuku.
Taro-NOM   snow.road-ACC   go
'Taro goes along a snowy road.'

   b. V-*yuku* 'V-go' (infinitive form)

Taroo-ga   yukimiti-o   hasiri-yuku   kookei.
Taro-NOM   snow.road-ACC   run-go   scene
'The scene of Taro running along a snowy road.'

   c. V-*te-yuku* 'V-CON-go' (-*te* converb form)

Taroo-ga   yukimiti-o   hasit-te-yuku.
Taro-NOM   snow.road-ACC   run-CON-go
'Taro runs along a snowy road.'

Of the three forms, V-*yuku* 'V-go', has not been exhaustively explored in the literature in contrast to extensive descriptive and theoretical research on the other two forms (Morita 1968, 1994; Yoshikawa 1976; Teramura 1984; Imani 1990; Yoshida 2012; Hidaka and Arai 2012; Nakatani 2013). Lin (1996), Kojima (2001), and Shibatani and Chung (2007) show that V-*yuku* 'V-go' used to be productive in Old and Middle Japanese, while becoming less productive as the -*te* converb form increases. Additionally, it has been argued that V-*yuku* 'V-go' has an aspectual meaning as V-*te-yuku* 'V-CON-go' does (Kojima 1998, 2001; Arai and Hidaka 2013). Based on previous research, the historical development can be sketched as Table 1, in which the infinitive form seems to have been replaced by the -*te* converb form.

Old/Middle Japanese	Modern Japanese
yuku	*yuku*
V-*yuku* (productive)	**V-*yuku*** (less productive)
V-*te-yuku* (less productive)	**V-*te-yuku*** (productive)

TABLE 1 Overview of the historical development of *yuku* 'go'.

In this paper, we argue that the historical development of Japanese *yuku* 'go' is the consequence of renewal, which has been cross-linguistically witnessed in the emergence of aspectual morphemes (Smith 2006).

---

converb form in Present-day Japanese, we consistently use /yuku/ based on its historical origin.

[2] Abbreviations: ACC = accusative, CON = conjunctive particle, DAT = dative, GEN = genitive, NOM = nominative, PART = particle, PAST = past tense, PREF = prefix, TOP = topic.

2 Locus of Issues

While much previous research on *yuku* 'go' in Japanese has been done from synchronic viewpoints, including description and formalization of its semantics, there have been fewer historical analyses of the verb.

Descriptive studies (Morita 1968, 1994; Yoshikawa 1976; Kuno 1978; Teramura 1984; Imani 1990; Yoshida 2012) examine the meaning of *yuku*: the verb denotes movement away from the speaker. They further analyze the aspectual meaning of its *-te* converb form, V-*te-yuku* 'V-CON-go', attributing its ambiguity to lexical meaning of the preceding verbs (Morita 1968, 1994; Yoshikawa 1976; Imani 1990). While these descriptive studies have revealed the semantic characteristics of the motion verb, the infinitive form, V-*yuku* 'V-go', is yet to be explored.

Theoretical analyses (Nakatani 2008, 2013; Hidaka and Arai 2012; Arai and Hidaka 2013) formalize the semantics of the motion verb in Present-day Japanese within the framework of Generative Lexicon (Pustejovsky 1995). However, they have not addressed the grammaticalization process.

Historically speaking, research from the grammaticalizationist viewpoint (Shibatani 2007; Shibatani and Chung 2007) shows that the once-predominant V-*yuku* 'V-go' is gradually replaced by V-*te-yuku* 'V-CON-go' by the 19th century (Shibatani and Chung 2007:29). The displacement has also been discussed in the historical development of verbal compounds (Lin 1996; Kojima 1998, 2001; Hyakutome 2003; Tokumoto 2009). These researchers argue for early auxiliarization of *yuku* and show that V-*yuku* used to be highly productive in Old/Middle Japanese, while becoming less productive in Modern Japanese. They further argue that the infinitive form emerges earlier than V-*te-yuku*. While these historical studies recognize the facts that V-*yuku* diachronically differs in productivity and is displaced by V-*te-yuku*, they have not examined concrete motivations for the process.

In this paper, we specifically aim to elucidate the following remaining questions: i) how the three forms involved in the grammaticalization process interrelate with one another, ii) why V-*yuku* became less productive in Modern Japanese, and iii) how V-*te-yuku* denotes a similar meaning as V-*yuku*.

3 Hypothesis

Based on the preceding arguments, we hypothesize that grammaticalization of Japanese *yuku* 'go' passes through four stages as shown in Table 2. We will give detailed explanation of Table 2 in Section 5, but first let us present a brief exposition of our semantic representation.

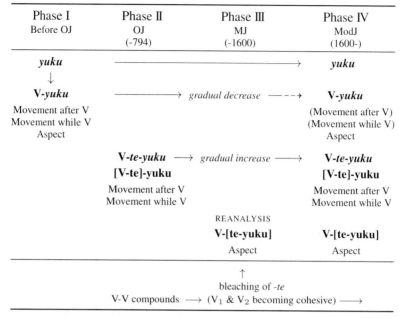

Phase I	Phase II	Phase III	Phase IV
Before OJ	OJ (-794)	MJ (-1600)	ModJ (1600-)

yuku ———————————————————→ *yuku*

↓

V-*yuku* ——————→ *gradual decrease* ——-→ **V-*yuku***

Movement after V (Movement after V)
Movement while V (Movement while V)
Aspect Aspect

V-*te-yuku* ⟶ *gradual increase* ⟶ **V-*te-yuku***
[V-te]-yuku **[V-te]-yuku**

Movement after V Movement after V
Movement while V Movement while V

REANALYSIS
V-[te-yuku] **V-[te-yuku]**

Aspect Aspect

↑
bleaching of -*te*
V-V compounds ⟶ (V$_1$ & V$_2$ becoming cohesive) ⟶

TABLE 2 Our view of the grammaticalization process of *yuku* 'go' in Japanese.

4   Framework

Our semantic representation is based on Hidaka (2012) as in (2). It divides the qualia structure (Pustejovsky 1995) into two semantic levels, Truth-conditional Section (TS) and Non-truth-conditional Section (NTS), and gives a more precise definition of each quale. The elements in TS are directly projected to the argument structure, while those in NTS are not.

(2)
```
⎡ lexeme
⎢ ARG = [ Syntactic arguments ]
⎢          ⎡ ⎡ Truth-conditional Section (TS)
⎢          ⎢ ⎢ FORMAL:  Temporal feature,
⎢          ⎢ ⎢          Distance function (DIS),
⎢          ⎢ ⎢          Point-of-view function (POV)
⎢ QUALIA = ⎢ ⎣ CONST:   Lexical conceptual structure (LCS)
⎢          ⎢ ⎡ Non-truth-conditional Section (NTS)
⎢          ⎢ ⎢ TELIC:    The potential resultative state
⎣          ⎣ ⎣ TRIGGER: The external factors of the verb
```

The temporal feature is adopted from Igarashi and Gunji (1998) and Gunji (2004), who propose that a verb has three temporal points, s, f and r, to describe its aspectual property; s is the start time of the event, f the finish time of the event, r the reset time at which the individual goes back to the original state. (3a–c) exemplify the temporal feature of *kiru* 'put on', *aruku* 'walk' and *sinu* 'die'.

(3) a. *kiru*: $s < f < r < \infty$ (recoverable transitional activity)

 b. *aruku*: $s < f = r < \infty$ (nontransitional activity)

 c. *sinu*: $s = f < r = \infty$ (nonrecoverable transtional achievement)

(Gunji 2004:25)

Based on the arguments that the point-of-view holder of *yuku* can be either the speaker or the speaker's empathy focus as in (4) (Kuno and Kaburaki 1977; Kuno 1987), we introduce two semantic functions: **DIS** and **POV**.

(4) a. POV holder = speaker

Taroo-ga yukimiti-o   yuku kookei-o mi-ta.
Taro-NOM snow.road-ACC go   scene-ACC see-PAST
'[I] saw the scene of Taro having gone along a snowy road.'

 b. POV holder = Mary (= speaker's empathy focus)

Mari-ga   Taroo-ga yukimiti-o   yuku kookei-o mi-ta.
Mary-NOM Taro-NOM snow.road-ACC go   scene-ACC see-PAST
'Mary saw the scene of Taro having gone along a snowy road.'

DIS (distance function) outputs the spatial/psychological distance between the POV holder (p) and the point in the event which p looks at. Its value of *yuku* 'go' is $\mathbf{DIS}(Loc(e, s')) < \mathbf{DIS}(Loc(e, f))$: p is nearer to the point of the event which s/he looks at than to the endpoint of the event (Figure 1).[3]

POV (point-of-view function) consists of **POINT** and **VIEW**. As for *yuku* 'go', **POINT**, which specifies the point which p looks at in the event, is $\mathbf{POINT}(e) = Loc(e, s')$: p looks at a random point after the event started. **VIEW**, which specifies the range of the whole event which p assumes, is $\mathbf{VIEW}(y) = \langle s, f \rangle$: p views the whole process (Figure 2).

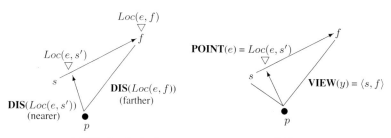

FIGURE 1 **DIS** of *yuku* 'go'.   FIGURE 2 **POV** of *yuku* 'go'.

---

[3] $Loc(e, s')$ refers to a random point after the starting point in the event procession.

5   Analysis

5.1   Phase I: The Emergence of V-*yuku*

The grammaticalization process of *yuku* 'go' is seen as early as Old Japanese. We first examine full-verb usage. The full-verb *yuku* denotes the subject's physical movement as in (5).[4]

(5)   wa ga   **yuku** miti no   ka-gupasi   panatatibana   pa
      I   NOM **go**   road GEN   balmy   citrus.tachibana TOP
      'Balmy citrus tachibana along the road we **go**. . .'   (*Kojiki Kayô*.43)

The semantics of the full-verb *yuku* is presented in (6). The temporal feature ($s < f$) shows that an interval exists between the start time and the finish time of the movement. While the motion verb encodes movement along a path, it does not lexically entail the arriving event (Nakatani 2013:199-207); the former (GO $(x$, VIA $(y))$ is set in CONST in TS, and the latter (BE-AT (x, z_{place})) in TELIC in NTS.

(6)
$$
\begin{bmatrix}
yuku \text{ 'go'} \\
\text{ARG} = \begin{bmatrix} \text{ARG1: } p, \ \text{ARG2: } VP \end{bmatrix} \\
\text{QL} = \begin{bmatrix}
\begin{bmatrix}
TS \\
\text{FL:} \begin{bmatrix} \boxed{s < f}, \\ \textbf{DIS}(\text{Loc}(e, s')) < \textbf{DIS}(\text{Loc}(e, f)), \\ \textbf{POV}(p) \text{: } \textbf{POINT}(e) = \text{Loc}(e, s'), \\ \textbf{VIEW}(y) = \langle s, f \rangle \end{bmatrix} \\
\text{CT:} \quad \text{GO } (x, \text{VIA } (y)) \\
NTS \\
\text{TC:} \quad \text{BE-AT } (x, z_{place})
\end{bmatrix}
\end{bmatrix}
\end{bmatrix}
$$

In Old Japanese, the main verb began to appear in the infinitive form, V-*yuku*, which was used productively (Lin 1996; Kojima 2001; Shibatani and Chung 2007). At the early stage, V-*yuku* expressed the subject's spatial movement to be interpreted in two different ways, depending on context: movement after the event denoted by the V ends as in (7a), or movement during the event denoted by the V as in (7b).

(7)   a.   aratama no   tukwi pa   **ki-pe-yuku**
           epithet   moon TOP **come-pass-go**
           'As time goes by, the moon **comes and then leaves**.'   (*Kojiki Kayô*.28)

      b.   matubara   ni   **watari-yukite**
           pinetree.forest DAT **cross-go**
           '[We] **approach** the pinetree forest to fight. . .'   (*Nihon Shoki Kayô*.28)

---

[4] Examples are taken from two databases: Oxford Corpus of Old Japanese (Frellesvig et al. 2013) and Japanese Text Initiative (of Virginia Library Electronic Text Center and the University of Pittsburgh East Asian Library 2006).

The semantics of the infinitive form *watari-yuku* 'cross-go' in (7b) is (9), in which the meaning of *wataru* 'cross' in (8) is compositionally combined with that of *yuku* 'go' in (6).

What made the simultaneous-moving interpretation possible in (7b) is the common temporal feature of the two verbs, $s < f$, which can be unified as $s_1 = s_2 < f_1 = f_2$ in (9).

(8)
$$\begin{bmatrix} watar\text{-}u \text{ 'cross'} \\ \text{ARG} = \begin{bmatrix} \text{ARG1: } x, \text{ ARG2: } y \end{bmatrix} \\ \text{QL} = \begin{bmatrix} \begin{bmatrix} TS \\ \text{FL: } \boxed{s < f} \\ \text{CT: GO } (x, \text{ VIA } (y)) \end{bmatrix} \end{bmatrix} \end{bmatrix}$$

(9)
$$\begin{bmatrix} watari\text{-}yuku \text{ 'cross-go'} \\ \text{ARG} = \begin{bmatrix} \text{ARG1: } p \end{bmatrix} \\ \text{QL} = \begin{bmatrix} \begin{bmatrix} TS \\ \text{FL: } \begin{bmatrix} \boxed{s_1 = s_2 < f_1 = f_2}, \\ \textbf{DIS}(\text{Loc}(c, s')) < \textbf{DIS}(\text{Loc}(e, f)), \\ \textbf{POV}(p)\text{: } \textbf{POINT}(e) = \text{Loc}(e, s'), \\ \textbf{VIEW}(y) = \langle s, f \rangle \end{bmatrix} \\ \text{CT: } \quad \text{GO } (x, \text{ VIA } (y)) \end{bmatrix} \\ \begin{bmatrix} NTS \\ \text{TC: } \quad \text{BE-AT } (x, z_{place}) \end{bmatrix} \end{bmatrix} \end{bmatrix}$$

Why does V-*yuku* show the above-mentioned ambiguity? We argue that the ambiguity stems from the fact that verbal compounds are underdeveloped in Old/Middle Japanese; the integrity between the two verbs in V-V sequences is not semantically tight enough to inhibit other elements (e.g., adverbs, different subjects, etc.) from being inserted (Sannoumaru 2009), and there exist few fixed semantic strategies to synthesize V and -*yuku* as well. Thus, the two interpretations in V-*yuku* expressing movement are determined only by the context where the form appears.

Auxiliarization of -*yuku* in V-*yuku* as movement (Inoue 1962; Tokumoto 2009) allows the form to denote aspectual meaning, exemplified by *saki-yuku* 'bloom-go' and *puke-yuku* 'deepen-go' in (10ab).

(10) a. topo-ki konure no **saki-yuku** mireba
      far   treetop GEN **bloom-go** see.if
      '. . .as I see treetops among mountains **bloom**.'   (*Man'yôshû*.10.1865)

    b. kwopwi mo sugwi-neba ywo pa **puke-yuku** mo
       love   PART pass-not.if   night TOP **deepen-go** PART
       '[Though Vega and Altair haven't met yet], dawn **breaks**.'
       (*Man'yôshû*.10.2032)

We represent the semantics of the aspectual -*yuku* as in (11). Aspectualization of -*yuku* is captured by removing LCS values from the CONST quale of the main verb; the verb has the temporal and POV features only. The vacant CONST quale (ϕ) is to be filled by LCS of the preceding verb.

$$(11) \quad \begin{bmatrix} \textit{-yuku} \text{ '-go' (aspect)} \\ \text{ARG} = \begin{bmatrix} \text{ARG1: } p, \text{ ARG2: } VP \end{bmatrix} \\ \text{QL} = \begin{bmatrix} \begin{bmatrix} TS \\ \text{FL:} \begin{bmatrix} s < f, \\ \textbf{DIS}(\text{Loc}(e, s')) < \textbf{DIS}(\text{Loc}(e, f)), \\ \textbf{POV}(p) : \textbf{POINT}(e) = \text{Loc}'(e, s'), \\ \textbf{VIEW}(y) = \langle s_e, f_e \rangle \end{bmatrix} \\ \text{CT:} \quad \phi \end{bmatrix} \\ \begin{bmatrix} NTS \\ \text{TC:} \quad \text{BE}_{Ident}(x, z_{state}) \end{bmatrix} \end{bmatrix} \end{bmatrix}$$

For example, the semantics of *puke-yuku* 'deepen-go' in (10b) is (13), which is the result of semantic composition of (11) with (12). The common temporal feature of *pukeru* 'deepen' and *-yuku* '-go' ($s < f$) make it possible for the start time and the finish time of the two verbs to be identified with each other ($s_1 = s_2 < f_1 = f_2$), and the resultative state of *pukeru* follows it. While the vacant CONST quale of *-yuku* is filled with *pukeru*, the resultative meaning of *pukeru* is synthesized in TELIC quale in the composite, since it matches with that of *-yuku*. This is induced by **POINT** and **VIEW** functions. That is, the POV holder of *-yuku* '-go' looks at a certain point of the ongoing change in state which *pukeru* denotes, whereas the end point of the change is just implied in his/her view.

$$(12) \quad \begin{bmatrix} \textit{puker-u} \text{ 'deepen'} \\ \text{ARG} = \begin{bmatrix} \text{ARG1: } x \end{bmatrix} \\ \text{QL} = \begin{bmatrix} \begin{bmatrix} TS \\ \text{FL: } s < f < r \\ \text{CT: GO}_{Ident}(x, \text{VIA-PATH TO } \textit{DEEPENED}) \end{bmatrix} \end{bmatrix} \end{bmatrix}$$

$$(13) \quad \begin{bmatrix} \textit{puke-yuku} \text{ 'deepen-go'} \\ \text{ARG} = \begin{bmatrix} \text{ARG1: } p \end{bmatrix} \\ \text{QL} = \begin{bmatrix} \begin{bmatrix} TS \\ \text{FL:} \begin{bmatrix} \boxed{s_1 = s_2 < f_1 = f_2 < r}, \\ \textbf{DIS}(\text{Loc}(e, s')) < \textbf{DIS}(\text{Loc}(e, f)), \\ \textbf{POV}(p) : \textbf{POINT}(e) = \text{Loc}'(e, s'), \\ \textbf{VIEW}(y) = \langle s_e, f_e \rangle \end{bmatrix} \\ \text{CT:} \quad \boxed{\text{GO}_{Ident}(x, \text{VIA-}\textit{PATH})} \end{bmatrix} \\ \begin{bmatrix} NTS \\ \text{TC:} \quad \boxed{\text{BE}_{Ident}(x, \textit{DEEPENED})} \end{bmatrix} \end{bmatrix} \end{bmatrix}$$

As has been shown so far, we argue that the infinitive form, V-*yuku*, in Old Japanese bears aspectual meaning as well as movement. Such ambiguity in V-*yuku* could be attributed to the undivided concept of space and time in ancient Japanese, as Yamaguchi (2004) and Hyakutome and Hyakutome (2008) discuss. It is assumed that the unclear division between space and time makes linguistic expressions less analytic, and V-*yuku* in Old Japanese could have ambiguous meanings: movement and aspect.

5.2 Phase II: The Emergence of V-*te-yuku*

Let us move on to Phase II, in which V-*te-yuku* 'V-CON-go' emerges. While previous research (Kojima 2001; Hyakutome and Hyakutome 2008) argues that the -*te* converb form has gradually replaced V-*yuku* since Middle Japanese, (14) suggests the transition begins earlier.

(14) **oki-te-ik**aba   imo ba   ma-kanasi
put-CON-go.if you TOP PREF-sad
'I feel sorry for you, my wife, if I **put you here and go away**.
(*Man'yôshû*.14.3567)

In (14), *oki-te-ikaba* 'put-CON-go.if' is to be construed as two events occurring in succession: the husband moves away after he left his wife behind. The role of -*te* induces such an interpretation. Since -*te* originates from the completive auxiliary -*tu* (Nishida 1971), it functions as an event sequencer, which puts an end to the first event and introduces the second event (Yoshida 2012): the two events are arranged in chronological order ($e_1 < e_2$). Thus, with *yuku* behaving as a main verb, the -*te* converb form in early usage expresses a successive event: the subject moves after the event denoted by the preceding verb ends.

(15)
$$
\begin{bmatrix}
oku \text{ 'put'} \\
\text{ARG} = \begin{bmatrix} \text{ARG1: } x, \text{ ARG2: } y \end{bmatrix} \\
\text{QL} = \begin{bmatrix} \begin{bmatrix} TS \\ \text{FL: } \boxed{s = f} \\ \text{CT: CAUSE ([ACT ON } (x, y)], \\ \quad\quad\quad\quad [\text{BE-AT-BY } (y, x)]) \end{bmatrix} \end{bmatrix}
\end{bmatrix}
$$

(16)
$$
\begin{bmatrix}
yuku \text{ 'go'} \\
\text{ARG} = \begin{bmatrix} \text{ARG1: } p, \text{ ARG2: } te\text{-}P \end{bmatrix} \\
\text{QL} = \begin{bmatrix} \begin{bmatrix} TS \\ \text{FL: } \begin{bmatrix} \boxed{s < f}, \\ \textbf{DIS}(\text{Loc}(e, s')) < \text{DIS}(\text{Loc}(e, f)), \\ \textbf{POV}(p)\text{: } \textbf{POINT}(e) = \text{Loc}(e, s'), \\ \quad\quad\quad \textbf{VIEW}(w) = \langle s, f \rangle \end{bmatrix} \\ \text{CT: } \quad \text{GO } (x, \text{VIA } (w)) \end{bmatrix} \\ \begin{bmatrix} NTS \\ \text{TC: } \quad \text{BE-AT } (x, z_{place}) \end{bmatrix} \end{bmatrix}
\end{bmatrix}
$$

(17)
$$
\begin{bmatrix}
oki\text{-}te\text{-}yuku \text{ 'put-CON-go'} \\
\text{ARG} = \begin{bmatrix} \text{ARG1:}\, p \end{bmatrix} \\
\text{QL} = \begin{bmatrix}
\begin{bmatrix}
\text{TS} \\
\begin{bmatrix}
\text{FL:} & \begin{bmatrix}
\boxed{(s_1 = f_1) < (s_2 < f_2)}, \\
\text{DIS}(\text{Loc}(e_2, s')) < \text{DIS}(\text{Loc}(e_2, f)), \\
\text{POV}(p): \text{POINT}(e_2) = \text{Loc}(e_2, s'), \\
\text{VIEW}(w) = \langle s, f \rangle
\end{bmatrix} \\
\text{CT:} & \begin{array}{l} \text{CAUSE ([ACT ON } (x, y)], \\ \text{[BE-AT-BY } (y, x)]) \\ \wedge \text{ GO } (x, \text{VIA } (w)) \end{array}
\end{bmatrix} \\
\begin{bmatrix}
\text{NTS} \\
\text{TC:} \quad \text{BE-AT } (x, z_{place})
\end{bmatrix}
\end{bmatrix}
\end{bmatrix}
\end{bmatrix}
$$

In addition to event succession, the -te converb form expresses a simultaneous moving event as V-*yuku* does in the same period. Previous research assumes that V-*te-yuku* came to allow a simultaneous interpretation in Middle Japanese (Kojima 2001; Hyakutome and Hyakutome 2008; Aoki 2012). However, *sugwi-te-yuku* 'pass-CON-go' in (18) suggests that the semantic change in V-*te-yuku* 'V-CON-go' had already begun in Old Japanese.

(18) wagipye no kadwo wo **sugwi-te-yuku** ramu
       my.house GEN gate   ACC **pass-CON-go** would
       'My sweetheart will **go passing** the gate of my house...'
       (*Man'yôsyû*.11.2401)

A plausible interpretation of *sugwi-te-yuku* in (18) is that the two events, *sugwu* 'pass' and *yuku* 'go', occur simultaneously. We argue that a new function of -te enables V-*te-yuku* to bear similar meaning as the older form, V-*yuku*. That is, -te functions as event connector which links the two events involved simultaneously ($e_1 = e_2$).[5] Compositionally, the simultaneous interpretation of *sugwi-te-yuku* 'pass-CON-go' in (18) is computed as follows.

(19)
$$
\begin{bmatrix}
sugwu \text{ 'pass'} \\
\text{ARG} = \begin{bmatrix} \text{ARG1:}\, x, & \text{ARG2:}\, y \end{bmatrix} \\
\text{QL} = \begin{bmatrix}
\begin{bmatrix}
\text{TS} \\
\text{FL:} \boxed{s < f} \\
\text{CT: GO } (x, \text{VIA } (y))
\end{bmatrix}
\end{bmatrix}
\end{bmatrix}
$$

---

[5] Our view of -te's function as event connector is roughly equivalent to "event-interlacing" proposed by Nakatani (2013:92-98).

(20)
$$
\left[
\begin{array}{l}
\textit{yuku} \text{ 'go'} \\
\text{ARG} = \left[\; \text{ARG1}: p, \;\; \text{ARG2}: \textit{te-P} \;\right] \\
\text{QL} = \left[
\begin{array}{l}
\left[
\begin{array}{l}
\textit{TS} \\
\text{FL:} \left[
\begin{array}{l}
\boxed{s < f}, \\
\mathbf{DIS}(\text{Loc}(e, s')) < \mathbf{DIS}(\text{Loc}(e, f)), \\
\mathbf{POV}(p): \mathbf{POINT}(e) = \text{Loc}(e, s'), \\
\qquad\qquad \mathbf{VIEW}(y) = \langle s, f \rangle
\end{array}
\right] \\
\text{CT:} \quad \text{GO}(x, \text{VIA}(y))
\end{array}
\right] \\
\left[
\begin{array}{l}
\textit{NTS} \\
\text{TC:} \quad \text{BE-AT}(x, z_{place})
\end{array}
\right]
\end{array}
\right]
\end{array}
\right]
$$

(21)
$$
\left[
\begin{array}{l}
\textit{sugwi-te-yuku} \text{ 'pass-CON-go'} \\
\text{ARG} = \left[\; \text{ARG1}: p \;\right] \\
\text{QL} = \left[
\begin{array}{l}
\left[
\begin{array}{l}
\textit{TS} \\
\text{FL:} \left[
\begin{array}{l}
\boxed{s_1 = s_2 < f_1 = f_2}, \\
\mathbf{DIS}(\text{Loc}(e, s')) < \mathbf{DIS}(\text{Loc}(e, f)), \\
\mathbf{POV}(p): \mathbf{POINT}(e) = \text{Loc}(e, s'), \\
\qquad\qquad \mathbf{VIEW}(y) = \langle s, f \rangle
\end{array}
\right] \\
\text{CT:} \quad \text{GO}(x, \text{VIA}(y))
\end{array}
\right] \\
\left[
\begin{array}{l}
\textit{NTS} \\
\text{TC:} \quad \text{BE-AT}(x, z_{place})
\end{array}
\right]
\end{array}
\right]
\end{array}
\right]
$$

We consider that having common temporal features as well as -*te* functioning as an event connector plays a key role in making V-*te-yuku* express a simultaneous event; the interlacing interpretation is possible only when a continuous or an activity verb, whose temporal feature is the same as that of *yuku* ($s < f$), precedes the -*te* converb form.

5.3 Phase III: Reanalysis of V-*te-yuku*

We propose that V-*te-yuku* 'V-CON-go' as a whole comes to bear aspectual meaning as a result of reanalysis illustrated in (22), and the reanalysis is instigated by the historical development of Japanese V-V compounds. According to Hyakutome (2003) and Aoki (2012), genuine V-V compounds started to develop in Middle Japanese as the two verbs in the composite had semantically become more cohesive.[6] This development of verbal compounds motivates semantic reduction of -*te*. Specifically, the semantic strategy of simultaneous interpretation for verbal compounds penetrates into V-*te-yuku*, which triggers the semantic bleaching of the conjunctive particle. Thus, the -*te* converb form began to bear aspectual meaning exemplified by *tumat-te-yuku* 'shorten-CON-go' in (23).

---

[6] Hyakutome (2003:20) argues for semantic cohesiveness in verbal compounds in Middle Japanese, presenting quantitative evidence which shows that the total number of verbal compounds increases although verbs appearing in the second position diminish in number.

(22) Reanalysis of V-*te-yuku*

    Before: [V-*te*] -*yuku*   (event succession / event simultaneity)

    After: V-[*te-yuku*]   (aspect)

(23) hi-no   tumat-te-yuku   sewasinai aki-ni

    daytime-NOM   **shorten-CON-go** busy   autumn-by

    '[It was when everyone was attracted] by the bustle of autumn, with daytime

    getting short.'   (*Kokoro*)

We give the same semantic representation as that of V-*yuku* for the reanalyzed aspectual *te-yuku* as in (24). The correspondence in semantics between the two forms prompts the aspectual meaning of V-*yuku* to flow into V-*te-yuku*: renewal took place in transition from the former to the latter. Given that renewal has been attested in the development of tense/aspect morphemes cross-linguistically (Smith 2006) and the newer form in the process usually undergoes morphophonological attrition, renewal is a reasonable scenario to explain the grammaticalization of Japanese *yuku* 'go'.

(24)
$$\left[\begin{array}{l} \text{\textit{te-yuku} 'CON-go' (aspect)} \\ \text{ARG} = \left[\ \text{ARG1}: p, \ \text{ARG2}: VP \ \right] \\ \text{QL} = \left[\left[\begin{array}{ll} \text{TS} \\ \text{FL:} & \left[\begin{array}{l} \boxed{s < f}, \\ \textbf{DIS}(\text{Loc}(e, s')) < \textbf{DIS}(\text{Loc}(e, f)), \\ \textbf{POV}(p): \textbf{POINT}(e) = \text{Loc}'(e, s'), \\ \quad\quad \textbf{VIEW}(y) = \langle s_e, f_e \rangle \end{array} \right] \\ \text{CT:} & \phi \end{array} \right] \left[\begin{array}{l} \text{NTS} \\ \text{TC:} \quad \text{BE}_{Ident}\ (x, z_{state}) \end{array} \right] \right] \end{array} \right]$$

(25)
$$\left[\begin{array}{l} \text{\textit{(hi-no) tumar-u} 'shorten'} \\ \text{ARG} = \left[\ \text{ARG1}: x \ (= \text{days}) \ \right] \\ \text{QL} = \left[\left[\begin{array}{l} \text{TS} \\ \text{FL:} \boxed{s < f < r} \\ \text{CT: } \text{GO}_{Ident}\ (x, \text{VIA-TO } (\textit{SHORT})) \end{array} \right] \right] \end{array} \right]$$

(26)
$$\left[\begin{array}{l} \text{\textit{tumat-te-yuku} 'shorten-CON-go'} \\ \text{ARG} = \left[\ \text{ARG1}: p \ \right] \\ \text{QL} = \left[\left[\begin{array}{ll} \text{TS} \\ \text{FL:} & \left[\begin{array}{l} \boxed{s_1 = s_2 < f_1 = f_2 < r_1}, \\ \textbf{DIS}(\text{Loc}(e, s')) < \textbf{DIS}(\text{Loc}(e, f)), \\ \textbf{POV}(p): \textbf{POINT}(e) = \text{Loc}'(e, s'), \\ \quad\quad \textbf{VIEW}(y) = \langle s_e, f_e \rangle \end{array} \right] \\ \text{CT:} & \text{GO}_{Ident}\ (x, \text{VIA-\textit{PATH}}) \end{array} \right] \left[\begin{array}{l} \text{NTS} \\ \text{TC:} \quad \text{BE}_{Ident}\ (x, \textit{SHORT}) \end{array} \right] \right] \end{array} \right]$$

5.4 Phase IV: Coexistence of Three Forms

As a result of the grammaticalization process which we have discussed in previous sections, the three forms, *yuku*, V-*yuku* and V-*te-yuku*, came to coexist in Modern Japanese (Phase IV), in which the -*te* converb form has become predominant and driven the infinitive form into near-extinction. This transition is illustrated empirically by Figure 3, showing V-*te-yuku* are on the increase, whereas V-*yuku* decreases.

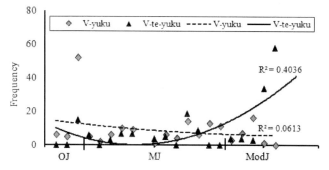

FIGURE 3 Chronological change from V-*yuku* to V-*te-yuku*.

6 Conclusion

This study has explored the grammaticalization process of the Japanese motion verb *yuku* 'go' within the framework of Generative Lexicon. We have elucidated the historical process, assuming four phases (see Table 2).

We discussed that -*yuku* in V-*yuku* had already converbalized in as early as Phase I and the infinitive form has aspectual meaning as well as two movement meanings: event-sequential movement and simultaneous movement, which are determined exclusively by context. V-*te-yuku* later emerges in Phase II. At its earliest usage, we proposed that -*te* functions as an event successor, which induces the event-sequential interpretation of the -*te* converb form. We demonstrated that the form is to be construed as simultaneous movement when the aspectual properties of the two verbs involved coincide. In Phase III, V-*te-yuku* acquires the aspectual meaning which V-*yuku* has originally denoted. Aspectual intepretation is added to V-*te-yuku* as -*te* semantically bleached in tandem with the development of verbal compounds in Japanese, which causes the -*te* converb form to be reanalyzed: [V-*te*]-*yuku*>V-[*te-yuku*]. We argued that the difference in productivity between V-*yuku* and V-*te-yuku* in diachrony (see Table 1) is the consequence of renewal from the infinitive form to the -*te* converb form, thereby motivating the latter to be used more productively in wider contexts afterwards.

Our system of semantic representation not only elucidates the interrelationships of the three forms during the diachronic process of *yuku* 'go' but can also model the historical process of other *-te* converb forms in Japanese (e.g., V-*te-kuru* 'V-CON-come', V-*te-iru* 'V-CON-be', etc.). We believe that this study helps illustrate how such linguistic forms might develop as well.

References

Aoki, H. (2012). Fukugoodoosi no rekisiteki henka. Paper presented at NINJAL Collaborative Research Project Meetings on Syntactic, Semantic, and Morphological Characteristics of the Japanese Lexicon, September 24, Tohoku University, Sendai, Japan.

Arai, F. and Hidaka, T. (2013). V-yuku no toogo koozoo to imi koozoo. Paper presented at the 38th Annual Meeting of the Kansai Linguisitc Society, June 8-9, Doshisha University, Kyoto, Japan.

Frellesvig, B., Horn, S. W., Russell, K. L., and Sells, P. (2013). The oxford corpus of old japanese. http://vsarpj.orinst.ox.ac.uk/corpus/index.html, (retrieved on September 10, 2013).

Gunji, T. (2004). Japanese aspects and counterfactuals. *TALKS: Theoretical and applied linguistics at Kobe Shoin*, 7:21–34.

Hidaka, T. (2012). *Word formation of Japanese V-V Compounds*. Ph.D. dissertation, Kobe Shoin Women's University.

Hidaka, T. and Arai, F. (2012). V-teiku no imi to hasei ni tuite. Paper presented at the 145th annual meeting of the Linguistic Society of Japan, November 24-25, Kyushu University, Fukuoka.

Hopper, P. J. and Traugott, E. C. (2003). *Grammaticalization*. Cambridge: Cambridge University Press, 2 edition.

Hyakutome, Y. (2003). Tyuuko-doodi-hyoogen ni okeru doosi-rensetu no tenkai. *Kokugogaku Kenkyu*, 42:14–42.

Hyakutome, Y. and Hyakutome, E. (2008). Idoodoosi no bunpooka no tuuziteki koosatu–'renyookei+v' no katati o tyuusin ni. Paper presented at The 9th Annual Conference of the Japanese Congitive Linguistics Association, September 13-14, Nagoya University, Nagoya, Japan.

Igarashi, Y. and Gunji, T. (1998). The temporal system in japanese. In Gunji, T. and Hashida., K., editors, *Topics in constraint-based grammar of Japanese*, pages 81–97. Kluwer, Dordrecht.

Imani, I. (1990). V-tekuru to v-teiku ni tuite. *Nihongogaku*, 9(5):54–66.

Inoue, N. (1962). Doosi no setuzi-ka: Manyoo-no *iku* to *ku*. *Manyoo*, 43:27–37.

Kojima, S. (1998). *Yuku* to *ku*–genji monogatari ni okeru yoohoo–. In *Tookyoodaigaku kokugo kenkyuusitu soosetu hyakusyuunenkinen kokugokenkyuu ronsyuu*, pages 325–344. Kyuko Shoin, Tokyo.

Kojima, S. (2001). Heian-zidai no hukugoo-doosi. *Nihongogaku*, 20(8):71–78.

Kuno, S. (1978). *Danwa no bunpoo*. Tokyo: Taishukan Shoten.

Kuno, S. (1987). *Functional syntax: Anaphora, discourse, and empathy*. Chicago: The University of Chicago Press.

Kuno, S. and Kaburaki, E. (1977). Empathy and syntax. *Linguistic Inquiry*, 8:627–672.

Lin, C. (1996). Kotengo fukugoodoosi kara gendaigo fukugoodoosi e. *Doshisha Kokubungaku*, 44:13–24.

Morita, Y. (1968). "iku kuru" no yooho. *Kokugogaku*, 75:75–87.

Morita, Y. (1994). *Doosi no imiron teki kenkyuu*. Meijishoin, Tokyo.

Nakatani, K. (2008). Tekuru teiku no doosikyookiseigen no hasei. In *Lexicon Forum 4*, pages 63–89. Tokyo: Hituzi Syobo.

Nakatani, K. (2013). *Predicate concatenation: A study of the V-te-V predicate in Japanese*. Kurosio Publishers, Tokyo.

Nishida, N. (1971). *Te* (kotengo). In Matsumura, A., editor, *Nihon Bunpoo Daiziten*, pages 502–506. Meiji Shoin, Tokyo.

of Virginia Library Electronic Text Center, T. U. and the University of Pittsburgh East Asian Library (2006). The japanese text initiative. http://etext.virginia.edu/japanese/, (retrieved on April 1, 2013).

Pustejovsky, J. (1995). *The Generative Lexicon*. The MIT Press, Cambridge, Mass.

Roberts, I. and Roussou, A. (2003). *Syntactic Change: A Minimalist Approach to Grammaticalization*. Cambridge: Cambridge University Press.

Sannoumaru, Y. (2009). Zyoodai fukugoodoosi no ketugoozizyoo ni tuite no iti koosatu. In goisi kenkyuukai, K., editor, *Kokugo goisi no kenkyuu 28*. Osaka: Izumi Shoin.

Shibatani, M. (2007). Grammaticalization of converb constructions: The case of japanese -*te* conjunctive constructions. In Jochen Rehbein, C. H. and Pietsch, L., editors, *Connectivity in Grammar and Discourse*, pages 21–49. John Benjamins, Amsterdam/Philadelphia.

Shibatani, M. and Chung, S. Y. (2007). On the grammaticalization of motion verbs: A japanese-korean comparative perspective. In McGloin, N. H. and Mori, J., editors, *Japanese/Korean Linguistics 15*, pages 21–40. CSLI Publications, Stanford.

Smith, A. (2006). The universal tendency for renewal among grammatical expressions for anterior and related aspect. *Journal of Universal Language*, 7:139–160.

Teramura, H. (1984). *Nihongo no sintakusu to imiII*. Kurosio Publishers.

Tokumoto, A. (2009). Zyoodai no fukugoodoosi–zenkoo to kookoo no imikankei kara–. *Rikkyodaigaku Nihonbungaku*, 102:114–124.

Yamaguchi, A. (2004). *Nihongo no ronri kotoba ni arawareru sisoo*. Taishukan Shoten, Tokyo.

Yoshida, T. (2012). *Nihongodoosi tekei no asupekuto*. Koyo Syobo, Kyoto.

Yoshikawa, T. (1976). Gendai nihongo doosi no asupekuto no kenkyuu. In Kindaichi, H., editor, *Nihongo doosi no asupekuto*. Tokyo: Mugi Shobo.

A Novel *wh*-Indeterminate in Korean: *wh-inka* as a Marker of Referential Vagueness*

ARUM KANG
University of Chicago

1 Introduction

In this paper, I identify a novel *wh*-indeterminate in Korean, *wh-inka*, as a marker of *referential vagueness* (à la Giannakidou and Quer 2013, henceforth GQ). Close parallels between the *wh*-words and indefinite NPs are frequently observed in Korean and Japanese. In these languages, *wh*-words are termed as *wh-indeterminates* in the sense that they change their function depending on the particles they are associated with (Kuroda 1965; Kratzer and Shimoyama 2002; Shimoyama 2001, 2006). Depending on which particles *wh*-words are attached to, Korean indefinite expressions which give rise to the existential quantificational interpretation of 'someone' can be divided into two groups: the bare *wh*-word *nwukwu* 'who' combined with a nominative marker *ka* in (1) or an overtly marked particle *inka* (*wh-inka*, henceforth) in (2):

* I would like to thank Anastasia Giannakidou for valuable discussions and suggestions about this material. I am also grateful to Junko Shimoyama for her generous commentary. Many thanks to Satoshi Tomioka, Suyeon Yun, Suwon Yoon, Michael Yoshitaka Erlewine, Ji Young Shim, Michael Kenstowicz, Chungmin Lee, and to the editors, reviewers and audience at the J/K 23 conference for their helpful comments, insightful suggestions and questions.

Japanese/Korean Linguistics 23.
Edited by Michael Kenstowicz, Theodore Levin and Ryo Masuda.
Copyright © 2016, CSLI Publications.

(1) Nwukwu-ka o-ass-ta.
who-NOM   come-PAST-DECL
'Someone came.'

(2) Nwukwu-**inka** o-ass-ta.
who-INKA   come-PAST-DECL
'Someone (I don't know) came.'

Although the use of *wh-inka* appears to be akin to a typical bare *wh*-indeterminate in (1), a closer look reveals that *wh-inka* never induces epistemically specific interpretations. In fact, *wh-inka* is generally associated with the inference that the speaker is unable to identify the individual in question. This type of indefinite is anti-specific; it cannot be used in contexts where the speaker has a specific value in mind (Haspelmath 1997; Farkas 2002a).

Wh-based anti-specificity in Korean also include a free choice items (FCIs), *wh-na*, since they exhibit a kind of deficiency in drawing values (Giannakidou 1998, 2001; Giannakidou and Cheng 2006):

(3) Nwukwu-**na** o-lswu.iss-ta.
who-NA   come-can-DECL
'Anyone/everyone/all the people can come; it doesnt matter which.'

Whereas the anti-specificity of the FCI *wh-na* has received huge attention (Gill et al. 2004; Kim and Kaufmann 2007; Choi 2007; Park 2009, inter alia), to my knowledge, the interpretation of *wh-inka* has been discussed only recently (Ha 2004; Choi 2011; Yun 2013). An immediate question raised by the above data would be whether any difference exists between the two different types of *wh*-based anti-specificity. My basic assumption is that the class of Korean anti-specificity is not homogeneous, and fine-grained constraints govern their value assignment. In this paper, the discussion leads to the following suggestions: First, a speaker's indeterminacy comes with the preconditions of individual alternatives. Second, the precondition of individual alternatives for *wh-inka* is only partial variation, as opposed to domain exhaustification, which is the core property of the FCI *wh-na*.

2 Markedness and indefinites

2.1 Marked indefinites

It is generally agreed upon that the indefinite article $a(n)$ is 'unmarked':

(4) **A** student came to see me.

It is an 'unmarked' argument marker since it contributes no constraints on the variable it introduces (Hawkins 1991; Farkas 2002c).

In contrast to this, there are 'marked' indefinite Ds with which the speaker intends to convey something more than just existential $\exists$ as shown in (5). Whereas indefinite Ds such as *a particular* and *a certain* in (5a) are used to indicate a rigid reference in the speaker's mind, indefinite Ds such as *any* and *some* in (5b-c) convey information about the speaker's lack of knowledge.

(5) a. **A certain/A particular** student came to see me.

  b. **Any** student can come to see me.

  c. **Some** student came to see me.

The marked Ds have more constrained distribution than the indefinite with the indefinite article a. Unlike the non-marked article-headed indefinite that scopes freely, the value of the indefinite in (5a) is fixed and the resulting reading is truth conditionally equivalent to a reading where the indefinite has wide scope. A wide scope reading is not available for *any student* in (5b) and *some student* in (5c), since they do not lend themselves naturally to a referential use.

The distinction between specificity and anti-specificity markers depends on the nature of the constraint D which contributes different values. With the use of morphologically overt D as a specificity marker, the value of indefinites is fixed; while by choosing to use an anti-specific D the speaker makes clear that she has no particular individual in mind, and the value of indefinites is not fixed. In what follows, each type of (anti)specificity marker will be reviewed.

2.2 Specificity

My description of the use of specificity markers utilize the felicity condition developed by Ionin (2006). Epistemically, specificity is non-varying reference, a kind of *rigid reference in the mind of the speaker* (Groenendijk and Stokhof 1981; Fodor and Sag 1982; Farkas 2002b,c; Schwarzschild 2002; Ionin 2006; Giannakidou and Quer 2013, inter alia). Ionin (2006) proposes that the indefinite *this* encodes the semantic feature that she called *specificity as noteworthiness*, a concept built upon Fodor and Sag's view of referentiality. Drawing a distinction between *presupposition* and *felicity conditions*, Ionin treats the deictic *this* and the referential indefinite *this* (i.e., *this$_{ref}$*) as two separate lexical items.

The referential indefinite *this* introduces a new discourse referent such that the speaker has a "unique individual in mind", which contributes a noteworthy property to the introduced referent. This noteworthiness is formulated with a felicity condition:

(6) Felicity condition (Ionin 2006: (23a)):
   $\lambda i.\ [\![\text{sp } \alpha]\!]^{c,i}$ is defined for a given context c, iff s_c in w_c at t_c intends to refer to exactly one individual x_c, and $\exists \varphi_{<s,et>}$ which s_c in w_c

at t_c considers noteworthy, and $\alpha(w_c)(x_c) = \varphi(w_c)(x_c) = 1$. If this condition is fulfilled, $\lambda i.\ [\![sp\ \alpha\ ]\!]^{c,i} = \lambda i.\ x_c$.

The lexical entry in (6) ensures that a referential *this*-indefinite obligatorily takes scope above intensional verbs and modals. Since the speaker intends to refer to a particular individual in the world of utterance, this individual must exist in the world of utterance. The felicity condition makes the $this_{ref}$ like a uniqueness marker. A felicity condition is crucially different from a presupposition, in the sense that a presupposition is a statement presupposed to be true by both speaker and listener whereas a felicity condition focuses on the knowledge state of the speaker.

2.3 Anti-specificity

2.3.1 Free choice as exhaustive variation

In the definites approach, the free choice effect gives rise to exhaustive variation. Exhaustive variation means that the possible values for the FCI in the domain of quantification are all exhausted. The existence of multiple *individual alternatives* is a prerequisite to the felicitous use of the FCI and comes with the presupposition that we *exhaust all values* in the domain:[1]

(7) **Free choice item** (Giannakidou and Cheng 2006: (39)):
Let W_i be a non-empty, non-singleton set of possible worlds. A sentence with a free choice item $[\![OP\ DET_{FC}\ (P, Q)]\!]$ is true in WE_0 with respect to W_i iff: (where OP is a nonveridical operator; P is the descriptive content of the FC-phrase; Q is the nucleus of the tripartite structure; W_0 is the actual world):

    a. Presupposition: $\forall w_1, w_2 \in W_i$: $[\![\alpha]\!]^{w1} \neq [\![\alpha]\!]^{w2}$, where α is the free choice phrase.

    b. Assertion: $[\![OPw, x\ [P(x,w); Q(x,w)]]\!] = 1$ where x, w are the variables contributed by α

Therefore, the free choice effect amounts to *domain exhaustification*. The FCI requires that there be a plural domain.

It has been argued that Korean FCIs exhibit a domain exhaustification (Park 2009). According to Park, free choice *wh-na* in Korean is a definite

---

[1] In Giannakidou (2001) the idea was implemented by using i(dentity)-alternatives (borrowed from Dayal 1997):

(1)   *i-alternatives* (= epistemic alternatives: Giannakidou 2001)
    A world w_1 is an i-alternative wrt α iff there exists some w_2 such that $[\![\alpha]\!]^{w1} \neq [\![\alpha]\!]^{w2}$

i-alternatives ensure that in each world, a different value will be drawn for the FCI, and this occurs until we exhaust all values.

plural FCI.[2] The definite nature of FCI *wh-na* can be attested by the following example, in which *wh-na* requires the maximality marker ta 'lit. all' for the definite plural reading (Park 2009, p.49):

(8) Nwukwu-**na ta**, sihem-ey thongkwaha-yess-ta.
who-NA   all test-in   pass-PAST-DECL
'Everyone/all the people, no matter who they are, passed the test.'

What is important here is that exhaustive variation is not a grammatical condition, but a presupposition; thus if the FCI fails to satisfy exhaustive variation, the sentence is infelicitous, not ungrammatical.

2.3.2 Referential vagueness as non-exhaustive variation

We have another defective indefinite, which we call "referentially vague indefinites (RVIs, henceforth)" (GQ 2013). Crosslinguistically RVIs, along with FCIs, are instances of anti-specific indefinites:

(9)   a.   **some** professor **or other**   ENGLISH
      b.   **algún** profesor   SPANISH
      c.   **kapjon** kathijiti   GREEK

Although they have in common that they impose a non-fixed value constraint, the difference between FCIs and RVIs is that the constraint for referential vagueness exhibits a weaker form of indeterminacy (non-exhaustive).

In what follows, I introduce two different types of RVIs – *kápjos* in Greek, and *algún* in Spanish/Catalan. As an anti-specificity marker, an RVI should signal the speaker's ignorance. This constraint can be tested with an epistemic judgment, using three methods (ostension, naming, description) originally suggested by Aloni and Port (2010). As shown below, none of them is compatible with *algún,* and *kápjos* (GQ 2013: (77)-(82)):

(10)   Naming

      a.   Tengo que quedar con **algún** profesor. #Se llama Regine Eckardt.
         'I have to meet with some professor or other. #Her name is Regine Eckardt.'   SPANISH
      b.   Thello na miliso me **kapjon** kathijiti. # To onoma tu ine Veloudis.
         'I want to meet some professor or other . #His name is Veloudis.' GREEK

---

[2] Semantically, *wh-na* is a definite FCI which strongly suggests the existence of an individual in the sense that it tends to excludes the empty set and is closely related with the contextually determined set of individuals. Syntactically, FCI *wh-na* requires the maximality marker *ta* 'all' for the definite plural reading. Thus Park argues that *na* acts as an iota operator (Park 2009).

(11) Ostension

    a. Tengo que leer un artáculo de **algún** profesor. #Es aquella senora de allí, pero no sé cójo se llama.

       'I have to read an article of some professor or other. ??It's that lady over here, but I don't know her name.'   SPANISH

    b. Thelo na miliso me **kapjon** glosologo. #Ine aftos o kirios eki.

       'I want to meet some linguist or other. ??It's that guy over there.' GREEK

(12) Description

    a. Tengo que quedar con **algún** profesor. #Es el director del Departamento de Filosofía.

       'I have to meet some professor or other. #He is the Head of the Philosophy Department.'   SPANISH

    b. Thelo na miliso me **kathijiti.** # Ine o propedros tu tmimatos filosofias.

       'I want to meet some professor or other. #He is the head of the Philosophy Department.'   GREEK

The second sentence in examples (10)-(12) introduces a specific value, and the previous use of the indefinite becomes odd. Another test is the "guess who" test (Haspelmath 1997, Aloni 2011), which detects the incompatibility of the *or-other* indefinite with fixed value:

(13) a. **Kapjos** fititis tilefonise. #Mandepse pjos!   GREEK

     b. Ha llamado **algún** estudiante. #Adivina quién!   SPANISH

     c. Ha trucat **algun** estudiante. #Endevina qui!   CATALAN
       'Some student or other called. #Guess who!'

Hence all these indefinites are sensitive to the knowledge of the speaker. It is necessary for the speaker to be in a state of uncertainty.

    The main contrast between FCIs and RVIs is that FCIs require individual alternatives that come with the presupposition that we exhaust all values in the domain; RVIs' individual alternatives do not exhaust these alternatives, in particular that there be different values:

(14) **Referential vagueness** (Giannakidou and Quer 2013: (96)):
    A sentence containing a referentially vague indefinite α will have a truth value iff:
    $\exists w_1, w_2 \in W$: $[\![\alpha]\!]^{w1} \neq [\![\alpha]\!]^{w2}$; where α is the referentially vague variable.

Referential vagueness exhibits a weaker form of indeterminacy in that there are at least two alternative worlds where the RVI receives distinct values. As a result, RVIs are weaker than FCIs, having domain non-exhaustification. We can think of this condition as a felicity condition (Ionin 2006) that concerns only the speaker only, thus weaker than presupposition. Given that a referential vagueness crucially depends on the speaker's epistemic state and is interpreted with respect to the speaker, the world for assessment is assumed to come from the speaker's belief model:

(15) **Belief model of an individual** (Giannakidou 1999: (45)):
Let c=<cg(c), W(c), M, s, h, w0, f,...> be a context.
A model MB(x) $\in$ M is a set of worlds associated with an individual x representing worlds compatible with what x believes.

(16) a. John won the race.

b. [John won the race] = 1 iff
$\forall$w [w $\in$ MB(s) $\rightarrow$ w $\in$ λw'. John wins the race in w']

By using the RVI, the speaker believes that there is more than one value in the contextual domain for RVI. The truth conditions for the RVI will be as follows:

(17) Particular individual in mind = fixed value in $M_B(s)$:
w1 $\rightarrow$ Bill, w2 $\rightarrow$ Bill, w3 $\rightarrow$ Bill

(18) No particular individual in mind = no fixed value in $M_B(s)$:
w1 $\rightarrow$ Bill, w2 $\rightarrow$ Nicholas, w3 $\rightarrow$ John, w4 $\rightarrow$?

Via the individual anchor, the belief worlds are available. Variation is modeled as different values in at least two worlds.

3 A new *wh*-indeterminate: Korean *wh-inka*

3.1 Hallmark properties of *wh-inka*

Similar to many other articleless languages, Korean employs the same morphological forms for *wh*-words and corresponding indefinites. For example, when the sentence is marked with interrogative markers in (19) at the end of the clause, the *wh*-word *nwukwu* is interpreted as an interrogative word 'who', whereas *nwukwu* that is suffixed with a case marker in a declarative sentence is interpreted as an existential quantifier 'someone' as in (20):

(19) Nwukwu-ka o-ass-**ni**?
Who-NOM come-PAST-Q
'who came?'

(20) Nwukwu-**ka** o-ass-ta.
Who-NOM come-PAST-DECL
'Someone came – the speaker may or may not know who.'

Anti-specific *wh*-indeterminates are realized by three distinct lexical items marked with special morphology: (i) one with *-na* for FCIs, (ii) one with *-(la)to* for NPIs, and (iii) one with *-inka* for RVIs, as shown in Table 1:

Wh-words		NPI: *wh-(la)to*	FCI: *wh-na*	RVI: *wh-inka*
nwukwu	(person)	*nwukwu-(la)to*	*nwukwu-na*	*nwuku-inka*
mwues	(thing)	*mwue(s)-(la)to*	*mwue(s)-na*	*mwu(es)-inka*
etten-N	(which-N)	*etten-N-(la)to*	*etten-N-na*	*etten-N-inka*
enu-N	(which-N)	*enu-N-(la)to*	*enu-N-na*	*enu-N-inka*
eti	(where)	*eti-(la)to*	*eti-na*	*eti-inka*
ence	(when)	*ence-(la)to*	*ence-na*	*ence-inka*
ettehkey	(manner)	*ettehkey-(la)to*	*ettehkey-na*	*ettehkey-inka*

TABLE 1 The inventory of Korean anti-specific *wh*-indeterminates

Similar to other anti-specific *wh*-indeterminates, *wh-inka* is the one that carries the epistemic condition of the speaker's lack of knowledge on the value of the referent:

(21) a. Nwukwu-**inka**(-ka) o-ass-ta.
         who-INKA-NOM   come-PAST-DECL
         'Someone (that I don't know) came.'

      b. Swuni-ka   mwues-**inka**(-lul) mek-ess-ta.
         Swuni-NOM what-INKA-ACC   eat-PAST-DECL
         'Swuni ate something (that I don't know).'

      c. Swuni-ka   cha-lul ettehkey-**inka** kochi-ess-ta
         Swuni-NOM car-ACC how-INKA   fix-PAST-DECL
         'Swuni fixed the car somehow (that I don't know).'

Wh-inka is generally associated with the inference that the speaker is unable to identify the individual in question. The speaker's ignorance induced by *wh-inka* can be identified by the following three identification methods: naming, ostension and description. As shown below, none of them is compatible with *wh-inka*:

(22) a. Naming
         Na-nun kyoswu   nwukwu-**inka**(-lul) manna-kosiph-ta.
         I-TOP professor who-INKA-ACC   meet-want-DECL
         #Kyoswu-uy ilum-un   con-i-ta.
         Professor-of name-TOP John-be-DECL
         'I want to meet some professor or other. # His name is John.'

    b. Ostension

        Na-nun kyoswu nwukwu-**inka**(-lul) manna-kosiph-ta.

        I-TOP   professor who-INKA-ACC   meet-want-DECL

        #Ceki-ey ku kyoswu-ka   i-ss-ta.

        there-Loc that professor-NOM be-PRES-DECL

        'I want to meet some professor or other. #That professor is over there.'

    c. Description

        Na-nun kyoswu nwukwu-**inka**(-lul) manna-kosiph-ta. #Ku

        I-TOP   professor who-INKA-ACC   meet-want-DECL. that

        kyoswu-nun   pwulkun meli-i-ta.

        professor-TOP red   haired-be-PRES-DECL

        'I want to meet some professor or other. #He is red haired.'

The second sentence introduces a specific value, and when the speaker knows what the target value is, the previous use of the *wh-inka* becomes odd. This difference parallels the one we find with *algún* in Spanish, and *kápjos* in Greek. Hence *wh-inka* feels like the constrained indefinite, sensitive to the knowledge of the speaker: it requires that the speaker be in a state of ignorance with a non-fixed value.[3]

Additionally, *wh-inka* necessarily takes narrow scope with respect to intensional operators. As shown below, bare-*wh* in (23) arises with de re/de dicto readings while *wh-inka* in (24) is de dicto only:

(23) a. Mary-nun uisa nwukwu-wa kyelhonha-ko sipehan-ta.

         Mary-TOP doctor who-with   marry-COMP want-DECL

     b. de re: $[\exists\, x\text{ in } w_0\text{ WANT (marry } (x \text{ at } w))]$

     c. de dicto: $[\text{WANT } [\exists\, w \exists\, x\text{ doctor}(x,w) \wedge\text{ marry } (x \text{ at } w)]]$

(24) a. Mary-un uisa nwukwu-**inka**-wa kyelhonha-ko sipehan-ta.

         John-TOP doctor who-INKA-with   marry-COMP want-DECL

     b. de dicto: $[\text{WANT } [\exists\, w \exists\, x\text{ doctor}(x,w) \wedge\text{ marry } (x \text{ at } w)]]$

Summing it up, as in our earlier discussion, the core properties of *wh-inka* can be characterized as follows:

---

[3] Note that we are not dealing with a polarity phenomenon here. *Wh-inka* can appear in a simple past, which is veridical, and it is not subject to "licensing". As *wh-inka* is not a polarity item, it cannot contain dependent variables.

(25) Properties of *wh-inka*

    a. *wh-inka* is indefinite;

    b. *wh-inka* takes NARROW scope with respect to intensional operators;

    c. *wh-inka* signals that the speaker has some LACK of information concerning the identity of the mentioned referent.

In terms of Ionin's account of the scope facts and the speaker's epistemic constraints (recall ex. (6)), the RVI *wh-inka* is the total opposite of *this$_{ref}$*. I therefore propose that *wh-inka* is the dual of the referential *this*-indefinite, signaling the *speaker's ignorance*. Although RVI *wh-inka* and FCI *wh-na* are both anti-specific, only *wh-inka* forms a dual with *this$_{ref}$* because we see that their inherent epistemic constraints are imposed differently. In what follows, I will show how they are distinct.

3.2 RVI *wh-inka* as non-exhaustive variation

3.2.1 FCIs and RVIs with necessity modals

We will now consider the imperatives and universal modals, where FCIs and RVIs contrast in bringing about their distinct exhaustive variation. In the discussion here, I compare with Greek, Catalan and Spanish RVIs because the effect is exactly parallel. Consider first deontic universal modals, where the FCI is infelicitous:

> *Context: The family is in a dire financial situation and Mary must save the family's face by marrying a rich guy. Lawyers are rich guys, so she needs to marry some lawyer or other, a member of the set 'lawyer'.*

(26)   a. #I Maria prepi na pandrefti **opjondhipote** dhikighoro.   GREEK

        b. #Maria-nun pyenhosa nwukwu-**na**-hako

            Mary-TOP   lawyer   who-NA-with

            kyelhonhay-yaha-n-ta.

            marry-must-PRES-DECL

            'lit. Maria must marry any lawyer.'   KOREAN

The presupposition imposes that there will be a value for FCI/any doctor in each w we consider. The result is an undesirably strong statement, because Maria cannot marry all the lawyers. In contrast, the use of the RVI is felicitous:

> *Context: The family is in a dire financial situation and Mary must save the family's face by marrying a rich guy. Lawyers are rich guys, so she needs to marry some lawyer or other, a member of the set 'lawyer'.*

(27) a. I Maria prepi na pandrefti **kapjon** dhikighoro. GREEK
      b. Maria-nun pyenhosa nwukwu-**inka**-hako
          Maria-TOP lawyer   who-INKA-with
          kyelhonhay-yaha-n-ta.
          marry-must-PRES-DECL
          'Maria must marry some lawyer or other.' KOREAN

The sentence becomes plausible in this case, since Maria needs to marry some lawyer or other, a member of the set lawyer, without running all the values in the set.

Likewise, in epistemic necessity modals, we get a similar contrast:

Context: I am talking with John and I see that he is very informed about Mary's illness.

(28) a. (Tha) prepi na milise me {**kapjon**/#**opjondhipote**} giatro. GREEK
      b. Ku-nun uysa   nwukwu-**inka**/#**na**-hako iyakiha-nkey
          He-TOP doctor who-INKA/NA-with   talk-REL
          pwunmyengha-ta.
          must.be-DECL
          'He must have talked with {some doctor or other/#any doctor}.' KOREAN

The FCI creates a too strong statement that forces John to have talked to every doctor in the hospital; in order to be informed about one's illness you do not have to talk with all doctors.

3.2.2 FCIs and RVIs in imperatives (Invitations and suggestions)

We conclude with two more cases: invitations and suggestions. FCIs and RVIs influence the imperative in different ways:

Context: A variety of delicious desserts are presented at the buffet in front of Maria. But she does not show much of an appetite. A says:

(29) a. Fae **opjodhipote** ghliko! GREEK
      b. Prueba **cualquier** dulce! SPANISH
      c. Kwaca mwes-**ina** tusey-yo.
          Cookie what-NA eat-IMP
          'Eat all of these cookies!' KOREAN

(30) a. Fae **kanena** ghliko/**kanena** ap'afta ta ghlika! GREEK
      b. Prueba **algún** dulce/**alguno** de estos dulces! SPANISH
      c. Kwaca mwes-**inka**-lul   tusey-yo.
          Cookie what-INKA-ACC eat-IMP
          'Eat some (or other) of these cookies!' KOREAN

Here the domain is specific, and contained by the context and the partitive. See the different situations between the FCI vs. RVI-imperatives in (29) and (30). The contrast between the interpretations induced by exhaustive vs. non-exhaustive indefinites leads us to the fact that FCIs and RVIs have different behaviors with respect to domain exhaustification. With the FCI in (29) we have a strong imperative to eat as many cookies as the addressee wants; we exhaust all available values in the domain of quantification. Whereas with the RVI in (30), the imperatives are gentle invitations to eat some sweet or other. In the context, the speaker invites the addressee to try. In uttering the sentence, the speaker is not inviting the addressee to consider *all* sweets; she is only inviting the addressee to consider some and try. In this sense, RVIs do not exhaustify the domain. What they require is only partial variation in their domain.

3.3   *Wh-inka* as RVI

I propose now that RVI *wh-inka* requires individual alternatives, with non-exhaustive alternative variations:

(31) **Referential vagueness of *wh-inka*** (à la GQ 2013):
A sentence containing a referentially vague indefinite *wh-inka* as α will have a truth value iff: $\exists w_1, w_2 \in W$: $[\![\alpha]\!]^{w1} \neq [\![\alpha]\!]^{w2}$; where α is the referentially vague variable.

(32) Nwukwu-**inka**(-ka) o-ass-ta.
who-INKA-NOM   come-PAST-DECL
'Someone (that I don't know) came.'

This imposes a weaker demand on the context, in which there are at least two alternative worlds where the RVI receives different values.

4   Conclusion and further implications

In this paper, I have shown that the RVI *wh-inka* is a marker of the speaker's ignorance, not free choice. The speaker's ignorance is referential vagueness, which requires only partial variation in their domain.

Before closing this paper, let me consider some remaining data. As shown below, the *wh-inka* RVIs never receive question meaning.

(33) a. Nwukwu-**inka** o-ass-ni?
who-INKA   come-PAST-Q
(i) 'Did someone come?'
(ii) 'Who came?'   RVI

b. Nwukwu-**na** o-lswu.iss-ni?
who-NA   come-can-Q
(i) 'Can anyone come?'
(ii) ~~'Who can come?'~~   FCI

c. Nwukwu-ka o-ass-ni?
who-NOM   come-PAST-Q
(i) 'Did someone come?'
(ii) 'Who came?'   bare *wh*-indeterminate

Since in the indefinite approach, FCIs and RVIs exhibit a kind of deficiency in drawing values, in this sense, no propositional semantics is needed (*pace* Kratzer and Shimoyama 2002). In fact, the RVI *wh-inka* and FCIs are never used as question words; then why do we generate propositional alternatives? Therefore, FCIs and RVIs jointly challenge the need for propositional alternatives of all *wh*-indeterminates.

References

Aloni, M. 2011. Modal inferences with marked indefinites. Presentation, Department of Linguistics, University of Chicago.

Aloni, M, and A Port. 2010. Epistemic indefinites and methods of identification. Talk presented at the Workshop on Epistemic Indefinites, University of Göttingen and Lichtenberg-Kolleg.

Choi, J. 2007. Free choice and negative polarity: A compositional analysis of Korean polarity sensitive items. Doctoral Dissertation, University of Pennsylvania.

Choi, Y.-J. 2011. Correlation between disjunction and modality: focused on 'inka' (written in Korean). *Journal of Korean linguistics* 60:146–181.

Dayal, V. 1997. Free relatives and *ever*: Identity and free choice readings. In *Proceedings of SALT*, volume 7, 99–116.

Farkas, D. 2002a. Extreme non-specificity in Romanian. *Romance Languages and Linguistic Theory* 127–151.

Farkas, D. F. 2002b. Specificity distinctions. *Journal of Semantics* 19:213–243.

Farkas, D. F. 2002c. Varieties of indefinites. In *Proceedings of SALT*, volume 12, 59–83.

Fodor, J. D, and I. A Sag. 1982. Referential and quantificational indefinites. *Linguistics and Philosophy* 5:355–398.

Giannakidou, A. 1998. *Polarity sensitivity as (non)veridical dependency*, volume 23. John Benjamins.

Giannakidou, A. 1999. Affective dependencies. *Linguistics and Philosophy* 22:367–421.

Giannakidou, A. 2001. The meaning of free choice. *Linguistics and philosophy* 24:659–735.

Giannakidou, A, and L. L.-S Cheng. 2006. (In)Definiteness, Polarity, and the Role of wh-morphology in Free Choice. *Journal of Semantics* 23:135–183.

Giannakidou, A, and J Quer. 2013. Exhaustive and non-exhaustive variation with free choice and referential vagueness: Evidence from Greek, Catalan, and Spanish. *Lingua* 126:120–149.

Gill, K.-H, S Harlow, and G Tsoulas. 2004. Connectives, indeterminates, and quantificational variability. *Empirical Issues in Formal Syntax and Semantics* 5:75–88.

Groenendijk, J, and M Stokhof. 1981. A pragmatic analysis of specificity. In *Ambiguities in intensional contexts*, 153–190. Springer.

Ha, S. 2004. The existential reading of wh-words and their scope relations. In *Proceedings of CLS*, volume 40, 83–95.

Haspelmath, M. 1997. *Indefinite pronouns*. Oxford University Press.

Hawkins, J. A. 1991. On (in)definite articles: implicatures and (un)grammaticality prediction. *Journal of linguistics* 27:405–442.

Ionin, T. 2006. This is definitely specific: specificity and definiteness in article systems. *Natural language semantics* 14:175–234.

Kim, M.-J, and S Kaufmann. 2007. Domain restriction in freedom of choice: A view from Korean indet-*na* items. In *Proceedings of Sinn und Bedeutung*, volume 11, 375–389.

Kratzer, A, and J Shimoyama. 2002. Indeterminate pronouns: The view from Japanese. In *3rd Tokyo conference on psycholinguistics*.

Kuroda, S.-Y. 1965. Generative grammatical studies in the Japanese language. Doctoral Dissertation, MIT.

Park, E.-H. 2009. Wh-indeterminates, free choice, and expressive content in Korean. Doctoral Dissertation, University of Chicago.

Schwarzschild, R. 2002. Singleton indefinites. *Journal of Semantics* 19:289–314.

Shimoyama, J. 2001. Wh-constructions in Japanese. Doctoral Dissertation, University of Massachusetts.

Shimoyama, J. 2006. Indeterminate phrase quantification in Japanese. *Natural Language Semantics* 14:139–173.

Yun, J. 2013. Wh-indefinites: meaning and prosody. Doctoral Dissertation, Cornell University.

On the Stativity of the Fourth Class Verbs and their Cousins in Japanese*

KIYOMI KUSUMOTO
Kwansei Gakuin University

1 Introduction

Certain classes of verbs in Japanese are known to be unable to occur in their simple tensed form to express a stative meaning. They must be in the *tei-(ru)* form. One such case is what Kindaichi (1950) calls the fourth class verbs. A fourth class verb *sobie-(ru)*, for instance, cannot be used in its simple present tense form.

(1) a. mukoo-ni yama-ga sobie-teiru
         there-at mountain-nom tower-tei-pres
         'A mountain towers over there'
     b. *mukoo-ni yama-ga sobie-ru
         there-at moutain-nom tower-pres
         'A mountain towers over there'

---

*This work is supported by JSPS KAKENHI (Grant-in-Aid) No. 24520443, to which I am grateful.

Japanese/Korean Linguistics 23.
Edited by Michael Kenstowicz, Theodore Levin and Ryo Masuda.

Motion verbs, when used nonagentively, are another instance of such cases, as noted in Tsujimura (2002).

(2) a. dooro-ga mati-no   mannaka-o hasit-tei-ru
         road-nom town-gen middle-acc run-tei-pres
         'A road runs in the middle of the town'
    b. *dooro-ga mati-no   mannaka-o hasi-ru[1]
         road-nom town-gen middle-acc run-pres

These verbs, however, can be used to express a stative meaning in a simple present tense form in noun modifying clauses, as noted in Takahashi (1973), Kinsui (1994) and Ogawa (2004) among others:

(3) a. [mukoo-ni sobie-ru] yama-o   mite-goran
         there-at   tower-pres mountain-acc look-please
         'Look at the mountain that towers over there'
    b. [mati-no mannaka-o hasir-u] dooro-ga mie-ru
         town-gen middle-acc run-pres road-nom visible-pres
         '(I) see a road that runs in the middle of the town'

Among what are called the fourth class verbs, we distinguish two sub-classes; spatial fourth class verbs like *sobie-* used above and property fourth class verbs as below. Property verbs behave similarly to spatial verbs in that they need to occur in the *tei-(ru)* form in root clauses.

(4) a. kono-otoko-wa Taroo-yori sugure-tei-ru
         this-man-top   T-than   excel-tei-pres
         'This man is superior than Taroo'
    b. *kono-otoko-wa Taroo-yori sugure- ru
         this-man-top   T-than   excel-pres

They are different from spatial verbs in that their simple present tense form is not allowed in noun modifying clauses:[2]

---

[1] Note that the present tense *–(r)u* can have a future meaning. The sentence is marginally acceptable when understood to refer to a future event.

[2] Judgment varies. The following example may be more acceptable than (5):

(i)   kiokuryoku-ni sugure-ru hito
         memory-in   excel-pres person
         'person who has a good memory'

(5) * Taroo-yori sugure-ru otoko-ga i-ru
       T-than   excel-pres man-nom be-pres
       'There is a man who is superior than Taroo'

Another construction we would like to look at is what is called a nonpast, adjectival usage of the so-called past tense morpheme –*ta*, whose distribution is limited to noun-modifying clauses. See Abe (1993), Kinsui (1994), Kusumoto (2001) and Ogihara (2004) among others for detailed data and analyses of nonpast –*ta*. Consider the following examples.

(6) a. taoru-ga   kawai-ta.
         towel-nom dry-past
         'The towel dried'
     b. [kawai-ta] taoru-o   mottekite kudasai
         dry-past   towel-acc bring   please
         'Please bring a dry towel/a towel that dried'

When –*ta* is used in root clauses as in (6a), it only has a past interpretation, by which we mean that it locates the relevant event in the past. When used in a noun modifying clause as in (6b), it is ambiguous and crutially has an adjectival stative meaning. On this nonpast interpretation, there is no implication of any past event of drying. That is, the towel refered to in (6b) may be coompletely new and has never gone throug a drying proess.

Not all noun modifying clauses allow such an interpretation, however. The nonpast interpretation is available only with change-of-state verbs like *kawak-* 'dry' above.

(7) [hasi-ta] hito
     run-past person
     'a person who ran'

The verb *hasi-* 'run' is not a change-of-state verb and –*ta* in the modifying clause only has a past reading.

The simple present tense with fourth class verbs may be accepted statively in poems, songs, and novels. We believe that they are used to create a certain stylistic effect, similar to what is called the historical present in English. In such contexts, even agentive motion verbs are accepted with the simple present tense.

(ii)   hookago-no   kootei-o   hasi-ru kimi-o   mi-ta
        after-school-gen ground-acc run-pres you-acc see-past
        '(I) saw you, running in the ground after school'('hatukoi' by Kozo Murashita)

Two subclasses of the fourth class verbs behave similarly with respect to the nonpast –*ta*, and distinguish themselves from (nonagentive) motion verbs.

(8) a. [mukoo-ni sobie-ta] yama-o   mite-goran   spatial
         there-at   tower-past moutain-acc look-please
         'Look at the mountain that towers over there'

     b. [Taroo-yori sugure-ta] otoko-ga i-ru   property
         T-than   excel-past man-nom be-pres
         'There is a man who is superior than Taroo'

     c. *[mati-no mannaka-o hasit-ta] dooro-ga mie-ru   motion
         town-gen middle-acc run-pres road-nom visible-pres
         '(I) see a road that runs in the middle of the town'

Here are some more examples of these three types of verbs:

(9) a. Spatial fourth class verbs
         maga-(ru) 'curve', *oisge-(ru)* 'thrive', *tat-(u)* 'stand',
         hiroga-(ru) 'spread', *yokotawa-(ru)* 'lay'

     b. Property fourth class verbs
         bagage-(ru) 'fool', *tom-(u)* 'abound', ni-(ru) 'resemble',
         kuroi-me-o su-(ru) 'have black eyes'

     c. Nonagentive motion verbs
         too-(ru), *nagare-(ru)* 'run', *yokogi-(ru)* 'across'

Their behaviors are summarized below:

clause type	tense morpheme	fourth-class (spatial)	fourth-class (property)	nonagentive motion
root	-(r)u	*	*	*
relative	-(r)u	ok	*	ok
	-ta	ok	ok	*

Table 1: The availability of stative interpretation with different verb classes

In this paper, we compare the behaviors of these verbs in root and relative clauses in reference to the present tense form and the so-called nonpast adjectival use of the past tense morpheme –*ta*.[3] We claim that these

---

[3] Another intersting class of verbs is noted in Kinsui (1994). The class includes verbs like *kotona-* 'differ', *kanrens-* 'relate' and *mot-* 'have (some property)' and is named the fifth class by Kinsui. Their stative interpretations are acceptable in all environments examined in this

three types of verbs are semantically different. That is, the observed difference in their behavior, especially among the fouth class verbs, is not just apparent but is a reflex of their semantic difference. We also propose a structural difference between root and relative clauses in that what look like relative clauses in Japanese may be reduced relatives without TP or higher projections. We then derive the availability of stative interpretations shown in the table above.

2 Assumptions

Ontologically, we assume the following:

(10) a. D_e the set of individuals
    b. D_t the set of truth values
    c. D_s the set of possible worlds
    d. D_i the set of intervals
    e. D_{ev} the set of eventualities, including events and Davidsonian-states
    f. D_k the set of Kimian-states

Verbal predicates are often divided into two classes, eventive and stative predicates. Maienborn (2005, 2008) argues that stative predicates are further classified into two sub-classes, Davidosonian statives and Kimian statives[4]. The former includes verbs like *sit, sleep* and *wait* and the latter includes verbs like *know* and *resemble* as well as copular constrcutions like *be-intelligent* and *be-tired*. Davidsonian statives are so-named because they are analyzed to have a Davidsonian eventuality argument just like ordinary eventive predicates. Kimian statives, on the other hand, do not denote events. They are "abstract objects for the exemplification of a property P at a holder x and a time t" (Maienborn 2008: 113).

Let us review some linguistic contrast. Davidsonian statives are located in space whereas Kimian statives are not. Thus we find a difference in the use of locative modifiers. The former allows them while the latter does not.

(11) a. John sleeps in bed.
    b. * John resembles his father in their house.

See Maienborn (2005, 2008) and Rothmayr (2009) for more linguistic evidence for the distinction. We will come back to this distinction when

---

paper; root and relative clauses with the present tense ending and with nonpast *–ta*. We do not have much to say about this class and leave their semantic analysis for future research.

[4] Named after Kim (1969).

necessary. For now, we use regular eventive verbs for explanatoory purposes.

We assume that verbs are predicates of eventualities:

(12)　$[\![\mathbf{run}]\!]^g = \lambda e \in D_{ev}.\ [\lambda w \in D_s.\ run(e)(w)]$

We adopt Kratzer's (1994) hypothesis and assume that external arguments are not true arguments of their verbs. They are introduced by an independent functional phrase called Voice.

(13)

```
                VoiceP
              /        \
        NP_agent      Voice'
                      /      \
                  Voice       VP
                    |        /    \
                  Agent    V   (NP_theme)
```

The semantics of this agent-intorducing head is given below:

(14) $[\![\mathbf{Agent}]\!]^g = \lambda x \in D.\ [\lambda e \in D_{ev}.\ [\lambda w \in D_s.\ Agent(x)(e)(w)]]$

The VP and the Voice head are composed together via an operation called Event Identification.

(15) Event Identification (slightly modified from Kratzer 1994, p.20)
If α is a branching node and β and γ its daughters, and β denotes a function f of type $<e, <ev, <s, t>>>$, and γ a function of g of type $<ev, <s, t>>$, then α denotes a function h of type $<<e, <ev, <s, t>>>$ such that for all $x \in D$, $e \in D_{ev}$, and $w \in D_s$, $h(x)(e)(w) = 1$ iff $f(x)(e)(w) = 1$ and $g(e)(w) = 1$.

3　Syntax and Semantics of Relative Clauses

Root clauses are full-fledged clauses, which means that they always project TPs, and do not stop at Voice-levels as in (17b).

(16) a.　Taroo-ga　hasit-ta
　　　　Taroo-nom run-past
　　　　'Taroo ran'

(17) a. [$_{TP}$ Taroo-nom$_1$ [$_{VoiceP}$ t$_1$ [$_{VP}$ run] Voice] past]
　　b. *[$_{VoiceP}$ Taroo-nom [$_{VP}$ run] Voice]

Noun modifiers, on the other hand, may be either full-fledged or 'reduced' clauses. Consider the following example, where the adjective *utukusi-i* 'beautful' modifies the noun *hana* 'flower'. This modifying clause may be structurally ambiguous between a simple untensed adjetive as in (18b) and a relative clause as in (18c).

(18) a. utukusi-i　　hana(-o　　mi-ta)
　　　　beautiful-pres flower(-acc) see-past
　　　　'(I) saw a beautiful flower /a flower which is beautiful'
　　b. [[$_{AP}$ beautiful] [$_{NP}$ flower]]
　　c. [[$_{CP}$ Op$_1$ [$_{TP}$ t$_1$ [$_{AP}$ beautiful] pres]] [$_{NP}$ flower]]

Examining the behavior of adjectival modifiers, Yamakido (2000) and Shimoyama (2011) argue that the parse in (18b) is in fact possible. This means that the so-called present tense ending of adjectives –*i* is not (always) a tense morpheme.[5]

One of the distinguising criteria for this structal ambiguity, proposed by Shimoyama (2011), is to use different interpretations in superlative constructions. Superlatives are said to show semantic ambiguity between an absoute reading and a comparative reading (Szabolcsi 1986, Heim 1985, 1999 among others). Consider the following example:

(19) John climbed the highest mountain.
(20) a. Absolute reading
　　　　John climbed a mountain that is higher than any other contextually salient mountain.
　　b. Comparative reading
　　　　John climbed a higher mountain than anyone else did.

The sentence (19) on its absolute interpretation compares the heights of (contextually salient) mountains. On the other hand, on its comparative reading, it compares people (i.e., climbers) according to the heights of the mountains they climbed.

Interestingly, when the superlative is embedded within a relative clause as in (21), the comparative reading disappears.

(21) John climbed the mountain that is highest.　　√absolute/*comparative

---

[5] For an opposing view, see Nishiyama (1999).

Heim (1999) accounts for this fact by assuimng that the superlative morpheme *–est* must move out to adjoin the matrix predicate in order to yield a comparative interpretation. This movement is syntactically banned when the morpheme is embedded in a relative clause.

(22)   John climbed a mountain [_CP_ that [_TP_ is [est high]]]

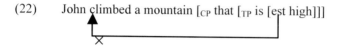

Shimoyama applies this ambiguity test to Japanese noun modifiers. Consider the following example, where the superlative *mottomo ookina* (literally) 'most large' modifies the following noun.

(23) kono-sankakukei-ga [mottomo ooki-na] en-ni   sessi-tei-ru
     this triangle-nom   most   large-pres circle-dat touch-tei-pres
     'This triangle touches the largest circle'

The sentence is ambiguous and curutially has a comparative reading, in which *mottomo ookina en* refers to the largest circle among those that touch a triangle, excluding circles that do not touch any triangle irrespective of their sizes. Shimoyama concludes from this fact that the modifier has a reduced structure.

    Also observed is the contrast between the present and past tense edndings. As shown in the following examples, the ambiguity arises only when the relevant predicate ends with the so-called present tense morpheme.

(24) a.   Ken-ga [mottomo sinsen-na] sakana-o hurumat-ta
          K-nom most   fresh-pres fish-acc   treat-past
          'Ken treated (the guests) to the freshest fish'   √comparative
     b.   Ken-ga [mottomo sinsen-dat-ta] sakana-o hurumat-ta
          K-nom most   fresh-cop-past fish-acc treat-past
          'Ken treated (the guests) to the fish that had been the freshest'
                                                              *comparative

Shimoyama only examines adjectival forms (adjectives with *–i* ending and adjectival nouns with *–na/da* endings). Let us consider verbal forms.

(25) a.   Taroo-ga [mottomo yuuki-ga   a-ru]   hito-o   syuzaisi-ta
          T-nom   most   courage-nom be-pres person-acc interview-past
          Taroo interviewed the most courageous person'   √comparative

b.   Taroo-ga [mottomo kigi-ga   oisiger-u] miturin-o oudansi-ta
    T-nom   most   tree-nom thrive-pres jungle-acc cross-past
    Taroo crossed the jungle in which trees thrive the most'
                                                        √comparative

In these examples, the predicates in noun modifying clauses have the verbal present tense ending –(r)u, and the sentences have a comparative reading as well as an abosolute reading.

The nonpast –ta construction also passes Shimoyama's test.[6]

(26)   Taroo-ga [mottomo kawai-ta] taoru-o   mot-tei-ru
       T-nom   most   dry-past towel-acc have-tei-pres
       'Taroo have the driest towel'   √comparative

This is in accordance with the conclusion arrived at in Kusumoto (2001) and Ogihara (2004) that nonpast –ta clauses have a more reduced structure than full relative clauses.

In this section, we have examined the behavior of what look like relative clauses in Japanese. It is shown based on the amibiguity of superlative interpretations that not all of them are full-fleged clauses but may be reduced. A corelation is found between reduced structures and the ending forms of the predicates. When reduced structures are available, we find the present tense ending –(r)u or the nonpast –ta.

4   Present and Past Tenses

Following Kusumoto (2001), we assume that –ta is ambiguous between true past tense and nonpast adjectival one. The former belongs to the category of T(ense) and the latter to some aspectual category, which in Kusumoto (2001) is called Part(icipial).

(27) a. $[\![\textbf{-ta}_{past}]\!]^g = \lambda P \in D_{<ev,<s,t>>}. [\lambda t \in D_i. [\lambda w \in D_s. \exists e \in D_{ev} [P(e)(w) \& \tau(e) < t]]]^7$

   b. $[\![\textbf{-ta}_{nonpast}]\!]^g = \lambda P \in D_{<ev,<s,t>>}. [\lambda s/z \in D_{ev/k}. [\lambda w \in D_s. \exists e \in D_{ev} \exists w' \in D_s. [P(e)(w') \& TARGET(e')(s/z)(w)]]$
      $[\![\textbf{-ta}_{nonpast}]\!]^g (P)(e)(w)$ is undefined when $TARGET(e)$ is undefined for all e such that $P(e)(w)$.

The past tense –ta is an existential quantifier that locates the relevant eventuality in the past with respect to some reference time. The nonpast –ta

---

[6] This fact is noted in Shimoyama (2011).
[7] τ is a trace function that takes an eventuality and gives its run time.

has some modal-like property and it does not necessarily locate the eventuality in the evaluation world. In addition, it comes with a definedness condition, by which we explain why this interpretation is only available with change-of-state verbs but not with other types of verbs.

Given that the nonpast adjectival –*ta* is not of the category of T, it explains why it can be found only in noun modifying clauses: Root clauses have to bear a tense whereas modifying clauses may be tenseless.[8]

We argue that what look like relative clauses with the present tense ending may not be full-fledged clause, either. This means that the so-called present tense morpheme –*(r)u* is also ambiguous. We argue that the morpheme –*(r)u* is ambiguous between the true tense (i.e., the morpheme that appears in the T head position) and vacuous place holder.[9]

(28) a. $[\![\text{-(r)u}_{\textbf{pres}}]\!]^g = \lambda P \in D_{<ev,<s,t>>}. [\lambda t \in D_i. [\lambda w \in D_s. \exists e \in D_{ev} [P(e)(w)$
  & $t \leq \tau(e)]]]$

  b. $[\![\text{-(r)u}_{\textbf{vacuous}}]\!]^g = \lambda P \in D_{<ev,<s,t>>}. P.$

The present tense morpheme is an existential quantifier just like the past tense one. It locates the relevant eventuality simultaneous or posterior to some evaluation time. The vacuous –*(r)u* is semantically vacuous.

Now we are ready to analyze the semantics of different verb types and explain their different behaviors in modifying clauses. We will do so in the following two sections.

5 Motion Verbs

Motion verbs may be used agentively or nonagentively.

(29) a. Taroo-ga hasit-tei-ru
     T-nom   run-tei-pres
     'Taroo is running'

  b. dooro-ga mati-no   mannaka-o hasit-tei-ru
     road-nom town-gen middle-acc run-tei-pres
     'A road runs in the middle of the town'

---

[8] What if it occurs in root clauses and the projection is further selected by T? Kusumoto (2003) argues that this is in fact possible, but when followed by a tense morpheme, the nonpast –*ta* morphologically alternates with –*te* and the result is the well-known –*tei(ru)* construction. See Teramura (1984) and Kusumoto (2003) for semantic similarities with nonpast –*ta* and the stative interpretation of the –*tei(ru)* construction

[9] We leave open the lexical status of this vacuous moprpheme. It may project a parallel structure to nonpast –*ta* an should be analyzed as some type of aspectual morpheme. Or it does not have any semantic component, even the vacuous one in (28b), and is a true place holder inserted at PF for morphophonological reasons.

We argue that they share the same verb stem, which denotes sets of eventualities. For instance, *hasi-* 'run' denotes the set of all running eventualities.

(30) $[\![\textbf{hasi-} (\text{run})]\!] = \lambda e \in D_{ev}. [\lambda w \in D_s. \text{run}(e)(w)]$

When used agentively, the agentive subject is introduced under the VoiceP. When used nonagentively, the subject is introduced in the Locative Phrase.[10]

(31) a.   [$_{VoiceP}$ Taroo-nom [$_{VP}$ run] Agent]
     b.   [$_{VP}$ [$_{LocP}$ road-nom [the-middle-of-the-town Loc] run]]

The Locative head has the following semantics.

(32) $[\![\textbf{Loc}]\!] = \lambda x \in D_e. [\lambda y \in D_e. [\lambda e \in D_{ev}. [\lambda w \in D_s. \text{Loc}(x)(y)(e)(w)]]]$ [11]

We argue that this is an obligatory head since nonagentive motions verbs are quite odd without modifying phrases.

(33) a.   [mati-no mannaka-o hasir-u] dooro-ga mie-ru
        town-gen middle-acc run-pres road-nom visible-pres
        '(I) see a road that runs in the middle of the town'
     b.?? [hasir-u] dooro-ga mie-ru
        run-pres road-nom visible-pres

Now let us recall the behavior of nonagentive motion verbs. With the present tense ending, they do not have a stative meaning in roon clauses but they do in noun modifying clauses. Moreover, they are incompatible with the nonpast interpretation of *–ta*.

    In root clauses, vacuous *–(r)u* cannot be used since it does not project TP. Therefore, the following structure is the only possible parse, yielding a future interpretation.

(34) [$_{TP}$ road-nom$_1$ [$_{VP}$ t$_1$[$_{LocP}$ [the-middle-of-the-town Loc] run] pres]]

In relative clauses, vacuous present tense may be used.

---

[10] Or the Manner Phrase in the case of *dooro-ga kunekuneto hasitteiru* 'A road runs tortuously'.

[11] For semantic composition, we use Event Identification in (15).

(35) [[$_{VP}$ [$_{LocP}$ [in-the-middle-of-the-town Loc] run]-pres$_{vacuous}$] [$_{NP}$ road]]

Finally, the nonpast –*ta* cannot be used since *hasi-* 'run' is not a change-of-state verb.

6   Fourth Class Verbs

We have identified two subclasses of the so-called fourth class verbs, spatial and property verbs. They are both unacceptable in the stative interpretation in root clauses when they do not accompany the *tei-ru* form. This is due to the same reason as motion verbs: When they accompany the present tense morpheme –*(r)u*, they do not yield a stative interpretation. But they differ in their behavior in relative clauses.

(36) a.   [mukoo-ni sobie-ru]   yama-o   mite-goran
         there-at   tower-pres mountain-acc look-please
         'Look at the mountain that towers over there'
     b. *[Taroo-yori sugure-ru] otoko-ga i-ru
         T-than   excel-pres man-nom be-pres
         'There is a man who is superior than Taroo'

We argue that they are both change-of-state verbs, based on their behavior with nonpast –*ta* (see examples (8)).

(37) Spatial: $[\![$**sobie-** (tower)$]\!]$ $= \lambda x \in D_e$. [$\lambda e \in D_{ev}$. $\lambda w \in D_s$. [tower$(e)(x)(w)$ & TARGET(e) = $\lambda s \in D_{ev}$. $\lambda w' \in D_s$. [towering$(x)(s)(w')$]]]

   Property: $[\![$**sugure-** (excel)$]\!]$ $= \lambda x \in D_e$. [$\lambda e \in D_{ev}$. $\lambda w \in D_s$. [excel$(e)(x)(w)$ & TARGET(e) = $\lambda z \in D_k$. $\lambda w' \in D_s$. [$z \approx$ excellent$(x)(w)$]]]]^{12}

They differ in their target state arguments. For spatial verbs, it is a Davidsonian state whereas that of property verbs is a Kimian state in the sense of Maienborn (2005, 2008). The former is rather like an eventive while the latter is an abstract object for "exemplification of a property P at a holder x and a time t", which is neither directly perceived nor spatially located according to Maienborn.

When nonpast –*ta* takes VPs with fourth class verbs, the resulting phrases denote some target state. With spatial verbs, the resulting states are

---

[12] $z \approx P(x)(w)$ should be read as 'z is exemplified by the predicate P applying to the individual x in w.'

Davidsonian statives. Like Davidsonian eventives, they allow locative modification as in (8a), repeated here as (38).

(38) [mukoo-ni sobie-ta]   yama-o   mite-goran
     there-at   tower-past moutain-acc look-please
     'Look at the mountain that towers over there'

Property verbs, on the other hand, yield Kimian statives when combined with nonpast –ta. Locative modifiers with property verbs are not acceptable.

(39) a.   [Taroo-yori sugure-ta] otoko-o sagas-ou
          T-than   excel-past man-acc search-let's
          'Let's look for a man who is superior to Taroo'
     b. * [Taroo-yori nyuuyooku-de sugure-ta] otoko-o sagas-ou
          T-than   N.Y.-in   excel-past man-acc search-let's
          'Let's look for a man who is superior to Taroo'

This is on par with the following English example:

(40)   * This man is superior to Taroo in N.Y.

Assuming that fourth class verbs are change-of-state verbs, the behavior of property verbs with the present tense ending in relative clauses is expected. Change-of-state verbs by themselves do not yield a stative interpretation. Consider other change-of-state verbs that are not fourth class verbs.

(41) [go-zi-ni   ak-u]   mise
     five-o'clock-at open-pres shop
     'a shop that will open at five/regularly open at five'

The example only has a future or habitual interpretation.

     Spatial verbs, too, are expected to behave the same way, contrary to the fact. We argue that the individual argument of spatial verbs is also introduced in the Locative Phrase.

(42) [$_{VP}$ [$_{LocP}$ mountain-nom [over-there Loc] tower]

Compare the following examples. We find a similar contrast to motion verbs showing that the Locative Phrase is obligatory.

(43) a. [mukoo-ni sobie-ru] yama-o   mite-goran
          there-at   tower-pres mountain-acc look-please
          'Look at the mountain that towers over there'
     b. ??[sobie-ru] yama-o   mite-goran
          tower-pres mountain-acc look-please

My tentative solution to the odd behavior of spatial verbs is to assume that the Locative head optionally moves to the verb head and binds off the event argument of the verb in a similar manner as the nonpast –*ta*.

7   Concluding Remarks

We have seen that different behaviors of fourth class verbs and their cousins in the availability of stative interpretations are explained by their semantic difference and structural difference between root and relative clauses.

We have based our discussion of statives on the works by Maienborn and others, who distinguish two ontologically different types of statives. In this respect, it is interesting to see other distinctions such as stage-level and individual-leve predicates discussed in the literature. For instance, Chierchia (1995) treats individual-level predicates as inherent generics and analyzed with an obligatory generic operator. He claims that this operator, when occurs with eventive verbs such as *smoke* and *run*, yields the so-called habitual interpretation. Putting aside the details, the following sentences are both analyzed with the generic operator.

(44) a.   John knows Mary.
     b.   John smokes.

The current data in Japanese go against such a unified treatment. Japanese behaves similarly to English in that its counterpart of (42b) has a habitual interpretation. If the same mechanism is available, we do not expect the observed odd behaviors of the fourth class and nonagetive motion verbs.

References

Abe, Y. 1993. Dethematized Subjects and Property Ascription in Japanese. *Language, Information and Computation; Prceedings of the Asuian Conference 1992*, ed. C. Lee and B. Kang, 132-144. Seoul: Thaehaksa.

Chierchia, G. 1995. Individual-Level Predicates as Inherent Generics. *The Generic Book*, eds. G. Carlson and F. J. Pelletier, 176-223. Chicago: University of Chicago Press.

Heim, I. 1985. Notes on Comparatives and Related Matters, ms. University of Texas at Austin.

Heim, I. 1999. Notes on Superlatives, ms. MIT.

Kim, J. 1969. Events and their Descriptions: Some Considerations. *Essays in the Honor of Carl G. Hempel*, ed., N. Rescher, 1980215. Dordrechit: Reidel.

Kindaichi, H. 1950. Kokugo Doosi no Itibunrui. (A classification of Japanese verbs) *Gengo Kenkyuu* 15: 48-63.

Kinsui, S. 1994. Rentai Syuusyoku-no '-ta'-nituite. (On noun modifying –ta) *Nihongo-no Meisiku Syuusyoku Hyoogen* (Noun modifying expressions in Japanese), ed. Y. Takubo, 29-66, Tokyo: Kurosio Publishing.

Kratzer, A. 1994. Severing the external argument from its verb. *Phrase Structure and the Lexicon*, eds. J. Rooryck and . Zaring 109-138. Dordrecht: Kluwer.

Kusumoto, K. 2001. The Semantics of Non-past *–ta* in Japanese. *Proceedings of the Third FAJL*, 163-180. Cambridge, Mass.: MIT Working Papers in Linguistics.

Kusumoto, K. 2003. The Semantics of *–teiru* in Japanese. *Japanese/Korean Linguistics* 11: 367-380.

Maienborn, C. 2005. On the Limits of the Davidsonian Approach: The Case of Copula Sentences. *Theoretical Linguistics* 31: 275-316.

Maienborn, C. 2008. On Davidosonian and Kimian States. *Existence: Semantics and Syntax,* eds. I. Comorovski and K. von Heusinger 107-130. Dordrecht: Springer.

Nishiyama, K. 1999. Adjectives and the Copulas in Japanese. *Journal of East Asian Linguistics* 8:183-222.

Ogawa, Y. 2004. The Simple Present Tense in Japanese and the Phonetically Empty Universal Quantifier. *Exploration in English Linguistics* 19.

Ogihara, T. 2004. Adjectival Relatives. *Linguistics and Philosophy* 27; 557-608.

Rothmayr A. 2009. *The Structure of Stative Verbs*. Amsterdam: John Benjamins.

Shimoyama, J. 2011. Degree Quantification and the Size of Noun Modifiers. *Japanese/Korean Linguistics* 18: 356-367.

Szabolcsi, A. 1986. Comparative Superatives. *MIT Working Papers in Linguistics* 8, ed. N. Fukui et al., 245-265. Cambridge, Mass.: MIT Working Papers in Linguistics.

Takahashi, T. 1973. Doosi-no Rentaikei 'suru' 'sita' nituite-no Iti-Kousatu (A note on noun modifying forms of verbs 'suru' and 'sita') *Kotoba-no Kenkyuu* (A study of language), 101-132. Tokyo: National Institute of Japanese Language and Linguistics.

Teramura, H. 1984. *Nihongo-no SIntakkusu-to Imi* II (The Syntax and Semantics of Japanese). Tokyo: Kuroshio Publishing.

Tsujimura, N. 2002. A Constructional Approach to Stativity in Japanese. *Studies in Language* 25: 601-629.

Yamakido, H. 2000. Japanese Attributive Adjectives are not (all) Relative Clauses. *Proceedings of WCCFL* 19: 588-602.

E-Type Anaphora of Degree in *Izyooni*(than)-Comparatives*

Toshiko Oda
Tokyo Keizai University

1 Introduction

Japanese comparatives have attracted wide attention in syntax and semantics. When it comes to clausal-comparatives, one of the central issues is how the standard of comparison is provided.

There are at least two assumptions regarding this question in the literature. One is that the standard of comparison is compositionally provided, as in the case of clausal *than*-comparatives in English. A comparative morpheme plays a central role under this assumption. (1) presents an invisible comparative morpheme that appears in clausal *yorimo*(than)-comparatives and (2) does

* This study is inspired by Yasutada Sudo (p.c.) and Erlewine and Gould (2013). I thank the audience of the talk at Eberhard Karls University, Tübingen, in August, 2013, where an earlier version of this paper was presented. I also thank the audience of Japanese/Korean Linguistics 23 at MIT in October 2013. I am especially grateful to Junko Shimoyama for her insightful comments on the presentation at JK23. All remaining errors are my own.

Japanese/Korean Linguistics 23.
Edited by Michael Kenstowicz, Theodore Levin and Ryo Masuda.

the same for clausal *izyooni*(than)-comparatives. [1] Both of these are practically the same as *-er* for clausal *than*-comparatives. In both cases, the standard degree of comparison is compositionally calculated by applying the maximality operator to the set of degrees provided by *yorimo*- or *izyooni*-clauses. This assumption is widely accepted in the analysis of Japanese clausal comparatives (Hayashishita 2007, Shimoyama 2012, a.o.).

(1.) $[\![\varnothing_{\text{-er}}]\!] = \lambda D_{<d,t>} \lambda D'_{<d,t>}.\max(D')>\max(D)$

(2.) $[\![izyooni(\text{than})]\!] = \lambda D_{<d,t>} \lambda D'_{<d,t>}.\max(D')>\max(D)^2$

(Hayashishita 2007:98)

Another assumption is that the standard of comparison is contextually provided. Beck et al. (2004) assume an invisible comparative morpheme such as the one in (3), where the standard of comparison is represented as c, a contextually given degree. The value of c is pragmatically inferred from the information given in a *yorimo*-clause. In other words, *yorimo*-clauses are not part of the compositional calculation, but are instead loosely connected to their matrix clauses via pragmatics.[3]

(3.) $[\![-er_J(c)]\!] = \lambda P \lambda x.\max(\lambda d.P(d)(x))>c$
  (where P is type $<d,<e,t>>$, an adjective meaning)

(Beck et al. 2004:329)

The purpose of this paper is to propose a third option. I will argue that in clausal *izyooni*-comparatives the standard of comparison is provided via E-type anaphora of degree. More specifically, there is E-type anaphora of degree in the complement of *izyooni*, and the standard degree of comparison is obtained by applying a maximality operator to a set of degrees provided by

---

[1] *Yorimo*(than)-comparatives and *izyooni*(than)-comparatives are different in that the former do not allow subcomparatives of degree, while the latter do and their embedded clauses have standard-oriented implication. See Hayashishita (2007) for more details.

[2] In Hayshishita (2007), *izyooni* 'than' is presented as *izyoo(ni)*. In this paper, however, I present it as *izyooni*, because *-ni* is obligatory in all of my examples, as in (i), which corresponds to (11) in the main text.

(i) X-wa [cpY-ga   nagai]-izyoo*(ni) nagai.
  X-Top [Y-Nom long]-than   long
  'X is longer than Y is.'

It is also worth noting that *-ni* must be deleted in some cases.

(ii) Watashi-wa kore-izyoo*(ni) aru-ke-nai,
  I-Top   this-than   walk-can-Neg
  'I cannot walk any more than this.'

[3] A contextually provided standard of comparison has been proposed only for clausal *yorimo*-comparatives, not for *izyooni*-comparatives.

the E-type anaphora. *Izyooni*-clauses are rather interpreted independently of their matrix clauses.

The organization of this paper is as follows. Section 2 reviews Shimoyama's (1999) E-type analysis of internally headed relative clauses (IHRCs) in Japanese. Practically the same analysis applies to clausal *izyooni*-comparatives. The only relevant difference between Shimoyama's analysis and ours is that in our case, relevant E-type anaphora denotes sets of degrees rather than sets of individuals. Section 3 presents evidence for our E-type analysis of *izyooni*-comparatives. In Section 3.1, I will argue that the positive interpretation of *izyooni*-clauses, which was first pointed out by Hayashishita (2007), is a natural outcome of the E-type analysis. Section 3.2 presents data for clausal *izyooni*-comparatives whose degree positions in their *izyooni*-clauses are filled by overt degree arguments. Some of these have ambiguous and context dependent interpretations, which is straightforwardly accounted for by assuming E-type anaphora of degree. Section 3.3 discusses clausal *izyooni*-clauses with wh-phrases. The interpretation of these suggests that the embedded clauses are interpreted as independent questions, providing another piece of evidence for the E-type analysis. Section 3.4 presents data where the relevant standard degree of comparison needs to be pragmatically calculated. Section 4 has some concluding remarks.

2 Framework: Shimoyama (1999)

I will follow the framework of E-type anaphora that Shimoyama (1999) proposes for the interpretation of IHRCs in Japanese. [4] Shimoyama's framework is built on Heim and Kratzer's (1999) analysis.[5] Let us consider their example.

(4.)   Every host bought just one bottle of wine and served it with the dessert.
   ⇨   For every host x, there is just one bottle y such that x bought y, and
       x served **the bottle that x brought** with the dessert.
            (Heim and Kratzer 1999:293, cited from Shimoyama 1999:165)

As shown in the following LF structure, the pronoun *it* is an E-type anaphor, which consists of the definite determiner *the* and two pronouns. *R* is a free pronoun that is given its interpretation via the assignment function g_c, while *pro* is bound by the antecedent *every host*. With these pronouns, the interpretation in which each host served his own bottle of wine is successfully derived.

---

[4] An analysis of IHRCs with E-type anaphora was originally proposed by Hoshi (1995).

[5] Heim and Kratzer (1999) follow the analysis of E-type anaphora by Cooper (1979).

(5.)

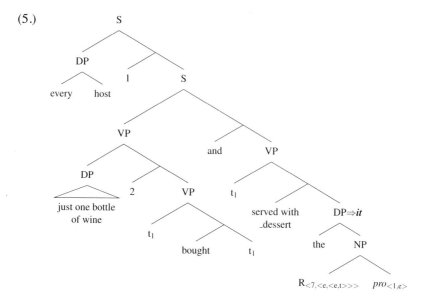

(Heim and Kratzer 1999:293, cited from Shimoyama 1999:165)

(6.) $g_c := [7 \rightarrow \lambda x \in D_e.\ \lambda y \in D_e.$ y is a bottle that x brought]

(Heim and Kratzer 1999:293, cited from Shimoyama 1999:165)

Shimoyama (1999) applies this analysis to IHRCs in Japanese. In (7), the external head *no* 'nominalizer' (henceforth NM) is coindexed with *dono shimbun-mo* 'every newspaper'. The interpretation of (7) indicates the involvement of E-type anaphora. *Them* in the translation refers to the newspapers Hanako bought.

(7.) Taro-wa [[$_{CP}$Hanako-ga [dono simbun-mo]$_i$ katte kita]-
Taro-Top [[Hanako-Nom [every newspaper] buy came]-
no$_i$]-o tana-ni narabeta.
NM]-Acc shelf-on placed
'Hanako bought and brought every newspaper, and Taro shelved *them*.'[6]

Under Shimoyama's analysis, the embedded clause of (7) is dislocated in the LF and interpreted as an independent clause. The unpronounced E-type anaphora *P* of type <e,t> in the complement of *no* receives its denotation via the assignment function.

---

[6] As for *and*, which logically connects two propositions, Shimoyama (1999) leaves its exact semantic mechanism open. Pragmatics may play a role in determining the relation. (fn.26, p. 179)

(8.)

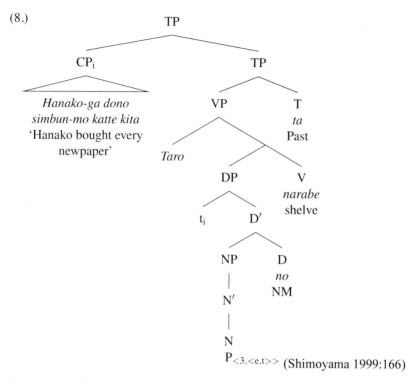

$P_{<3,<e,t>>}$ (Shimoyama 1999:166)

(9.) $g_c := [3 \rightarrow \lambda x \in D_e.$ x is newspapers that Hanako bought]

(Shimoyama 1999:167)

Shimoyama further assumes that the nominalizer *no* serves as a definite determiner. This brings the interpretation *the newspapers Hanako bought and brought*, which corresponds to *them* in the translation of (7).

(10.) $[\![no]\!]^{\,g} \in D_{<<e,t>,e>}$
       $[\![no]\!]^{\,g}$ (f) denotes the maximal individual *a* such that f(*a*)=1.

(Shimoyama 1999:167)

This E-type analysis is motivated by the fact that internal heads of IHRCs, like *dono shimbun* 'every news paper' in (7), do not move to the head position and thus do not show any scope interaction with other QPs in their matrix clauses. This is contra the so-called head-raising analysis.[7] Shimoyama's E-type analysis allows the internal head *dono shimbun* 'every newspaper' to

---

[7] The LF raising analysis of Japanese IHRC constructions was proposed by Ito (1986). LF raising analyses have also been adopted in analyzing IHRC constructions for Choctaw, Quechua, and other languages. See Lefebvre and Muysken (1988) and others.

remain clause internal and at the same time serve as the object of the matrix verb *narabeta* 'placed'.

Essentially the same analysis applies to *izyooni*-comparatives. In what follows, I will present four types of data that are best analyzed using E-type anaphora.

3 Evidence for E-Type Anaphora in *Izyooni*-Comparatives

3.1 *Izyooni*-Clauses with Predicative Adjectives as Positives

It has been pointed out by Hayashishita (2007) that predicative adjectives in *izyooni*-clauses have positive interpretations. Therefore, in (11), *Y* in the *izyooni*-clause is considered 'long'. In other words, it is longer than a contextually given standard length, $d_{\text{std-length in c}}$. Consequently, X in the matrix clause must be considered 'long' as well.

(11.) X-wa   [$_{CP}$Y-ga   nagai]-izyooni   nagai.
      X-Top   [Y-Nom   long]-than   long
      'X is longer than Y is.'
      (Implication: Both X and Y are long.)

Such standard-oriented implication in the *izyooni*-clause is a natural outcome if the clause is dislocated and interpreted independently of the matrix clause. In fact, the *izyooni*-clause in (11) can be uttered as an independent positive sentence, as shown in (12). The LF structure of (11) is given in (13).

(12.) Y-ga   nagai.
      Y-Nom   long
      'Y is long.'

(13.)

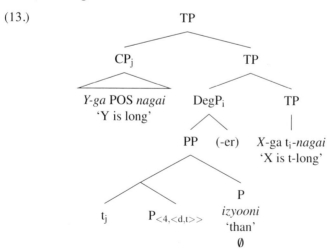

Importantly, the free variable P is type $<d,t>$. The function g_c assigns to the index a set of degree d such that Y is d-long and d is considered 'long'. The maximality operator, which is part of the lexical entry of the comparative operator, serves as a definite article and provides the interpretation of 'the degree of Y'. The truth conditions of the sentence are given in (16).

(14.) $g_c := [4 \rightarrow \lambda d \in D_d.$ Y is d-long $\wedge$ $d > d_{\text{std-length in c}}]$

(15.) $[\![\text{-er}_{\text{JPN}}]\!] = \lambda D_{<d,t>}. \lambda D'_{<d,t>}.\max(D') > \max(D)$

(16.) $[\![(13)]\!]^{\,g} = 1$ iff
　　　　$\exists d[$Y is d-long $\wedge$ $d > d_{\text{std-length in c}}] \wedge$
　　　　$\max(\lambda d.$ X is d-long$) > \max(\lambda d.$ Y is d-long $\wedge$ $d > d_{\text{std-length in c}})$

In short, the best paraphrase of the sentence (11) is 'Y is long, and X is longer than that'.

3.2　Ambiguous *Izyooni*-Clauses

The interpretation of E-type anaphora is context dependent. Our analysis predicts that ambiguity will arise when a context is complex enough. This prediction is borne out in this subsection, which shows that one *izyooni*-clause can have more than one interpretation depending on the denotation of the E-type anaphora assigned by g_c.

　　In the *izyooni*-clause in (17), the standard-oriented implication is visibly expressed by *maisuuseigen yorimo ni-peeji* 'two pages (more) than the page limit'.

(17.) X-wa　　[Y-ga　　**maisuuseigen yorimo ni-peeji**　　nagai]-izyooni
　　　　X-Top　[Y-Nom page.limit　　　than　　　two-page　　long]-than
　　　　nagai
　　　　long
　　　　Lit.'X is longer than Y is **two pages longer than the page limit**.'
　　　　(Implication: Y's length exceeds the page limit by two pages.)

The sentence compares the length of X and that of Y, which is two pages longer than (some given) page limit. A paraphrase of (17) is given in (18), where 'that' refers to 'two pages longer than the page limit'.

(18.) Y is **[two pages longer than the page limit]**$_i$, and X is longer than **that**$_i$.

This sentence is interpreted as comparing direct degrees, and it is judged true in the following scenario. These is a standard of comparison shared by X and Y, namely fifteen pages (the page limit). Y is two pages longer than the page limit, and X is longer than Y's length.

(19.)   X:|-------------------------------| 20 pages
              Y:|--------------------|17 pages
Page limit:|-----------------|15 pages

Notice that in (17) *maisuuseigen yorimo ni-peeji* 'two pages (more) than a page limit' seems to occupy the degree position of *nagai* 'long'. Such degree positions in 'than'-clauses are normally abstracted over and left as gaps, as shown in (20).

(20.)   X is longer than Y is.
          than-clause: [than [Op$_i$ Y is **d$_i$** ~~long~~]]

Under our E-type analysis, the filled degree position is not a problem, because the embedded clause is independently interpreted, as shown in the LF structure in (21).[8] Thus, degree abstraction is not necessary.

(21.)

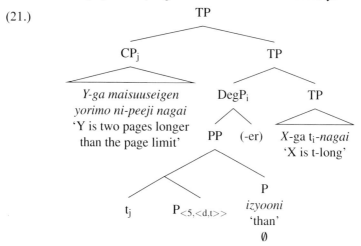

Importantly, g$_c$ assigns the index the denotation of a set of direct degrees.

---

[8] The embedded clause of (17) is well formed when uttered as an independent sentence.

(i) Y-ga   maisuuseigen yorimo   ni-peeji   nagai
    Y-Nom   page.limit   than   two-page   long
    'Y is two pages longer than the page limit.'

(22.) $g_c := [5 \rightarrow \lambda d \in D_d$. Y is d-long $\wedge$ d is two pages longer than the page limit]

(23.) $\llbracket (21) \rrbracket^g = 1$ iff $\exists d$[Y is d-long $\wedge$ d is two pages longer than the page limit] $\wedge$ max(λd. X is d-long) > max(λd.Y is d-long $\wedge$ d is two pages longer than the page limit)

Interestingly, the same *izyooni*-clause can be used to derive comparisons of differential degrees as well.[9] This flexibility strongly suggests the involvement of pragmatics. In (24), a *yorimo*-phrase is added in the matrix clause. Otherwise, it is identical to (17).

(24.) X-wa   [Y-ga   maisuuseigen yorimo **ni-peeji**   nagai]-izyooni
      X-top   [Y-Nom page.limit   than   two-page   long]-than
      [maisuuseigen   yorimo]   nagai.
      [page.limit   than]   long
      Lit. 'X is longer than a page limit (by) more than Y is two pages longer than a page limit.'

The sentence compares the gap between X and its relevant page limit and another gap between Y and its relevant page limit. An English paraphrase is given in (25) where 'that' refers to 'two pages'.

(25.) The length of Y exceeds (its relevant) page limit by **[two pages]**$_j$, and the length of X exceeds (its relevant) page limit by a larger number of pages than **that**$_j$.

(24) is judged true in the following scenario. Notice that in X's length is shorter than that of Y. This is because it is not absolute lengths that are being compared.

(26.)

                  X:|-----------------------------------|20 pages
      X's page limit:|-----------------------|15 pages
                  Y:|-------------------------------------|22 pages
      Y's page limit:|-----------------------------------|20 pages

---

[9] Hayashishita (2007) describes *izyooni*-comparatives as "comparisons of deviation", following Bierwisch (1989) and Kennedy (2001).

Again, notice that in (24) the differential degree position of the embedded clause (*ni-peeji* 'two pages') is filled. The embedded clause is independently interpreted; thus, degree abstraction is not necessary.[10]

(27.)

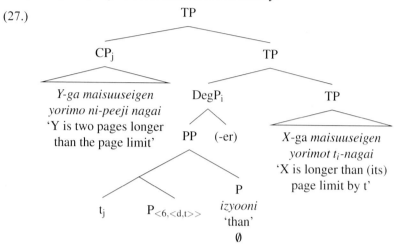

(28.) $g_c := [6 \rightarrow \lambda d \in D_d.$ Y is d-longer than Y's page limit $\wedge$ d=two pages]

(29.) $⟦(27)⟧^g = 1$ iff $\exists d[$Y is d-longer than Y's page limit $\wedge$ d=two pages] $\wedge$ max($\lambda d.$ X is d-longer than X's page limit) > max($\lambda d.$ Y is d-longer than Y's page limit $\wedge$ d=two pages)

Both a comparison of absolute degrees and a comparison of differential degrees can be derived from the same *izyooni*-clause, because the value of the free variable *P* can be flexibly determined by the assignment function g_c.

3.3   Degrees Given Only by Pragmatics

In some IHRCs, there is no obvious internal head, and so a relevant interpretation can be given only by resorting to pragmatics. In (30) Wasaburo read 3×n papers, where n is a number of students. There is no internal head that corresponds to 3×n; thus, it needs to be pragmatically calculated.

(30.) Wasaburo-wa   [dono gakusei-mo   peepaa-o   san-bon
      Wasaburo-Top   [every student   term.paper-Acc   three-CL
      dasita   no]-o   itiniti-de   yonda.
      turned.in   NM]-Acc   one.day-in   read
      'Every student turned in three term papers and Wasaburo read them
      in one day.'
                                               (Shimoyama 1999:176)

---

[10] The embedded clause of (24) is well-formed when uttered as an independent sentence, as already shown in ft. 8.

Parallel data is available in *izyooni*-clauses. The meaning of (31) described in (32) can be obtained only by pragmatically calculating the amount of money donated by Taro's classmates, that is, 500 yen×n.

(31.) Taro-wa   [minna-de   go-hyaku-en-zutu   kifu-o   sita]
      Taro-Top   [everyone-DE   five-hundred-yen-each donation-Acc   did]
      -izyooni takusan kifu-o   sita.
      -than   much   donation-Acc did
      'Everyone donated 500 yen each, and Taro made a bigger donation than that.'

(32.) Taro made a bigger donation than 500 yen×n, where n is the number of Taro's classmates.[11]

(33.) Set of degrees obtained by E-type anaphora:
      $\lambda d \in D_d.$ $\forall x.$ x is Taro's classmate $\wedge$ $|x|=n$ $\wedge$ donate(500 yen)(x) $\wedge$
      500 yen×n=d

3.4   *Izyooni*-Clauses with Wh-Phrases

When a wh-phrase appears within an *izyooni*-clause, it is expected under our E-type analysis that such clauses become wh-questions that are independent of their matrix questions, and that relevant E-type anaphora is paraphrased with a variable x. This is borne out.

Let us first see Shimoyama's example of IHRC. In (34) the subject of *nigedasita* 'ran away' is paraphrased by the definite description 'the cat that x brought along', where x ranges over people.

(34.) Taro-wa   [[[dare-ga   neko$_i$-o   turete kita]-no$_i$]-ga
      Taro-Top   [[[who-Nom   cat-Acc   brought.along]-NM]-Nom
      nigedasita   ka]   sitteiru.
      ran.away   Q]   know
      'Taro knows who$_x$ brought along a cat and that the cat that x brought along ran away.'   (Shimoyama 1999:159)

Here, (34) is compatible with (35) but not with (36). Shimoyama reports that for some speakers the sentence does not sound perfectly felicitous under the scenario in (36). I share this intuition.

(35.) Carol brought along Lucky, Yoko brought along Nyaaon, and Isadora brought along Spencer. Lucky, Nyaaon and Spencer ran away.
                                                          (Shimoyama 1999:160)

---

[11] Note that (31) seems to have another reading where Taro donated more than the amount that one single classmate donated, for example 600 yen. This reading is much more easily obtained when *takusan* 'much' is deleted. The ambiguity is explained on par with the data in 3.2.

(36.) Carol brought along Lucky, Yoko brought along Nyaaon, and Isadora brought along Spencer. Lucky and Nyaaon ran away.

(Shimoyama 1999:159)

In sentence (34), Taro has to know two sets of true propositions, as in (37); further, according to the first proposition, Taro has to know the complete answer to the question "Who brought along a cat?" The answer is in (38).

(37.) [that x brought along a cat] and [that the cat that x brought along ran away]

(38.) {that Carol brought along a cat, that Yoko brought along a cat, that Isadora brought along a cat}

Based on (38), Taro knows the following set of propositions. In other words, all the cats mentioned in (38) need to have run away.

(39.) {that the cat that Carol brought along ran away, that the cat that Yoko brought along ran away, that the cat that Isadora brought along ran away}

The point is that the set is different from the answer to a possible question when the embedded clause is *not* interpreted independently, namely *that a cat that x brought along ran away*, which cares only about runaway cats and does not ask for every single person who bought a cat. Thus, the question is compatible with the scenario in (36).

Parallel judgments are obtained in the case of *izyooni*-comparatives. Below, (40) is compatible with (41) but not with (42). The judgment of (40) under the scenario in (42) is very subtle, but I feel the same awkwardness for it that I do for (36). It is odd not to know what the situation is with Cathy when I utter (40). However, I admit that the judgment is not very clear and it needs to be clarified by more native speakers.

(40.) (Taro is coaching Hanako for the upcoming women's marathon. There will be many good runners, but Taro thinks that Hanako has a good chance to win the race, because:)

Taro-wa [[dare-ga hayai]-izyooni Hanako-ga hayai ka]
Taro-wa [[who-Nom fast]-than   Hanako-Nom fast Q]
sitteiru.
know
Lit. 'Taro knows Hanako is faster than x is fast.'
(Implication: x and Hanako are fast.)
(Taro knows that who$_x$ is fast and that Hanako is faster than the person x is.)

(41.) Amy, Beth, and Cathy are fast runners. Taro also knows that Hanako is faster than all three of them.

(42.) Taro knows that Amy, Beth, and Cathy are fast. He also knows that Hanako is faster than Amy and Beth.

Taro has to know two sets of true propositions of the form in (43), and the standard degree of comparison must contain a variable x that ranges over people.

(43.) [that x is fast] and [that Hanako is faster than x is]

According to the first proposition in (43), then, Taro has to know the complete answer to the question "Who is fast?"

(44.) {that Anne is fast, that Beth is fast, that Cathy is fast}

Consequently, Taro knows the following set of propositions.

(45.) {that Hanako is faster than Anna is, that Hanako is faster than Beth is, that Hanako is faster than Cathy is}

In summary, the parallelism between IHRC constructions and *izyooni*-comparatives suggests that both types of construction adopt the same mechanism, namely E-type anaphora.

4 Conclusion and Issues for Further Study

I have proposed that in clausal *izyooni*-comparatives, the value of the standard degree of comparison is provided by E-type anaphora of degree. The proposal accounts for the observed behaviors of *izyooni*-clauses, namely:

(46.) a. Predicative adjectives function in *izyooni*-clauses as positives
       b. Some *izyooni*-clauses are interpreted ambiguously
       c. Some degrees are obtained only by pragmatics
       d. *Izyooni*-clauses with wh-phrases function as independent questions

E-type anaphora is a new source of standard degrees of comparison in Japanese (that is, one other than the compositionally provided standard degrees and contextually provided standard degrees that have been suggested in previous studies).

   Our E-type analysis of *izyooni*-comparatives is quite different from conventional compositional analyses of clausal comparatives in Japanese, in that it relies more on pragmatics and does not necessarily require degree movement in the embedded clauses. This is contra Hayashishita (2007) and

Kubota (2012), who employ standard compositional analyses of clausal *izyooni*-comparatives.[12]

One serious problem that our E-type analysis of *izyooni*-comparatives comes across is the lack of appropriate constraints for their interpretations. In this paper, I have simply let g_c pick relevant degrees rather freely. However, this would give any interpretation to E-type anaphora. The first thing we might want to do is to check the already proposed constraints on E-type anaphora in IHRC constructions and see whether they also apply to *izyooni*-comparatives. In what follows I would like to give a list of some constraints on the interpretation of IHRCs proposed in the literature.

Hoshi (1995) points out that E-type pronouns in IHRC constructions require overtly realized NP antecedents in the preceding discourse. Shimoyama (1999) revised Hoshi's (1999) analysis, and argues that the properties recovered by E-type anaphora obligatory include the predicative part of the internal heads of IHRCs. Thus, non-predicative properties such as proper names cannot be heads of IHRCs. Shimoyama (2001) further argues that the denotations of E-type pronouns in IHRC constructions are restricted by the semantic roles of the embedded clauses. Kim (2007) proposes that there is a "formal link" between the main clauses and the embedded clauses of the IHRC constructions, via state variables.

It would also be worth investigating non-E-type analysis in IHRC constructions. Grosu and Landman (2012) may be of interest to us here. They assume a functional category called "ChR (choose role)." ChR re-opens closed embedded clauses of IHRC constructions by providing a variable to which abstraction can apply.

References

Beck, S., T. Oda, and K. Sugisaki 2004. Parametric Variation in the Semantics of Comparison: Japanese vs. English. *Journal of East Asian Linguistics* 13:289-344.

Bierwisch, M. 1989. The Semantics of Gradation. *Dimentional Ddjectives*, eds. M. Bierwisch and E. Lang, 71-261. Berlin: Springer.

Cooper, R. 1979. Interpretation of Pronouns. *Syntax and Semantics* 10:61-92.

Erlewine, M. Y. and I. Gould 2013. Domain Readings of Japanese Head-Internal Relative Clauses. *Paper presented at the 87th Meeting of the Linguistic Society of America.*

Grosu, A. and F. Landman 2012. A Quantificational Discourse approach to Japanese and Korean Internally Headed Relatives. *Journal of East Asian Linguistics* 21:159-196.

---

[12] Hayashishita (2007) and Kubota (2012) differ in that the former considers *izyooni*-comparatives as comparisons of deviation, whereas the latter considers them as comparisons of absolute degrees with standard-oriented presuppositions. See Kubota (2012) for details.

Hayashishita, J.-R. 2007. *Izyoo(ni)-* and *Gurai-* Comparatives: Comparison of Deviation in Japanese. *Gengo Kenkyu* 132:77-109.

Heim, I. and A. Kratzer 1999. *Semantics in Generative Grammar*. Oxford: Blackwell.

Hoshi, K. 1995. Structural and Interpretive Aspects of Head-Internal and Head-External Relative Clauses. Doctoral dissertation, University of Rochester.

Ito, J. 1986. Head-Movement at LF and PF. *University of Massachusetts Occasional Papers in Linguistics* 11:109-138.

Kennedy, C. 2001. Polar Opposition and the Ontology of 'Degrees'. *Linguistics and Philosophy* 24:33-70.

Kim, M.-J. 2007. Formal Linking in Internally-Headed Relatives. *Natural Language Semantics* 15:279-315.

Kubota, Y. 2012. The Presuppositional Nature of *Izyoo(-ni)* and *Gurai* Comparatives: A Note on Hayashishita (2007). *Gengo Kenkyu* 141:33-46.

Lefebvre, Claire and Pieter Muysken. 1988. *Mixed Categories: Nominalizations in Quechua*. Dordrecht: Kluwer Academic Publishing.

Shimoyama, J. 1999. Internally Headed Relative Clauses in Japanese and E-Type Anaphora. *Journal of East Asian Linguistics* 8:147-182.

Shimoyama, J. 2001. Wh-Constructions in Japanese. Doctoral dissertation, University of Massachusetts, Amherst.

Shimoyama, J. 2012. Reassessing Crosslinguistic Variation in Clausal Comparatives. *Natural Language Semantics* 20:83-113.

von Stechow, A. 1984. Comparing Semantic Theories of Comparison. *Journal of Semantics* 3:1–77.

On Two Varieties of Negative Polar Interrogatives in Japanese[*]

SATOSHI ITO
Cornell University

DAVID Y. OSHIMA
Nagoya University

1 Introduction

It has been observed in the literature (Ladd 1981, Romero and Han 2004, among others) that negative polar interrogatives often convey an epistemic bias toward a specific answer, and that the bias could be either toward a positive or negative answer.

(1) Isn't Ken home?

    a. 'I expect Ken to be home – am I correct?' (positive bias)

    b. 'I infer that Ken is not home – am I correct?' (negative bias)

This work demonstrates that Japanese has two varieties of the negative polar interrogative that are differentiated *information-structurally* as well as *tonally*, and discusses semantic properties of each type.

---

[*] Thanks to John Whitman, Christopher Tancredi, Makoto Kanazawa, Mats Rooth, Dorit Abusch, Christopher Davis, Hyun Kyung Huang, and the audience of JK23 for valuable comments. All remaining errors are our own.

Japanese/Korean Linguistics 23.
Edited by Michael Kenstowicz, Theodore Levin and Ryo Masuda.

2 Three Interpretations of Negative Polar Interrogatives

The seminal work by Ladd (1981) demonstrates that there are two varieties of negative polar interrogatives. With one version (which he calls the "outside NEG" question), "the speaker believes a proposition **P** and wants confirmation" and "what is being questioned is the speaker's belief **P**". With the other (the "inside NEG" question), "the speaker has just inferred a proposition ¬**P**" and "what is being questioned is the inference ¬**P**". He also points out that the "outside NEG" type is compatible with positive polarity items (PPIs) such as *too* but not with negative polarity items (NPIs) such as *either*, and the opposite pattern holds for the "inside NEG" type. The following examples, adapted from Romero and Han (2004), illustrate this point.

(2) A: Ok, now that Stephen has come, we are all here. Let's go!

B: Isn't Jane coming too?   ("outside NEG")

(3) A: Pat is not coming. So we don't have any phonologists in the program.

B: Isn't Jane coming either?   ("inside NEG")

Romero and Han (2004) point out that some negative polar interrogatives do not carry an epistemic bias. In languages such as English and Spanish, while negative polar interrogatives with preposed negation (e.g., *Won't he come?*) always convey a positive or negative epistemic bias, ones with non-preposed negation (e.g., *Will he not come?*) allow a "neutral" interpretation.

(4) (**Situation**: B is organizing a party and is in charge of supplying all the non-alcoholic beverages for teetotalers. She is going through a list of people that are invited. She has no previous belief or expectation about their drinking habits.)

A: Jane and Mary do not drink.

B: OK. What about John? {Does he not/#Doesn't he} drink (either)?

(Romero and Han 2004: 610)

Unbiased negative polar interrogatives are compatible with an NPI, as shown in (4B), but not with a PPI (ibid.: 621–622). Romero and Han do not elaborate on the discourse conditions under which unbiased negative polar interrogatives are felicitous; we suggest that they are appropriate only when the meaning of the negated predicate — in the case of (4), 'not drink', or $\lambda w[\lambda x[\neg\textbf{drink}(x, w)]]$ — is contextually prominent. Table 1 summarizes the points discussed so far.

In the following, we will tentatively adopt the rather simple definitions of the two kinds of epistemic biases presented in (5). We will look into more

kind of epistemic bias	positive	negative	no bias
Ladd's label	outside NEG	inside NEG	(inside NEG)
NPI licensing	no	yes	yes
PPI licensing	yes	no	no
preposed negation	OK	OK	*
non-preposed negation	OK	OK	OK

TABLE 1 Three interpretations of negative polar interrogatives

subtle aspects of meanings conveyed by negative polar interrogatives in Sections 7 and 8.

(5) a. **Positive epistemic bias**: Speaker considers **P** to be likely,[1] where **P** is the proposition denoted by the radical of the negative polar interrogative minus the negation.
(e.g., for the negative polar interrogative with a positive bias: *Isn't Ken home (already)?*, **P** will roughly be: $\lambda w[\textbf{home}(\textbf{ken}, w)]$)

b. **Negative epistemic bias**: Speaker considers **P** to be likely, where **P** is the proposition denoted by the radical of the negative polar interrogative.
(e.g., for the negative polar interrogative with a negative bias: *Isn't Ken home (yet)?*, **P** will roughly be: $\lambda w[\neg\textbf{home}(\textbf{ken}, w)]$)

We will use the term "core proposition" in the sense of **P** in (5a), and the term "proposition denoted by the radical" in the sense of **P** in (5b).

3 Two Varieties of Japanese Negative Polar Interrogatives

The central claim of the current work is that Japanese has two tonally differentiated varieties of the negative polar interrogative, and this tonal contrast has an information-structural basis.[2]

To illustrate the two varieties with an example, (6) will have different tonal properties in contexts (7) and (8).[3] Actual tokens are presented in Figure 1.[4]

---

[1] See Lassiter (2011) for discussion of the semantics of 'likely'.

[2] The existence of two semantic varieties of Japanese polar interrogatives was first pointed out by Kuno (1973: 273–281), who discusses (i) negative questions that are "semantically neutral" and (ii) ones that "contain the questioner's expectation of a positive answer".

[3] The abbreviations in the glosses are: Acc = accusative, Aux = auxiliary, Ben = benefactive, Cop = copula, Dat = dative, DP = discourse particle, Ger = gerund, Inf = infinitive, Ipfv = imperfective, Neg = negation, Nom = nominative, Plt = polite, Prs = present, Pst = past, Top = topic.

[4] The adjective form *amaku* has multiple accepted accent patterns (see fn.8); the tokens of *amaku* here happen to be accented on /ma/.

(6) Amaku   nai?
    sweet.Inf NegAux.Prs
    'Isn't it sweet?'

(7) A is eating an orange. B has heard that oranges this year are excep-
    tionally sweet (although he has not eaten one so far). B utters (6).

(8) A eats a piece of orange and makes a grimace. B utters (6).

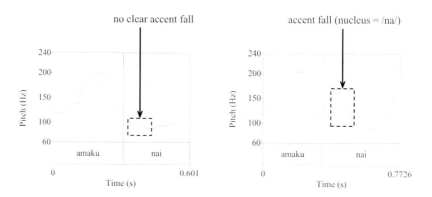

FIGURE 1 "Amaku nai?" uttered in situations (7) (left) and (8) (right)

The key contrast here is the absence/presence of the steep pitch fall within
the string /nai/ that is attributable to the accent nucleus on the mora /na/. In
more general terms, the two varieties of Japanese negative polar interrogative contrast in the size of pitch movements within the phrase containing the
negation that are caused by a phrase tone[5] and/or a lexical accent (but not
by an utterance-final intonation, namely a question rise). In one of them, the
movements are often compressed (Section 5 discusses cases where the compression does not take place); in the other, they are retained.[6]

The former often (but not always; Section 8) conveys a positive epistemic
bias, as in (6) uttered in context (7); we will refer to it as the P-type (positive
type). The latter often conveys a negative epistemic bias, as in (6) uttered in
context (8), but is compatible with the neutral interpretation, as shown in (9);
we will refer to this type as the NN-type (negative/neutral type).

(9) (**Situation**: A and B are organizing a Japanese sake party. Having
    been asked to bring some bottles of sweet sake to the party venue, B

[5] A phrase tone is the rise that takes place after the first mora within an accent phrase except
when the first mora carries an accent nucleus (Venditti 2005, Vance 2008).

[6] The term "(tonal) compression" will be understood to subsume total disappearance, as well as
mere subdual/weakening, of pitch movements.

comes to the liquor storage room. She does not know which bottles
are sweet and which are not, so asks A for help.)

A: Kore-to kore-wa amaku   nai.
   this-and this-Top sweet.Inf Neg.Prs
   'This one and this one are not sweet.'

B: Kore-wa? Amaku   nai?
   this-Top   sweet.Inf Neg.Prs
   'How about this one? Is it not sweet?'

(10) and (11) are additional examples of the P-type and the NN-type, respectively; *warito* 'quite' in (10) is a PPI, or at least has a strong tendency to
occur in positive contexts, and *amari* 'particularly' in (11) is an NPI.

(10)   Ano hito,   warito tetsudatte kurenai?
       that person quite   help.Ger BenAux.Neg.Prs
       'Isn't he pretty helpful?'

(11)   Ano hito,   amari   tetsudatte kurenai?
       that person particularly help.Ger BenAux.Neg.Prs
       'Is he not so helpful?'

Observe that in (10) not only the lexical accent but also the phrase tone
(the potential rise after /ku/) within /kurenai/ is suppressed (Figure 2).

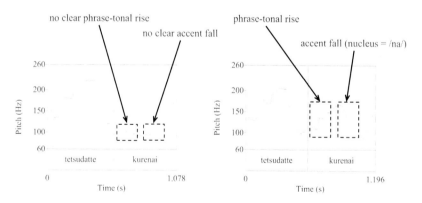

FIGURE 2 The string "tetsudatte kurenai" in (10) (left) and (11) (right)

It is worth mentioning that the P-type and NN-type are answered differently. When the core proposition of the P-type holds, the answer is "yes", as
in the case of English negative interrogatives. When the core proposition of
the NN-type holds, the answer is "no" (cf. Kuno 1973: 280).

(12) (in reply to (6) uttered in context (7))

a. Un, amai.
    yes sweet.Prs
    'Yes, it is sweet.'

b. Iya, amaku   nai.
    no sweet.Inf NegAux.Prs
    'No, it is not sweet.'

(13) (in reply to (6) uttered in context (8))

a. Un, amaku   nai.
    yes sweet.Inf NegAux.Prs
    'Yes, it is not sweet.'

b. Iya, amai.
    no sweet.Prs
    'No, it is sweet.'

In the next section, we review certain facts about the relation between prosody and information structure in Japanese, which are relevant to a better understanding of the P/NN-distinction.

4   Tonal Compression and Focus/Ground Configuration

The tonal contrast between the P- and NN-types can be attributed to the independently attested phenomenon known as *post-focus reduction* (Kori 1997, Sugahara 2003), whereby phrase-tonal rises and lexical accent falls within the phrases following the information-structural focus are obligatorily compressed.[7] The term "phrase" here refers to a syntactic word potentially followed by one or more particles (e.g., case particle).

To exemplify, when sentence (14) is uttered in reply to "When did you go to Rome last year?", the two phrases following the focus phrase (*haru*) must be tonally compressed, as in (15) (square brackets indicate phrase boundaries; apostrophes indicate lexical accent nuclei; boldface indicates focushood, which implies retention of pitch movements; italicization indicates obligatory tonal compression).

(14) Kyonen-wa   haru   Rooma-ni ikimashita.
      last.year-Top spring Rome-Dat go.Pst.Plt
      'Last year, I went to Rome in the spring.'   (Kori 1997: 173)

(15) Q: "When did you go to Rome last year?"

      A: [kyo'nenwa] [**ha'ru**] [*ro'omani*] [*ikima'shita*]

"Phrases" syntactically defined here typically correspond to accent phrases (APs) in the sense of Venditti (2005) and Vance (2008). It is commonly acknowledged that under certain conditions multiple syntactic phrases may be merged into a single accent phrase; this process is called *dephrasing*. Thus,

---

[7] Non-focus (ground) phrases *preceding* the focus may undergo tonal compression, but only optionally (Kori 1997).

at least in theory, it is possible for *Rooma-ni* and *ikimashita* in (14) to form, or belong to, a single AP. For the purpose of the current paper, the issue of AP-phrasing can be safely put aside; we remain neutral about the question of how tonal compression is related to dephrasing.

We propose (i) that in the P-type, the phrase containing the negation is *part of ground* (i.e., not part of the focus), so that it is tonally compressed, and (ii) that in the NN-type, the phrase containing the negation is *part of the focus*, so that it is not tonally compressed.[8]

(16)   The P-type

   a.   (6) in context (7): {[**amaku**]/[**a᾿maku**]/[**ama᾿ku**]} [*na᾿i*]

   b.   (10): ... [**tetsuda᾿tte**] [*kurena*$^{(᾿)}$*i*]

(17)   The NN-type

   a.   (6) in context (8): {[**amaku**]/[**a᾿maku**]/[**ama᾿ku**]} [**na᾿i**]

   b.   (11): ... [**tetsuda᾿tte**] [**kurena**$^{(᾿)}$**i**]

At the present time, we are not certain how exactly groundhood and focushood of negation lead to the positive and negative biases, respectively. It can be said, however, that the focushood of the negation in the NN-type is resonant with the fact that the NN-type is compatible with an NPI but not with a PPI. As pointed out by Kori (1997: 182), a negated predicate — in the case of a complex predicate where the auxiliary carries negation, both main and auxiliary predicates — tends to be part of the focus and not tonally compressed.[9]

(18)   (in reply to: "Why don't you ask John for help?")

   Ano hito-wa   kitto   tetsudatte kurenai-yo.
   that person-Top probably help.Ger BenAux.Neg.Prs-DP

   'He probably won't give me a hand.'
   ... [**tetsuda᾿tte**] {[**kurena᾿iyo**]/[**kurenai᾿yo**]}

A positive auxiliary, in contrast, tends to be part of ground and thus tonally compressed.

---

[8] Some predicate forms, including *amaku* and *kurenai*, have multiple accepted accent patterns (Vance 2008: 162–180). An apostrophe put between parentheses (e.g., [ama$^{(᾿)}$i]) indicates that the versions with and without a lexical accent are both acceptable.

[9] It is possible for a negative predicate to be part of ground, as in *Hiroshi-ga konai.* 'Hiroshi will not come.' uttered in reply to *Dare-ga konai-no?* 'Who will not come?'

(19)   (in reply to: "Were you able to finish your work by yourself?")

Iya, Hiroshi-ga tetsudatte kureta-yo.
no H.-Nom   help.Ger BenAux.Pst-DP

'No, Hiroshi gave me a hand.'
… [**tetsuda'tte**] [*kureta'yo*]

Thus, the negation in the NN-type patterns the same as the negation in a declarative in two respects: (i) it has the ability to license an NPI while it is not compatible with a PPI, and (ii) it is part of the focus. The negation in the P-type, on the other hand, lacks both properties. The tonal contrast and the occurrence patterns of PPIs/NPIs concurrently suggest that, in the pretheoretical sense, the negation in the NN-type is a "genuine" or "true" negation, while that in the P-type is "fake".

5   Tonal Neutralization

In the examples of the P- and NN-types presented so far, the negation occurs on an auxiliary predicate. In (6), the negative auxiliary *nai* follows the infinitive form (also called the adverbial form) of an adjective. In (10), the derivational negation affix /(a)na/ occurs within the auxiliary *kureru*, which follows the gerund form (also called the *te*-form) of the main verb.

The exactly same tonal contrast can be observed with other constructions where negation is expressed on the auxiliary; i.e., the copular construction where the copula *da* follows a noun or a nominal adjective (e.g., *Shinsetsu-ja nai?* 'Isn't he kind?'), and complex verbs with an auxiliary (that selects for a gerund form) other than *kureru*, e.g., V-(*i*)*te iru* 'be V-ing, have V-ed', V-(*i*)*te miru* 'try V-ing', V-(*i*)*te shimau* 'end up V-ing'.

Things are more complicated with constructions with "simple" verbs, whose negative forms, as well as positive forms, do not involve an auxiliary. For these constructions, the retention of pitch movements within the phrase containing the negation does not guarantee the NN-interpretation (while the tonal compression does guarantee the P-interpretation). To illustrate with an example, utterance (20) is felicitous not only in context (21), where the NN-type is expected, but also in context (22), where the P-type is expected. In other words, in this case the tonal contrast between the two types is neutralized.

(20)   Iwashi tabenakatta?
sardine eat.Neg.Pst
'Didn't she eat the sardine?'
… [**tabe'nakatta**]

(21)   Mrs. Abe gave sardine to her cat. 15 minutes later, Mr. Abe notices that the sardine is still in her food bowl. He asks his wife (20).

verb stem	negation	tonal compression	example
in focus	in focus (= NN-interpretation)	no	(20) in (21)
in focus	in ground (= P-interpretation)	no	(20) in (22)
in ground	in ground (= P-interpretation)	yes	(23)

TABLE 2 Focus/ground configurations within simple verbs in their negative forms

(22) In the morning, Mrs. Abe tells her husband that she will give sardine to their new cat, who has been fussy about her food. Later in the day, Mr. Abe comes across the previous owner of the cat and learns that she loves sardine and never refuses to eat it. He comes home in the evening and asks his wife (20).

The neutralization happens because tonal compression takes place only when all semantic components of the phrase are ground. The negative form of a simple verb has, as its sematic components, the meaning of the verb stem and the negation, among others; tonal compression happens only when both components are ground (Table 2).

(23) illustrates a case where the meaning of the verb stem and the negation are both parts of ground; in such a case, the P-interpretation is singled out.

(23) (in reply to: "The cat had mackerel for her dinner yesterday.")

E? Iwashi-o   tabenakatta?
huh sardine-Acc eat.Neg.Pst

'Huh? Didn't she eat sardine?'
... [**iwashio**] [*tabe'nakatta*]

6 Attachment of *No/Noda*

Negative polar interrogatives, like declaratives and other kinds of interrogatives, may be accompanied by the discourse particle *no* or the auxiliary *noda*, which have largely overlapping functions. (The semantic effect of addition of *no/noda* is a complicated matter and will not be discussed here.)

The NN- and P-types exhibit interesting differences in the ways in which they are combined with *no/noda* (cf. Kuno 1973: 278). When *no* or *noda* follows a negated predicate, as in (24), the NN-interpretation is singled out.[10]

---

[10] The construction where *no/noda* follows a negated copula exceptionally allows the P-interpretation, as well as the NN-interpretation.

(i) Kore, tamago-ja   nai-no?
     this   egg-Cop.Inf NegAux.Prs-*no*
     'Isn't this an egg?'

(24)　Amaku　nai-{no/ndesu-ka}?
　　　sweet.Inf NegAux.Prs-{*no/noda*.Prs.Plt-DP}
　　　'Isn't it sweet?' (the NN-interpretation only)
　　　{[**amaku**]/[a`maku]/[ama`ku]} {[**na`ino**]/[na`indesuka**]}

When *noda* is negated, in contrast, the P-interpretation is preferred.

(25)　Amai-nja　　　　　nai(-desu-ka)?
　　　sweet.Prs-*noda*.Inf NegAux.Prs-PltAux.Prs-DP
　　　'Isn't it sweet?' (the P-interpretation preferred)
　　　{[ama`inja]/[amai`nja]} [*na`i(desuka)*]
　　　??{[ama`inja]/[amai`nja]} [na`i(desuka)]

It is possible for a polar interrogative with negated *noda* to be further followed by *no* or (another instance of) *noda*; in such cases, prosody determines the interpretation.

(26)　Amai-nja　　　　　nai-{no/ndesu-ka}?
　　　sweet.Prs-*noda*.Inf NegAux.Prs-{*no/noda*.Prs.Plt-DP}
　　　'Isn't it sweet?'
　　　... [**na`ino**]/[**na`indesuka**] ⇒ the NN interpretation
　　　... [*na`ino*]/[*na`indesuka*] ⇒ the P interpretation

7　More on the Meaning of the NN-type Interrogative

In this section, we will take a closer look at the function of the NN-type on its "negative" (as opposed to "neutral") interpretation.

It has been claimed in the literature (Ladd 1981, Romero and Han 2004, among others) that the English inside-NEG interrogative (with a negative epistemic bias) is felicitous only if the negative bias is formed in the discourse situation, rather than had been present beforehand. This "inference on the spot" condition is relevant to the NN-type interrogative in Japanese too. (27), for example, is felicitous in context (28), but not in context (29) (note that the "inference on the spot" condition is met only in the former).

(27)　Hottodoggu-ya-san, kite　　　(i)nakatta?
　　　hotdog-seller-Suffix come.Ger IpfvAux.Neg.Pst
　　　'Wasn't the hotdog vendor there?'
　　　... [**ki`te**] [**(i)na`katta**]

[kore] [**tama`goja**] [**na`ino**] ⇒ the NN-interpretation
[kore] [**tama`goja**] [*na`ino*] ⇒ the P-interpretation

This fact is resonant with Noda's (1997: 83) observation that under certain discourse conditions, the use of *noda* is compulsory in verbal constructions but is optional in copular constructions. That is, (i) on the P-interpretation can be understood to be formed by "omitting" *noda* (*nja*) from "*Kore tamago-na-nja nai-no?*" (cf. (26)).

(28) In most days, a hotdog wagon comes to the park near the office where A and B work. One afternoon, A says to B: "Let's have lunch. I'll go get us hotdogs". A few minutes later, A comes back with boxes of Chinese food, instead of hotdogs, in his hand. B utters (27).

(29) A and B work in the same office. In most days, in the lunch break A goes to a hotdog wagon in the nearby park and eats there. B has heard the rumor that the hotdog vendor has been ill. When A comes back to the office after the lunch break, B utters (27).

Note that in context (29), the P-type interrogatives (30a,b), whose denotational meanings are roughly equivalent to that of the NN-type interrogative (27), will be felicitous.

(30) a. Hottodoggu-ya-san, yasumi-ja   nakatta?
          hotdog-seller-Suffx day.off-Cop.Inf NegAux.Pst
          'Wasn't the hotdog vendor on a day off?'
          . . . [**yasumi'ja**] [*na'katta*]

      b. Hottodoggu-ya-san, kite   naku   nakatta?
          hotdog-seller-Suffx come.Ger IpfvAux.Neg.Inf NegAux.Pst
          'Wasn't the hotdog vendor not there?'
          . . . [**ki'te**] [**na'ku**] [*na'katta*]

Unlike the English inside-NEG interrogative, however, the NN-type can also be used when (the "inference on the spot" condition is not met but) the speaker considers the proposition denoted by the radical *both likely and desirable*.

(31) (**Situation**: A and B have been working all day in a room without a window. They hope that it is not raining. They believe that it is unlikely to be raining on the basis of the morning weather forecast, but still are worried that it might. Around 2 p.m., A goes out to check the weather and comes back. B asks A:)

      Doo? Futte   nakatta?
      how   fall.Ger Ipfv.Neg.Pst

      'How was it? Was it raining? (lit. Wasn't it raining?)'
      . . . [**fu'tte**] [**na'katta**]

It must be noted that the desirability alone is not a sufficient condition of the felicitous use of the NN-type. In the context of (31), speaker B would not use the NN-type if he had estimated the chance of rain to be, say, 80%.

8 More on the Meaning of the P-type Interrogative

The P-type interrogative has several other uses besides the "positive epistemic bias" use, so that it may occur in certain environments where the English "outside NEG" interrogative may not.

8.1 The P-type and Information Gaps

The P-type has a distinct use where it does not convey an epistemic bias but indicates that the speaker considers the core proposition possible based on some information that may not be available to the hearer.[11]

(32) (**Situation**: The speaker is looking for her friend Yamada. She has been informed that Yamada is visiting one of the 10 residents on the second floor of the dormitory, but does not know in which room he actually is. She decides to check the rooms one by one. She first goes to room #201, and asks the resident:)

Nee, Yamada-kun kite   nai?
hey Y.-Suffix   come.Ger IpfvAux.Neg.Prs

'Hey, is Yamada here?' (lit. 'Hasn't Yamada come?')
. . . [**ki'te**] [*na'i*]

Note that in (32), the chance of the core proposition's holding is a mere 10%; the speaker will likely be surprised by her good luck if the answer is "yes". In the same situation an English negative polar interrogative ("Isn't Yamada here?") would be infelicitous.

The effect of using the P-type in such a situation is similar to adding a phrase like: "You may be surprised by my asking this, but (is **P** the case?)" or "I have a reason to suspect that **P** is the case. (Is it?)". It preemptively justifies the speaker's asking a question in a situation where the hearer might think it is unreasonable for her to even suspect that the core proposition holds. Indeed,

---

[11] Note that the P-type can be licensed either by the "information gap" condition (described here) alone or the "positive epistemic bias" condition alone. Example (i) is a case where only the latter is met.

(1) (**Situation**: The speaker comes into her office, which she shares with her colleagues Yamada and Suzuki. Suzuki is sitting at his desk. Yamada is supposed to take a day off today, but she notices that Yamada's bag in on his chair. The bag is visible from Suzuki too. She asks Suzuki:)

Are, Yamada-kun kite   nai?
oh   Y.-Suffix   come.Ger IpfvAux.Neg.Prs

'Oh, isn't Yamada here?'
. . . [**ki'te**] [*na'i*]

in the context of (32), the corresponding positive polar interrogative would sound a little abrupt and less natural.

8.2 The P-type as a Means of Expressing One's Belief

The P-type interrogative has a use whereby the speaker expresses her belief, opinion, or judgment. Compared to regular statements in the form of declaratives, P-type interrogatives in this "expression of belief" use appear to convey the speaker's wish to avoid being overly self-assertive.[12]

(33) (**Situation**: A and B are eating cookies that their colleague brought to their office. A finds the cookies distasteful, and says:)

    a. Kore, mazuku   nai?
       this   distasteful.Inf NegAux.Prs
       'Doesn't this taste bad?'
       {[**mazuku**]/[**mazu`ku**]/[**ma`zuku**]} [*na`i*]

    b. Kore, oishiku naku   nai?
       this   tasty.Inf NegAux.Inf NegAux.Prs
       'Doesn't this not taste good?'
       [**oishi**$^{(`)}$**ku**] [**na**$^{(`)}$**ku**] [*na`i*]

One might be tempted to consider the illustrated use as a mere pragmatic effect (conversational implicature) of the P-type as a question. It can be shown, however, that there is a conventional aspect in it. If (33a,b) have the illocutionary force of question, they would be interchangeable with the NN-type interrogative given in (34), which has the antonymous propositional content. This prediction is not borne out; (34) would not be acceptable in the same situation.

(34) Kore, oishiku nai?
     this   tasty.Inf NegAux.Prs
     'Doesn't this taste good?'
     [**oishi**$^{(`)}$**ku**] [**na`i**]

Note that the speaker's inclination to the belief: "The cookies do not taste good (they taste bad)" is formed in the discourse situation, implying that the unacceptability of (34) in the described situation cannot be attributed to the "inference on the spot" condition discussed in Section 7.

---

[12] Based on experimental data, Hara and Kawahara (2012) propose that the unaccented pronunciation of the adjective (e.g., [amaku] rather than [a`maku] or [ama`ku]; see fn.8) in its infinitive form tends to be chosen when "public evidence" for the core proposition is available in the discourse situation. Their experimental findings seem compatible with the alternative interpretation that the unaccented pronunciation of the adjective is preferred when a P-type interrogative receives the "expression of belief" interpretation.

The P-type interrogative with *noda* (see Section 6) can likewise be used as a statement, but it conveys that the speaker merely infers, rather than believes, the core proposition. In the context of (35), the P-type interrogative with *noda* is appropriate while the one without it (*Chuushi-ni naranai?*) would be less natural.

(35) (**Situation**: A and B are talking about the outdoor concert scheduled tomorrow. A asks B: "What will happen if it rains tomorrow?" B does not know the answer, and says:)

Shiranai.   Chuushi-ni   naru-nja
know.Neg.Prs cancellation-Cop.Inf become.Prs-*noda*.Inf
nai?
NegAux.Prs

'I don't know. I guess it will be canceled.'

8.3   The P-type as a Means of Making a Suggestion or Polite Request

The P-type interrogative is commonly used to make a suggestion or polite request (Nihongo Kijutsu Bunpo Kenkyukai 2007: 296–298). Comparing (36a) and (36b), the latter would be a more natural choice in most situations where the speaker's intention is to suggest the hearer to go to the café, rather than seeking information about his current plan. (37a,b) are both naturally interpreted as requests, but the negative version sounds more polite.[13]

(36) Kafe, yotte   {a. iku/   b. ikanai}?
      café stop.by.Ger go.Prs go.Neg.Prs
      a. 'Are you going to stop by the café?'
      b. 'How about stopping by the café?'

(37) Ato-de tetsudatte {a. kureru/   b. kurenai}?
      later help.Ger   BenAux.Prs BenAux.Neg.Prs
      '{a. Will/b. Would} you give me a hand later?'

It is worth noting that in English it is much less common to use negative polar interrogatives for the purpose of making a suggestion/request (cf. "Won't you come visit me?").

9   Summary

We have demonstrated that Japanese has two distinct varieties of negative polar interrogatives: the P-type and the NN-type. In the P-type, the negation is

---

[13] For the "request" interpretation of (37a,b), the presence of the benefactive auxiliary *kureru* is essential. The potential form of another benefactive auxiliary verb *morau* could instead be used (*Ato-de tetsudatte {moraeru/moraenai}?*).

part of ground; this information-structural property is often reflected by tonal compression of the word containing the negation morpheme. The P-type is similar to the English outside-NEG interrogative, in that it often conveys a positive epistemic bias, and is compatible with a PPI. However, its distribution and functions are not exactly the same as those of the outside-NEG interrogative; it can, for example, be used to make a polite request.

In the NN-type, the negation is part of the focus, so that the tonal movements within the word containing the negation morpheme are always retained. The NN-type is similar to the English inside-NEG interrogative, in that it often conveys a negative epistemic bias, and may contain a NPI. Like the English negative polar interrogative with non-preposed negation, the NN-type allows the neutral interpretation when the meaning of the negated predicate is contextually prominent. On the negative-bias interpretation, it indicates either that the bias has been formed in the discourse situation, or that the speaker considers the proposition denoted by the radical desirable.

References

Hara, Y. and Kawahara, S. 2012. The Prosody of Public Evidence in Japanese: A Rating Study. *Proceedings of the 29th West Coast Conference on Formal Linguistics*, 353–361. Somerville: Cascadilla Press.

Kori, S. 1997. Nihongo no Intonēshon: Kata to Kinō (Intonation in Japanese: Patterns and functions). *Akusento, Intonēshon, Rizumu to Pōzu (Accent, intonation, rhythm, and pause)*, eds. T. Kunihiro, H. Hirose, and M. Kono, 169–202. Tokyo: Sanseido.

Kuno, S. 1973. *The Structure of the Japanese Language*. Cambridge: MIT Press.

Ladd, D. R. 1981. A First Look at the Semantics and Pragmatics of Negative Questions and Tag Questions. *Proceedings of the Chicago Linguistic Society*, vol.17, 164–171.

Lassiter, D. 2011. *Measurement and Modality: The Scalar Basis of Modal Semantics*. Doctoral dissertation, New York University.

Nihongo Kijutsu Bunpo Kenkyukai. 2007. *Gendai Nihongo Bunpō (A Contemporary Grammar of the Japanese Language)*, vol.3. Tokyo: Kurosio Publishers.

Noda, H. 1997. *"No(da)" no Kinoo (The Functions of no(da))*. Tokyo: Kurosio Publishers.

Romero, M. and Han, C. 2004. On Negative "Yes/No" Questions. *Linguistics and Philosophy* 27:609–658.

Sugahara, M. 2003. *Downtrends and Post-Focus Intonation in Tokyo Japanese*. Doctoral dissertation, University of Massachusetts.

Vance, T. J. 2008. *The Sounds of Japanese*. Cambridge: Cambridge University Press.

Venditti, J. J. 2005. The J_ToBI Model of Japanese Intonation. *Prosodic Typology: The Phonology of Intonation and Phrasing*, ed. S.-A. Jun, 172–200. Oxford: Oxford University Press.

Apparent Vehicle Change Phenomena in the Absence of Ellipsis

JUNKO SHIMOYAMA
McGill University

ALEX DRUMMOND
McGill University

1 Introduction: Vehicle Change Phenomena

1.1 Vehicle Change Phenomena

This paper is concerned with so-called vehicle change phenomena that are found in unexpected places. Let us first present two well-known examples of vehicle change phenomena. First, Condition A effects are sometimes obviated in elided VPs, as shown in (2). In the strict identity reading of (2) paraphrased in (3b), it is *as if* in the elided constituent, *himself* was replaced by *him* as shown in (4b).

(1) John$_1$ defended himself$_1$ better than his lawyer$_2$ defended himself$_2$. (unambiguous)

(2) John$_1$ defended himself$_1$ better than his lawyer did. (ambiguous)

(3) a. John$_1$ defended himself$_1$ better than his lawyer$_2$ defended himself$_2$. (sloppy identity reading)

    b. John$_1$ defended himself$_1$ better than his lawyer$_2$ defended John$_1$. (strict identity reading)

Japanese/Korean Linguistics 23.
Edited by Michael Kenstowicz, Theodore Levin and Ryo Masuda.

(4)   a. John$_1$ defended himself$_1$ better than his lawyer$_2$ did [defend himself$_2$].

  b. John$_1$ defended himself$_1$ better than his lawyer did [defend himself$_1$ $\Rightarrow$ him$_1$].

 Further, the example in (6) shows that Condition C effects are sometimes obviated in elided VP. Without ellipsis, the sentence is ungrammatical due to a Condition C violation, as shown in (5). In this case, it is *as if* in the elided constituent, *John's* was replaced by *his* as in (7).

(5)   *I like John$_1$'s friends more than he$_1$ likes John$_1$'s friends.

(6)   I like John$_1$'s friends more than he$_1$ does.

(7)   I like John$_1$'s friends more than he$_1$ does [like John$_1$'s $\Rightarrow$his$_1$ friends]

As far as we are aware, such phenomena have been identified only in elided structures (VP or larger).

1.2 "Vehicle Change" Analysis

Fiengo and May (1994) propose that when an antecedent VP is copied into an ellipsis site, reflexives and R-expressions may indeed be replaced by pronominal correlates. This process is known as Vehicle Change. Given only the data above, Vehicle Change would appear to be an *ad-hoc* mechanism. There is, however, significant evidence favouring a Vehicle Change analysis. For instance, as shown in (9a), Condition B effects appear to be triggered by the pronominal correlate *him* of *John* as a result of Vehicle Change.

(8)   a. *I like John$_1$ more than he$_1$ does.

  b. I like John$_1$ more than he$_1$ wants me to.

(9)   a. *I like John$_1$ more than he$_1$ does [like John$_1$$\Rightarrow$him$_1$].

  b. I like John$_1$ more than he$_1$ wants me to [like John$_1$$\Rightarrow$him$_1$].

 In this paper, we will first present a movement analysis of the Condition A obviation phenomenon by Hestvik (1995), which builds on Heim (1993) (section 2). We then observe that apparent vehicle change phenomena are found even in the absence of ellipsis, namely in phrasal comparatives in Japanese and Hindi-Urdu (section 3), as well as in superlative constructions in English and Japanese (section 4). We show that only the Hestvik/Heim analysis of the Condition A obviation phenomenon extends straightforwardly to such cases with no ellipsis. We also explore an alternative analysis based on Kennedy and Lidz (2001) and conclude that it does not extend to Japanese (section 5). Section 6 summarizes the paper.

2 Strict Readings of Reflexives in VP Ellipsis

2.1 Deriving Strict Readings via QR

Hestvik (1995), building on Heim (1993), argues against a Vehicle Change analysis of the Condition A cases in subordinate structures, proposing instead that a reflexive undergoes short QR to VP so that it binds traces in both the antecedent and elided VPs following LF copying.

(10) a. $John_1$ defended $himself_1$ before his lawyer did.

  b. $John_1$ defended $himself_1$ before his $lawyer_2$ defended $John_1$. (strict)

  c. John [$_{VP}$ himself [$_{VP}$ defended t] before his lawyer did [$_{VP}$ ~~defend t~~]].

The derivation of (4a) has two steps: First, the reflexive undergoes short QR to adjoin to VP; second, the VP containing the trace of *himself* is copied into the ellipsis site at LF. The tree in (13) illustrates Hestvik (1995:226)'s analysis in more detail. We use the double indexation system of Heim (1993), as indicated in (11). The intuition here is that we want to create a non-reflexive predicate in the antecedent VP while making sure that *John* binds *himself*.

(11) $[himself_1]_2$
  a. Inner indices encode what they are bound by.
  b. Outer indices encode what they bind.

(12) $John_1$ $\lambda 1[himself_1$ $\lambda 2[[t_1$ defended $t_2]$ before his lawyer $\lambda 1[\underline{t_1$ defended $t_2}]]]$

(13)

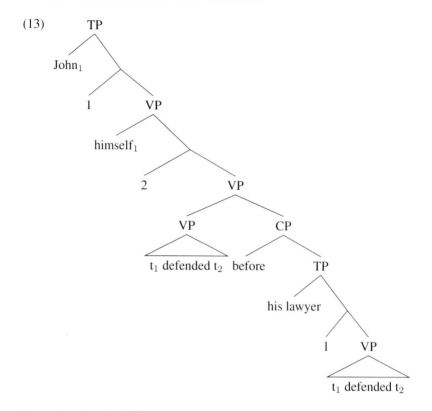

2.2 Subordination Effect

One of Hestvik's main arguments for the movement analysis above is a difference in the availability of strict readings in coordinate vs. subordinate structures. In general, syntactic coordination disfavours strict interpretation of reflexives, while subordination facilitates it (see Hestvik (1995) for a review of the literature). This is illustrated in the examples of subordination structure in (14) and those of coordination structure in (15) below.

(14) a. John defended himself better than Bill/his lawyer did. (subordination-comparative)

  b. John defended himself before Bill did. (subordination-temporal adjunct)

  c. John laughed at himself because Bill did. (subordination-causal adjunct)

  d. John introduced himself to everyone that Bill did (subordination-ACD)

(15) John defended himself well, and Bill did, too.

    a. John defended John well, and Bill defended Bill well, too.
(sloppy)

    b. ?John defended John well, and Bill defended John well, too.
(strict)

Hestvik's QR-based analysis of strict readings for reflexives captures the asymmetry between coordination and subordination structures: *himself* cannot be high enough in the coordination structure to generate the strict reading.[1]

(16) a. John defended himself well, and Bill did, too.

    b. *John [himself$_1$ [defended t$_1$ well]], and Bill did [defended t$_1$ well]

3 Vehicle Change Phenomena in the Absence of Ellipsis

Support for the availability of Heim/Hestvik-style derivations comes from Hindi-Urudu and Japanese phrasal comparatives. Phrasal comparatives in Hindi-Urdu and Japanese have been argued to have non-ellipsis derivations (Bhatt and Takahashi 2011; Heim 1985). Surprisingly, however, they allow strict readings of reflexives. A Vehicle Change analysis of this phenomenon is impossible in principle in the absence of ellipsis. The Heim/Hestvik analysis applies straightforwardly to derive the unexpected strict reading.

3.1 Phrasal Comparatives in Japanese and Hindi-Urdu

Bhatt and Takahashi (2011) argue that some phrasal comparatives in Japanese and all phrasal comparatives in Hindi-Urdu have a "direct" analysis, or non-ellipsis derivations (Heim 1985). One type of argument comes from binding facts. An ellipsis analysis predicts that the remnant (the complement of *than*) is c-commanded by everything that c-commands the associate, as schematically illustrated in (18b) for ditransitive V (Lechner 2004).

(17) Takumi likes [$_{associate}$natto] more than [$_{remnant}$ chocolate].

(18) a. DP$_{subj}$ V DP DP$_{associate}$ than DP$_{remnant}$ (direct)

    b. DP$_{subj}$ V DP DP$_{associate}$ than ~~DP$_{subj}$ V DP~~ DP$_{remnant}$ (ellipsis)

As Bhatt and Takahashi (2011) show, in Hindi-Urdu and Japanese, binding properties of the remnant do not correlate with the structural position of its associate. Rather, the remnant PP patterns with other PPs with respect to binding properties. We can see this by looking at the example in (22) from Bhatt

---

[1] The analysis is too strong, however, as it would rule out any strict readings in coordinate structure as ungrammatical.

and Takahashi (2011). A simpler sentence in (20) is added here just to show the basis for (22). Coreference between *Taroo* and *kare* 'he' is fine in (22). This is not expected in an ellipsis analysis, as (23) below is ungrammatical.[2]

(19) DP_{subj} [$DP_{remnant}$]-than $DP_{ind.obj}$ $DP_{associate}$ Adv V

(20) Hanako-wa [$_{remnant}$ kono shashin]-yori Taroo-ni [$_{associate}$ ano
      Hanako-TOP   this picture-than Taro-DAT   that
      shashin]-o hinpanni miseta.
      picture-ACC frequently showed
      'Hanako showed that picture$_{associate}$ more frequently to Taro than this picture$_{remnant}$.'

(21) DP_{subj} [R-Expression$_{remnant}$]-than Pron$_{ind.obj}$ $DP_{associate}$ Adv V

(22) Hanako-wa [$_{remnant}$ Taroo$_i$-no imooto-no   shashin]-yori
      Hanako-TOP   Taro-GEN younger.sister-GEN picture-than
      kare$_i$-ni [$_{associate}$ Keiko-no imooto-no   shashin]-o
      he-DAT   Keiko-GEN younder.sister-GEN picture-ACC
      hinpanni miseta.
      frequently showed
      'Hanako showed him Keiko's sister's picture$_{associate}$ more frequently than (Hanako showed him) Taro's sister's picture$_{remnant}$.'

(23) *Hanako-wa kare$_i$-ni [Taro$_i$-no imooto-no shashin]-o hinpanni
      Hanako-TOP he-DAT Taro-GEN sister-GEN picture-ACC frequently
      miseta.
      showed
      'Hanako showed him$_i$ Taro$_i$'s sister's picture frequently.'

Bhatt and Takahashi (2011)'s derivation exploits "parasitic scope" (Nissenbaum 2000; Barker 2007; Kennedy and Stanley 2008). Using example (24a), we see in (25) that (i) movement of the subject out of vP introduces a λ-abstractor over individuals; and (ii) the degree phrase then "tucks in" between the subject and the λ-node to introduce an abstractor over degrees. As shown in (24b), the degree head first composes with the complement of *than*, then with the predicate of degrees and individuals, and finally with the subject.

---

[2] See Bhatt and Takahashi (2011) for more arguments for the non-ellipsis analysis of phrasal comparatives in Hindi-Urdu and Japanese, based on scopal properties of quantifiers in the *than*-complement. Phrasal and clausal comparatives show distinct patterns there.

(24) a. Hahaoya-wa [chichioya-yori] hageshiku kodomo-o
mother-TOP father-than   severely   child-ACC
hihan-shi-ta.
criticize-do-PAST
'The mother criticized the child more severely than the father.'

b. Deg(Father)(λdλx. x criticized Child d-severely)(Mother)
(where Deg(x)(P)(y) $\leftrightarrow$ $\exists$d[P(y,d) $\wedge\neg$ P(x,d)])

c. $\exists$d[Mother criticized Child d-severely $\wedge$ $\neg$[Father criticized Child d-severely]]

(25)

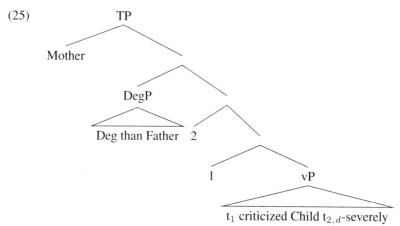

On the face of it, a reflexive in VP should be bound by the (trace of) the subject, yielding a sloppy reading. Surprisingly, however, phrasal comparatives in both Japanese and Hindi-Urdu permit both strict and sloppy readings. This is shown for Japanese in (26) from Kishida (2012) and Hindi-Urdu in (27).[3]

(26) Mary-ga   Bill yorimo hageshiku zibun-o hihan-shi-ta.
Mary-NOM Bill than   severely   self-ACC criticize-do-PAST

a. 'Mary criticized Mary more severely than Bill criticized Bill.' (sloppy)

b. 'Mary criticized Mary more severely than Bill criticized Mary.' (strict)

(27) John apnii hifaazat Tim se   behtar kartaa hai.   (Hindi-Urdu)
John self's defense Tim than better do   is

a. 'John defended John better than Tim defended Tim.' (sloppy)

b. 'John defended John better than Tim defended John.' (strict)

---

[3] We thank Dave Kush and Rajesh Bhatt for providing Hindi-Urdu data.

As a side note, Korean and Chinese phrasal comparatives also seem to allow strict readings in the following examples.[4] If phrasal comparatives in these languages had non-ellipsis derivations as well (Xiang 2005; Lin 2009; Sung 2011), then they also present a puzzle for ellipsis-based analyses.

(28) John-un pyunhosa-pota cal caki-lul pyunho-haet-ta. (Korean)
     John-TOP lawyer-than   well self-ACC defended

     'John defended himself better than the lawyer.'

(29) Mary duidai ziji bi   John hao. (Chinese)
     Mary treat self compare John well.

     'Mary treats herself better than John.'

3.2 Extending Hestvik's Analysis to Non-Ellipsis Derivations

In the absence of ellipsis, a Vehicle Change analysis of the strict reading is impossible in principle. Hestvik's movement analysis, on the other hand, combines neatly with the analysis of Bhatt and Takahashi (2011) of phrasal comparatives to derive the strict reading. The reflexive QRs above the degree operator and is bound by the raised subject, as in (30). The internal and external arguments of *criticize* then translate as distinct non-covarying variables.

(30) [Mary [$_{vP}$ herself [$_{vP}$ λy [$_{vP}$ [$_{DegP}$ Deg than John] [λd [λx [$_{vP}$ x criticized y d-severely]]]]]]]

(30) can be derived as shown in (33)/(34) using the indexation system of Heim (1993). We assume the variant of Heim's system in which a binder need not delete its outer index immediately once this index is copied to a λ, so long as all outer indices are eventually deleted from NPs. The key assumptions are (31) and (32).[5] We use superscripts for outer indices, and subscripts for inner indices.

(31) All outer indices must delete (consequence of Heim's requirement that all indices be variables, p. 230).

(32) In the configuration [α^ι [λ_ι ...]] the outer index of α may (but need not) delete.

---

[4] We thank Hye Young Bang, Donghyun Kim and Jiajia Su for the examples and judgments.

[5] The transition from (iii)–(iv) of (33) assumes that *Mary* is in an A-position prior to QR.

(33) [$_{vP}$ Mary^1 criticized herself$^2_1$ more severely [Deg than Bill]^3]   (i)

'Mary' raises from vP-internal subject position:

[$_{TP}$ Mary^1 [λ_1 [$_{vP}$ t_1 criticized herself$^2_1$ more severely [Deg than Bill]^3]]]   (ii)

'herself' QRs to adjoin between 'Mary' and its index node:

[$_{TP}$ Mary^1 [herself$_1$ [λ_2 [λ_1 [$_{vP}$ t_1 criticized t_2 more severely [Deg than Bill]^3]]]]]   (iii)

'Mary' QRs to bind 'herself' via introduction of λ_1:

[Mary [λ_1 [$_{TP}$ t_1 [herself$_1$ [λ_2 [λ_1 [$_{vP}$ t_1 criticized t_2 more severely [Deg than Bill]^3]]]]]]]   (iv)

DegP tucks in below raised subject and QRed reflexive:

[Mary [λ_1 [$_{TP}$ t_1 [herself$_1$ [λ_2 [[Deg than Bill] [λ_3 [λ_1 [$_{vP}$ t_1 criticized t_2 t_3-severely]]]]]]]]]   (v)

(34)

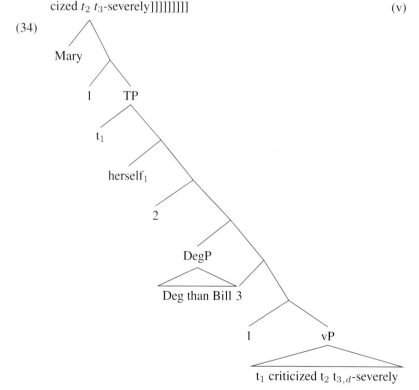

Before we end this section, let us make a few side-notes. First, the strict reading disappears when we use a morphologically reflexive verb, e.g. *self-criticize*, as observed by Kishida (2012). A similar behavior is reported for

Kannada in Lidz (2001).

(35) Mary-ga   Bill-yorimo hageshiku ziko-hihan-shi-ta.
Mary-NOM Bill-than   severely self-criticism-do-PAST

a. 'Mary criticized herself more severely than Bill criticized himself.' (sloppy)

b. *'Mary criticized herself more severely than Bill criticized her' (strict)

Second, a question that requires investigation is how complex reflexives such as *zibun-zisin* 'self-self' and *kare-zisin* 'he-self' are interepreted in the context under discussion, as in (36) and (37). Judgments are not as clear-cut as one wants them to be, and we leave further examination for future research.

(36) John-ga   Bill-yorimo hageshiku zibun-zisin-o
John-NOM Bill-than   severely zibun-zisin-ACC
hihan-shi-ta.
criticize-do-PAST

a. 'John criticized himself more severely than Bill criticized himself.' (sloppy)

b. ?'John criticized himself more severely than Bill criticized John' (strict)

(37) John-ga   Bill-yorimo hageshiku kare-zisin-o hihan-shi-ta.
John-NOM Bill-than   severely he-zisin-ACC criticize-do-PAST

a. ??'John criticized himself more severely than Bill criticized himself.' (sloppy)

b. ?'John criticized himself more severely than Bill criticized John' (strict)

A final note before moving on is that strict readings are possible with bound variable uses of reflexives in both English and Japanese (*himself* and *zibun*).

(38) Every defendant defended himself better than his lawyer did.
a. Every defendant$_1$ defended himself$_1$ better than [his$_1$ lawyer]$_2$ defended himself$_2$ (sloppy: local)
b. Every defendant$_1$ defended himself$_1$ better than his$_1$ lawyer defended him$_1$ (strict: non-local)

(39) Dono oya-mo   *zibun*-no   kodomo-o Tanaka-sensei-yori
      which parent-every zibun-GEN child-ACC Tanaka-teacher-than
      umaku bengo-shi-ta.
      well   defend-do-PAST

      a. 'Every parent$_1$ defended his$_1$ child better than Mr. Tanaka$_2$ de-
      fended his$_2$ child.' (sloppy: local)
      b. 'Every parent$_1$ defended his$_1$ child better than Mr. Tanaka defended
      his$_1$ child'. (strict: non-local)

3.3 Some Consequences to be Explored

In this section, we note two empirical areas that need to be explored in future
research. First, if the QR analysis of reflexives is on the right track, we should
be able to see some consequences of a reflexive raising to a high position. For
instance, a high reflexive should take scope over other materials in a sentence,
as suggested to us by Mitcho Erlewine (p.c.). One way of testing this is to
take the example in (26) and create a variation of it that has the structure in
(40). One might expect that in the strict reading in (41b) the inverse scope
reading would become available if 'every student of self' needs to undergo
QR. The result, however, is that in both the sloppy reading in (41a) and the
strict reading in (41b), only the surface scope interpretation is available.

(40) Mary [than Bill] QP1 [$_{QP2}$ ...self...] V

(41) Mary-wa Bill-yori hayaku nanika-o   {[dono zibun-no
      Mary-TOP Bill-than quickly something-ACC which self-GEN
      gakusee]-ni-mo/[zibun-no [dono gakusee]]-ni-mo} okutta.
      student-DAT-every/sef-GEN which student-DAT-every sent

      a. 'Mary$_1$ sent something to every student of self$_1$ more quickly
      than Bill$_2$ sent something to every student of self$_2$' (sloppy; sur-
      face scope $\exists > \forall$ only)
      b. 'Mary$_1$ sent something to every student of self$_1$ more quickly
      than Bill$_2$ sent something to every student of self$_1$' (strict; surface
      scope $\exists > \forall$ only)

In this particular example, one could say that only the reflexive *zibun* 'self'
is moving, hence it does not affect the scope relation between the two quantificational phrases. The scope rigid nature of Japanese is also a confounding
factor here. We thus need to construct better examples to test the prediction
made by the QR analysis.

Another area where further investigation needs to be left for future research has to do with the example in (42), brought to our attention by Satoshi
Tomioka (p.c.). The strict reading of the sentence is perfectly fine, and is
even the more pragmatically natural reading than the sloppy reading. In the

QR analysis of the strict reading of reflexives, it seems that the structure (43b) must be assumed, which is a weak crossover configuration. (43b) is derived from (43a) by raising $[t_2\text{'s mother}]_4$ to the position between $\lambda 2$ and DegP, and the non-c-commanding pronoun *kanojo-no* 'she-GEN' ends up intervening between *zibun-no hahaoya* 'self-GEN mother' and its trace.

(42) Daremo-ga   zibun-no hahaoya-o   kanojo-no bengoshi-yori
     everyone-NOM self-GEN mother-ACC she-GEN   lawyer-than
     umaku bengoshita.
     well   defended
     'Everyone$_1$ defended [self$_1$'s mother]$_4$ better than her$_4$ (=the mother of 1's) lawyer defended her$_4$.' (strict)

(43) a. everyone$_1$ self$_1$ [λ_2[[Deg than her$_4$ lawyer] [λ_3 [λ_1 t$_1$ defended [t$_2$'s mother]$_4$ t$_{3,d}$-well]]]]

   b. everyone$_1$ self$_1$ [λ_2 [[t$_2$'s mother]$_4$ [[Deg than her$_4$ lawyer] [λ_3 [λ_1 t$_1$ defended t$_4$ t$_{3,d}$-well]]]]]

One thing we need to investigate is the nature of the overt pronoun *kanojo* 'she' in (42), which is receiving a bound-variable-like interpretation in this example, while it usually cannot be interpreted as a bound variable pronoun.[6] As far as we could see, the English correlate of (42) in (44) in its strict reading raises similar issues.

(44) Every boy defended his mother better than her lawyer.
   a. Every boy$_1$ defended [his$_1$ mother]$_4$ better than her$_4$ lawyer (direct analysis)
   b. Every boy$_1$ defended [his$_1$ mother]$_4$ better than her$_4$ lawyer defended her$_4$ (ellipsis analysis)

4 VC Effect Without Ellipsis Structure Elsewhere

If the extension of Hestvik's analysis to non-ellipsis derivations that we just presented is on the right track, we make a prediction. If we find other constructions where no ellipsis structure is involved but an apparent 'ellipsis copy' is created in the semantics, the prediction will be that strict readings of reflexives should be available, if we follow Hestvik's analysis. A case in point is the superlative construction in English and Japanese. An apparent vehicle change phenomenon (strict reading of reflexives) is observed in (45)–(47), where it is reasonable to assume that no ellipsis structure is involved. Instead, in the meaning assigned to the superlative degree operator Deg$_{\text{sup}}$ in

---

[6] The weak crossover effect shows up with *zibun* 'self', which allows bound variable interpretation (Saito and Hoji 1983).

(48), the degree predicate is 'recycled' in semantics, just as in the case of the three-place degree operator in (24b) (see, for example, Heim 1999; Sharvit and Stateva 2002; Aihara 2009).

(45) Out of all the boys, John painted the best picture of himself.
a. ..., John painted the best self-portrait. (sloppy)
b. ..., John painted the best picture of John. (strict)

(46) Out of all the boys, John defended himself most skillfully.
a. ..., John did the most skillful self-defending. (sloppy)
b. ..., John defended John most skillfully. (strict)

(47) We all love to google John since he won the Nobel Prize, but John googles himself the most.[7] (strict)

(48) $Deg_{sup}(C)(P)(y) \leftrightarrow \exists d[P(y,d) \wedge \forall x[x \in C \wedge x \neq y \rightarrow \neg P(x,d)]]$
(C for comparison set)

The strict reading of (46), for instance, is expected to be derived from the structure in (49a) (or (52)).

(49)   a. $John_1 \ himself_1 \ \lambda 2 \ [most_C \ \lambda 3. \ \lambda 1. \ [t_1 \ defended \ t_2 \ t_{3,d} \ skillfully]]$

b. John defended himself more skillfully than any one else [defended John].

c. $\exists d[John \ defended \ John \ d\text{-}skillfully \wedge \forall \ x[x \in C \wedge x \neq John \rightarrow \neg[x \ defended \ John \ d\text{-}skillfully]]]$

(50) Hanako-ga   zibun-o mottomo umaku bengoshita.
Hanako-NOM self-ACC most   well   defended

a. 'Hanako did the most skillful self-defending.' (sloppy)
b. 'Hanako defended Hanako most skillfully among the defenders of Hanako.' (strict)

(51) Hanako-ga   mottomo umaku zibun-o bengoshita.
Hanako-NOM most   well   self-ACC defended

a. 'Hanako did the most skillful self-defending.' (sloppy)
b. (?)'Hanako defended Hanako most skillfully among the defenders of Hanako.' (strict)

---

[7] Thanks to Maayan Adar for this example.

(52)

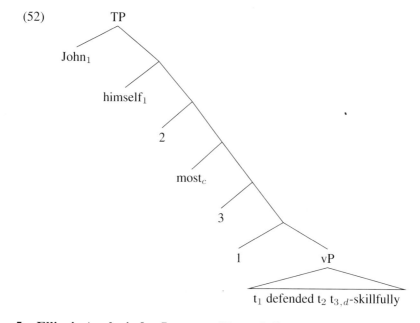

TP

John$_1$

himself$_1$

2

most$_c$

3

1   vP

t$_1$ defended t$_2$ t$_{3,d}$-skillfully

5 Ellipsis Analysis for Japanese Phrasal Comparatives?

What we have shown so far is that, given the non-ellipsis derivations of Japanese and Hindi-Urdu phrasal comparatives (and of Japanese and English superlatives), the availability of the strict reading of reflexives provide evidence for the Hestvik/Heim-style analysis. A Vehicle Change analysis is not an option there. The big assumption made, of course, is the non-ellipsis analysis of Japanese and Hindi-Urdu phrasal comparatives. If these phrasal comparatives did indeed have ellipsis derivations, the Hestvik analysis and the Vehicle Change analysis would work equally well (though even in such a case, the observation on the superlatives can only be handled by the Hestvik analysis).[8] In this final section we look at a third possible analysis of the stric reading of reflexives in Japanese within an ellipsis analysis of phrasal comparatives that capitalizes on the long distance nature of *zibun* 'self'. We conclude that even though such an analysis is proposed for English phrasal comparatives by Kennedy and Lidz (2001), the analysis does not successfully extend to Japanese.

5.1 Exploiting the Long Distance Nature of *zibun*

Kennedy and Lidz (2001) propose that English possesses an inaudible long distance anaphor, a counterpart of audible *ziji* in Chinese. According to their

---

[8] In Drummond and Shimoyama (2013) we show that Condition C obviation cases can be handled by a Hestvik-style analysis, in a more satisfactory way than by a Vehicle Change analysis.

analysis, English phrasal comparatives involve ellipsis structure, in particular, stripping. For the strict reading of (53a), the Hestvik-style analysis is not possible because the elided constituent is clausal rather than verbal, and therefore includes an occurrence of the moved reflexive, which leads to a sloppy reading.[9]

(53) a. John defended himself better than the lawyer.

   b. John [himself [defended t better]] than the lawyer [~~himself [defended t better~~]] (stripping)

Therefore the long distance *ziji* (inaudible in English) has to be used in order to derive a strict reading, as in (54), according to Kennedy and Lidz (2001).

(54) John$_1$ defended himself$_1$ better than the lawyer [$_{FP}$ ~~[$_{VP}$ defended ziji$_1$]~~] (stripping)

This is an intriguing proposal for English, and it does seem to make sense to extend the analysis to Japanese, namely to assume ellipsis derivations for phrasal comparatives and take advantage of the long-distance nature of *zibun* 'self' to account for its strict reading. It turns out, however, that an immediate prediction of this analysis is not borne out.[10]

5.2 Predictions on the Blocking Effect

Japanese *zibun* shows a number of properties similar to Chinese *ziji*. A prediction is made then that the so-called Blocking Effect would show up in Japanese phrasal comparatives. We will show below, however, that the Japanese phrasal comparatives do not exhibit the expected behaviour. This leads us to conclude that an ellipsis analysis combined with the long distance nature of *zibun* is not a viable alternative to the QR analysis of strict readings of *zibun*.

Example (55) illustrates what is known as a Blocking Effect caused by an intervening 1st person or 2nd person subject in Chinese: the long distance anaphor *ziji* cannot be bound by *Zhangsan* due to the intervening 1st or 2nd person pronoun (see, for example, Huang and Liu 2001).

---

[9] Thanks to Takeo Kurafuji (p.c.) for pointing out another reading available in (53a) where *than* is interpreted more or less like *compared to*, giving rise to the interpretation of the complement of *than* as setting up an appropriate standard, as in 'compared to how lawyers defend in general' (See, for example, Beck, Oda, and Sugisaki 2004). The same observation applies to its Japanese counterpart.

[10] Kishida (2012) assumes an ellipsis analysis of phrasal comparatives in Japanese and proposes an analysis of strict readings of reflexives along the lines of 'near reflexives' in the sense of Lidz (2001).

(55) Zhangsan danxin wo/ni hui piping   ziji.
Zhangsan worries I/you will criticize self

'Zhangsan is worried that I/you will criticize myself/yourself/*him (=Zhangsan).'

Similar Blocking Effects are found in Japanese, as shown in (56) and (57).[11]

(56) Sota-wa watashi/anata-ga zibun-o   urikonda yori umaku zibun-o
Sota-TOP I/you-NOM   self-ACC promoted than well   self-ACC
urikonda.
promoted

a. 'Sota promoted himself better than I promoted myself/*him.'
b. 'Sota promoted himself better than you promoted yourself/*him.'

(57) Takashi-wa watashi/kimi-ga zibun-o   kizutsukeru kamoshirenai
Takashi-TOP I/you-NOM   self-ACC hurt   may
to   shinpaishiteiru yo
that worried   PRT

a. 'Takashi is worried that I might hurt myself/?him (=Takashi).'
b. 'Takashi is worried that you might hurt yourself/?him (=Takashi).'

Note that Kennedy and Lidz (2001) report that the same kind of Blocking Effect is found in English phrasal comparatives (their (15)). A strict reading is reported to be unavailable in (58a), which is attributed to the intervening second person pronoun *you* blocking the inaudible *ziji* to be bound by *the lawyer*, as shown in (58b). This is supposed to contrast with the situation in sentence (59a), where a strict reading is available because there is no 1st or 2nd person pronoun in the *than* clause blocking the long-distance bound interpretation of inaudible *ziji* as in (59b).

(58) a. The lawyer defended himself better than **you**.
      b. The lawyer$_3$ defended himself$_3$ better than **you**$_2$ [defended *ziji*$_{2/*3}$]. (strict reading blocked)

(59) a. You defended yourself better than **the lawyer**.
      b. You$_2$ defended yourself$_2$ better than **the lawyer**$_3$ [defended *ziji*$_{2/3}$]

Going back to Japanese, the prediction now is that we should find the same pattern of Blocking Effects. That is, we should find the following pattern:

[11] The effect is felt to be weak in (57), especially if one sets up a context properly. This seems to relate to the use of the psych verb *shinpaisuru* 'worry' and empathy. (See Oshima 2004, 2007). Also, the 2nd person pronoun may be a weaker blocker than the 1st person pronoun in Japanese.

(60)   a. DP_{3rd} defended *zibun* better than $DP_{1st/2nd}$. $\Rightarrow$ should lack a strict reading

   b. $DP_{1st/2nd/3rd}$ defended *zibun* better than DP_{3rd}. $\Rightarrow$ should be ambiguous

It turns out that the prediction is not borne out. Despite the intervening first person pronoun *watashi* in (61), the sentence is ambiguous – crucially, it allows for a strict reading. Thus, whether we have a first person pronoun in the complement of *yori* 'than' as in (61) or a third person pronoun as in (62), the availability of the strict reading is not affected, contrary to the prediction.

(61)   Sota-wa **watashi**-yori umaku zibun-o   urikonda.
       Sota-TOP I-than   well   self-ACC promoted

   a. 'Sota promoted himself better than **I** promoted **myself**.' (sloppy)
   b. 'Sota promoted himself better than **I** promoted **him**(=Sota).' (strict)

(62)   Sota-wa **Yuya**-yori umaku zibun-o urikonda.
       Sota-TOP Yuya-than well self-ACC promoted

   a. 'Sota promoted himself better than **Yuya** promoted **himself**.' (sloppy)
   b. 'Sota promoted himself better than **Yuya** promoted **him**(=Sota).' (strict)

   The data above show that the strict readings of *zibun* in phrasal comparatives in Japanese do not arise from long-distance binding of *zibun* in the putative ellipsis site. Note that it is telling that strict readings of *zibun* in overt clausal comparatives do show the Blocking Effect, as illustrated in (56) above, as well as in the contrast between (63) and (64) below.

(63)   Mary-wa John-ga   zibun-o hihan-shi-ta-yorimo   hageshiku
       Mary-TOP John-NOM self-ACC criticize-do-PAST-than severely
       zibun-o hihan-shi-ta.
       self-ACC criticize-do-PAST

   a. 'Mary criticized herself more severely than John criticized himself.' (sloppy)
   b. 'Mary criticized herself more severely than John criticized her' (strict)

(64)   Mary-wa watashi-ga zibun-o hihan-shi-ta-yorimo   hageshiku
       Mary-TOP I-NOM   self-ACC criticize-do-PAST-than severely
       zibun-o   hihan-shi-ta.
       self-ACC criticize-do-PAST

   a. 'Mary criticized herself more severely than I criticized myself.' (sloppy)
   b. *'Mary criticized herself more severely than I criticized her' (strict)

The following Chinese example in (65) is from Erlewine (2010). In a similar sentence in Japanese, the sloppy reading is preferred, but with appropriate contexts and the choice of lexical items, the strict reading seems to be available also.

(65) Yuehan$_1$ bi wo$_2$ geng   xihuan ziji$_{1/2}$-de xuesheng.
      John   BI I   even.more like self-DE   student
      'John likes his own students more than I like my own students.'
      (sloppy)

6 Summary

In this paper, we presented evidence for a Heim/Hestvik-style analysis of strict readings of reflexives. More specifically, we observed the availability of strict readings of reflexives in non-ellipsis derivations (phrasal comparatives in Japanese, Hindi-Urdu, Korean and Chinese; superlatives in English and Japanese). In the absence of ellipsis structure, a Vehicle Change analysis is not an option. We also presented evidence that strict readings of *zibun* in Japanese phrasal comparatives do not arise from a long-distance binding relation between *zibun* in a putative elided constituent and its matrix antecedent. Many important questions remain. For example, are we in a position to despense with the 'Vehicle Change' analysis all together? In an attempt to provide a partial answer to this question, in Drummond and Shimoyama (2013), we examine vehicle change phenomena in Condition C obviation cases, as well as vehicle change phenomena outside of subordicate structure.

Acknowledgments

For valuable feedback, we would like to thank the audience at the 23rd Japanese/Korean Linguistics Conference (October 2013, MIT) and the McGill Syntax-Semantics Research Group, in particular, Maayan Adar, Marcel den Dikken, Mitcho Erlewine, Sayaka Goto, Takeo Kurafuji, Jeff Lidz, Bernhard Schwarz, and Satoshi Tomioka. We would also like to thank Symon Stevens-Guille for help with type-setting. The research reported here is supported in part by research grants from SSHRC (410-2010-1264 and 435-2013-0103), for which we are grateful. All remaining errors are our own.

References

Aihara, M. 2009. The Scope of -*est*: Evidence from Japanese. *Natural Language Semantics* 17:341–367.

Barker, C. 2007. Parasitic Scope. *Linguistics and Philosophy* 30:407–444.

Beck, S, T Oda, and K Sugisaki. 2004. Parametric Variation in the Semantics of Comparison: Japanese and English. *Journal of East Asian Linguistics* 13:289–344.

Bhatt, R, and S Takahashi. 2011. Reduced and Unreduced Phrasal Comparatives. *Natural Language and Linguistic Theory* 581–620.

Drummond, A, and J Shimoyama. 2013. QR as an Agent of Vehicle Change. Handout for NELS 44, University of Connecticut, October 2013.

Erlewine, M. Y. 2010. Independent Dependency in the Mandarin *bi* Comparative. Handout for MIT Workshop on Comparatives, November 2010.

Fiengo, R, and R May. 1994. *Indices and Identity*. Cambridge, Massachusetts: MIT Press.

Heim, I. 1985. Notes on Comparatives and Related Matters. Unpublished manuscript, University of Texas-Austin.

Heim, I. 1993. Anaphora and Semantic Interpretation: A Reinterpretation of Reinhart's Approach. *SfS-Report* 07-93 University of Tübingen (Reprinted in 1998 in The Interpretive Tract, ed. Orin Percus and Uli Sauerland, MIT Working Papers in Linguistics 25, 205-246, Department of Linguistics and Philosophy, MIT).

Heim, I. 1999. Notes on Superlatives. Ms. MIT.

Hestvik, A. 1995. Reflexives and Ellipsis. *Natural Language Semantics* 3:211–237.

Huang, C.-T. J, and C.-S. L Liu. 2001. Logophoricity, Attitudes, and *ziji* at the Interface. In *Syntax and semantics 33: Long-distance reflexives*, ed. P Cole, G Hermon, and C.-T. J Huang, 141–195. Academic Press.

Kennedy, C, and J Lidz. 2001. A (Covert) Long Distance Anaphor in English. In *Proceedings of the 20th West Coast Conference in Formal Linguistics*, ed. K Megerdoomian and L. A Bar-el, 318–331. Somerville, Massachusetts: Cascadilla Press.

Kennedy, C, and J Stanley. 2008. What an" Average" Semantics Needs. In *Proceedings of SALT*, volume 18, 465–482.

Kishida, M. 2012. Reflexives in Japanese. Doctoral Dissertation, University of Maryland, College Park.

Lechner, W. 2004. *Ellipsis in Comparatives*. Berlin/New York: Mouton de Gruyter.

Lidz, J. 2001. Condition R. *Linguistic Inquiry* 32:123–140.

Lin, J.-W. 2009. Chinese Comparatives and their Implicational Parameters. *Natural Language Semantics* 17:1–27.

Nissenbaum, J. 2000. Investigations of Covert Phrase Movement. Doctoral Dissertation, Massachusetts Institute of Technology, Cambridge, Massachusetts.

Oshima, D. Y. 2004. *Zibun* Revisited: Empathy, Logophoricity and Binding. In *Proceedings of the 20th NWLC*, volume 23, 175–190. University of Washington Working Papers in Linguistics.

Oshima, D. Y. 2007. On Empathic and Logophoric Binding. *Research on Language and Computation* 5:19–35.

Saito, M, and H Hoji. 1983. Weak Crossover and Move α in Japanese. *Natural Language and Linguistic Theory* 1:245–259.

Sharvit, Y, and P Stateva. 2002. Superlative Expressions, Context, and Focus. *Linguistics and Philosophy* 25:453–504.

Sung, M. 2011. Comparative Constructions in Korean with Two Types of -*Kes* Constructions. MA Research Paper, McGill University.

Xiang, M. 2005. Some Topics in Comparative Constructions. Doctoral Dissertation, Michigan State University.

The Derivation of *Soo-su*: Some Implications for the Architecture of Japanese VP[*]

HIDEHARU TANAKA
Osaka University / JSPS Research Fellow

1   Introduction

The concern of this paper is the anaphoric verbal expression in Japanese, namely, *soo-su* 'do so.' In (1), for example, the expression *soo-su* refers back to the content of the VP in the preceding clause (i.e. *play the piano*):

(1)   *Taro-ga   piano-o   hii-ta-node,   Ziro-mo   **soo** si-ta.*
        Taro-Nom piano-Acc play-Past-because Ziro-also so   do-Past
        'Because Taro played the piano, Ziro did so, too.'

[*] For their valuable advice, I wish to thank JK reviewers and the following people: Takeo Kurafuji, Hiroshi Mito, Kenta Mizutani, Akiemo Mukai, Sadayuki Okada, Yuta Sakamoto, Koji Shimamura, and Yuta Tatsumi. This study was supported by the Japan Society for the Promotion of Science, Grant-in-Aid for JSPS Fellows, No. 241177.

Japanese/Korean Linguistics 23.
Edited by Michael Kenstowicz, Theodore Levin and Ryo Masuda.
Copyright © 2016, CSLI Publications

Specifically, this paper addresses how to generate the syntactic and semantic structures of *soo-su*. Traditionally, *soo-su* has been analyzed as replacing the VP by a syntactic transformation when its content is recovered from the context (e.g. Nakau 1973). However, under the Minimalist Program, this replacement rule is prevented by the Inclusiveness Condition (Chomsky 1995), which bans a syntactic computation from adding any new items that are not selected from the numeration. Then, what analysis is possible for the derivation of *soo-su*, if we keep to the Minimalist Program?

In this paper, we offer a strictly compositional analysis of *soo-su* that treats *soo* 'so' and *su* 'do' as independent lexical items. In particular, we claim that *soo* is an item anaphoric to event properties, and *su* describes its event argument as an action event. Under this view, the derivation of *soo-su* is not in violation of the Inclusiveness Condition, because *soo* and *su* are introduced independently in the numeration stage, then merged into a unit by the syntactic computation, and lastly, that unit is interpreted as an anaphoric expression at semantics. This analysis, if tenable, implies that the architecture of the Japanese VP may consist not only of V and *v* but also of further argument-introducing heads (cf. Chomsky 1995).

This paper is organized as follows. Section 2 describes the syntactic and semantic properties of *soo* and *su* in *soo-su*. Section 3 gives a compositional analysis of *soo-su*. Finally, Section 4 concludes with some implications of the analysis for the Japanese VP architecture.

2 Data

2.1 Non-compound Nature of *Soo-su*

To argue that the expression *soo-su* is composed of at least two independent lexical items, *soo* and *su*, in syntax, we must begin by showing that it is not a compound word. According to Kageyama (1993), compounds in Japanese are morphologically single words (i.e. atomic units of syntax), because they comply with morphological integrity in that their lexical parts cannot be affected by syntactic operations. Thus, if *soo-su* is a syntactically structured unit, it should not show sensitivity to morphological integrity. As illustrated below, this is empirically the case.

To make the point, let us first show that compound words such as *nomi-aruk* 'drink-walk' cannot be cut off by displacement, as illustrated in (2c):

(2) a. *Taro-ga* **nomi-aruk**-*u-no-wa* *yosoodekita-ga* ...
   Taro-Nom drink-walk-Pres-C-Cont expected-though
   'I could expect that Taro walked around drinking, but ...'
 b. *Ziro-mo* **nomi-aruk**-*u-nante* *odoroki-da*.
   Ziro-also drink-walk-Pres-C surprise-Cop
   'It was surprising that Ziro walked around drinking, too.'

c. * *Nomi*_i *Ziro-mo* *t*_i *aruk-u-nante odoroki-da.*

By contrast, *soo-su* can be cut off by displacement, as noted by Kageyama (1993: 82) and shown in (3c):

(3) a. *Taro-ga*   *nomi-aruk-u-no-wa*   *yosoodekita-ga ...*
          Taro-Nom drink-walk-Pres-C-Cont expected-though
          'I could expect that Taro walked around drinking, but ...'
    b. *Ziro-mo*   *soo*   *su-ru-nante*   *odoroki-da.*
          Ziro-also so do-Pres-C surprise-Cop
          'It was surprising that Ziro walked around drinking, too.'
    c. *Soo*_i *Ziro-mo* *t*_i *su-ru-nante*   *odoroki-da.*

This suggests that *soo-su* is not a compund word in that it is insensitive to morphological integrity.[1]

Now we have reason to believe that *soo-su* is syntactically composed of at least two lexical items, *soo* and *su*. In Sections 2.2 and 2.3, we will examine the syntactic and semantic properties of *soo* and *su*, respectively.

2.2 Properties of *Soo* 'So' in *Soo-su*

First, the syntactic category of *soo* is adverb (Adv) and not V. To argue for this, let us consider the nominalizing suffix *-kata* 'way.' This suffix is attached to verbs and realizes their expected arguments and adjuncts in the nominalized domains (e.g. Kageyama 1993, Kishimoto 2006). For example, sentence (4a) can be nominalized by adding *-kata*, as in (4b):

(4) a. *Taro-ga*   *butai-de*   *karei-ni/*karei-na*   *odot-ta.*
          Taro-Nom stage-on beautifully/beautiful dance-Past
          'Taro danced beautifully on the stage.'
    b. *Taro-no* *butai-de-no* *karei-na/*karei-ni*   *odori-kata*
          Taro-Gen stage-on-Gen beautiful/beautifully dance-way
          'Taro's beautiful way of dancing on the stage'

Importantly, (4b) shows that the *-kata* construction excludes only adverbial expressions, as summarized in (5):

(5) Unavailable category for the *-kata* construction

✓DP[+Gen]	✓PP[+Gen]	✓Adj	*Adv	✓V
e.g.	e.g.	e.g.	e.g.	e.g.
Taro	*butai-de*	*karei-na*	*karei-ni*	*odori*
'Taro'	'on the stage'	'beautiful'	'beautifully'	'dance'

---

[1] This is also shown by the fact that *soo-su* can be separated by inserting focus particles such as *-wa* 'at least' (e.g. Kageyama (1993: 81)). I would like to thank JK reviewers for bringing this fact to my attention.

In (4b), the adverb *karei-ni* 'beautifully' must be excluded and converted into its adjectival (Adj) counterpart, namely, *karei-na* 'beautiful.' Thus, the -*kata* construction is used as a diagnostic for identifying syntactic categories. Let us compare *soo-su* with the Japanese counterpart of 'do that' anaphora, namely, *sore-o su* 'that-Acc do.' The point is that there are some contexts where these two expressions are semantically interchangeable. For example, context (6a) allows both to occur, with the same meaning:

(6) a. *Taro-ga   sono-sigoto-o   si-ta-node* ...
Taro-Nom   that-work-Acc   do-Past-because
'Because Taro did the work ...'

　　 b. *Ziro-mo **soo** **si**-ta.*　　　c. *Ziro-mo **sore-o** **si**-ta.*
Ziro-also so   do-Past　　　　　Ziro-also that-Acc do-Past
'Ziro did so, too.'　　　　　　　'Ziro did that, too.'
soo-su = "do the work"　　　　*sore-o su* = "do the work"

Now suppose we have the same context in mind for the minimal pair in (7):

(7) a. * *Ziro-no **soo(-no)si**-kata*　b. *Ziro-no **sore-no** **si**-kata*
Ziro-Gen so-Gen do-way　　　　Ziro-Gen that-Gen do-way
'Ziro's way of doing so'　　　　'Ziro's way of doing that'

However, this minimal pair shows that the -*kata* construction excludes *soo-su*, and suggests that the ungrammaticality of (7a) should be attributed to the lexical item *soo*. Accordingly, given that the -*kata* construction is incompatible only with adverbs, the category of *soo* should be adverb.

　　Second, *soo* is the locus of anaphora in the expression *soo-su*. In other words, only the lexical part *soo* is responsible for the anaphoric nature. To see this, let us again compare *soo-su* and *sore-o su*. The point is that there are also some contexts where they are *not* semantically interchangeable. For example, context (8a) allows *soo-su* but excludes *sore-o su*:

(8) a. *Taro-ga   ne-ta-node* ...
Taro-Nom   sleep-Past-because
'Because Taro went to bed ...'

　　 b. *Ziro-mo **soo** **si**-ta.*　　　c. * *Ziro-mo **sore-o** **si**-ta.*
Ziro-also so   do-Past　　　　　Ziro-also that-Acc do-Past
'Ziro did so, too.'　　　　　　　'Ziro did that, too.'
soo-su = "go to bed"　　　　　*sore-o su* = "go to bed"

This contrast suggests that whether the $\alpha + su$ anaphora can be contextually used depends on what the part α is. We take this situation to mean that the verbal part *su* does not contribute to make the whole expression anaphoric, and that *soo* determines the anaphric nature of the whole expression *soo-su*.

Third, *soo* is a semantically controlled anaphora — i.e., it does not require syntactic identity for its antecedents. For example, (9) shows that *soo* can refer back to the content of DP, even though it is an adverb:

(9) [DP ***Huyu-no-tozan***]ᵢ-*wa*   *kikenda-to*   *iwareta-node*,
       winter-Gen-climbing-Top dangerous-C was.told-because
       Taro-wa   *soo*ᵢ   *su-ru-no-o*   *yame-ta*.
       Taro-Top   so   do-Pres-C-Acc stop-Past
       'Because he was told that climbing in winter was dangerous, Taro
       gave up the idea of doing so.'

In this case, the antecedent of *soo* is the subject DP in the precedeing clause, and the *soo-su* clause means that Taro gave up the idea of climbing mountains in winter. This suggests that *soo* is not sensitive to the syntactic category of its antecedent and that its antecedent is defined at semantics.[2,3]

Finally, the semantics of *soo* involves contextually-given eventualities. To set the stage, let us assume a semantic model that includes at least the following three domains: D_e (the set of entities), D_v (the set of eventualities), and D_t (the set of truth values) (e.g. Davidson 1967, Parsons 1985). Thus, it consists of elements of type e, v, and t. In this model, we regard the notion of event as a linguistically relevant primitive. In fact, Grimshaw (1990) divides nominal expressions into two kinds: *event nominals* vs. *non-event nominals*. Under our model, event nominals denote properties of eventualities, for example, the noun *uwaki* 'love affair,' while non-event nominals denote properties of individuals, for example, the noun *uwaki-gokoro* 'unfaithfulness' (cf. Kageyama 1993). This distinction is crucial, as (10) shows that *soo* can take nominal antecedents only when they are event nominals:

(10) a.   [DP***Uwaki***]ᵢ-*wa* *yokunai-to*   *iwareta-node*,
           affair-Top   not.good-C   was.told-because
           Taro-wa   *soo*ᵢ   *su-ru-no-o*   *yame-ta*.
           Taro-Top so   do-Pres-C-Acc stop-Past
           'Because he was told that affairs were not good,
           Taro gave up the idea of doing so.'

---

[2] In Hankamer and Sag's (1976) terminology, *soo* is considered deep anaphora. Hoji (1990) also argues for this view by offering the utterance in (i), where *soo-su* is used deictically:
(i)   [After a meal, John put his hands together in front of his face, showing gratitude.]
       Yoko: *Ara, watashi-no-haha-mo   itumo   soo   suru wa.*
              Hey   I-Gen-mother-also   always   so   do
              'Hey, my mother always does so too.'   (Hoji 1990: Ch. 5, 57)
[3] Yuta Sakamoto (p.c.) points out that it is difficult for *soo-su* to refer back to the content of DP if it is not embedded in clausal nominals headed by the nominalizer C *no*. Thus, for the second clause in (9), if we say *Taro-wa soo si-nakat-ta* 'Taro did not do so,' the use of *soo-su* is judeged as marginal. We leave this fact unexplained.

b. * [DP***Uwakigokoro***]ᵢ-wa yokunai-to iwareta-node,
      unfaithfulness-Top not.good-C was.told-because
      Taro-wa **soo**ᵢ **su***-ru-no-o*   *yame-ta.*
      Taro-Top so   do-Pres-C-Acc stop-Past
      'Because he was told that unfaithfulness was not good,
      Taro gave up the idea of doing so.'

In (10a), *soo* refers back to the content of the subject DP *uwaki*, and its clause means that Taro gave up the idea of having a love affair. In (10b), by contrast, it is impossible to identify the antecedent of *soo* with the content of the subject DP *uwakigokoro* and its use is judeged as infelicitous. Given this contrast, the semantics of *soo* should have to do with contextually-given eventualities.

2.3 Properties of *Su* 'Do' in *Soo-su*

Let us turn to consider the syntactic and sematic properties of *su*. First, it is a substantial verb in that it makes an independent semantic contribution. To make the point, let us compare *soo-su* with the Japanerse counterpart of the 'try in that way' anaphora, namely, *soo-yar* 'so-try.' Again, the point is that there are some contexts that distinguish these two expressions. For example, the context of (11) allows only *soo-su* and excludes *soo-yar*:

(11) a.   *Taro-ga*   *mado-o*   *wat-ta-node* ...
         Taro-Nom window-Acc break-Past-because
         'Because Taro broke a window ...'
    b. *Ziro-mo* **soo** *si-ta.*   c. * *Ziro-mo* **soo** **yat***-ta.*
       Ziro-also so   do-Past   Ziro-also so   do-Past
       'Ziro did so, too.'   'Ziro tried in that way, too.'
       soo-su = "break a window"   *soo-yar* = "break a window"

The context of (12), on the other hand, excludes *soo-su* and allows *soo-yar*:

(12) a.   *Taro-ga*   [*mado-o*   *wat-te*]   *ie-ni*   *haitta-node*...
         Taro-Nom window-Acc break-Infl house-Dat   entered-because
         'Because Taro got into his house by breaking a window ...'
    b. ??*Ziro-mo* [**soo** *si-te*] *ie-ni*   *hait-ta.*
       Ziro-also so   do-Infl   house-Dat enter-Past
       'Ziro got into his house by doing so, too.'
       soo-su = "break a window"
    c. *Ziro-mo* [**soo** **yat***-te*] *ie-ni*   *hait-ta.*
       Ziro-also so   try-Infl   house-Dat enter-Past
       'Ziro got into his house by trying in that way, too.'
       soo-yar = "break a window"

In particular, this minimal pair shows that the marginality of (12b) should be attributed to the semantics of *su*. Thus, we must reject the idea that the lexical part *su* is a semantically vacuous verb (i.e. a dummy verb) while *soo* solely determines the semantics of the whole unit *soo-su*. This is because, if the semantics of *soo* rules out (12b), it should also rule out (12c), but this is not true. Accordingly, to explain the contrast in (12), *su* should be analyzed as a semantically substantial verb.

Second, *su* is associated with agency. To illustrate this, let us begin with the fact that *soo-su* cannot be anaphoric to non-agentive predicates such as unaccusative verbs.[4] For example, the minimal pair in (13) demonstrates that *soo-su* can refer back to the content of an unergative predicate, but cannot refer back to that of an unaccusative predicate:

(13) a. **Unergative: *muka* 'direct'**
       Taro-ga   MIT-ni   mukat-ta-ato, Ziro-mo soo si-ta.
       Taro-Nom MIT-Dat direct-Past-after Ziro-also so do-Past
       'After Taro left for MIT, Ziro did so, too.'
   b. **Unaccusative: *tuk* 'arrive'**
       * *Taro-ga   MIT-ni   tui-ta-ato,   Ziro-mo soo si-ta.*
       Taro-Nom MIT-Dat arrive-Past-after Ziro-also so do-Past
       'After Taro arrived at MIT, Ziro did so, too.'

Let us reduce this contrast to the semantics of *su* and analyze it as involving the notion of agency. This means that *su*, not *soo*, makes (13b) unacceptable because it forces *soo-su* to take agentive predicates as its antecedents. Thus, it should be true that *soo* itself does not care about the non-agency of its antecedent. This prediction is borne out by the minimal pair in (14), in which *soo-su* is compared with the Japanese counterpart of the 'become so' anaphora, namely, *soo-nar* 'so-become':

(14) a. *Taro-ga   netsu-o dasi-ta-ato ...*
       Taro-Nom fever-Acc show-Past-after
       'After Taro ran a fever ...'

b. * *Ziro-mo soo si-ta.*	c. *Ziro-mo soo nat-ta.*
Ziro-also so do-Past	Ziro-also so become-Past
'Ziro did so, too.'	'Ziro became so, too.'
soo-su = "run a fever"	*soo-nar* = "run a fever"

In (14), the antecedent predicate "run a fever" is not agentive and makes the use of *soo-su* infelicitous, but that of *soo-nar* acceptable. What is important here is that *soo* itself is compatible with the non-agency of its antecedent

---

[4] Nakau (1973) makes the generalization that *soo-su* can "replace" action predicates but not state predicates. However, a more adequate statement should be made in terms of agency, as we claim here.

predicate, as in (14c). This result supports our claim that it is the semantics of *su* that is associated with agency.[5]

Finally, *su* takes *soo* as its argument in *soo-su*. To make the point, let us consider the verb *wasure* 'forget.' According to Yumoto (2005), this verb can combine with another verb to make a complex head V⁰. For example, the VP structure for (15a) can be represented as in (15b):

(15) a. *Ken-wa   niku-o   itame-wasure-ta.*
Ken-Top meat-Acc fry-forget-Past
'Taro forgot to fry the meat.'

b.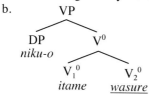

The diagram in (15b) shows that the first verb V_1^0 in the complex-head structure must keep an X^0 projection and realize its argument DP in the sister position of the complex head V^0. Yumoto (2005) argues for this analysis based on the fact that adjuncts fail to modify V_1^0 alone. Let us compare (16a) with (16b), in which *wasure* takes a clausal complement:

(16) a. *Ken-wa   niku-o   (??sio-de)   itame-wasure-ta.*
Ken-Top meat-Acc salt-with   fry-forget-Past
'Ken forgot to fry the onions with salt.'

b. *Ken-wa [niku-o   (sio-de)   itame-ru-no]-o   wasure-ta.*
Ken-Top meat-Acc salt-with fry-Pres-C-Acc   forget-Past
'Ken forgot that he should fry the onions with salt.'

The PP adjunct, *sio-de* 'with salt,' cannot modify the first verb 'fry' in (16a), but it can in (16b). The marginality of the adjunction in (16a) is explained by the complex-head structure in (15b) because it extends the projection level of the first verb, and such extension violates the complex-head condition that the first verb must keep an X^0 projection. Thus, the generalization is that the first verb can be associated only with its arguments. Let us now consider whether the adverb *soo* serves as an argument or adjunct for *su*. As

---

[5] Takeo Kurafuji (p.c.) points out that *soo-su* has a non-agentive use, as shown in (i):

(i)   A: *Kanozyo-ni   huraremasita.* B: [[**Soo si**-*ta*]   *koto*]-*wa   yoku   arusa.*
girlfriend-by was.dumped   so do-Past fact-Top often   exist
'She dumped me.'   'A lot of people have things like that.'

However, note that the non-agentive use of *soo-su* is allowed only if it is in the past form and modifies nouns. Here, we assume this "past + adnominal" form of *soo-su* as an idiom.

shown in (17a), *soo* and *su* can enter into a complex-head formation with *wasure*, generating an acceptable instance of the expression *soo-su*:

(17) a. *Ken-wa niku-o   itame-wasure-ta; Ai-mo* **soo** *si-wasure-ta.*
         Ken-Top meat-Acc fry-forget-Past   Ai-also so   do-forget-Past
         'Ken forgot to fry the meat; Ai forgot to do so, too.'

   b.

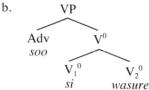

Thus, as shown in (17b), *soo* should occupy the same argument position as the object DP *niku-o* does in (15b). This suggests that *soo* serves as an argument of *su*, even though its category is adverb.

2.4   Summary

In summary, the properties of *soo* and *su* in *soo-su* are described as in (18):

(18) a. *Soo* is an adverb and an event anaphor under semantic control.
   b. *Su* is an agentive verb that takes *soo* as its argument.

3   Analysis

3.1   Proposals

We now present a compositional analysis of *soo-su* that can accommodate both descriptions in (18). Let us begin with the assumptions under which we make the proposal. We adopt Heim and Kratzer's (1998) framework for syntax-semantics interface issues and assume the mapping rule in (19):

(19) *Functional Application* (cf. Heim and Kratzer 1998)
     Let α be a merged unit $\{\beta, \gamma\}$, where $[\![\beta]\!]$ is a function whose domain contains $[\![\gamma]\!]$. Then $[\![\alpha]\!] = [\![\beta]\!]([\![\gamma]\!])$.

We also assume, with Kratzer (1996), that external arguments are not true arguments of lexical verbs and that they are introduced by a functional head, say, *little v* (e.g. Chomsky 1995). However, we depart from Kratzer's view of agentive *v* as an element of type <e, <v, t>> and adopt Ramchand's (2007) ideas that it is of type <<v, t>, <e, <v, t>>> and denotes relations between event properties. Specifically, we assume that the agentive *v* has an event-composition component, as shown in (20):

(20) *Ag(ent)-introducing v* (cf. Kratzer 1996, Ramchand 2007)
     $[\![v]\!] = \lambda P_{<v, t>}.\lambda e.\lambda v_1. [\mathbf{Ag}(e)(v_1) \ \& \ \exists v_2. [v_2 \leq v_1 \ \& \ P(v_2)]]$
     where '$v_2 \leq v_1$' means that v_2 is part of v_1.

Under these assumptions, for example, the vP structure for (21a) derives its denotation via Functional Application as in (21b):

(21) a. *Taro-ga   LGB-o   yom-da.*
         Taro-Nom   LGB-Acc   read-Past
         'Taro read LGB.'

   b.

$$[[vP]] = \lambda v_1.[\textbf{Ag}(\textbf{taro})(v_1) \ \& \ \exists v_2.[v_2 \leq v_1 \ \& \ \textbf{read}(\textbf{lgb})(v_2)]]$$

$[[DP]] \quad [[v']] = \lambda e.\lambda v_1.[\textbf{Ag}(e)(v_1) \ \& \ \exists v_2.[v_2 \leq v_1 \ \& \ \textbf{read}(\textbf{lgb})(v_2)]]$
  Taro

$\lambda v.[\textbf{read}(\textbf{lgb})(v)] = [[VP]] \quad [[v]] = \lambda P.\lambda e.\lambda v_1.[\textbf{Ag}(e)(v_1) \ \& \ \exists v_2.[v_2 \leq v_1 \ \& \ P(v_2)]]$

$[[DP]] \quad [[V]] = \lambda e.\lambda v.[\textbf{read}(e)(v)]$
 LGB *yom*

The denotation of vP, if existentially closed, conveys that there are v_1 and v_2 such that Taro is the Agent in v_1, v_2 is part of v_1, and LGB is the participant in v_2 which is a reading event. Importantly, the events described by V and v are potentially non-identical ones, roughly speaking, v_2 and v_1, respectively (cf. Kratzer 1996).

   With these assumptions, we propose syntactic and semantic properties of *soo* and *su* as stated in (22):

(22) Syntactic and semantic properties of *soo* and *su* in *soo-su*[6]
   a. *Soo* is Adv$_{<v, \triangleright>}$; $[[soo_i]] = \lambda v. [P_i(v)]$
   b. *Su* is V$_{<<v, \triangleright>, <v, \triangleright>>}$; $[[su]] = \lambda P_{<v, \triangleright>}.\lambda v. [\textbf{act}(v) \ \& \ P(v)]$
   c. *Su* is merged with v [+Agent] due to its unergative semantics.

First, *soo* is an Adv, and its meaning is an event description (i.e. of type $<v, t>$). Importantly, it ascribes an anaphoric property P_i to its event argument, and this P_i takes a contextually-given property as its antecedent. Next, *su* is a V, and its meaning is of type $<<v, t>, <v, t>>$. In particular, it makes a semantic contribution in that it describes its event argument as an action. Consequently, as stated in (22c), this semantic component requires that *su* be merged with the agentive v, because it is an unergative verb; it is normal to assume that the unergative V is merged with the agentive v.

   Let us now elaborate on the semantics of *soo*. To begin, we define antecedent property P_A for P_i as in (23):

(23) *Antecedent property* P_A
   Every P counts as P_A iff P is contextually given and is of type $<v, t>$.

---

[6] Hallman (2004) analyzes *do so* in English and proposes that *do* is a realization of v with *so* in its sister position. If his analysis is correct, then *soo-su* and *do so* differ in structure: The former is a VP, while the latter, vP.

We also assume that *soo* poses an output condition on the result of identifying P_i with P_A. Let P_C be a property co-occurring with P_A in the sense that they share the same event variable. Then, the output condition requires that the actual antecedent P_A be a "hyponym" of any P_C, or a "more specific" property than any P_C. Put in terms of entailment, the condition is defined as stated in (24):

(24) *Hyponymy Condition*
For every P_A, the result of identifying P_i with P_A is licensed only if for every P_C and every event v, if $P_A(v)$ is true, then $P_C(v)$ is true.

3.2 Demonstration

We now demonstrate how our proposals work. Let us begin with the case of verbal antecedents. For example, the *soo-su* clause in (25a) derives its *v*P structure and its denotation, as in (25b):

(25) a. *Taro-ga   LGB-o   yom-da*; *Ziro-mo **soo** si-ta.*
Taro-Nom LGB-Acc read-Past Ziro-also so   do-Past
'Taro read LGB; Ziro did so, too.'

b.

$$[[vP]] = \lambda v_1.[\mathbf{Ag}(\mathbf{ziro})(v_1)\ \&\ \exists v_2.[v_2 \leq v_1\ \&\ \mathbf{act}(v_2)\ \&\ P_i(v_2)]]$$

$[[DP]]\quad [[v']] = \lambda e.\lambda v_1.[\mathbf{Ag}(e)(v_1)\ \&\ \exists v_2.[v_2 \leq v_1\ \&\ \mathbf{act}(v_2)\ \&\ P_i(v_2)]]$
Ziro

$\lambda v.[\mathbf{act}(v)\ \&\ P_i(v)] = [[VP]]\quad [[v]] = \lambda P.\lambda e.\lambda v_1.[\mathbf{Ag}(e)(v_1)\ \&\ \exists v_2.[v_2 \leq v_1\ \&\ P(v_2)]]$

$\lambda v.[P_i(v)] = [[Adv]]\quad [[V]] = \lambda P.\lambda v.[\mathbf{act}(v)\ \&\ P(v)]$
soo$_i$ *su*

In this case, and actually all cases, the denotation of *soo-su* is characterized as shown in (26):

(26) a. $[[\{_{VP}\ soo_i, su\}]] = \lambda v_2.\ [\mathbf{act}(v_2)\ \&\ P_i(v_2)]$
b. P_i's co-occuring property $P_C = P_{act} = \lambda v.\ [\mathbf{act}(v)]$
(because P_{act} and P_i share the same event variable v_2.)

Now let us consider how the *soo-su* clause in (25a) is assigned an actual reading such as "Ziro read LGB, too." The task for interpretation is two-fold. The first step is to determine what property counts as an antecedent P_A for P_i. Suppose that context (25a) renders the following property given: $P_1 = \lambda v.\ [\mathbf{read}(\mathbf{lgb})(v)]$ (i.e. the denotation of VP in (21b)). Because P_1 is of type $<v, t>$, it meets the definition of P_A in (23). Here, let P_A be P_1. Then, the second step is to check the result of identifying P_i with that P_A by applying the Hyponymy Condition in (24), which says that the actual antecedent P_A must be more specific than any P_C. This process is summarized in (27):

(27) a.   Suppose P_A = λv. [**read**(**lgb**)(v)] and P_C = λv. [**act**(v)].
      b.   Then the result of identifying P_i with P_A is licensed, because
            for every v, if **read**(**lgb**)(v) is true, then **act**(v) is true.

As stated in (27b), the result satisfies the Hyponymy Condition, because we can assume that reading LGB is an action. Thus, there is no problem with the logical inference that, for every event, if it is an LGB-reading event, then it is an action event. As a result, the *soo-su* clause in (25a) is allowed to obtain an actual reading such as "Ziro read LGB, too."

Let us turn to the case of nominal antecedents (see (10)). The point is that *soo-su* can take DP antecedents if they are event nominals (e.g. *uwaki* 'affair'), but not non-event nominals (e.g. *uwakigokoro* 'unfaithfulness'). This fact also follows under our proposals, as the former can be regarded as event descriptions, but the latter should be viewed as entity descriptions:

(28) a.   [[*uwaki*]] = λv. [**have-affair**(v)]   i.e. type <v, t>
      b.   [[*uwakigokoro*]] = λe. [**unfaithfulness**(e)] i.e. type <e, t>

Thus, only [[*uwaki*]] meets the definition of P_A. Moreover, the Hyponymy Condition licenses the result of identifying P_i with [[*uwaki*]], because we can assume that having affairs is an action. Thus, it is always true that, for every event, if it is a having-affair event, then it is an action event. This is how our compositional analysis derives the syntax and semantics of *soo-su*.[7]

3.3   Further Predictions

Let us consider further predictions of our proposals. First, the semantics of *su* predicts that there are some cases where *soo-su* fails to realize potential internal arguments. This is correct, as illustrated in (29) (e.g. Nakau 1973):

(29) *Taro-ga   LGB-o   yom-da*; *Ziro-mo (*MP-o)* ***soo si**-ta.*
      Taro-Nom LGB-Acc read-Past Ziro-also   MP-Acc so   do-Past
      'Taro read LGB; Ziro did so (MP), too.'

The reason is that the semantics of *su* (i.e. λP.λv. [**act**(v) & P(v)]) does not introduce any argument of type e, such as *MP*.

Second, the Hyponymy Condition predicts that *soo* alone cannot directly "replace" adjunct phrases of type <v, t>, such as *hayaku* 'fast.' Again, this is correct, as illustrated in (30):

(30) *Taro-ga   hayaku$_i$ hasit-ta*; *Ziro-mo   hayaku/*soo$_i$ hasit-ta.*
      Taro-Nom fast   run-Past Ziro-also fast/so   run-Past
      'Taro ran fast; Ziro ran fast/so, too.'

---

[7] However, the contrast in (12) remains to be explained: Why is *soo-su* not allowed in an infinitival manner-clause? Still, (12) is important in showing the substantial semantics of *su*.

Here, *soo* is never interpreted as referring back to the content of *hayaku* in the precedeing clause. To see what blocks the "direct replacement" use of *soo*, let us consider the denotations of $\{_{VP}$ *hayaku, hasit*$\}$ and $\{_{VP}$ *soo, hasit*$\}$. Suppose that both VPs are interpreted via an event-semantics version of Heim and Kratzer's (1998) Predicate Modification, shown in (31):

(31) *Predicate Modification* (cf. Heim and Kratzer 1998)
    Let α be a merged unit $\{\beta, \gamma\}$, where both $[\![\beta]\!]$ and $[\![\gamma]\!]$ are elements of type $<v, t>$. Then $[\![\alpha]\!] = \lambda v. [[\![\beta]\!](v)\ \&\ [\![\gamma]\!](v)]$.

As all items *hasit, hayaku*, and *soo* are of type $<v, t>$, the rule in (30) turns both VPs into the following interpretations:

(32) a. $[\![\{_{VP}$ *hayaku, hasit*$\}]\!] = \lambda v. [\mathbf{run}(v)\ \&\ \mathbf{fast}(v)]$
    b. $[\![\{_{VP}$ *soo, hasit*$\}]\!] = \lambda v. [\mathbf{run}(v)\ \&\ P_i(v)]$

In this case, we can pick out just the denotation of *hayaku* (i.e. $\lambda v. [\mathbf{fast}(v)]$) as the antecedent property P_A for P_i, given that it is of type $<v, t>$. However, the Hyponymy Condition does not license the result of identifying P_i with $[\![hayaku]\!]$, because that P_A is not a "hyponym" of the P_C, as shown in (33):

(33) a. Suppose $P_A = \lambda v. [\mathbf{fast}(v)]$ and $P_C = \lambda v. [\mathbf{run}(v)]$.
    b. Then the result of identifying P_i with P_A is *not* licensed, because for every v, if $\mathbf{fast}(v)$ is true, then $\mathbf{run}(v)$ is *not necessarily* true.

That is, it is not true that every fast event is a running event; for example, there may be a fast walking event. Thus, the Hyponymy Condition correctly rules out the use of *soo* in (30).[8]

4 Conclusion

In summary, we undertook a compositional analysis of the Japanese anaphoric verbal expression *soo-su* that treats *soo* and *su* as independent lexical items. Under our analysis, *soo* is anaphoric to event properties, while *su* describes its event argument as an action, and these items are merged into *soo-su* by a syntactic computation. Thus, our analysis ensures that the derivation of *soo-su* complies with the Inclusiveness Condition.

    Finally, in light of the syntax and semantics of *soo-su* developed here, we discuss the architecture of the Japanese VP. Our suggestion is that there

---

[8] Note another possiblity, that P_i is identified with $[\![\{_{VP}$ *hayaku, hasit*$\}]\!]$ itself: $P_A = \lambda v. [\mathbf{run}(v)$ & $\mathbf{fast}(v)]$. This P_A is a "hyponym" of the P_C, satisfying the Hyponymy Condition; it is a valid inference that, for every v, if $[\mathbf{run}(v)\ \&\ \mathbf{fast}(v)]$ is true, then $\mathbf{run}(v)$ is true. However, such a reading is not allowed. This fact can be reduced to Condition C. On the impossible reading, *soo* violates Condition C in that it c-commands the co-indexed R-expression *hasit*, as shown in (i):

(i) * *Taro-ga   hayaku$_i$ hasit$_j$-ta; Ziro-mo   soo$_{i,j}$ hasit$_j$-ta.*
    Taro-Nom fast   run-Past Ziro-also so   run-Past

are further functional heads between VP and vP that introduce some types of dative and accusative internal arguments (IA), as shown in (34):

(34) [$_{vP}$ EA [$_{XP}$ IA$_{Dat/Acc}$ [$_{VP}$ V] **X**] v] (NB, EA = external argument)

To make the point, let us recall the fact in (29) that *soo-su* does not license potential IAs. However, as noted by Mihara (2004), *soo-su* is not completely incompatible with the existence of IA. We show this point by adopting a predicate classification on the notion of scale (see Levin 2010 for an overview). Put simply, some predicates introduce scales by which they measure out the amount of state/location change that their arguments undergo. Note that there are two types of "scalar" predicates: One inherently encodes a scale, and the other creates a scale compositionally with its incremental-theme or path XP (cf. Levin 2010). Thus, there are three predicate types in terms of scale, shown in (35):

(35) a.   Non-scalar (NS)   e.g. *apologize [$_{Dat}$ DP], order DP*
     b.   Inherent-scale (IS)   e.g. *freeze DP*
     c.   Compositional-scale (CS)   e.g. *move [$_{Dat}$ DP], eat DP*

We now point out that *soo-su* can occur only with (i) **the NS type's dative IA** and (ii) **the IS type's accusative IA**, as illustrated in (36) to (40):

[Dative IA]
(36) **Compositional-scale Pred: *idoo-su* 'move-do'**
     Ken-ga   *MIT-ni*   *idoosita*;   *Ai-mo*   (*NYU-ni)   *soo*   *sita*.
     Ken-Nom   MIT-Dat moved   Ai-also   NYU-Dat   so   did
     'Ken moved to MIT; Ai did so (to NYU), too.'
(37) **Non-scalar Pred: *syazai-su* 'apology-do'**
     Ken-ga   *MIT-ni*   *syazaisita*;   *Ai-mo*   (?*NYU-ni*)   *soo*   *sita*.
     Ken-Nom   MIT-Dat apologized   Ai-also   NYU-Dat   so   did
     'Ken apologized to MIT; Ai did so (to NYU), too.'

[Accusative IA]
(38) **Non-scalar Pred: *tyumon-su* 'order-do'**
     Ken-ga   *udon-o*   *tyumonsita*;   *Ai-mo*   (*piza-o)   *soo*   *sita*.
     Ken-Nom   udon-Acc ordered   Ai-also   pizza-Acc   so   did
     'Ken ordered udon; Ai did so (a pizza), too.'
(39) **Compositional-scale Pred: *kansyoku-su* 'eat.up-do'**
     Ken-ga   *udon-o*   *kansyokusita*;   *Ai-mo*   (*piza-o)   *soo*   *sita*.
     Ken-Nom   udon-Acc ate.up   Ai-also   pizza-Acc   so   did
     'Ken ate the udon up; Ai did so (the pizza), too.'

(40) **Inherent-scale Pred:** *reitoo-su* **'freeze-do'**
 Ken-ga udon-o reitoosita; Ai-mo (?piza-o) soo sita.
 Ken-Nom udon-Acc froze   Ai-also pizza-Acc so did
 'Ken froze the udon; Ai did so (the pizza), too.'

If our proposals for *soo-su* are correct, then it should be true that the dative IA in (37) and the accusative IA in (40) are introduced by heads other than *su*, as *su* does not introduce any argument of type e. This suggests that there are further argument-introducing heads between VP and *v*P. We leave investigations of this possibility for future research.

References

Chomsky, N. 1995. *The Minimalist Program*. Cambridge, MA.: MIT Press.

Davidson, D. 1967. The Logical Form of Action Sentences. *The Logic of Decision and Action*, ed. N. Rescher, 81-95. Pittsburgh: University of Pittsburgh Press.

Grimshaw, J. B. 1990. *Argument Structure*. Cambridge, MA.: MIT Press.

Hallman, P. 2004. Constituency and Agency in VP. *WCCFL* 23: 101-14.

Hankamer, J. and I. A. Sag. 1976. Deep and Surface Anaphora. *Linguistic Inquiry* 7: 391-426.

Heim, I and A. Kratzer. 1998. *Semantics in Generative Grammar*. Oxford: Blackwell.

Hoji, H. 1990. *Theories of Anaphora and Aspects of Japanese Syntax*. ms.. University of Southern California.

Kageyama, T. 1993. *Bunpoo to Go Keisei (Grammar and Word Formation)*. Tokyo: Hituzi Shobo.

Kishimoto, H. 2006. Japanese Syntactic Nominalization and VP-internal Syntax. *Lingua* 116: 771-810.

Kratzer, A. 1996. Severing the External Argument from Its Verb. *Phrase Structure and the Lexicon*, ed. J. Rooryck and L. Zaring, 109-37. Dordrecht: Kluwer.

Levin, B. 2010. Lexicalized Scales and Verbs of Scalar Change. Handout given at 46th Annual Meeting of the Chicago Linguistic Society, University of Chicago, Chicago, IL, April 8-10, 2010.

Mihara, K. 2004. *Asupekuto Kaisyaku to Toogo Gensyou (The Interpretation of Aspect and Syntactic Phenomena)*, Tokyo: Shohakusya.

Nakau, M. 1973. *Sentential Complementation in Japanese*. Tokyo: Kaitakusha.

Parsons, T. 1985. Underlying Events in the Logical Analysis of English. *Actions and Events: Perspectives on the Philosophy of Donald Davidson*, ed. E. LePore and B. Basil, 235-267. Oxford: Blackwell.

Ramchand, G. C. 2007. *Verb Meaning and the Lexicon: A First Phase Syntax*, ms.. University of Tromsø.

Yumoto, Y. 2005. *Fukugoo Dooshi/Hasee Dooshi no Imi to Toogo (The Meaning and Syntax of Compound Verbs/Derived Verbs)*. Tokyo: Hituzi Shobo.

Part IV

Historical Linguistics

Ubiquitous Variability in the Phonological Form of Loanwords: Tracing Early Borrowings into Japanese over Five Centuries of Contact

AARON ALBIN
Indiana University

1 Introduction

It is well known that many changes can occur in a word's phonological form when it is borrowed from one language (the 'Source Language', or SL) into another (the 'Borrowing Language', or BL) as a loanword.[1] The present paper examines loanword phonology from a sociohistorical

---

[1] In this paper, the term 'loanword' refers specifically to a lexical item within the BL that even monolinguals (i.e. individuals with no second language knowledge of the SL) can use. For example, native speakers of English can use the words *karaoke* and *kimchi* to communicate with each other in English discourse, even without any second language knowledge of Japanese or Korean.

Japanese/Korean Linguistics 23.
Edited by Michael Kenstowicz, Theodore Levin and Ryo Masuda.
Copyright © 2016, CSLI Publications

perspective, focusing specifically on the issue of segmental variation. Relatively few studies have examined loanword phonology from this angle. The majority of studies in this field begin by laying out data in the format 'source word X in the SL = loanword Y in the BL' (e.g. English *blanket* = Japanese *buranketto*), inherently suppressing variation before the analysis even begins. Moreover, the most common data sources have been modern synchronic dictionaries, perception experiments, and linguistic informants, all of which can only tap loanword forms that happened to survive into the modern language. Due to these methodological biases, our understanding of the mechanisms of phonological variation in loanwords is still rather limited.

The present paper is organized as follows. Section 2 establishes the theoretical background for the present study, first reviewing two previous studies examining synchronic variation and diachronic change in loanword phonology and then by laying out the goals of the study. Section 3 describes the methods used in the construction of a database of segmental loanword variation. Section 4 presents the empirical results of two analyses applied to this database – first on the overall extent of variation (4.1) and then on the network structure that can be observed in the variation (4.2). Section 5 proposes a theoretical explanation for why the variation is so extensive (5.1), and argues how the results of the present study lend support to this explanation (5.2). Section 6 concludes the paper with a discussion of limitations and future directions (6.1) and a statement of the broader implications for the field of Loanword Phonology (6.2).

2 Background

One important study that directly addresses the issue of variation and change in loanword phonology is Crawford (2009). Crawford argues that the process of loanword borrowing can be broken into two separate processes: (1) the *adaptation* of the word by BL speakers in direct contact with the spoken or written form of the original SL word, and (2) the *transmission* of the adapted word forms throughout the BL community. If the BL and SL communities remain in sustained language contact, adaptation and transmission are both simultaneously operative. Crucially, however, if language contact ceases, then adaptation ceases as well and only transmission continues. Crawford (2009) bases this model on a series of computational simulations in which foreign structures (e.g. [ti], as opposed to [tʃi], in Japanese) enter and spread through the BL, drawing on historical dates of loanwords' first written attestation as data. In the simulations, members of the BL community are represented as different nodes within a social network, each of which spreads loanword forms to other nodes (with some fixed probability of miscommunication). At the level of the BL community as a whole, the foreign structure and the nativized structure (e.g.

[ti] and [tʃ i]) coexist and compete with each other. After enough time has elapsed, one of the two forms ultimately emerges as dominant within the community due to a 'telephone game' type effect.

The study by de Jong and Cho (2012) makes it clear that it is not always the case that a single form emerges as dominant, and that instead a significant amount of variation may survive to the present day. In this study, the authors constructed a database of English (SL) to Korean (BL) obstruent mappings, drawing on data from two loanword dictionaries published in Korea, other published sources, and surveys of native speakers of Korean. The extent of variation found in this dataset is described as follows:

> A general perusal of this database shows one aspect of loanword mapping that is generally not discussed in much of the earlier linguistic literature on the topic, namely, that loanword adaptations are often variable in form. That is, for a substantial minority of the corpus (27.6% of the words [...]), there is more than one form in circulation. (de Jong & Cho 2012:348)

In both this study and Crawford (2009), each individual loanword is taken to represent one or more instances of a pre-determined set of segments, which serve as the data points for analysis. As of yet, no study has taken the opposite perspective – examining loanwords' phonological variation at the level of the entire word, irrespective of segmental makeup. With this change in perspective, the resulting picture may look quite different. Considering that any segment of a word can, in principle, exhibit variation, the proportion of words with more than one variant may be even greater than the 27.6 percent reported in de Jong & Cho (2012).

The goal of the present study is to explore this alternative perspective. In particular, the present study examines how much segmental variation is attested for a sample of early loanwords into Japanese (borrowed in or before the 1890s). The overall goal is document the full spectrum of variation that has been historically attested for each loanword in this sample. As such, forms that have become archaic are valid data points to be included in the sample, as are variant forms only found in modern Japanese dialects.

The present study takes a panchronic approach, examining how much variation is attested for each loanword across all time (i.e. between the time each word was originally borrowed and the present day). In order to yield as comprehensive a picture as possible, rather than restricting attention to one specific SL-BL pairing (e.g. just English-SL loanwords into Japanese), loanwords from five different 'Western' languages (Portuguese, Dutch,

German, French, and English) are included in the sample.[2] Of these, for historical reasons, the earliest borrowings are from Portuguese in the 1500s, hence the present study traces this set of early loanwords over approximately five centuries (from the 1500s up to and including the 1900s).

The following section describes the methodological steps involved in constructing the database used in the present study.

3   Construction of Database

The first step in constructing the database was to identify a sample of early Western loanwords borrowed into Japanese. Toward this end, all headwords for loanwords of Portuguese, Dutch, German, French, and English origin were located in an approximately 120 year old Japanese dictionary: *Nihon Daijisho* (Yamada 1892-1893). Since, unlike modern Japanese, the *katakana* writing system was generally not used for writing loanwords at the time, the dictionary entries containing Roman print were first manually located and then filtered down to *bona fide* loanword entries (for which the Roman print represented the orthography of the source word in the SL). By searching for variant forms at the end of each entry, and by following cross references to other entries, it was ensured all variant forms of each loanword given in *Nihon Daijisho* were included in the database. In total, this resulted in a set of 256 loanwords, each with its own 'family' of one or more variant forms (all corresponding to the same SL word). Taken as a whole, this set of loanwords gives a rough picture of the kinds of loanwords that enjoyed common currency in the 1890s.[3]

The second step in constructing the database was to cross reference these 256 loanwords in three other modern dictionaries, with the goal of finding all other historically attested variant phonological forms for each word. Three data sources were triangulated (rather than relying on just one) in order to get a richer and more realistic picture of the full scope of variation. The first dictionary was the second edition of *Nihon Kokugo Daijiten* (Nihon Daijiten Kankōkai 2000-2001), the largest dictionary of the

---

[2] Due to their geographic proximity, Japanese has engaged in language contact with Chinese and Korean for many centuries, unlike the much more recent contact between Japanese and the Western languages considered here. This vast difference in historical depth makes it unsafe to collapse the two cases and treat them on the same grounds. As such, words of Chinese and Korean origin were excluded from the present study. Moreover, since Latin and Sanskrit are both classical languages that are no longer spoken natively, the only means by which they could enter Japanese is through native speakers of other languages (e.g. Portuguese for Latin and Chinese for Sanskrit). Due to this potential complication, loanwords from these languages were also excluded.

[3] While pitch accent information is provided in Nihon Daijisho (and was therefore also recorded in the database), the present study examines segmental variation only. Thus, each variant in the present study is defined in terms of segmental makeup alone.

Japanese language. With over 500,000 entries it is sometimes likened to the Oxford English Dictionary in size and scope. Not surprisingly, a substantial portion of variants were only found in this source. The other two data sources were the second edition of *Daijisen* (Matsumura 1998) and the third edition of *Daijirin* (Matsumura 2006). While these two dictionaries share the same supervising editor, since the goal is merely to find as many variants as possible, this overlap is not especially problematic. Moreover, the two dictionaries are in fact rather different – having been compiled by different publishers' staff for different target markets. These three data sources were searched electronically for all of the variants found in *Nihon Daijisho*. Whenever a new variant was found, that variant was searched for in the other dictionaries. By iterating this process, it was possible to exhaustively sample the historically-attested phonological variation for each of the 256 loanwords.

Two methodological hurdles are of note. First, the four dictionaries sometimes occasionally disagreed as to the true SL and/or source word for a given loanword. Special attention was given to this problem throughout the process of compiling the database. For each of the 256 loanwords, the SLs and source forms posited in the four dictionaries were compared and any discrepancies were resolved. While this involved arbitrating on a case by case basis based on the given evidence, the selected SL and source form generally represented either the majority opinion of the four dictionaries or the most historically plausible source (given the detailed etymological notes and historical attestation dates in *Nihon Kokugo Daijiten*).

Secondly, in *Nihon Kokugo Daijiten*, certain variants are marked as representing *hōgen* 'dialect' or *namari* '(regional) accent'. For example, in addition to *hankachi* and *hankechi* (from English *handkerchief*), the form *hanketsu* is listed as occurring in a dialect in Nagasaki. It is not immediately clear whether such variants should be included or excluded from the present analysis. On the one hand, such forms can be thought of a perfectly valid representation of phonological variation, hence excluding them would yield an incomplete picture. On the other hand, it could be argued that the variation incurred as a word spreads through multiple dialects is an orthogonal process, hence including dialectal variants would artificially inflate the extent of variation. The solution to this conundrum adopted in the present study is to explicitly code each variant as [+/–dialectal] and use this information throughout the analysis. Specifically, any variant that was *only* found in the *hōgen* or *namari* sections of an article in *Nihon Kokugo Daijiten* was marked as [+dialectal]. All other variants were marked as

[–dialectal].[4] In all analyses presented in the rest of this paper, parallel analyses are shown – both including and excluding the [+dialectal] variants.

4 Results

4.1 Overall Extent of Variation

Overall, a total of 750 variants were found across the 256 loanwords in the sample, yielding an overall ratio of 750/256=2.9 variants per loanword on average. Of these 750 variants, 136 (18.1%) were classified as [+dialectal] according to the criteria given above. With these dialectal variants excluded, the ratio becomes 614/256=2.4 variants per loanword on average.

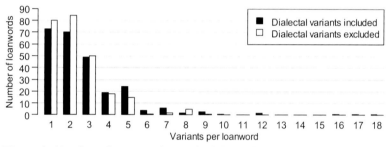

Figure 1: Number of variants for each of the 256 loanwords

Figure 1 captures the distribution of the number of variants per loanword in the database. Black bars represent the number of variants per loanword if dialectal variants are included, whereas white bars represent the number of variants if they are excluded. For example, if dialectal variants are excluded, the loanword for 'handkerchief' discussed above would be classified under '2' (for *hankachi* and *hankechi*), whereas if dialectal variants are included, this loanword would be classified under '3' (adding a third form *hanketsu*).

Inspection of Figure 1 reveals that, while N=1 variant is a numerous case, a substantial portion of the distribution lies at or above N=2 variants. If dialectal variants are included, only 73 (28.5%) of the 256 loanwords have just one variant, as opposed to 183 (71.5%) with more than one. (If dialectal variants are included, this shifts only slightly to 80/256 (31.2%) for N=1 versus 176/256 (68.8%) for N=2 and above.)

---

[4] Forms classified as [–dialectal] represented two clases of cases: (1) either a variant was found in neither the *hōgen* nor *namari* sections, or (2) a variant was found in one of these sections but was also attested in historical documents. In the latter case, since the variant has a historical attestation, it cannot be a recent innovation within a modern dialect, hence that variant would need to be included even in a conservative analysis in which dialectal variants are removed. The classification of such variants as [–dialectal] achieves this result.

It can also be observed in Figure 1 that the exclusion of dialectal variants has the effect of trimming the tail of the distribution and shifting the overall distribution to the left. Thus, if dialectal variants are included, the highest number of variants is N=18; if they are excluded, this number drops to N=9. The overall shape of the distribution, however, remains largely unaffected by the inclusion vs. exclusion of dialectal variants.

Source	Variants	N
shovel (English): 'shovel'	**shaberu**, shaveru, shavuru, shaburu, shoeru, shoberu, shooberu, shoburu, (*shaboru, safuro, saburo, shafuro, shapuro, shaboro, shaburo, shabero, shoburo, chaberu*)	18 (8)
vidro (Portuguese): 'glass'	**biidoro**, hiitoro, (*hiidoro, biizoro, biitoro, bindoro, bindoroo, binzoro, bin, bidoro, bijiro, biroodo, biiboro, biiroro, beedoro, biidoru, biduru*)	17 (2)
chapeau (French): 'hat'	**shappo**, shiapoo, shappu, shappoo, shapu, shapoo, chappo, (*appon, sappu, sappo, shiappu, shiyappu, shappon, shapo, chapo, happo*)	16 (7)
confeito (Portuguese): 'confection'	**konpeitoo**, konpei, (*konpeito, konpetoo, konpeto, konpento, konpentoo, konpenpo, konpeko, konheito, kopeto, kobento*)	12 (2)
blanket (English): 'blanket'	**buranketto**, furanketto, furangetto, furankeeto, puranken, furanken, furanke, ketto, kettoo, (*furanketsu, keton, ketton*)	12 (9)
Camboja (Portuguese): 'pumpkin'	**kabocha**, kanboocha, (*kabucha, abocha, boocha, kabuchiya, kabo, kaboccha, kaboja, kwabocha*)	10 (2)

Table 1: Variant forms for the six loanwords with ten or more total variants

For illustration purposes, the variant forms of all loanwords with ten or more total variants are listed in Table 1. The 'Source' column gives the spelling of the original word in the source language, which source language the word comes from, and a gloss representing the loanword's meaning (as used in Japanese). The 'Variants' column lists the variants for that loanword. The first variant (given in bold) is the dominant form of that word in modern Japanese. This is followed by one or more other historically attested forms for that loanword (most of which are now archaic). This is then followed by the dialectal variants (given in italics and surrounded by parentheses) – that is, variants that are only found in modern dialects (and not in any historical documents). Finally, the 'N' column lists the total number of variants for each loanword – both with dialectal variants included (listed first) and excluded (in parentheses).

4.2 Network Structure in the Variation

In Table 1 above, the variants of each loanword are displayed as entries in an unstructured list. This representation obscures the intricate structure of interrelatedness among the variants. In particular, closer inspection of the variant lists in Table 1 reveals that many pairs of variants form minimal pairs, raising the possibility that one may have historically derived from the other through some sort of phonological process. On a global level, such relationships can be thought of as forming the ties in a network of the sort that can be visualized as an undirected graph. In such a graph, each vertex (node) represents a variant form, and each edge (connection) represents some minimal phonological change (such as devoicing or deletion).

Figure 2 below depicts the network structure for the variant loanword forms of English *shovel* – an ideal candidate since this loanword has the largest number of variants (N=18).[5] In order to formally capture the notion of minimal phonological change, all variants were first recoded from *katakana* into a broad phonemic transcription, equivalent to *Nihonshiki* Romanization with three exceptions: The first mora in a geminate consonant is represented as Q, a moraic nasal as N, and the second mora in a long vowel as ':'. The string distances between all logically possible pairs of variants were then computed using the 'adist()' function in R 3.0.2 (R Core Team 2013), with string distance operationalized as follows:

> The (generalized) Levenshtein (or edit) distance between two strings *s* and *t* is the minimal [...] number of insertions, deletions and substitutions needed to transform *s* into *t* (so that the transformation exactly matches *t*). (R Core Team 2013)

---

[5] While, by definition, this data point represents an outlier, examination of similar network graphs for other more 'typical' loanwords with fewer variants suggests that the same patterns described below also obtain there, just on a smaller scale.

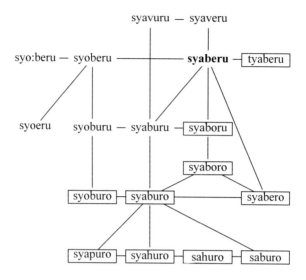

Figure 2: Network structure in the loanword variants of English shovel

In Figure 2, the variant in boldface (/syaberu/) is the main form at both time points (in the 1890s and in the present day). The ten variants surrounded by boxes are dialectal forms.[6] Only the edges (connections) representing a string distance of 1 are shown, thus connecting variants differing by only one segment.[7] As a consequence, different phonological features can be mapped onto different regions of the network. For example, the forms with /o/ in the first syllable (/syo-/, /syo:-/) are localized in the left half; all other forms have /a/ in the first syllable (/sya-/, /sa-/, /tya-/). Similar observations can be made of other segments as well, such as the second syllable's onset (v/b/h/p/Ø) or the final vowel (u/o).

---

[6] The two variants at the top of the graph (/syavuru/ and /syaveru/) include the segment /v/. This is a representation of the words' spellings as シャヴル and シャヴェル, respectively. Given the fact Japanese does not natively have /v/ in its phonemic inventory, these spellings could possibly be an element of orthography only. These were nonetheless included in the dataset because it is possible some members in the Japanese-speaking community produced these forms with /v/. This methodological decision had only a minor impact on the dataset as a whole, as only 3 of the 256 loanwords in the entire dataset have /v/: English *shovel* (/syavuru/, /syaveru/), English *octavo* (/okuta:vo/), and French *vermouth* (/verumoQto/).

[7] While this connects all vertices (nodes) in Figure 2, this is not always the case – occasionally a variant has no minimal pair neighbor (e.g. in cases of truncation where multiple segments are elided together, like *konpei* vs. *konpeito(o)* in Table 1).

Interestingly, the phonological network structure maps quite closely onto the attested temporal and spatial information available for the word. The distribution of forms is described in *Nihon Kokugo Daijiten* as follows:

(1)   Various word forms are seen, but to divide roughly, it can be said that the original spelling reading /syo/ first appeared, and after that, the original sound form /sya/ appeared. Among these, /syoburu/ was used until the middle of the Meiji period and /syaburu/ was used until the end of the Taisho period. /syoberu/ and /syaberu/ were used together, but after the Showa period, /syaberu/ became dominant.

(2)   Looking at the whole country's dialects, /syoberu/ is West Japan, and the forms that changed from /syaberu/ – /syaboro/, /syaboru/, /saburo/, etc. – are distributed in East Japan, hence the /sya/ form and the /syo/ form constitute an East-West division.

(Nihon Daijiten Kankōkai. 2000-2001)

These observations coincide with other information included inside the article for this loanword in *Nihon Kokugo Daijiten*. Forms with /o/ have an earlier date of first historical written attestation (e.g. /syoeru/ in 1869) and are found in dialects in West Japan (/syoburo/ in Shimane prefecture). In contrast, forms with /a/ appeared later (e.g. /syaberu/'s appearance in *Nihon Daijisho* (1892-1893)) and are distributed widely in East Japan (e.g. /syaburo/ in Tochigi, /syafuro/ in Iwate, and /safuro/ in Aomori).

5   Discussion

5.1   A Proposed Explanation for the Observed Variation

One central finding from Section 4 is that phonological variation is pervasive in loanwords. For example, it was found that 71.5 percent of the 256 loanwords in the sample had more than one variant attested either in historical documents, modern dialects, or both. The natural question, then, is *why* is there so much variation – that is, what sorts of processes led to so much variation being created? One promising explanation, pursued here, is that new variant phonological forms of a loanword can arise through both of the processes described in Crawford's (2009) model – adaptation and transmission – the combined force of which produces extensive variation.

Recall that *adaptation* occurs when BL speakers come in direct contact with the spoken or written form of the original SL word. In the process of adaptation, variation could arise from at least three sources. First, it could derive from variation in SL speakers' own pronunciations and spellings of the source word. For example, the modern Japanese word for 'paint', *penki*, has two earlier forms *pekki* and *pikki*, which may correspond to variation within the SL (Dutch), where this word (meaning 'tar') alternates as either *pek* or *pik*. Second, the members of the BL community may perceive the spoken form of the source word in the SL differently based on differences in how proficient the members of the BL community are in the SL as a second language. For example, some BL speakers may perceive the spoken form of English *shovel* as *shaberu* while others perceive it as *shaveru*, depending on each individual's perceptual capabilities (Peperkamp 2005). Third, there may be an opaque orthography-pronunciation mapping in how the word is spelled in the SL. This is also tied to proficiency differences within the BL community – more specifically, different degrees of familiarity with the SL's writing system. For example, the English chemical name *aniline* /ˈæ.nə.lɪ n/ has both *anirin* and *anirine* as variants in the present study's database. BL community members who are more proficient in this SL may have adapted this word as *anirin*, faithfully representing the word's pronunciation, whereas others less proficient may have adapted it as *anirine*, faithfully representing the word's spelling (Smith 2006).

Put together, these three factors have the cumulative effect of introducing new variation into the BL 'system' during the process of adaptation.[8] The exact weighting of these three factors (i.e. the extent to which they combine to create the observed variation) is likely dependent on the nature of the contact situation. For example, the perception-driven factor is only relevant for contact situations involving face to face interaction (where such spoken input is possible). In contrast, the orthography-driven factor is only applicable to contact situations where the BL speakers are literate in the SL (hence can access SL texts in the first place). In sum, then, adaptation is not a monotonic process that unconditionally occurs across the board to all kinds of contact situations.

In addition to adaptation, the transmission component of Crawford's (2009) model can also explain why the present study found such extensive variation. Recall from above that *transmission* refers to the dissemination of adapted word forms throughout the BL community. Variation may arise during this transmission process by means of a miscommunication from one BL speaker to another. In principle, this may happen in any of the four linguistic modes, i.e. misperceptions, misproductions, misreadings, and miswritings. These miscommunications are made possible due to differences in the linguistic knowledge ('grammars') of BL speakers across the BL community. These differences may be partially due to differences in second language proficiency in the SL across the BL community. However, there may be other contributing factors as well. For example, it would be difficult to ascribe the phonological changes occurring between the three

---

[8] It is important to keep in mind that adaptation does not occur all at once. Rather, the three sources of variation just described can lead to the same SL word being adapted in different ways at different points in time, e.g. the 19th vs. 20th century 'doublets' in Smith (2006).

forms /syaburo/, /syapuro/, and /syahuro/ to second language proficiency factors given that all three phones (/b/, /p/, and /h/) are licensed in that environment in Japanese. Examples such as this suggest that the processes that create phonological variation in loanwords during transmission may be partially due to more general mechanisms of language change – that is, processes not restricted to loanwords alone (e.g. analogy).

5.2   Supporting Evidence from the Present Study

The empirical results of the present study provide evidence for the above account that adaptation and transmission combine to create the observed phonological variation. First, note that the extent of variation documented in Section 4.1 above is most likely much larger than that found for native words. While, at present, fully comparable data for native words are not available, anecdotal evidence suggests that there are generally not, for example, nine (historically related) non-dialectal variants for common native words like 'apple' or 'walk' in the same way that there are nine non-dialectal variants of the loanword for 'blanket'. If, in the absence of systematic empirical investigation, this anecdotal insight is indeed correct, then there must be some difference between loanwords and native words that can explain the difference in the extent of variation. One likely candidate is the presence vs. absence of Crawfordian adaptation. While adaptation continues to occur for loanwords as long as language contact is sustained, native words lack the process of adaptation entirely. (Native words are already inside the BL, hence it is not necessary to adapt anything foreign.) This line of reasoning suggests that the extent of variation may be higher for loanwords because loanwords have an additional process – adaptation – fueling the variation.

In addition to adaptation, the present study provides evidence that transmission is also at work in creating the observed variation. This evidence takes two forms. First, while the network structure shown in Section 4.2 was created based on purely phonological information, it was shown to closely mirror the available temporal-spatial information for the loanword. In particular, certain phonologically-defined regions of the network could be mapped onto dates of first written attestation (for historically attested variants) and onto actual areas within Japan (for the dialectal variants). This is precisely what is expected if variation arises from transmission: Since time is required for a loanword to disseminate through the BL community during transmission, and since the BL community itself is spread across some geographic expanse, transmission inherently has both spatial and temporal components.

The second piece of evidence that transmission is at work in creating the observed variation lies in how many of the peripheral nodes in Figure 2 (such as /safuro/) are heavily warped from the original SL form *shovel* /ʃ ʌ vl/. Recall how each individual graph edge (connection) in the network structure of Figure 2 is a phonologically minimal change. As such, it is only possible for such heavy warping to occur if individual changes can cascade into a chain, one feeding into another. Inspection of Figure 2 suggests that this indeed appears to be the case. For example, *safuro* might have arisen through the path *shaveru-shaberu-shaburu-shaburo-shafuro-safuro* (among numerous other possibilities). Crawfordian transmission is a prerequisite for such iterative warping to occur, hence these findings serve as evidence that transmission contributes to the variation observed in the present study.

In sum, then, both adaptation and transmission appear to be at work in generating the variation documented above. Consequently, the observed variation cannot be attributed entirely to just one of these two processes.[9]

6 Conclusion

6.1 Limitations and Future Directions

Four limitations of the present study are worthy of mention. First, since the present dataset was tied to a single point in history – the 1890s – the present study can only make direct claims about *early* loanwords. By design, any words that had died out before the 1890s or had not entered Japanese by that time were not included in the present dataset and therefore remain to be analyzed in future research. Second, the present study only examined the case of loanwords from borrowed from five specific SLs into one specific BL. It is left to future research to determine whether the above results generalize to other SL-BL pairings. Third, the evidence used to argue for the role of adaptation relied on the untested assumption that the extent of variation for native words is less than that of loanwords. A natural next step would be to empirically verify this assumption by analyzing the extent of variation found in at native words from the same dictionaries used in the present study. Fourth and finally, the network analysis presented in Section 4.2 was applied in an ad hoc fashion to a single loanword. This method must be systematically applied to a larger sample of loanwords in order for the results of such an analysis are to be conclusive.

While the present study documented that variability in the phonologial form of loanwords is ubiquitous, it is most likely not random. As such, in addition to rectifying the above limitations, a promising future direction of the present research is to try to explain *why* some loanwords have more

---

[9] Kang, Kenstowicz, & Itō (2008) discuss 'hybrid loans' that enter a BL from a SL indirectly through some other carrier language (in their case, English words entering Korean through Japanese). In contact situations where such words exist, the resultant warping can be thought of as a third source of variation, occurring parallel to adaptation and transmission.

variant phonological forms than others. Toward this end, at least four different kinds of external 'predictors' can be brought in to explain the observed variation. The first of these is the segmental makeup of the source word in the SL. It is surely not a mere coincidence that there is only one variant loanword form of Dutch *pen* (whose segmental and phonotactic structure largely conform to Japanese phonology) whereas there are 18 variants for English *shovel* (which contains multiple structures that are foreign to Japanese phonology). This observation suggests that, to some extent, the extent of phonological variation for a given word should be predictable from the degree to which the segmental makeup of the original SL word (as BL speakers would have encountered it) is licensed by the phonology of the BL. The second predictor is the specific SL a loanword comes from. Note that all analyses in the present paper collapsed the five SLs in the dataset together. It would be of theoretical interest to ascertain whether the overall distribution of variation presented in Figure 1 above is stable across each of the five different SLs independently. The third predictor is the date at which a variant first appears in writing. Since the present study used a panchronic analysis, whereby all variants from all epochs were pooled, the results of the present study indicate merely that the pool of phonological variation in loanwords is extensive *when viewed across all time*. The internal temporal dynamic to this variation (e.g. when new variants arise within the history of each loanword) is still unclear. The fourth predictor is frequency. Note that the loanwords in Table 1 all represent objects encountered in daily life (*shovel, glass, hat, confection/candy, blanket, and pumpkin*). This observation suggests that usage frequency may predict the extent to which a loanword exhibits phonological variation. Clearly, the present study has only begun to scratch the surface of the many possible research questions of theoretical interest regarding the nature and structure of phonological variation in loanwords.[10]

6.2   Implications for Loanword Phonology

The present study's findings suggest a fundamental reconceptualization of the phenomenon of loanword phonology. If the line of reasoning pursued above is correct, then a modern 'loanword' (of the type usually analyzed in studies of Loanword Phonology) is merely a variant form that has happened to dominate from among a pool of other competing variants. Recall from the introduction that the majority of studies in the field begin by laying out data in the format 'source word X in the SL = loanword Y in the BL'. This study's findings suggest that this way of thinking about the data is

---

[10] To facilitate future research in this direction, both the dataset described in Section 3 as well as the script used to analyze it are available at the author's website.

oversimplistic. More specifically, rather than 'X → Y', the relation is more like 'X → {Y$_1$, Y$_2$, Y$_3$, Y$_4$, Y$_5$} → Y$_N$' (for a loanword with five variants, of which four are archaic). In this light, while previous studies in Loanword Phonology framed themselves as describing what happens in the 'X→Y' mapping, it may be more accurate to view their findings as accounting for which kinds of variants within the pool of variation are ultimately 'selected' diachronically (or, in the formalism above, which Y(s) are selected as Y$_N$).

In terms of methodology, the present study underscores the importance of choosing data sources that document the wider pool of variation (perhaps including archaic and/or dialectal variants) rather than data sources that lend themselves to simple deterministic X=Y mappings. If no such data source is available, then it is also possible to uncover the richness of the variation by triangulating multiple data sources (as done in the present study).

Traditional studies in Loanword Phonology are criticized in Crawford (2009:17) as merely describing 'the behavior of a single idealized speaker at a particular moment in time', as epitomized in static box and arrow diagrams. While such studies have been valuable in forming the conceptual foundations of the modern field, the time is ripe to transition a more dynamic view of loanword phonology – one that can account for variation and diachrony by allotting a role for both adaptation and transmission.

References

Crawford, C. 2009. Adaptation and transmission in Japanese loanword phonology. Doctoral dissertation, Cornell University. http://hdl.handle.net/1813/13947

de Jong, K., & M.-H. Cho. 2012. Loanword phonology and perceptual mapping: Comparing two corpora of Korean contact with English. *Language* 88(2):341-68.

Kang, Y., M. Kenstowicz, & C. Itō. 2008. Hybrid loans: A study of English loanwords transmitted to Korean via Japanese. *Journal of East Asian Linguistics* 17(4):299-316.

Matsumura, A. 1998. *Daijisen* [Great Fountainhead of Words]. 2nd ed. Tokyo: Shōgakukan.

Matsumura, A. 2006. *Daijirin* [Great Forest of Words]. 3rd ed. Tokyo: Sanseidō.

Nihon Daijiten Kankōkai. 2000-2001. *Nihon Kokugo Daijiten* [Great Dictionary of the Japanese National Language]. 2nd ed. Tokyo: Shōgakukan.

Peperkamp, S. 2005. A psycholinguistic theory of loanword adaptations. *Proceedings of 30th Annual Meeting of Berkeley Linguistics Society*, 341-352.

R Core Team. 2013. R: A language and environment for statistical computing. R Foundation for Statistical Computing, Vienna, Austria. http://www.R-project.org/.

Smith, J. L. 2006. Loan phonology is not all perception: Evidence from Japanese loan doublets. *Japanese/Korean Linguistics* 14:63-74. Palo Alto: CSLI.

Yamada, B. 1892-1893. *Nihon Daijisho* [Great Dictionary of Japan]. Tokyo: Nihon Daijisho Hakkōjo. http://babel.hathitrust.org/cgi/pt?id=mdp.39015030806726

Phonological Reduction and the (Re)emergence of Attributive Forms in Yaeyama Ryukyuan

TYLER LAU
Harvard University

CHRISTOPHER DAVIS
University of the Ryukyus

1 Introduction

In many Japono-Ryukyuan languages, there is a distinction between the con-clusive and attributive forms of verbs. This distinction was lost in the transi-tion from Old to Modern Japanese, in a process whereby a suffix that origi-nally marked verbs as attributive was reanalyzed as a present tense marker. In this paper, we adduce evidence from Yaeyama Ryukyuan for an ongoing re-analysis going in the opposite direction, where a present tense suffix is being reanalyzed as an attributive marker.

Section 2 describes the attributive marker in Old Japanese and its reanal-ysis as a present tense suffix in Modern Japanese. Section 3 provides an overview of the conclusive-attributive distinction in two Ryukyuan languages, Okinawan and Yaeyaman. Okinawan is seen to have overt conclusive and at-tributive markers, while Yaeyaman only has overt conclusive marking, ap-parently lacking any analog of the attributive marker found in Old Japanese and Okinawan. Section 4 complicates this picture, showing that Yaeyaman

Japanese/Korean Linguistics 23.
Edited by Michael Kenstowicz, Theodore Levin and Ryo Masuda.
Copyright © 2016, CSLI Publications.

299

stative present verbs show a surface contrast between attributive and conclusive forms that looks like the one seen in Okinawan. This is argued to derive from phonological reduction of the present tense suffix before the conclusive marker. The resulting surface forms, however, are driving a reanalysis of the present tense marker into an attributive marker. Section 5 considers the implications of the Yaeyaman reanalyis for how attributive marking has emerged in Ryukyuan. Section 6 concludes.

2 Attributive and Conclusive Forms in Japanese

In this section we present a basic overview of the attributive/conclusive distinction found in Old Japanese and the way in which this distinction was lost in Modern Japanese.

2.1 Old Japanese

Old Japanese was the language of Western Mainland Japan as spoken around the 7th to 8th centuries.[1] A comprehensive overview of the language can be found in Vovin (2004/2008), while Frellesvig (2010) describes Old Japanese and its later historical developments up to and including Modern Japanese.

Old Japanese verbs exhibit a morphological distinction between what are commonly known as the conclusive (*syuusi*) and attributive (*rentai*) forms. The conclusive form is alternatively known as the predicate form and generally appears sentence-finally, while the attributive form is alternatively known as the adnominal form and is generally used to modify noun phrases. The attributive form also appears in a construction known as *kakari-musubi*, in which it is used in sentences that contain any of the focus particles: =*zo*/=*so*, =*ka*, =*ja*, or =*namu*. It can also be used to head nominalized clauses.

The conclusive and attributive forms for exemplars from the eight verbal conjugational classes in Old Japanese are laid out in Table 1, modified from a chart in Frellesvig (2010:54).[2] As can be seen, all Japanese verb classes other than the quadrigrade class have distinct conclusive and attributive forms.[3] In all verb classes where the conclusive-attributive distinction is marked, except for the *r*-irregular class, the attributive form consists of the conclusive form

---

[1] "Old Japanese" refers to a particular variety of Mainland Japanese, which is attested in written records of the time. This variety served as the basis for a written standard that was used until relatively recently, which is often called Classical Japanese. Old Japanese thus refers to an actual language variety spoken at a particular time and place, while Classical Japanese refers to a written standard that was based on this variety.

[2] The class known as the lower monograde, which contains only one verb *keru* 'to kick', is omitted, since it did not appear until Early Middle Japanese (Frellesvig 2010:228).

[3] However, there is evidence of a difference in quadrigrade forms as well in Eastern Old Japanese (with -*o* in the attributive). See a longer discussion in the footnote in Frellesvig (2008:190).

TABLE 1 Old Japanese Attributive and Conclusive Verb Forms

Conjugation Type	Conclusive	Attributive	English
Quadrigrade	kaku	kaku	"write"
Upper Monograde	(mi)	mi<u>ru</u>	"see"
Upper Bigrade	oku	oku<u>ru</u>	"live"
Lower Bigrade	aku	aku<u>ru</u>	"receive"
n-Irregular	sinu	sinu<u>ru</u>	"die"
r-Irregular	ari	aru	"exist"
k-Irregular	ku	ku<u>ru</u>	"come"
s-Irregular	su	su<u>ru</u>	"do"

plus an additional *ru*.[4] The conclusive form itself is formed from the verb root and a final *u*. The upper and lower bigrade verb roots end in the vowels *i* and *e* respectively; these root-final vowels are deleted in both the attributive and conclusive verb forms.

2.2 Modern Japanese

In the transition to Late Middle Japanese, the conclusive forms were replaced by the attributive forms,[5] thought to be due to the increased usage of the *kakari-musubi* construction (Martin 1987:803), and the once-distinct conclusive and attributive markers fused into a single suffix. For the bigrade verbs, this apparently happened in two stages (Hattori 1959:344):

	Stage 1	Stage 2	Stage 3
conclusive	uku —//—→ ukuru ——→ ukeru		
attributive	ukuru ——→ ukuru ——→ ukeru		

Before the collapse, the attributive verb form received additional morphological marking beyond that found on conclusive forms, via the suffix *-ru*. The *-u* attached to the verb root in both conclusive and attributive forms is treated by Nishiyama (2000) as a present tense suffix, cognate with the one found in Modern Japanese. He argues that all Old Japanese attributive verbs forms contain an underlying attributive morpheme *-ru*, which ends up deleted or fused with the present tense suffix *-u* in the quadrigrade verbs, but preserved on the surface for the remaining verbs.[6] According to this analysis, the

---

[4] Martin (1987:805) reconstructs the stem as *a- with a *ra- formant originally, so there is potential evidence of the attachment of *-ru* as an attributive marker to the r-irregular stem as well.

[5] The n-irregular *sin-* 'to die,' however, regularized to the conclusive form.

[6] Nishiyama cites a different conclusive form for monograde verbs than that cited here; we ignore

underlying morphosyntactic structure of attributive verb forms is as follows
(Nishiyama 2000:268):

(1)

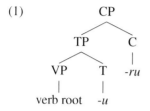

In this analysis, the "conclusive" suffix -*u* is a present tense marker, cognate
with the present/non-past tense marker found in Modern Japanese (Nishiyama
2000:265). Under this view, the conclusive form in Old Japanese is marked
only negatively, by the absence of the attributive suffix -*ru*.

As pointed out by Kaplan and Whitman (1995), the collapse of attributive and conclusive forms was due in effect to a reanalysis of the attributive
marker -*ru* as the present tense suffix -*u*. This reanalysis was made possible by
a partial homophony of the two suffixes, along with the fact that the quadrigrade verb class, to which belonged a bulk of Old Japanese verbs, lacked
a conclusive-attributive distinction. When this reanalysis was complete, the
attributive morpheme was lost from Japanese, and with it the system of C-
marking via inflectional morphology on the verb. The history of Japanese
thus presents a situation in which the attributive C marker was reanalyzed as
a tense morpheme and absorbed into the tense marking system, leading to a
loss of distinctive CP level morphology.[7]

---

this class in this discussion. The disparity likely stems from the fact that Nishiyama's analysis is
targeted at Classical Japanese, which as discussed earlier is an artificial written standard, rather
than a particular spoken language variety used at a particular time and place.

[7] Frellesvig (2010:53) argues that the conclusive suffix (or rather, the conclusive form) did not
encode present tense in Old Japanese, since the conclusive-attributive distinction was made on
various auxiliaries, some of which encoded past tense. According to Frellesvig, the collapse
of the conclusive-attributive distinction described above laid the ground for a reanalysis of the
resulting forms as encoding non-past tense, in opposition to past tense forms that derived from
Old Japanese auxiliaries that originally themselves exhibited the conclusive-attributive contrast.
This reanalysis of the conclusive-attributive verb forms as non-past tense forms occurred in Late
Middle Japanese (Frellesvig 2010:332). Although this complicates the picture described above,
the end result is still one in which the original attributive suffix is first lost through fusion with
the partially homophonous suffix that precedes it, and the resulting suffix is then absorbed into
the tense marking system, rather than the C system to which the attributive marker originally
belonged.

3 Conclusive and Attributive Forms in Ryukyuan

3.1 An Overview of Ryukyuan

The Ryukyuan languages constitute the only sister language group with (Mainland) Japanese. The Ryukyuan languages are spoken from the Amami islands in the southern part of Kagoshima Prefecture to Yonaguni island in the southwest reaches of Okinawa Prefecture next to Taiwan. Uemura (2003) and Shimoji and Pellard (2010) provide overviews in English of the Ryukyuan language group. There is a great deal of diversity within Ryukyuan, with recent research typically dividing the language group into 5 or 6 mutually unintelligible languages, which are divided at the topmost level into the Northern and Southern Ryukyuan language groups. Pellard (forthcoming) adduces a variety of evidence that the Ryukyuan language group as a whole split from Mainland Japanese before the Old Japanese period. Old Japanese and Proto-Ryukyuan are thus sister languages. All varieties of Ryukyuan are highly endangered, with the youngest fluent speakers typically in their forties or fifties in the healthiest varieties, and in their eighties or older in the most endangered varieties.

Many Ryukyuan languages show a distinction between attributive and conclusive verb forms similar to that found in Old Japanese. Although the details differ from Old Japanese and between individual Ryukyuan languages, many Ryukyuan languages require the attributive form in adnominal positions, as well as in clauses including focus particles like *du* and its cognates, a pattern that is typically treated on a par with the Japanese *kakari-musubi* construction. There is a large literature on this topic, in particular by Leon Serafim and Rumiko Shinzato; see for starters Shinzato and Serafim (2013). Here, we focus on data from Okinawan and Yaeyaman. To a first approximation, it appears as though Okinawan has complementary suffixes marking conclusive and attributive forms, while Yaeyaman lacks a distinct attributive marker.

3.2 Okinawan

In Okinawan, both conclusive and attributive marking exist for all verbs. For simple present tense verbs, the conclusive forms are marked by the suffix -*n*,[8] which follows tense markers such as the present tense suffix -*u*. Attributive forms are marked by -*ru*, paralleling what we saw for Old Japanese. The

---

[8] The -*n*-final form is traditionally treated on a par with the conclusive form in Old Japanese, because it is found in roughly the same set of environments, contrasts with the attributive form, and like the conclusive form seems to be blocked in certain *kakari-musubi* constructions. It seems very likely that this morpheme, variants of which are found throughout the Ryukyuan language family, is not simply a "conclusive" marker, but has particular semantic effects related to mood, modality, or evidentiality, varying across different Ryukyuan languages. The -*n* suffix surfaces as -*m* in those varieties that allow distinctive bilabial coda nasals, and is believed to be related to the final -*mu* appearing in the Old Japanese volitional/conjectural form (Uemura 2003:85).

attributive suffix follows tense morphology, including the present tense suffix *-u*. Comparisons of the conclusive and attributive forms are given below for simple present tense verbs from Shuri/Naha Okinawan (the de-facto standard dialect of Okinawa Ryukyuan):

(2) Shuri/Naha Okinawan Verb Forms

	Conclusive	Attributive
"write"	katʃ-u-**n**	katʃ-u-**ru**
"row"	kuudʒ-u-**n**	kuudʒ-u-**ru**
"go"	itʃ-u-**n**	itʃ-u-**ru**
"exist" (inanimate)	a-**n**	a-**ru**
"exist" (animate)	wu-**n**	wu-**ru**

Okinawan thus exemplifies a pattern in which there are complementary markers for both conclusive and attributive forms, in contrast to Old Japanese, in which only the attributive form is given additional marking. The attributive marker appears identical to that found in Old Japanese, but seems to have been regularized to the entire verbal paradigm.

Following Nishiyama's (2000) treatment of Old Japanese, we treat Okinawan *-ru* as spelling out a C head; although there are differences between the syntactic distribution of attributive-marked clauses in Old Japanese and Ryukyuan, we will assume that in both languages *-ru* fills the same morphosyntactic slot. The conclusive marker *-n* we also treat as filling the C slot.[9] This view receives support from those varieties of Ryukyuan (such as Okinawan) in which conclusive *-n* and attributive *-ru* markers are in complementary distribution (Miyara 2011). This picture is illustrated in the following diagrams:

(3)

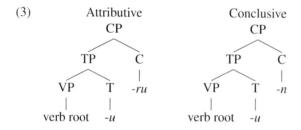

Okinawan thus presents a development that is essentially the opposite of that seen in Japanese. Whereas in Japanese the loss of the attributive marker

---

[9] Sugahara (1996) calls these morphemes in Okinawan "modal heads", and places them in a node labeled M, while Miyara (2011) calls them mood morphemes. For our purposes, these differences are immaterial. The crucial idea is that *-n* and *-ru* occupy the same morphosyntactic slot (and are thus in complementary distribution), and that this slot directly follows the one that encodes tense.

led to a verbal paradigm lacking any suffixes that occupy the C slot, Okinawan seems to have generalized the attributive marker across the entire verbal paradigm, and also innovated a novel conclusive C suffix that stands in complementary distribution with -ru.

3.3 Yaeyaman

Like Okinawan, simple present tense verbs in Yaeyaman can host the conclusive suffix -n.[10] Unlike Okinawan, however, they lack any additional marking of the attributive form. Comparisons of the conclusive and attributive forms of simple present tense verbs in Miyara Yaeyaman are given below:[11]

(4)   Miyara Yaeyaman Verb Forms

		Conclusive	Attributive
"write"		kak-u-n	kak-u
"row"		kuug-u-n	kuug-u
"go"		har-u-n	har-u
"exist" (inaminate)		a-ru-n	a-ru
"exist" (animate)		u-ru-n	u-ru

Patterns like these have often led researchers to the conclusion that Southern Ryukyuan (as exemplified here by Yaeyaman) lacks any overt attributive marking (Uemura 2003:84). Genuardi (2008:44), for example, writes: "Miyako and Yaeyama show no distinction between the Attributive and Conclusive [=predicative] outside of the nasal Conclusive form ... Otherwise, the Conclusive and Attributive are indistinct from each other in Miyako and Yaeyama, just as they are in Standard Japanese." Data from our own fieldwork paints a more complex picture. In the next section we show that Yaeyaman present tense verbs with stative aspectual morphology have surface forms with Okinawan-style contrasts between a final -ru and -n.

3.4 Summary

The attributive-conclusive marking paradigms for the four languages discussed above are summarized in Table 2. These languages represent the four logical possibilities for expressing the conclusive-attributive distinction. Okinawan has a designated morpheme for both forms, while Modern Japanese fails to make the distinction at all. In between we have Old Japanese, which marks only the attributive form with additional morphology, and Yaeyaman, which marks only the conclusive form.

---

[10] See Izuyama (2003:95-101) for a discussion of -n in Miyara Yaeyaman. Davis and Lau (forthcoming) call this morpheme in Miyaran an indicative mood marker.

[11] Yaeyaman data are from the authors' own fieldwork notes unless noted. Transcriptions follow the conventions laid out in Davis and Lau (forthcoming).

TABLE 2 Conclusive and Attributive Marking Contrasts

Language	Conclusive	Marked?	Attributive	Marked?
Okinawan	nindʒ-u-**n**	+	nindʒ-u-**ru**	+
Yaeyaman	nib-u-**n**	+	nib-u	−
Old Japanese	n-u	−	n-u-**ru**	+
Mod. Japanese	ne-ru	−	ne-ru	−

These distinctions are based on simple present tense verb forms in the four languages. As we show in the next section, verb forms with additional aspectual morphology suggest that Yaeyaman is in the process of developing a new attributive marker in a subset of its verbal forms.

4 A Closer Look at Yaeyaman

4.1 Stative Present Verb Forms

The observations made above were made on the basis of simple present tense verb forms, consisting of the verb root and the present tense morpheme -*u*. We now turn to the stative present[12] forms of these verbs in Yaeyaman. In Miyara Yaeyaman, the stative present is formed by insertion of the suffix -*í* between the verb root and the present tense suffix -*u* (Davis and Lau forthcoming:11). The acute accent on -*í* represents an inherent accent on this morpheme, realized as the locus of a pitch peak and subsequent fall in the resulting word. This lexical accent will be seen below to play a crucial role in the phonology of the resulting conclusive verb forms.

Given the above morphological breakdown of the stative present, and also that epenthetic *r* is systematically inserted to break hiatus between two vowels in separate morphemes,[13] we would predict the conclusive and attributive stative present forms for the regular consonant-final verb root *kak-* 'to write' to be as follows:

(5)   a.   Predicted Conclusive: /kak-í-u-n/ → *[kakírun]

   b.   Predicted Attributive: /kak-í-u/ → [kakíru]

The predicted attributive form is correct; however, the conclusive surfaces as [kakín] rather than the expected *[kakírun]. It appears that the present suffix -*u* is deleted in the conclusive, but not in the attributive. The same pattern holds for other verbs as well, as shown in Table 3. Shiraho, another distantly related variety of Yaeyaman, exhibits the same pattern, as shown in Table 4.[14]

---

[12] See Davis and Lau (forthcoming) for discussion of this form in Miyara Yaeyaman. This form could also be called the present progressive.

[13] This process is common in Japono-Ryukyuan, including in Modern Japanese .

[14] Phonetically, the attributive morpheme is -*ro* when used phrase-finally in Shiraho. However,

TABLE 3 Miyaran Stative Present Verb Forms

Attributive	Predicted Conclusive	Attested Conc.	
kak-í-ru	**kak-í-ru-n*	*kak-í-n*	'is writing'
jum-í-ru	**jum-í-ru-n*	*jum-í-n*	'is reading'
uk-í-ru	**uk-í-ru-n*	*uk-í-n*	'has gotten up'
ut-í-ru	**ut-í-ru-n*	*ut-í-n*	'has fallen'

TABLE 4 Shiraho Stative Present Verb Forms

Attributive	Predicted Conclusive	Attested Conc.	
kak-é-ru	**kak-é-ru-n*	*kak-é-n*	'is writing'
jum-é-ru	**jum-é-ru-n*	*jum-é-n*	'is reading'
ug-á-ru	**ug-á-ru-n*	*ug-á-n*	'has gotten up'
ut-á-ru	**ut-á-ru-n*	*ut-á-n*	'has fallen'

4.2 Phonological Analysis

Given that *-ru* marks present tense in the attributive stative forms seen above, its absence in the predicative form with final *-n* must result from deletion of the underlying present tense suffix. We call this the *phonological analysis*:

(6) Phonological Analysis: The stative present conclusive verb, whose surface form is [V-*í-n*], is derived from underlying /V-*í-u-n*/, from which the present tense marker *-u* has been deleted. The final *-ru* in the stative present attributive results from epenthesis of *r* before the present tense marker *-u*.

In this analysis, an underlying vowel sequence /iu/ is avoided by epenthesis of *r* in the attributive and by deletion of *u* in the conclusive. This raises the question of why the repair process should differ for the two forms.

We argue that this difference results from two related features of syllable accent in Yaeyaman, in combination with a need to eliminate vowel hiatus. The underlying vowel sequence /iu/ is eliminated in both conclusive and attributive forms, a fact that we attribute to the pressure of a NoHiATUS constraint:

(7) NoHiATUS: No vowels may be adjacent.

As mentioned above, the stative suffix bears a lexical accent; there is a phonological pressure for this accent to be faithfully realized in surface forms.[15] In

---

-ru is used in adnominal and pre-clitic positions.

[15] See Davis and Lau (forthcoming) for evidence for the existence of this accent in Miyara Yaeyaman. The existence of the accent in Shiraho Yaeyaman is based on currently unpublished data collected by Lau.

addition, there is a strong tendency (undescribed, as far as we are aware) in Yaeyaman for heavy syllables to host a pitch peak, phonetically identical to the pitch peak associated with lexical pitch accents.[16] These two pressures (the faithful encoding of underlying lexical accents and the surface accentualization of heavy syllables) are enforced by the following constraints:

(8) NOSHIFT: The location of a stress does not shift. (Alderete 1999)

(9) WEIGHT TO STRESS PRINCIPLE (WSP): Heavy syllables are stressed. (Prince 1983)

The conclusive suffix -*n* creates a coda, making the syllable it attaches to heavy. Given the requirement that heavy syllables are stressed, this triggers a prominence on the preceding present tense suffix -*u*. However, this leads to a clash of adjacent accents (**kakírún*), which is militated against by *CLASH.

(10) *CLASH: No stressed/accented syllables are adjacent. (Prince 1983)

The accentual clash in the conclusive form is resolved by deletion of the present tense suffix -*u*, giving a surface form that satisfies in a single accented syllable both the preservation of the lexical accent on *í* and the requirement that the heavy syllable formed by attachment of -*n* receive a prominence.

As illustrated by the tableaux in Table 5, the above four constraints need not be ranked with respect to one another, but must all outrank MAX and DEP. In order to account for the epenthesis of *r* in the attributive form, MAX must outrank DEP. This underlying preference for epenthesis over deletion is overridden in the conclusive form, due to the accentual pressures described above. The tableaux in Table 5 are based on a consonantal verb root in Miyaran. The same ranking can also account for vocalic verb roots, as well as for the stative present forms in Shiraho, but we leave out the relevant tableaux and discussion for reasons of space.

4.3 Grammatical Reanalysis and Flux

The deletion process described above results in surface forms in which -*n* sits in apparent opposition to -*ru*. This opens the way for the following reanalysis:

(11) Attributive (Re)Analysis: The present stative form of verbs consists of the verb root and the marker -*í*, / V-*í* /. The attributive is marked by -*ru*, while the indicative predicative form is marked with -*n*. The two markers are in complementary distribution.

This (re-)analysis leaves mysterious why there is no overt attributive marking in the simple present verb forms. It is also unclear where the present tense

---

[16] This generalization is also based on observations from the authors' own fieldwork; we put aside discussion of further details and evidence for reasons of space.

TABLE 5 Tableaux for Attributive and Conclusive Present Verb Forms in Miyara

Input: /kak-í-u/	NOHIATUS	*CLASH	NOSHIFT	WSP	MAX	DEP
a. kakíu	*!					
b. ☞ kakíru						*
c. kakí				*!		
d. kaku				*!		

Input: /kak-í-u-n/						
a. kakíun	*!			*!		
b. kakírun				*!		*
c. kakírún		*!				*
d. kakirún			*!			*
e. ☞ kakín					*	
f. kakún			*!		*	

verb semantics would come from in the absence of an underlying present tense suffix -u. Despite these obstacles to full reanalysis, there is evidence from past tense verb forms in both Miyaran and Shiraho that such a reanalysis may be taking place. The following examples illustrate conclusive and attributive past tense stative verbs in Miyaran:

(12)   a.   mizï   num-í-da
            water drink-STA-PST
            '(Someone) was drinking water.'

       b.   mizï   num-í-da(-ru)   pïtu[17]
            water drink-STA-PST(-ATT) person
            'A person who was drinking water.'

As seen in (12a), the conclusive marker -n is not found with the past tense suffix -da (see Davis and Lau forthcoming for discussion of this fact). In attributive position, however, there is an optional marker -ru that may be attached after the past tense suffix. Given the past tense semantics of the resulting form, this marker cannot be analyzed as a present tense suffix. Instead it seems to be an attributive marker, suggesting that the grammatical reanalysis sketched above may be occurring in Miyaran. The marker is not, however,

---

[17] In predicate position, however, -ru is not permitted: mizï(=du) num-í-da(*-ru).

mandatory. This area of the grammar, then, appears to be in a state of flux.

Past tense forms in Shiraho seem to be in a later stage of reanalysis than Miyaran, as illustrated by the following examples:

(13) a. mizi num-é-ta-n
water drink-STA-PST-IND
'(Someone) was drinking water.'

b. mizi(=du) num-é-ta-ro
water(=FOC) drink-STA-PST-ATT
'(Someone) was drinking water.'

c. mizi num-é-ta-ru[18] pitu
water drink-STA-PST(-ATT) person
'A person who was drinking water.'

The Shiraho form appears to be at a later stage of reanalysis than Miyaran, as both conclusive and attributive past tense forms *must* be followed by an additional ending (if not -n or -ru, then a clitic). We suggest that in Shiraho the reanalysis we proposed for Miyaran has been completed, so that in past tense forms the marker -ru has been fully reanalyzed as an attributive marker, and that this reanalysis has furthermore paved the way for complementary marking with the conclusive -n on past tense verbs (13a), which is not allowed in Miyaran (12a).[19]

In summary, while the simple present form does not have any attributive marking, the phonological deletion of the present tense marker -u in the stative present conclusive form, along with r epenthesis in the attributive, leads to a surface contrast between a conclusive form ending in -n and an attributive one ending in -ru.[20] The present tense marker -ru is then reanalyzed as an attributive morpheme and past tense forms subsequently may (in Miyaran) or must (in Shiraho) host an attributive marker. Yaeyaman languages show a transition period in which the attributive marker is becoming more productive, but is still blocked in simple present forms.

---

[18] -ru is alternatively pronounced -nu. At present, it is unclear whether -ru and -nu are in free variation. At the very least, however, -nu is not permitted when the attributive is in predicate position (as in the kakari-musubi construction).

[19] An alternative analysis would be that Shiraho exemplifies a more conservative system, in which attributive and conclusive marking were robustly distinguished on past tense verb forms, and that this distinction is being lost in Miyaran. It is beyond the scope of this paper to consider the relative merits of this alternative account, but we think it unlikely that the conclusive would drop off of past tense suffixes completely, leaving an optional attributive suffix. We instead think that the restriction of -n to present tense forms in Miyaran reflects a fact about the historical semantic content of -n, which has subsequently been bleached in other Ryukyuan varieties.

[20] An analogous pattern holds for the resultative present verb forms; see Davis and Lau (forthcoming) for data and discussion.

5 Comparison to Northern Ryukyuan

Hattori (1959) argues that the simple present in Northern Ryukyuan is derived from the *renyou* (continuative) form (created from the root combined with an -*i* formant) in combination with the existential *wor-. This form originally had the same meaning as the stative present forms discussed earlier, but eventually came to replace the simple present form and lose the original aspectual meaning.

The evidence for the derivation of Northern Ryukyuan simple present forms from stative present forms comes from the phonological process of palatalization in both coronal and velar stops *k*, *g*, *t*, *d* before front vowels *i* and *e*. Northern Ryukyuan verbs cognate with Japanese verbs ending in these consonants show palatalization in the simple present form. Shinzato and Serafim (2013:7-8) explain that by the 16th century, the forms involving the attached existential *jur* (< *-i + *wor-) had already begun to replace the simple present, creating a contrast between the conclusive and attributive forms that did not previously exist for quadrigrade verbs.

Genuardi (2008) points out that there is no good evidence that this process occurred in Southern Ryukyuan, due to the lack of palatalization in the relevant forms (notably, roots ending in -*k* and -*t*).

(14) Present Conclusive Forms

Language	'to write'	'to stand'
Okinawan	katʃ-u-n	tatʃ-u-n
Miyaran	kak-u-n	tats-ï-n

The Yaeyaman stative present forms described in the previous section derive from the same stative construction from which the Northern Ryukyuan simple present forms derived. This construction involves the combination of the *renyou* form of the verb, ending in -*i*, with the lexically accented existential verb *úr-*. This construction, which is still active in the varieties of Yaeyaman discussed in this paper, served as the historical source of the stative present, by reduction of *V-i úr-u* to *V-í-ru*. Unlike Northern Ryukyuan, both the reduced and unreduced stative present forms in Yaeyaman are still used with a stative meaning.[21] We suggest that Yaeyaman shows partial reanalysis of the -*ru* ending, which is blocked by the lack of attributive marking on the older simple present form. In Northern Ryukyuan, the replacement of the simple present by the stative present has eliminated this obstacle to full reanalysis of the present tense marker as an attributive marker.

---

[21] See Davis and Lau (forthcoming) for discussion of the unreduced stative present construction and its relation to the stative present form described in the previous section, including reasons why this reduction process should be considered a diachronic change, and not due to synchronic phonological reduction.

Given that in Northern Ryukyuan the existential verbs themselves show an opposition between *-n* and *-ru*, as seen for Okinawan in (2), one possible source of attributive versus conclusive marking in Northern Ryukyuan verbs is that the simple present forms inherited the opposition encoded on the existential verb when the simple present was replaced by the stative present, which was built using an existential verb. But the cognate existential verbs in the Yaeyaman varieties considered here do *not* show an opposition between *-n* and *-ru*, as seen for Miyara Yaeyaman in (4). This is thus not a possible source for the partial opposition between *-n* and *-ru* seen in Yaeyaman. The phonological reduction of the present tense suffix in conclusive stative forms is thus an alternative path by which the opposition between *-n* and *-ru* in Ryukyuan has been and is being accomplished.

6 Conclusion

The attributive marker *-ru* seen in Old Japanese, Okinawan, and Yaeyaman are not cognates, despite being strikingly similar on the surface. The Yaeyaman data adduced in this paper provide evidence for a grammaticalization path in which the tense suffix *-u*, found throughout Japono-Ryukyuan, is reanalyzed as an attributive marker *-ru*. This reanalysis is the opposite of what happened in the transition from Old Japanese to Late Middle Japanese, in which the old attributive suffix *-ru* was reanalyzed as the present tense suffix *-u*. Given the phonological similarity and morphosyntactic adjacency of the attributive *-ru* and the present *-u* in Japono-Ryukyuan, it is not implausible that reanalysis in both directions could have independently occurred in different Japono-Ryukyuan languages.

The reanalysis described in this paper was triggered by the existence of the conclusive morpheme *-n*. The existence of this morpheme provides overt evidence of C-marking in the verbal inflection system, and without it there would be no attributive-conclusive distinction in the varieties of Yaeyaman discussed here. This suggests that the development of inflectional C-marking in Ryukyuan was spurred in large part by the early grammaticalization of the conclusive marker *-n*. It may thus have been the development of explicit conclusive marking that allowed Ryukyuan to preserve and/or recreate explicit attributive verbal morphology like that seen in Old Japanese. We leave further investigation of this idea to future research.

Acknowledgements

We thank all of our informants, without whose generosity this work would not have been possible. Thomas Pellard provided critical commentary on prior work by Davis which has significantly informed the discussion of Old Japanese. Any errors of fact or analysis are the responsibility of the authors.

References

Alderete, John D. 1999. Morphologically governed accent in optimality theory. Doctoral Dissertation, UMass Amherst.

Davis, Christopher, and Tyler Lau. forthcoming. Tense, aspect, and mood in Miyara Yaeyaman. In *Handbook of the Ryukyuan languages*, ed. Patrick Heinrich, Shinsho Miyara, and Michinori Shimoji. Mouton de Gruyter.

Frellesvig, Bjarke. 2008. On reconstruction of proto-Japanese and pre-Old Japanese verb inflection. In *Proto-japanese: Issues and prospects*, ed. Bjarke Frellesvig and John Whitman. John Benjamins Publishing Co.

Frellesvig, Bjarke. 2010. *A History of the Japanese Language*. Cambridge: Cambridge University Press.

Genuardi, Marisa Ann. 2008. On the origins of attributive verb forms in the Ryukyuan languages. Master's thesis, Cornell University.

Hattori, Shiro. 1959. *Nihongo no keitou (the lineage of the Japanese language)*. Tokyo: Iwanami Shoten.

Izuyama, Atsuko. 2003. The Grammar of Ishigaki Miyara dialect in Luchuan. In *Studies on Luchuan grammar*, ed. Atsuko Izuyama, 1–162. Kyoto: ELPR.

Kaplan, Tamar I., and John B. Whitman. 1995. The category of relative clauses in Japanese, with reference to Korean. *Journal of East Asian Linguistics* 4:29–58.

Martin, Samuel. 1987. *The Japanese Language Through Time*. New Haven: New Haven Press.

Miyara, Shinsho. 2011. Clausal focus structure in Okinawan. *Ryudai Review of Euro-American Studies* 55:85–111.

Nishiyama, Kunio. 2000. Predicative and attributive forms in Old Japanese. In *MITWPL 36*, 263–275.

Pellard, Thomas. forthcoming. The linguistic archaeology of the Ryūkyū Islands. In *Handbook of the Ryukyuan languages*, ed. Patrick Heinrich, Shinsho Miyara, and Michinori Shimoji. Mouton de Gruyter.

Prince, Alan. 1983. Relating to the grid. *Linguistic Inquiry* 14:19–100.

Shimoji, Michinori, and Thomas Pellard, ed. 2010. *An introduction to Ryukyuan languages*. Tokyo: ILCAA.

Shinzato, Rumiko, and Leon Serafim. 2013. *Synchrony and diachrony of Okinawan kakari musubi in comparitive perspective with premodern Japanese*. Brill.

Sugahara, Mariko. 1996. Shuri Okinawan kakari-musubi and movement. In *Formal Approaches to Japanese Linguistics: Proceedings of FAJL 2*, ed. Koizumi Masatoshi, Masayuki Oishi, and Uli Sauerland, 235–254.

Uemura, Yukio. 2003. *The Ryukyuan language*. Kyoto: ELPR.

Vovin, Alexander. 2004/2008. *A descriptive and comparative grammar of Western Old Japanese [part 1 published 2004, part 2 published 2008]*. Brill.

Towards a Stronger Theory of Proto-Korean-Japanese*

ALEXANDER T. RATTE
The Ohio State University

1 Introduction

This paper presents a critical reassessment of the hypothesis of Korean-Japanese common origin, with the aim of creating a stronger theory of proto-Korean-Japanese (pKJ). In this paper, I will show that some of the cognates proposed by Martin (1966) and Whitman (1985) are indeed weak, but that they can be replaced by stronger matches that are less susceptible to criticism. In this way, this paper will address deficiencies and weaknesses in the theory of proto-Korean-Japanese. From a formal perspective, critics point to three main problems for the Korean-Japanese hypothesis.

First, there is an insufficient number of unimpeachable cognates. Although at least 300 cognates (many of them overlapping) have each been

*I would like to thank John Whitman and J. Marshall Unger for their helpful feedback on this paper and the ideas presented herein. I claim responsibility for all errors. I would also like to acknowledge the Office of International Affairs and The Council of Graduate Students at The Ohio State University for making this research possible through grants

Japanese/Korean Linguistics 23.
Edited by Michael Kenstowicz, Theodore Levin and Ryo Masuda.
Copyright © 2016, CSLI Publications

316 / ALEXANDER T. RATTE

proposed by Martin (1966) and Whitman (1985), it is not the case that every one of these lexical correspondences is of equal strength. As recently pointed out by Vovin (2010), a large number of Whitman's early proposed Korean-Japanese matches can be criticized on the basis of their form or meaning. Unger (2009), who disagrees with Vovin (2010) about the strength of the hypothesis, nevertheless admits that a K-J relationship requires better evidence than we currently have to be fully convincing.

Second, although a discrete set of regular Korean-Japanese sound correspondences has been established to account for a majority of lexical matches, some cognates proposed by both Martin and Whitman (as well as subsequent scholars) fall outside of these regular sound rules, or show idiosyncratic correspondences without a proper explanation.

Third, although Korean-Japanese lexical correspondences can be identified for nouns and verb roots, the important prize of shared morphology is elusive. A prime example of this is in nominal case-marking morphology, where it often appears that the morpho-syntactic *categories* of Japanese and Korean have close analogues (e.g. 'topic marker': 'genitive'), but the actual morphemes occupying those categories do not seem related.

This paper seeks to address each of these problems for the theory of K-J common origin by 1) proposing new K-J cognates, 2) scrutinizing previous theories and replacing weaker matches, and 3) addressing correspondences in morphology by proposing discrete theories of morphological change through reanalysis. In so doing, this paper seeks to build a stronger theory of proto-Korean-Japanese that synthesizes the results of K-J research with recent criticism and advances in our understanding through the in-depth internal work accomplished in the three decades since Whitman (1985).

1.1 Previous Accounts and Literature

The two major, relevant works that argue for a Korean-Japanese relationship are Martin (1966) and Whitman (1985). Martin (1966) is widely acknowledged as a major work focused solely on establishing a common origin for the Japanese and Korean languages, coming up with a list of over 300 systematic lexical correspondences that he considers valid. As an early attempt towards reconstructing a proto-Korean-Japanese, Martin's paper is monumental. However, Martin (1966) has faced a great deal of scholarly criticism, and much of it has been deserved, for in attempting to create a

---

This paper will employ the following abbreviations: pKJ (proto-Korean-Japanese), pJ (proto-Japanese), pK (proto-Korean), K-J (Korean-Japanese), OJ (Old Japanese), MK (Middle Korean), adn. (adnominal). and gen. (genitive). Italicized text indicates a romanized form, starred forms indicate reconstructions, and bracketed text implies a phonetic description. This paper uses the transcription of OJ in Frellesvig (2010), where *o* = *o2* [ə], *wo* = *o1* [o]. Korean is transcribed in Yale Romanization.

correspondence set, Martin was forced to inflate the phoneme inventory of his reconstructions to such an extent that now seems improbable. Whitman's (1985) dissertation builds on Martin (1966) by providing a more streamlined and reasonable set of Korean-Japanese phonological correspondences, as well as providing more potential cognates. Perhaps the greatest testament to Whitman (1985) is that proposals in this dissertation are still being cited by scholars three decades later, not merely as historical relics but as ideas worth considering. Once again, however, the correspondences and reconstructions are not without problems. Our understanding of the proto-Japanese vowel and consonant systems have changed considerably, in large part due to work by Whitman himself (Frellesvig and Whitman 2004; 2008), and this has made some of his correspondences and cognates obsolete. Others could be misidentified loans; Vovin (2010), who once favored a Korean-Japanese relationship but has now become its most staunch opponent, has recently levelled a great deal of criticism at Whitman's comparisons, and concludes that most of the lexical correspondences are early loans into Japanese[1]. Even proponents of a Korean-Japanese relationship agree that more work needs to be done before any relationship can be seen as established. I should note that it is in no way the intention of this paper to tear down or diminish the significance of Martin or Whitman's work, but after examining both the theories and the data, it seems clear that some of the matches could be correct, others are likely wrong, and still others are perhaps right, but not for reasons that have been thus far provided. Without new viewpoints and opinions, the validity of these proposals will remain clouded in doubt. Although I present new ideas about K-J correspondences based on a relatively small number of matches, it is evident that they have broad implications for the ultimate structure of the pKJ reconstruction as a whole. This paper thus underscores the critical need to consider alternative etymologies and sound correspondences before adopting a radically skeptical hypothesis such as Vovin's.

The rest of this paper takes the following form. Section 2 proposes new possible Korean-Japanese cognates, with an accompanying analysis for each proposal whose relationship is not immediately apparent. I also introduce and discuss a new correspondence of OJ *a* ~ MK *uy*. Section 3 discusses some problematic K-J matches that have been previously identified, and offers a revised cognate and/or correspondence. Section 4 discusses

---

[1] I do not agree with Vovin's loanword identifications, and many of his rejections of K-J cognates depend on an idiosyncratic theory of Korean consonant lenition not accepted by other scholars. It is unsurprising that Whitman's (1985) reconstructions are now susceptible to criticism, given the vast advances in our understanding of OJ and pJ in the past three decades. Nobody, not even Whitman himself, contends that these reconstructions are authoritative (p.c.).

correspondences in noun morphology, focusing on genitive particles in Japanese and Korean as a case study in grammatical change. Section 5 summarizes the main points of this paper, and concludes with a discussion of the Korean-Japanese question.

2 New Korean-Japanese Proposals

Against the perennial critique that the Japanese-Korean hypothesis lacks sufficient evidence, I offer new K-J matches, building on the framework in Martin (1966) and Whitman (1985) with subsequent improvements. Proposed cognates include core vocabulary unlikely to be borrowed.

2.1 OJ *wor-*, *wi-* 'is seated, present' ~ MK *wo-* 'comes'

This comparison is superior to the idea that OJ *wi-* 'is seated, present' < pJ **wo-* ~ MK *isi-* 'have, exists' mentioned passingly by Martin (1996) and explicitly by Miller (1971). The idea that OJ *wor-* and *wi-* go back to a single root **wo-* or **wu-* is now uncontroversial, which makes a comparison with any Korean or Altaic root in *i-* phonologically dubious. A comparison to MK *wo-* 'comes' is phonologically unimpeachable, but the meaning is obviously different; however, the semantic properties of OJ *wor-*, *wi-* show that it likely came from a verb of motion, which I reconstruct as proto-Japanese **'come'*. Satoshi Kinsui has objected to reconstructions of pJ **wo-* as generally 'be at, is present,' and his objection can be summed up in the following way: OJ *wor-* may mean 'be present' but its related form OJ *wi-* means 'be seated' or more likely 'lose movement' as an antonym of *tat-* 'stands up; begins moving'. It is easier to see how a proto-meaning of 'lose movement' developed into 'be at' as opposed to the opposite development of 'be at' > 'lose movement' (one can always 'be at' somewhere by losing movement, but one cannot lose movement if one is already stationary). These arguments together imply that the OJ *wor-* / *wi-* could not have come from a stative verb, but instead are more likely to have come from a verb of losing motion. If **wo-* originates from a verb meaning 'come,' then we can reconstruct the semantic development of pJ **wo-* as follows:

pKJ **'comes'* ~ 'comes and stops' > 'loses movement; is at a location'

Since 'come' in both Korean and Japanese involves a telic, speaker-oriented element, 'come' necessarily implies movement that stops at the speaker's current location. This provides a plausible scenario for semantic shift, where early Japanese speakers narrowed the meaning of 'comes; comes and stops' to simply 'ceases movement'. Thus, a comparison of pJ **wo-* to MK *wo-* 'comes' is not only phonologically strong, it actually has explanatory power to account for an otherwise mysterious Japanese-internal observation. This reinforces the case for their being cognate.

Furthermore, the fact that this same morpheme appears to be employed
as a verbal inflection in both Japanese (as the pJ adnominal *-o-ru) and Korean (as the Middle Korean volitive adnominal -wo/wu-l) further reinforces
the match. Scholars have long noted that the *rentai-kei* or adnominal form
of OJ verbs looks suspiciously as if it built on the *syuusi-kei* or conclusive
ending. Frellesvig (2013) has recently argued that the appearance of any
differences between the vowel formant in the adnominal and conclusive
endings for Eastern OJ verbs is illusory, and that the evidence points to reconstructing pJ *o in both the adnominal and conclusive forms of quadrigrade verbs. If correct, this would prove to be a significant piece of evidence for reconstructing a single morpheme, pJ *(w)o as a root affix formant in both the *syuusi-kei* (conclusive) and *rentai-kei* (adnominal) verbal
endings. Under the theory tentatively proposed here, both conclusive and
adnominal forms include the same auxiliary *-wo from pJ *wo- 'comes,'
with the adnominal form including an additional morpheme *-ru.

Reconstructing a pJ verb *wo- that functioned as an auxiliary also has
the potential to unravel the mysteries surrounding how and why verbal auxiliaries seem to be able to gain inflectional properties. The OJ fu-
ture/suppositional *-am- could derive from a nominalizer *-am- (cf. MK
nominalizer -m)[2], or *-am- could have the same origin as MK *ama* 'probably' and *amo* 'some, any' as Frellesvig (2010) suggests. However, either
theory leaves us handling an inescapable problem: how does *-am- gain the
inflectional properties of an auxiliary if it does not itself come from an inflecting stem? The same problem arises when we consider that the OJ negative auxiliary *-an- seems to have the verbal morphology necessary for
predication and modification, despite likely being cognate with the MK
negative *an*, which is not an inflecting stem. Under the theory being proposed here, *-am- and *-an- gained the inflectional properties of verbs by
root-suffixing the proto-Japanese verb *wo-, the same verb used as an auxiliary to form what we later call the 'conclusive' in OJ. After the reanalysis
of *-wo as an inflection rather than a separable auxiliary, *wo became incorporated into *-am- and *-an- to form new verbal auxiliaries. It is thus no
coincidence -u appears as a finite ending for verbs and auxiliaries alike;
under this theory, -u < *wo was not simply the conclusive morpheme, it was
the actual derivational means by which many auxiliaries gained inflectional
properties in the first place. This thus can explain how auxiliaries could
have been formed from uninflected material.

We can also identify a potential Korean cognate to this auxiliary usage
of pJ *wo-. The "volitive" suffix in Korean refers to a formant -wo/wu- (depending on vowel harmony) that affixes directly to the verb root. Its exact

---

[2]This idea was suggested by John Whitman (p.c.).

meaning is unclear, as it appears to be losing productivity by Late Middle Korean and survives mostly in nominalizations, but we can deduce that its use denotes some sort of agency, and its syntactic function is related to predication (Lee and Ramsey 2011). Isolated verbs in Middle Korean are nominalized with the suffix -(*u/o*)*m*, but the volitive suffix -*wu/wo*- is obligatorily affixed to the verb root when the predicate is a nominalization: *timchoy-lol mekwum* 'eating Kimchi' (vs. *mekum* 'eating'). This theory posits that the volitive suffix represents the remnants of a more widespread root affixation of the verb *wo*- 'come,' a morpheme that was originally an auxiliary used to denote active agency in the predicate. The semantic reconstructions of this hypothesis are speculative, but the only internally viable candidate for an origin of the volitive suffix is the verb *wo*- 'come,' and morphologizations of motion verbs 'come' and 'go' into auxiliaries are cross-linguistically common[3]. Returning once more to Japanese, now we can see the same structure [*verb-come-ADN] employed in both pre-MK and pre-OJ to express an adnominalized clause: pre-MK *kal-wo-l 'one who reaps,' pre-OJ *kar-wo-ru 'one who reaps'[4]. I reconstruct an auxiliary *wo that was employed in proto-Korean-Japanese as a root affix that marked the verb in question as a clausal predicate. This auxiliary usage of *wo 'come' survived as the volitive suffix in Korean; in Japanese, it was reanalyzed as an inflection on verbs and became the derivational means by which uninflected material became verbal auxiliaries.

2.2 OJ *pe*- 'time passes' < pJ *pə- 'sees it' ~ MK *pwo*- 'sees it'

Martin (1966) compares MK *pwo*- 'sees it' to OJ *wosipe*- 'instructs it,' but *wosipe*- is more likely related to *wosape*- 'applies force to it' and thus to *wos*- 'pushes it'. Instead, comparing OJ *pe*- 'time passes, elapses' < *pə- is a stronger match made possible by the theory that MK *wo* can originate from proto-Korean *wə; I reconstruct pKJ *pwə with the meaning 'see,' with the Japanese reflex shifting to '(*see >) experience a time' + *-e- 'transitivity flip' > 'time goes by'. As Unger (1993 [1977]), Frellesvig (2008) and Frellesvig and Whitman (2008) argue, the OJ bigrade conjugation, specifically the lower bigrade conjugation in -*e*-, should not be factored into a reconstruction of proto-Japanese stem shapes, as such verbs are in all likelihood derived with a 'transitivity switch' formant *-e- or *-(C)i-. The intransitive semantics of OJ *pe*- '(time) passes, (time) is passed' indicate that *pe*- is likely built with the bigrade formant *-e-, which implies a proto-Japanese verb of the shape *pə- whose transitivity is opposite to that

---

[3]This may also explain why *wo- affixed only onto verb roots, as adjectives are not operational predicates.
[4]Like Unger (1993 [1997]) and Whitman (1990), I find it likely that all verbs in proto-Japanese originally took an adnominal morpheme ending in *-*ru*.

of OJ *pe-*[5]. Since OJ *pe-* meant '(time) passes, (time) elapses,' a plausible transitive reconstruction for its transitive root *pə- could be '(subj.) passes time' or 'subject experiences a time go by'. In this case, we could reconstruct a motion verb 'passes' as the proto-meaning of the transitive verb, but this fails to take into account the fact that OJ *pe-* is only used to indicate temporal passage; the dual meaning of 'pass' in English here is deceptive, as the meaning really is 'time passes / elapses,' as opposed to 'the people pass (by)' or 'the birds pass (by)'. If *pə- had meant 'passes,' we would expect its distribution to look more like OJ *topor-*, which does mean 'it passes (a location)'. Instead, I propose reconstructing pJ *pə- as 'sees it (trans.),' whose intransitive pair 'is seen' develops narrowly into a temporal sense. 'Seeing' is related to 'experiencing' an event or time ('I have seen much in this life,' 'I have seen many tragedies'), but we can see this precise usage of 'see' to metaphorically mean 'pass a time' in archaic English expressions such as 'I have seen many winters' = 'I have experienced many winters (transitive); many winters have passed for me (intransitive)'.

Additional evidence from its interaction with aspect militates towards *pe-* originally deriving from a verb denoting an instantaneous action like 'see' rather than 'pass'. When functioning as the sentential predicate, OJ *pe-* is mostly attested in *Manyoshu* with the perfective auxiliary -*nu*: *tosi pa he-ni-tutu* (1080); *tukwi zo pe-ni-kyeru* (1464, 2093); *tosi zo pe-ni-kyeru* (2019, 2266); *tukwi no pe-nu-ramu* (1793). I hypothesize that the fact that *pe-* is mostly attested in the perfective can be interpreted as evidence that *pe-* refers to a state resulting from an action that has been done in the past. 'Having being seen' is semantically prior to the description of a resulting state as 'passing by,' and thus militates towards a morphologically perfective use for *pe-* in a meaning of 'pass'. By contrast, reconstructing pJ *pə- directly as 'pass' cannot explain the preference for perfective -*nu*, since 'pass' need not be perfective to describe the present. Based on this analysis, I reconstruct pJ *pə- 'sees it,' given that *pə+e would uncontroversially give OJ *pe-*. Reconstructing a transitive root *pə- 'sees it' now reveals the link to MK *pwo-* 'sees it'. This leads us to reconstruct proto-Korean-Japanese *pwə- 'sees it,' where MK *pwo-* < *pwə-. Given this highly complex derivation of OJ *pe-*, it is almost certainly not a borrowing from Korean; nor is the Korean form likely to be a borrowing from 'Koguryoic' either, since MK *pwo-* exhibits a labial that is not reconstructible for the Japanese form[6].

---

[5]Frellesvig (2008) reconstructs OJ *pe-* 'pass, elapse' as a *pəC-(i) or *paC-(i); however, this reconstruction attempts to identify monosyllabic bigrade verbs that might be from *a/ə + i crasis. There are no prima facie reasons for thinking OJ *pe-* does not incorporate the bigrade formant.

[6]Reconstructing *po- is not completely out of the question, since it is still unclear as to what stem-final vowels could combine with *-e- to create the lower bigrade conjugation.

Also related are MJ *fanare-* 'is sent away, released' / *fanas-* 'releases, sends it,' reconstructed as *pana-r/s- and further as pJ *pǝna-r/s- via Arisaka's so-called laws of OJ vowel combination. Proto-Japanese *pǝna-r/s- reflects a compound of *pǝ- (from *pwǝ- 'sees it') and *na-r/s- (the same root that gives OJ *nar-* 'becomes' and *nas-* 'makes it' by suffixed *-(a)r- 'intransitive' and *-(a)s- 'causative'). This is a parallel derivation to MK *pwonay-* 'sends it, releases it,' which is transparently a transitivized compound of pK *pwǝ- 'sees it' + *na-* 'goes out' (MK *nay-* is the transitive of *na-*). We can therefore reconstruct pKJ *pwǝ-na- as a word reflecting a compound in proto-Korean-Japanese itself of *pwǝ- 'sees it' + *na- 'goes out' to mean 'is sent out, released'. The reconstruction here does not rule out the possibility that OJ *po-si* 'desires' and OJ *por-* 'desires it' are related (they very well could be), and even MK *pola-* 'desires it' may be related, though the unrounded *o* and final *-la* are unexplained.

2.3   OJ *yoro-, yo-, ye-* 'good' ~ MK *cal* 'well,' *cul-keW-* 'joyous'

The OJ adjective *yo-si* is often reconstructed as pJ *yǝ-, but the existence of competing *ye-si* < *yǝy- in *Manyoshu* and the seemingly related *yorosi* all suggest reconstructing *yǝr- as the proto-Japanese root, with *r dropping before a consonant and becoming *y word-finally, as predicted by the apophonic vowel theory (Unger 1993 [1977]; Frellesvig 2010). This allows a comparison to the MK *cul* of *cul-keW-* 'joyous' (-W- being a common Korean adjective formant, and -k- here being the same formant we see in *pulk-* 'red' < *pǝ r 'fire' + *-k- '-adj.'), but more importantly MK *cal* 'good, well'. I reconstruct MK *cal* as pK *cǝr via analogy to the merger of *ǝ to *a in open stems; this means that MK *cul-keW-* displays what was once its harmonic variant. The reconstruction is thus pKJ *cyǝr or *cyɨ r. The oft-cited resemblance between MK *cul-keW-* 'joyous' and OJ *yorokob-* 'rejoices' is either coincidental or (more likely) a partial morpheme calque, Japanese *yor(o)* with a borrowed *-kob-* from MK *-keW-*. This would make it a later borrowing, since it displays a clear correlation to the *-keW-* structure that we know is innovative and compositional within Korean.

2.4   Regular Correspondence of OJ *a* ~ MK *uy*, pKJ *aj

The following Korean-Japanese lexical comparisons provide evidence for a regular correspondence of OJ *a* to MK *uy*, reconstructed here as pKJ *aj:

OJ *ma* 'interval' ~ MK *muy* 'time interval' (from *imuy, mili*), pKJ **maj**
OJ *ima* 'now' ~ MK *imuy* 'already,' pKJ **imaj**
OJ *ka* 'mosquito' ~ MK *mwo-kuy* 'id.,' pKJ **kaj**
OJ *-nap-* 'be afflicted with' ~ MK *nip-* < *nujp- 'id.; wears,' pKJ **najp-**
MJ *fasu* 'aslant' ~ K *pisutum*, MK *pisk-* 'slant' < pK *pujs-, pKJ **pajsu**
OJ *patwo* 'pigeon' ~ MK *pitwuli* < *pujtol 'id.,' pKJ **pajtol**

OJ *-ga* 'genitive' ~ MK *uy/oy* < *uj 'animate genitive,' pKJ ***nkaj**
OJ *tabi* 'occasion' ~ MK *tiWi* < *tujβi 'time when,' pKJ ***tarpi/*tajnpi**
OJ *-ra, -re* 'pron./deictic suff.' ~ MK *-li* < *luj 'pron./deictic suff.' pKJ ***laj**
OJ *nana* '7' ~ MK *nil-kwop* < *nujl- 'id.,' pKJ ***narta**
OJ *saru* 'monkey' ~ MK *wen-sungi* 'monkey' < *suj, pKJ ***saj(ru?)**

This paper is not necessarily committed to the hypothesis that these correspondences should be reconstructed as pKJ diphthongs in *aj; they could very well reflect a long vowel *a: that undergoes diphthongization ('breaking') in Korean. What is important here is not the specific phonetic reconstruction, but the identification of a regular correspondence between OJ *a* ~ MK *uy*. The diphthongal analysis is, however, supported by two observations. First, Vovin (1993) also suggests a possible diphthongal origin for the initial syllable *pa-* in OJ *patwo*. Second, it seems significant that a little less than half of the comparisons presented here are monosyllabic morphemes (*ma* 'interval,' *ka* 'mosquito,' *-ga* 'gen.,' *-ra/-re* 'plural; pron./deictic suffix'), of which two of them (*ma, ka*) are non-bound, monosyllabic nouns. Both Japanese and Korean appear to have very few free nominal morphemes with a true CV shape, and there are only a small number of comparisons involving such free nouns between Japanese and Korean; e.g. OJ *pa* 'topic marker' ~ MK *pa* 'situation; condition,' OJ *pi-* 'ice' ~ MK *pi* 'rain,' et cetera. That is, internal evidence and comparative evidence conspire to suggest that free CV nouns are rare in proto-Japanese and in proto-Korean. Thus, if we are able to reconstruct OJ *ma* 'interval' and *ka* 'mosquito' as originally CVC nouns *maj and *kaj respectively, this would decrease the number of free CV nouns in proto-Japanese and harmonize with our observations about Japanese and Korean lexical typology.

3 Revised Etymologies

3.1 OJ *posi* 'star' ≠ MK *pyel* 'id.'; instead, OJ *posi* ~ MK *pozoy-* 'it shines; is dazzled,' pKJ *posu-/pəsu- 'shines'

Outside of Whitman's (1985) dissertation, the comparison of OJ *s* to MK *l* has, it seems, been inextricably linked to a desire to see Japanese reflexes of the reconstructed Altaic *l² phoneme, which allegedly surfaces as *s* in some Altaic languages and *l* in others. However, there is otherwise no evidence at all to reconstruct a special type of lateral phoneme in proto-Korean-Japanese. In place of the oft maligned comparison of OJ *posi* 'star' to MK *pyel* 'star,' for which both the consonant and vowel correspondences are problematic, I propose that OJ *posi* matches a Korean verb stem *pozo-/pozoy-* 'it shines'. The comparison I present here is phonologically unproblematic and almost as close in its semantics. This hypothesis assumes pre-OJ *posi < *pos-i, a deverbal derivation from a reconstructed verb *pos- 'shines'. Alternate Middle Korean forms *pozoy/posoy* likely have incorporated the passivizer *-ki > *-Gi > *-i. I suspect that MK *pyel* 'star' in fact derives from an expression *pi-el 'light-spirit,' as stars are often conceived of as celestial beings of light across different cultures; in addition, an Old Korean word for 'star' has been reconstructed as *ili 伊利, which shows that MK *pyel* is some kind of internal innovation.

3.2   OJ *natu* 'summer' ≠ MK *nyelom* 'id.'; instead, OJ *natu* ~ MK *nac* daytime,' pKJ *natu 'daytime'

The usual comparison of OJ *natu* 'summer' to MK *nyelom* 'id.' is problematic for several reasons: 1) OJ *Ca* and MK *Cye* syllables do not regularly correspond in any other proposed cognate; 2) mid-vowel raising does not normally occur in word-final position, which makes it difficult to justify pJ *nato to make the comparison work; and 3) the final -*m* in *nyelom* is left unexplained and suggests the possibility that *nyelom* is a deverbal noun. Instead, a phonologically superior match to OJ *natu* is MK *nac* 'daytime'. Under the theory that pK *u caused a preceding *t to become affricated, we can reconstruct MK *nac* < *nacu < *natu. I hypothesize that the meaning of 'summer' for OJ *natu* is an innovation derived from the observation that summer is the period of the year with the most daylight.

3.3   OJ *swora* 'sky' ≠ MK *hanolh* 'id.'; instead, OJ *kamwi* 'god' ~ MK *hanolh*, pKJ *xa 'great'

The comparison of OJ *swora* 'sky' to MK *hanolh* 'sky' is phonologically irreconcilable. Whitman (1985) valiantly attempts to forge a link by reconstructing pKJ *šanora, but he cannot account for the vowel discrepancy or for the presence of final *h*. Moreover, OJ *swora* looks monomorphemic, but MK *hanolh* (with possibly 4 syllables in proto-Korean) looks to be too phonologically complex to be a simplex root. MK *hanonim* 'god' (an obvious compound with *ni:m* 'lord') must be related, which entails parsing *hanolh* as *ha-nolh*. I propose that *hanolh* 'sky' is an early compound of *ha-* 'great' (with the interpretation 'heavenly') with the adnominal form *-nə and a suffixed morpheme truncated as *lh*. This -*lh* is a bound locative suffix, as we can see in MK *nalah* 'country,' which is widely parsed as *na 'land' + *-lah/k 'locative'. This allows us to reconstruct the semantic derivation of *hanolh* as 'great-adn.-place' or 'celestial-adn.-place,' the celestial realm. MK *hanonim* 'god' is likewise derived from *ha-nə-ni:m 'celestial-adn.-lord'. This makes a comparison with OJ *swora* 'sky' impossible, but it does open up a new cognate match with Japanese, namely OJ *kamwi* 'god'. OJ *kamwi* / *kamu* 'god' < *kamuy has proven difficult to provide an etymology for, since it cannot be related to OJ *kami* 'above' due to the vowel discrepancy. I hypothesize that OJ *kamwi* is actually an early compound of a root *ka 'heavenly, great' and the root giving OJ *mwi* 'body' (pKJ *mom?), meaning 'heavenly bodies'. This leaves a prefix *ka that modifies *muy 'body' to give the meaning of 'god,' leading to the conclusion that *ka must have meant 'heavenly' or 'great'. The match to MK *ha-* and *hanolh / hanonim* is therefore semantically strong and phonologically perfect.

Whence then OJ *swora* 'sky'? Whitman (1985) assumes that *koorui-o* (*wo*) here must be secondary, but under a 6-vowel hypothesis for proto-Japanese, OJ *wo* can reflect pJ *o. Reconstructing pJ *sora 'sky' matches the Middle Korean *soy* 'dawn' < pK *sor under the theory espoused here that MK *o* in some environments reflects both pK *ə and *o.

3.4 OJ *yo* 'the earth, an age' ≠ MK *nwuy, nwuli* 'id.'; instead, OJ *ni* 'earth, dirt' ~ MK *nwuy, nwuli*, pKJ *nur/nuri 'earth'

This comparison is superior to OJ *yo* ~ MK *nwuy* proposed in Whitman (1985), and assumes that OJ *ni* 'earth' must be from pre-OJ *nwi according to Whitman's theory of coronal loss. Given this internal reconstruction, the match is phonologically close. Though we can see a clear continuity in meaning from 'earth (dirt)' to 'the earth,' the semantic differentiation between these reflexes and the broader meaning of OJ *ni* as 'earth (dirt)' also makes either of these forms unlikely to be a borrowings.

4 Morphological Correspondences

4.1 OJ *–no* 'genitive' ~ MK *(o/u)n* 'topic,' pKJ *nə 'genitive'

Whitman (1985) and Frellesvig (2001) have both proposed that OJ genitive *-no* is cognate with the MK topic marker *(u/o)n*. I agree in principle that this comparison is valid; however, the putative developments are problematic. Whitman explains the morpho-syntactic mismatch by appealing to how genitive particles can be employed to mark nominative case in subordinate clauses in both Japanese and Korean. However, MK *(u/o)n* is not a subject marker but a topic marker; its behavior is opposite, in that MK *-(u/o)n* is never attested in subordinate clauses and instead always attaches to the sentential node, so this correspondence remains unexplained. I propose that in Korean sentences where a noun phrase consisting of [noun1-*nə-noun2] constituted the subject noun phrase of a descriptive sentence, early Korean speakers reanalyzed the genitive particle *nə into a topic marker, and led to the reanalysis of all remaining *(u/o)n* forms (that were suffixed on nominals) from 'genitive' to 'topic'. In sentences where a description is provided (where the predicate is generally an adjective), virtually any Korean sentence with the pattern noun1-gen.-noun2 (where this noun phrase is the syntactic subject of the verb phrase) can be reanalyzed as a topic-comment structure, noun1-topic-noun2, with almost no change to the meaning: *khwo'kkili-uy khwo-ka kil-ta* 'The nose of the elephant is long'; *khwo'kkili-*

nun khwo-ka kil-ta 'As for elephants, their noses are long'. In genitive-marked sentences, the noun is described by virtue of the fact that the predicate describes the noun directly associated with it; in topic-marked sentences, the entire predicate is a comment or description of the topicalized noun. These sentences are pragmatically indistinguishable. Given that the genitive-marked input can easily be analyzed as topic-comment structure, I hypothesize that pK *-nə/nɨ underwent word-final vowel loss very early in the history of Korean, as *-n (after vowels) or *-Vn (before consonants with minimal vowel inserted). Subsequently, pK *-n/-Vn 'genitive' became re-analyzed as a topic marker. Competing genitives and noun-modifiers in proto-Korean (reflexes of MK *-uy* and MK *-s*) filled the place of the lost genitive *-(V)n, which explains why most genitive particles do not have direct K-J correspondences. I reconstruct pKJ *nɨ or *nə 'genitive' (the identity of the vowel is obscured by vowel harmony in Korean).

4.2   OJ *no* 'genitive' ~ MK (*o/u*)*n* 'adnominal,' pKJ *nə 'genitive'

The OJ genitive *-no* < *nə seems related to the Korean adnominal *-u/on* in its meaning as a noun-modifier, and the comparison has been a staple of Japanese-Korean and Altaic scholarship, but there is obviously a problem: OJ *-no* is purely a nominal suffix, whereas MK *-u/on* only suffixes on (un-inflected) verbs and adjectives. Without a viable theory of grammatical change for this morpheme in one or both languages, the comparison remains unexplained. We can already compare the Middle Korean topic marker *-u/on* to OJ *-no* 'genitive' via pKJ *nə/-nɨ 'genitive,' as explained in 4.1; given that the MK topic marker and adnominal morphemes appear to have the exact same shape, and given that adnominal modification is functionally similar to genitive modification, we can posit a single origin for morphemes. The best way to account for the adnominal *-u/on* is by hypothesizing that pKJ adjective roots were originally nominal, just as they are in proto-Japanese, and later gained the inflectional properties of verbs in Korean. This allows reconstructing a single proto-Korean-Japanese morpheme, *-nə/-nɨ 'genitive,' which becomes reanalyzed as the topic marker *-u/on* as in 4.1, and becomes an adnominal suffix *-u/on* as will be explained below.

It is now clear that adjective roots in Japanese reflect property nominals in proto-Japanese; adjectives as a class are formed from adding suffixes such as *-si or *-ke onto nominal roots. However, we also know from *rendaku* compounds that proto-Japanese adjective roots could modify a noun via a suffixed genitive *nə *without* the normal inflective paradigm that we expect for attributive adjectives. Examples of such modification include OJ *paya-busa* 'falcon (lit. fast-tassel)' < *paya-nə-pusa, and OJ *pisa-gwi* 'Chinese catalpa (lit. long-time-tree)' < *pisa-nə-kwi. Most cases of *rendaku* reflect the genitive particle *nə being inserted between compound elements

(Frellesvig 2010), so cases of *rendaku* between adjective roots and the noun they describe are indicative that genitive *nə could *directly* suffix onto adjective roots to modify a noun in proto-Japanese. I hypothesize that proto-Korean adjectives also originated from nominal roots, and *-nə/-nɨ 'genitive' could also be directly suffixed onto these roots to enable nominal modification, just as in proto-Japanese. After adjectives were reanalyzed as inflecting, this original genitive *-nə/-nɨ that suffixed directly onto the adjective root became reanalyzed as an adnominal or noun-modifying ending for inflecting stems. Curiously, adjectives permit the direct suffixation of *(u/o)n* onto the stem for present-tense modification, whereas action verbs with suffixed *(u/o)n* have only a past-tense interpretation, not present-tense. I hypothesize that this distinction originates from the fact that adjectives were originally nominal roots in proto-Korean that allowed the direct suffixation of genitive *-nɨ /nə onto the root for modification. When adjective roots became inflecting stems, they retained the direct suffixation of *-nɨ /nə for present-tense noun modification and thus became differentiated from verbs.

This paper does not offer a definitive account of adnominal morphology in Korean, but the use of the identical *-u/on* as a past-tense verbal adnominal is almost certainly connected to the cross-linguistic syncretism between past verb forms and modification. Adjectives in Korean are stative inflecting stems whose interpretations are removed from time; by contrast, in order for an action verb to have the sense of 'a quality removed from time' like a stative verb, the only possible interpretation is that the action was completed in the past, with the imbued quality being a result of the past action in question. Using this principle, we can understand why present-tense adjective morphology corresponds to past-tense adnominal morphology for action verbs; in order for the adnominal * -nɨ /nə to mean a 'quality removed from time' (which is the interpretation it naturally gains on stative verbs), the interpretation of *-nɨ /nə became 'past tense' for action verbs.

How do we know that the Korean topic marker *-u/on* and verbal adnominal *-u/on* were *nə with a final vowel, as opposed to *ən with a final consonant as in Middle Korean? The answer lies in examining instances where the morpheme was shielded from word-final vowel loss by virtue of being fossilized within a compound. The example I provide is *hanolh* 'sky,' which I reconstruct as *ha-nə-lh 'great-adn.-place'. Here, *ha- must represent the root for 'great' (compare *hanonim* 'god' < *ha-nə-ni:m 'great lord'), and the final consonants *-lh* are likely a truncation of *-lah*, which can be identified as a bound locative in words including *na-lah* 'country' *sil-lah* 'Silla' and possibly *kyezu-lh* 'winter'. This leaves *-nə- of *hanolh* as the adnominal ending, clearly indicating a final vowel.

5 Conclusions

This paper has presented new cognates, including some important verbs, that build a stronger case for K-J common origin. Contrary to recent arguments against K-J, this paper turns weaknesses of past proposals into strengths. Finally, discrete proposals of grammatical reanalysis help us to make sense of how important nominal morphology could be shared between MK and OJ. This paper has considered only a small number of Korean-Japanese etymologies, and a serious defense of the hypothesis entails far more analysis than has been possible in this paper. However, these reconstructions have broader implications for the morphological development of Japanese and Korean, which suggests that more remains to be discovered in the proto-histories of both languages. Going forward, it is important for us to take seriously the possibility that we have thus far underestimated the amount of phonological and semantic shift that has taken place. Regardless of one's stance on the question of Japanese-Korean common origin, it should be clear that comparing these two languages can still teach us a great deal about their history, and that the theory of proto-Korean-Japanese could be stronger than has previously been assumed.

References

Frellesvig, B. 2001. A common Korean and Japanese copula. *Journal of East Asian Linguistics 10*: 1–35.

Frellesvig, B. 2008. On reconstruction of proto-Japanese and pre-Old Japanese verb inflection. *Proto-Japanese: Issues and Prospects*, ed. B. Frellesvig and J. Whitman, 179-198. Amsterdam/Philadelphia: John Benjamins.

Frellesvig, B. 2013. Chronological Layering in proto-Japanese and pre-Old Japanese Verb Inflection. *Studies in Japanese and Korean Linguistics*, ed. B. Frellesvig, J. Kiaer, and J. Wrona, 28-47. Munich: Lincom.

Kinsui, S. 1983. Jōdai, chūko no *wiru* to *wori* - jyōtaika keishiki no suii [*Wiru* and *woru* in Old and Middle Japanese – Transition to a situationalized form]. *Ōsaka daigaku daigakuin bungaku kenkyūka kiyō, 42*: 1-25.

Martin, S. 1966. Lexical Evidence Relating Japanese to Korean. *Language 42.2*: 185-251.

Martin, S. 1987. *The Japanese Language through Time*. New Haven: Yale University Press.

Martin, S. 1996. *Consonant Lenition in Korean and the Macro-Altaic Question*. University of Hawai'i Press: Honolulu.

Nihon Daijiten Kankōkai and Shōgakkan. 2000. *Nihon kokugo daijiten* [Shogakukan's Japanese Dictionary]. Tōkyō:Shōgakkan.

Ramsey, R. and Lee, K.M. 2011. *A History of the Korean Language*. UK: Cambridge University Press.

Nam, K. 1960. *Ko'eo Sajeon* [Dictionary of Ancient Korean]. Donga Publishing: Seoul, Korea.

Unger, J.M. 1993 [1977]. *Studies in Early Japanese Morphophonemics.* Bloomington: IULC.

Unger, J.M. 2009. *The Role of Contact in the Origins of the Japanese and Korean Languages.* Honolulu: University of Hawai'i Press.

Vovin, A. 1993. Long Vowels in Proto-Japanese. *Journal of East Asian Linguistics,* 2, 2: 125-134.

Vovin, A. 2010. *Koreo Japonica: A Re-Evaluation of a Common Genetic Origin.* Honolulu: University of Hawai'i Press.

Whitman, J. 1985. *The Phonological Basis for the Comparison of Japanese and Korean.* Ph.D. Dissertation, Harvard University.

Whitman, J. 1990. A rule of medial *-r- loss in pre-Old Japanese. *Trends in Linguistics, 45*: 512-545.

Whitman, J. 2008. The source of the bigrade conjugation and stem shape in pre-Old Japanese. *Proto-Japanese: Issues and Prospects*, ed. B. Frellesvig and J. Whitman, 163-178. Amsterdam/Philadelphia: John Benjamins.

Whitman, J. 2012. The Relationship of Japanese and Korean. *The Languages of Japan and Korean*, ed. D. Tranter, 24-38. London: Routledge.

Part V

Discourse

Reference in Discourse: The Case of L2 and Heritage Korean

HYUNAH AHN
University of Hawai'i at Mānoa

1 Introduction

This study has two goals: The first is to investigate how referential expressions (null vs. overt NPs) interact with discoursal factors (e.g. topicality) in a null pronoun language and the second is to see how null arguments are processed by overt pronoun language speakers. Specifically, the paper examines how the use of null and overt arguments is influenced by topicality in Korean and how the argument drop pattern in Korean discourse is processed by Korean learners whose native language is English, an overt pronoun language.

Intriguing as the issue may be, taking any form of measurement on a nonexistent element may not be straightforward. The current study attempted to infer the thematic role of a null argument via the interpretations given of an overt argument. The inferred thematic role of a null argument will point to its antecedent, which will shed light on the relationship between referential expressions and topicality in Korean.

Japanese/Korean Linguistics 23.
Edited by Michael Kenstowicz, Theodore Levin and Ryo Masuda.
Copyright © 2016, CSLI Publications

Referential expressions in discourse have a long history of research in many subareas of linguistics. Givenness (Gundel, Hedberg, & Zacharski 1993), accessibility (Almor 1999, 2000; Almor & Eimas 2008), and centeredness (Gordon, Grosz, & Gillom 1993) are some of the factors that previous studies have used to describe how referential expressions take phonologically more costly or less costly forms. The issue has also been of great interest to second language researchers in that the relationship between NP forms and discoursal factors involves both syntax and discourse and has been found to be especially difficult for second language learners, even at near-native levels of proficiency (Sorace & Filliaci 2006).

Most of the studies conducted so far have focused on overt pronoun languages like English (Almor 1999, 2000; Almor & Eimas 2008; Gordon et al. 1993) or on null pronoun languages in which verb inflections reveal information about the grammatical role of the null *pro* (e.g. Italian) (Carminati 2002; Sorace & Filliaci 2006). Research on null pronoun languages without rich verbal agrement systems (e.g. Japanese) has used metalinguistic tasks, the results of which may not reflect second language speakers' actual use of the structures (Ueno & Kehler 2010).

This study uses an ambiguous construction in Korean, a null pronoun language without a rich verbal agreement system, where the interpretation of a sole overt NP can be used to infer the interpretation of the dropped argument, which in turn points to the antecedent of the dropped argument. Using this construction allows the relationship between null arguments and discourse to be investigated. The study also examines the differences between native speakers of Korean (L1ers), English native speakers who learn Korean as a second language (L2ers), and English native speakers who learn Korean as a heritage language (HLers). Comparing the three groups not only sheds light on how a first language with overt pronouns can influence the use of a second language with null pronouns, but also on how speakers who grow up learning both overt and null pronoun languages will differ from those who are exposed in early life to only either a null pronoun language (Korean) or an overt pronoun language (English). In the study, the L1ers showed sensitivity to topicality in using overt and null NPs, whereas the L2ers and the HLers did not. However, what appears to be the same insensitivity in L2ers and HLers may be attributable to different factors.

2 Background

2.1 Syntax-Discourse Interface

Syntax-discourse interface phenomena have been intensively studied due to their relative complexity, which often results in their incomplete acquisition even by L2ers with near-native competence (Sorace 2011; Sorace & Filliaci

2006, inter alia). One of the most well-known studies on the topic of the syntax-discourse interface is by Sorace and Filliaci (2006); they found that near-native L2ers displayed optionality in using null and overt pronouns in Italian. In Italian, the position of the antecedent determines whether a pronoun should be null (1) or overt (2) (Carminati 2002).

> (1) Quando Mario$_i$ ha telefonato a Giovanni, Ø$_i$ aveva appena finito di mangiare.
> When Mario$_i$ has telephoned to Giovanni, Ø$_i$ had just finished eating.
> (2) Quando Mario ha telefonato a Giovanni$_i$, lui$_i$ aveva appena finito di mangiare.
> When Mario has telephoned to Giovanni$_i$, he$_i$ had just finished eating.

Intrasententially, if the antecedent of a pronoun is located in the Spec-IP position, the pronoun is realized covertly, but it is realized overtly if the antecedent is located elsewhere. In (1), the NP in the Spec-IP position of the subordinate clause (*Mario*) is coindexed with the null pronoun (Ø) in the main clause. In (2), on the other hand, the overt pronoun (*lui*) in the main clause is coindexed with an NP that is not Spec-IP (*Giovanni*).

The decision to place a referent in the Spec-IP position or elsewhere is based on discoursal factors (e.g. topicality). Once the position of the antecedent is set, however, the realization of the pronoun either overtly or covertly is directed by the syntax; hence, the syntax-discourse interface. Based on their findings that even near-native L2ers did not interpret the pronouns like native speakers did, Sorace and Filliaci (2006) argued for the difficulty of mastering linguistic phenomena at the syntax-discourse interface: the Interface Hypothesis (cf. Slabakova & Ivanov 2011; White 2011).

Another prominent line of research on the syntax-discourse interface has investigated clitic left dislocation constructions (CLLDs) in Spanish. Montrul (2009) used the examples below (3–4) to explain obligatory clitic doubling when accusative or dative NPs are topicalized. This construction, however, can be used only when the topicalized NP has a specific referent. For nonspecific NPs, the construction is ungrammatical (4).

> (3) a. Juan tiene las carpetas en la oficina.
>   b. Las carpetas *las* tiene Juan en la oficina.
>   c. *Las carpetas tiene Juan en la oficina.
>   the folders *(them) has Juan in the office
>   'Juan has the folders in the office.'
> (4)   *Agua, me gusta tomarla.
>   'Water, I like to drink.'

Because the syntactic decision of doubling a clitic or not involves both specificity (semantics) and topicalization (pragmatics), the complexity of the structure makes it all the more difficult for even highly advanced learners to master. Montrul (2009) argued that Spanish HLers had advantages over L2ers in terms of age of first exposure and the quality of input. Indeed, if only the quantity of input matters in the acquisition of complex structures in the interface of syntax and discourse, the mastery of such interface structures will depend more on proficiency level than learning environment (i.e. heritage vs. L2 environment). If it is the quality of input that makes a difference, however, the language-learning environment may be an important factor. Therefore, comparing L2ers' and HLers' use of a syntax-discourse interface construction will shed light on the question of quantity versus quality of input.

2.2 Centering Theory

The centering theory (Gordon et al. 1993) argues that discourse coherence is maintained by the proper use of pronouns linking the previous discourse to the present and future discourse, using the notion of 'center' to talk about discourse coherence. A backward-looking center (Cb) is an entity that links the current utterance to the previous discourse while a forward-looking center (Cf) is a potential candidate to link the current utterance to the next.

In Example (5), from Gordon et al. (1993), a discourse-initial utterance does not have a Cb but a set of Cfs (5a); all noninitial utterances have a Cb and a set of Cfs (5b-c). The rule is that a Cb should be realized as a pronoun, and using a name (a full NP) for a Cb interferes with discourse processing.

(5) a. Susan gave Betsy a pet hamster.
$Cf = \{Susan, Betsy, hamster_1\}$
b. She reminded her such hamsters were quite shy.
$Cb = Susan, Cf = \{Susan, Betsy, hamsters\}$
c. She asked Betsy whether she liked the gift.
c'. Susan asked her whether she liked the gift.
$Cb = Susan, Cf = \{Susan, Betsy, gift = hamster_1\}$

The comparison of (5c) and (5c') shows that the coherence of the discourse is much more easily maintained when the third sentence is (5c) than when it is (5c'). The center of the discourse is consistent with *Susan* throughout the discourse; therefore, using the name (instead of the pronoun *she*) interferes with the processing of referents. Gordon et al. (1993), through a set of four experiments, showed that English speakers are slowed down in their reaction time when the name of a Cb is repeated (the repeated name penalty).

In Gordon et al.'s (1993) experiments, the realization of an entity either as a repeated name or as a pronoun is not influenced by intrasentential syntactic structures, unlike in Carminati's (2002) study. Extrasententially, the more expansive term 'center' can account for the role of a pronoun in maintaining discourse coherence. In addition, Carminati focused on null and overt pronouns in Italian while Gordon et al. delved into the role of pronouns (compared to full NPs) in English. These two characteristics of the centering theory make it a suitable theory to account for the role of referential expressions in maintaining discourse coherence in a language like Korean, in which an overt pronoun in spoken contexts is very rare and a null pronoun behaves in a very similar way to an unstressed pronoun in English. A parallel between a Korean null pronoun and an unstressed English pronoun can be assumed, as can a parallel between full NPs in Korean and English. The next section will illustrate how the shift of a discourse center can be instantiated in a null argument sentence with psych-predicates in Korean.

2.3   Psych-predicates and Double Nominative Constructions

Belletti and Rizzi (1988) classified psychological verbs into three different categories depending on the grammatical case of their two mandatory arguments: experiencer and stimulus (or theme). The example sentences in (6) are from Landau (2010). A Class I verb requires its experiencer and stimulus to be marked nominative and accusative, respectively, while a Class II verb will have the cases inverted for the two arguments. A Class III verb has a nominative theme and a dative experiencer.

(6)   a.   *Class I*: Nominative experiencer, accusative theme
            John loves Mary.
      b.   *Class II*: Nominative theme, accusative experiencer
            The show amused Bill.
      c.   *Class III*: Nominative theme, dative experiencer
            The idea appealed to Julie.

The Korean psych-predicates used in this study belong to Class III. Canonically, the experiencer should be marked as dative. For example, in (7a) and (7b), the experiencer is marked dative and the stimulus nominative.[1]

(7)   a.   Yenghuy-eykye   Chelswu-ka   mwusewu-n   ka   po-ta.
            Yenghuy-DAT   Chelswu-NOM   scary-ADJ   INF   AUX-DEC
            'To Yenghuy, Chelswu must be scary.'
      b.   Chelswu-eykye   Yenghuy-ka   mwusewu-n   ka   po-ta.
            Chelswu-DAT   Yenghuy-NOM   scary-ADJ   INF   AUX-DEC
            'To Chelswu, Yenghuy must be scary.'

When the context allows (Yang 1999), however, the dative experiencer in Class III Korean psych-predicates (7a-b) can be marked as nominative, which will lead to a double nominative construction (DNC) (8a-b).

(8)   a.   Yenghuy-ka   Chelswu-ka   mwusewu-n   ka   po-ta.
            Yenghuy-NOM   Chelswu-NOM   scary-ADJ   INF   AUX-DEC
            'To Yenghuy, Chelswu must be scary.'
      b.   Chelswu-ka   Yenghuy-ka   mwusewu-n   ka   po-ta.
            Chelswu-NOM   Yenghuy-NOM   scary-ADJ   INF   AUX-DEC
            'To Chelswu, Yenghuy must be scary.'

---

[1] Please note the word order of (7). Canonically, a dative experiencer precedes a nominative stimulus.

c. Yenghuy-ka   ~~Chelswu-ka~~   mwusewu-n   ka   po-ta.
    Yenghuy-NOM   ~~Chelswu-NOM~~   scary-ADJ   INF AUX-DEC
    'Yenghuy must be scared.'
d. ~~Chelswu-ka~~   Yenghuy-ka   mwusewu-n   ka   po-ta.
    ~~Chelswu-NOM~~   Yenghuy-NOM   scary-ADJ   INF AUX-DEC
    'Yenghuy must be scary.'

In DNCs, the word order will imply the thematic role of the two NPs; The experiencer precedes the stimulus. In addition, either (or both) of the arguments can be dropped depending on the context. When the stimulus is dropped from (8a), a one-argument sentence like (8c) will be produced; the omission of the experiencer in (8b) will result in (8d). However, the segmental information alone cannot indicate which argument was dropped. That is, the isolated sentence *Yenghuyka mwusewun ka pota* could mean either (8c) or (8d). The interpretation of the overt argument, which will suggest the interpretation of the null argument, will be based on the context.

The remaining question is what determines which argument will be dropped and which left overt. The hypothesis here is that the omission of either argument will be highly influenced by the centering mechanism of the discourse. Gordon et al. (1993) listed several factors that contribute to making a referent the center of a local discourse but did not pinpoint one most important factor. In this study, I argue that topicality is an important factor, and I will show how the manipulation of topicality[2] can influence the interpretation of the overt NP, hence the interpretation of the null NP.

2.4 Topicality and the Interpretation of an Overt NP

One way to manipulate the centeredness (topicality) of a referent comes from the fact that Cb should be realized as an unstressed pronoun (in English) or a null pronoun (in Korean) and that the use of a name indicates the shift of the center (or the topic) of a local discourse. Thus, an ambiguous sentence such as (8c-d) in different locations within a discourse will lead to different interpretations of the overt and null NPs. For example, a discourse could start with (9). The overt NP *Yenghuy* cannot possibly mean a topic shift (center shift), as there is no previously set topic. Rather, it will indicate a new topic.

(9) Yenghuy-ka   mwusewu-n   ka   po-ta.
     Yenghuy-NOM   scary-ADJ   INF   AUX-DEC

The question now is whether native speakers of Korean will start a story topicalizing an experiencer or a stimulus. According to Dowty (1991), experiencer and stimulus have proto-thematic roles of agent and patient, respectively. Given that agentivity plays an important role in topichood, one can assume that *Yenghuy* in this sentence will be used as an experiencer

---

[2] From here on, the terms *topicality* and *centeredness* will be used interchangeably.

REFERENCE IN DISCOURSE: THE CASE OF L2 AND HERITAGE KOREAN / 339

discourse-initially. At the end of a discourse, however, an existing topic is most likely to be continued, and the proto-agent experiencer will not have as high a chance of being overtly stated as in the beginning of a discourse. This will more likely lead to the interpretation of the overt NP as a stimulus.

If a Korean speaker is given the task of simply building a story on the sentence in (9), s/he could come up with a story where the overt NP *Yenghuy* could be interpreted either as an experiencer or as a stimulus. However, if the task is to start a story with the sentence (10a), the overt NP will more likely be used as an experiencer. If the task is to end a story with the same sentence, as in (10c), a stimulus interpretation is more likely. In the middle of a discourse, as in (10b), the choice to interpret the overt NP as either experiencer or stimulus will be at chance level.

(10) a. Create a story that starts with the following sentence:
   Yenghuyka mwusewun ka pota. _____
   _____

   b. Create a story that has the following sentence in the middle:
   _____. *Yenghuyka mwusewun*
   ka pota. _____

   c. Create a story that ends with the following sentence:
   _____
   _____. *Yenghuyka mwusewun ka pota.*

This study aims to investigate if the hypotheses in (11) can be verified for Korean L1ers and if the expected interpretations in each discourse location will be borne out by L2ers and HLers, who are exposed to different quantities and qualities of input. As studies on near-native L2ers and HLers have shown, these groups have difficulty distinguishing syntactic structures that vary with regard to a discourse factor (e.g. topicality) (Montrul 2009; Sorace & Filliaci 2006). The L2ers and HLers in this study are expected to show such difficulty as well.

(11) Hypothesis 1: Discourse-initially, the overt NP of an ambiguous construction such as that in (9) will be interpreted as an experiencer more often than as a stimulus, and the rate of the experiencer interpretation will decrease as the position of the critical sentence moves toward the end of the discourse.

Hypothesis 2: L2ers and HLers will not show significant differences in their interpretations of the overt NP in the three sentence locations.

3   Method

3.1   Participants

Twenty-seven Korean L1ers with less than five years' length of residence (LOR) in any non-Korean-speaking country were recruited. Nineteen

Korean L2ers and seventeen Korean HLers were also recruited. The mean age of the L2 group was twenty-nine, and of the HL group, twenty-five. Participants' LORs in Korea varied from three weeks to sixteen years; the two groups' mean LORs in Korea were significantly different, with L2ers (3.5 years) spending more time in Korea than HLers (1.5 years) $(t(30) = 2.14, p < .05)$.

3.2 Proficiency

The significantly different LORs of the two groups, however, did not indicate a significant difference in proficiency.[3] A Korean C-test (Lee-Ellis 2009) was used to measure participants' proficiency. The C-test was scored using Rasch Analysis (Bond & Fox 2007) to compute an index called 'person ability' that indicates a true interval between test-takers, which cannot be estimated by the mere raw number of right answers on a test. The person ability measures ranged from -3.96 to 2.96 ($\mu = 0.62$, $\sigma = 1.56$) and a Welch's two-sample t-test showed that the two groups were not significantly different in proficiency ($t(31) = 1.14, p = 0.27$).

All L2 and HL participants were put into three proficiency groups based on their person ability measures. The advanced group comprised participants with a person ability measure higher than 1.4 (L2ers: $N = 9$, HLers: $N = 6$); the intermediate group was made up of those whose measures were between 1.4 and -0.16 (L2ers: $N = 7$, HLers: $N = 5$); and the low proficiency group included those whose measures were below -0.16 (L2ers: $N = 3$, HLers: $N = 6$).

3.3 Stimuli

A Latin-square design of the eighteen experimental items with the three conditions ensured that each participant would see all items, but no item in more than one condition. Each item included one two-place psych-predicate that would require an experiencer and a stimulus. The psych-predicate was given alongside only one nominative-marked argument that was ambiguous in terms of whether it was an experiencer or a stimulus. The overt NPs were all common first names in Korean, which were carefully selected for their gender neutrality to avoid any bias from gender roles (e.g., a male person might be more easily perceived as a stimulus than as an experiencer of fear). Eighteen fillers with intransitive psych and nonpsych verbs were shuffled in among the experimental items.

---

[3] The discrepancy between LOR and proficiency could be due to the fact that HLers are exposed to the target language (Korean) from an early age without actually visiting Korea.

3.4 Procedure

Each participant first filled out a language background questionnaire. The participant was then seated in a sound-attenuated booth for the experiment session. Audio-recorded instructions were provided along with the written instructions on a computer screen, after which three practice items were given. After the practice session, the experimenter checked the recordings to ensure that there was no mechanical failure and that the participant understood the task. The actual trial session lasted from thirty minutes to one and a half hours, varying to a great degree depending on the participants' proficiency. After the experiment session, the L2ers and HLers took the C-test. Forty minutes maximum was given for the C-test, but most participants finished it within twenty-five minutes.

3.5 Task

As introduced in Section 2.4, the task was to build a story using a given sentence. The sentence was presented on the screen with empty lines that indicated where participants should add their sentences. The empty lines appeared after the critical sentence for the discourse-initial condition (10a), both before and after the critical sentence for the discourse-middle condition (10b), and before the critical sentence in the discourse-final condition (10c). For each item, participants were given the time they needed to come up with a story that filled the empty lines. Participants' stories were audio-recorded on the computer.

4 Analysis and Results

4.1 Analysis

The stories were coded according to the participants' interpretation of the critical overt NPs, which the overall contexts created by the participants made clear. (12) presents an example.

(12) a. Ywunswu$_i$ wants to help out Ciweni.

    b. e_i Ciweni-ka   kekcengsulewu-n ka   pwayo.[4]

       e_i Ciweni-NOM worry-ADJ   INF   AUX-DEC-HON

       '(To Ywunswu) <u>Ciweni</u> must be worrisome.'

    c. But Ciweni thinks that s/he can do it on his/her own.

The story shown in (12),[5] with the critical sentence in the middle of the discourse (12b), was created by an L1 participant. Two referents, *Ywunswu* and *Ciweni*, are introduced in the first sentence, and the next sentence starts with *Ciweni*. Because *kekcengsulewu* 'worry' is a two-place predicate, it

---

[4] The null pro marker *e* is added here to help readers understand how (12b) was interpreted by the Korean L1ers.

[5] The sentences in (12a) and (12c) were said in Korean by the participant, but to save space are presented here in English translation only.

requires both an experiencer and a stimulus regardless of whether both are overtly realized or not. The last sentence *But Ciweni thinks that s/he can do it on his/her own* makes it clear that *Ciweni* is not the experiencer of *worry* but the stimulus, and the dropped experiencer of (12b) is *Ywunswu*.

As this explanation of (12) demonstrates, the interpretation of the overt NP was inferred from the general context, and each story was coded for the thematic role of the overt NP and the discourse location of the critical sentence. Any item in which the interpretation of the overt NP was unclear or ambiguous was removed from the data analysis. With sentence location as a fixed factor and participants and items as random factors, a logistic mixed effects model was built to compute the ratio of experiencer reading in each discourse location.

4.2   Results

4.2.1   Sentence Location and Overt NP Interpretation

As hypothesized (11a), the overt NP in the discourse-initial condition was interpreted by the L1ers as an experiencer 91% of the time, and the experiencer reading showed a decrease in the discourse-middle condition (79%) and in the discourse-final condition (72%) (Figure 1).

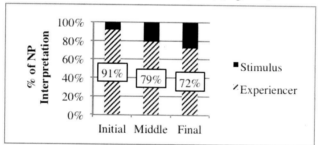

Figure 1. L1ers' overt NP interpretation

A nonlinear logistic mixed effects model showed that, for the L1ers, the effect of sentence location was significant in both the discourse-middle and discourse-final conditions (Table 1).

	Estimate	Std. Error	Z-value	Pr (>|z|)	
(Intercept)	3.63	0.57	6.41	0.00	***
Middle	-1.52	0.42	-3.66	0.00	***
Final	-2.03	0.41	-4.95	0.00	***

Table 1. Logistic mixed effects model of L1ers' overt NP interpretation

As Hypothesis 2 (11b) predicted, L2ers and HLers did not show sensitivity to sentence location in interpreting the overt NP in critical sentences; for L2ers, the decrease in the experiencer interpretation was not statistically significant in any condition ($p < 1$). For HLers, the decrease was significant only in the discourse-final condition ($p < .05$) (Figure 3). However, the data cannot explain why a significant decrease was not shown in the discourse-middle condition.

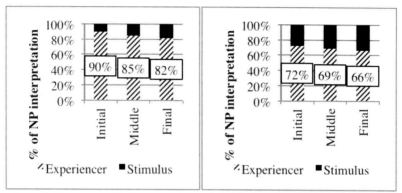

Figure 2. L2ers' overt NP interpretation   *Figure 3*. HLers' overt NP interpretation

4.2.2 Language Group and Overt NP Interpretation

The three language groups' overall rates of the experiencer reading, regardless of sentence location, differed numerically. The mean rate of experiencer reading across the three conditions in L1ers was 81%; in L2ers, it was 85%; and in HLers, 69%. The twelve–percentage point difference between L1ers and HLers, however, widens when only the upper level participants are included in the analysis. Figure 4 lists all HL participants in the order of proficiency. The participant on the leftmost side of the x-axis has the lowest proficiency and the one on the rightmost side has the highest. When the lowest proficiency group ($N = 6$) is eliminated from the analysis,[6] the rate of the experiencer reading in HLers goes down to 60%. This tendency is noteworthy in that the L2ers behave more like the L1ers than do the HLers, whereas previous findings have shown that HLers have an advantage over L2ers from higher quantity and quality of input (Montrul 2009). This matter will be further discussed in Section 5.

4.2.3 Proficiency and Overt NP Interpretation

With regard to proficiency, two interesting observations were made. One is that when advanced L2ers and HLers are grouped together, they seem to behave like L1ers, as they show a significant decrease in the experiencer reading by sentence location. The other is that HLers show an inverse correlation between the rate of experiencer reading and proficiency.

---

[6] The rationale for the elimination of the lowest proficiency learners is that these learners might not have benefited much from their status as heritage learners; their low proficiency indicates insufficient exposure to speech input from their parents/caregivers.

Regardless of the language group, advanced learners showed more sensitivity to sentence location. The advanced group (N = 16; 9 L2ers and 7 HLers) showed a decrease in the experiencer reading in both the discourse-middle and discourse-final conditions (p < .01), but, as with the L1ers, the difference between the discourse-middle and discourse-final conditions was not significant (p = .82). Before interpreting this seemingly native speaker–like performance in terms of the possible role of input quantity, which is expected to be larger in higher proficiency learners, one should note that advanced L2ers alone showed a difference in rates of experiencer reading only between discourse-initial and discourse-final conditions. Advanced HLers, on the other hand, showed a difference only between discourse-initial and discourse-middle conditions. That is, the apparently significant difference between discourse-initial and discourse-middle conditions and between discourse-initial and discourse-final conditions in the advanced group does not correctly represent the overall advanced group but may be an artifact of putting the two language groups together.

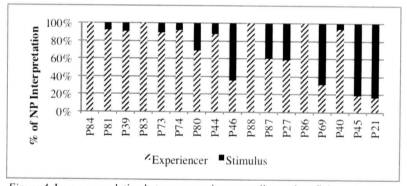

Figure 4. Inverse correlation between experiencer reading and proficiency in HLers

Looking at the HLers' individual data led to the interesting observation that the HLers' proficiency and rates of experiencer reading were inversely correlated. As explained before, on the x-axis in Figure 4 are listed all HL participants in the order of the least proficient to the most proficient from left to right. As the striped portion of each bar indicates, the participant with the lowest proficiency (P84) interpreted overt NPs as experiencers 100% of the time, while the participant with the highest proficiency (P21) did so only 17% of the time. This inverse correlation was significant (r = −.40, p < .000) and such a relationship was not observed in L2ers.

5   Discussion

Neither L2ers nor HLers showed sensitivity to sentence location in interpreting the overt NP in the null argument psych-predicate double nominative construction. The results could be interpreted as indicating that both L2ers and HLers (even at advanced levels) have not fully acquired the subtle phenomenon at the syntax-discourse interface tested by manipulating sentence location to modulate the topicality of the target overt NP. The results of this study seem to be in line with earlier findings from Sorace and Filliaci (2006) and Montrul (2009).

However, it is important not to overlook the fact that L1ers themselves, despite showing a significant decrease in the experiencer reading by sentence location, also showed quite a high rate of the experiencer reading even in the discourse-final condition. For topicality to be a decisive factor in the interpretation of the overt NP (i.e. experiencer for a new topic or topic shift, and stimulus for topic continuation), the rate of the stimulus reading in the discourse-final condition should have been higher than was found.

The current results can be attributed to the experimental design. The task was for participants to build a story with a given sentence in the beginning, in the middle, or at the end. Because the very first NP the participants read on the screen was the critical overt NP, they topicalized the critical NP regardless of the location of the sentence within the discourse and repeated full NPs even when there was no topic shift. About 11% of the time in the discourse-middle condition and 25% of the time in the discourse-final condition, participants used the experiencer reading when there was no topic shift.[7] This artifact of the experimental design weakens the claim that topicality plays an important role in the interpretation of the overt NP, and hence, the inferred interpretation of the null argument. A future study should pursure a method that can address this issue.

What is noteworthy in this study, however, is the inverse correlation found between the rate of experiencer reading and proficiency in HLers. There are two possible accounts for this observation: the quality of input and L1 transfer.

Despite the clear relationship between proficiency and overt NP interpretation in HLers, proficiency alone cannot fully account for the phenomenon. HLers are also exposed to more naturalistic speech input compared to L2ers, whose language learning experience largely occurs in the instructional environment. Thus, it is safe to assume that L2ers and HLers differ both in the quantity and quality of input. If only the quantity of input mattered, L2ers would have shown the same inverse correlation between experiencer reading and proficiency, which was not the case. Also, it is possible that low proficiency HLers and most L2ers, who all preferred the experiencer reading, may not even be aware that these constructions

---

[7] The stimulus reading for topic shift, however, was used in less than 1% of all trials.

allow a stimulus reading. If that is the case, it would be the quality of input that made the difference between the advanced HLers and the rest of the HL and L2 participants.

Another account is possible when the three language groups are compared in terms of the overall rates of experiencer reading. L1ers, L2ers, and HLers interpreted the overt NP as an experiencer 81%, 85%, and 69% of the time, respectively. Although the L2ers seem to have behaved more similarly to the L1ers than the HLers did, one should consider what the underlying representation for the ambiguous construction at issue here would be in each language group. The underlying structure of the Korean psych-predicates in this study requires a dative experiencer and a nominative stimulus as in (6c). The English equivalents of such psych-predicates, however, belong to Class II according to Belletti and Rizzi's (1988) classification. For example, *kekcengsulewun* in Korean can be translated into English as either *worried* or *worrying* (= *worrisome*), both of which are derived from *worry*, a two-place psych-verb that takes a nominative stimulus and an accusative experiencer (6b). These verbs are often passivized in English, and the sole overt NP in the passivized sentence is always an experiencer. Without passivization, both arguments are obligatorily overt. Thus, if L2ers resort to their L1 grammar (i.e. use the underlying structure of Class II English psych-verbs) in interpreting the critical NP in Korean, it is natural that they read it as an experiencer.

The quite high rate of the stimulus reading observed in the HLers, however, indicates their understanding that the stimulus of such psych-predicates can be marked nominative without resorting to the passivization of a Class II structure; that is, they understand that the psych-predicates in the study belong to Class III. What they do not understand, however, seems to be the fact that a dative experiencer can be marked nominative, too. Ahn (2012) showed that a nominative marked stimulus is preferred by L1ers when there is no topic shift. Therefore, at least the HLers' use of the stimulus reading can be safely argued to be like that of the L1ers despite their lack of understanding that topicality can influence the interpretation of the overt NP.

Neither the L2ers nor the HLers showed significant sensitivity to topicality in interpreting the overt NP, from which the interpretation of the null argument could be inferred. However, because they may have different underlying representations of the critical construction in the study, it is difficult to determine whether the two groups' insensitivity comes from the same sources. A future study will have to ensure that the constructions used to test the relationship between topicality and argument-drop patterns have the same underlying representations in both L2 and HL grammar.

References

Ahn, H. 2012. Prosodic Boundaries and Null Arguments in L2 Korean. *Proceedings of the 36th Annual Boston University Conference on Language Development*, vol. 1, ed. A. K. Biller, E. Y. Chung, & A. E. Kimball, 29–41. Sommerville, MA: Cascadilla Press.

Almor, A. 1999. Noun-Phrase Anaphora and Focus: The Informational Load Hypothesis. *Psychological Review 106* (4): 748–65.

Almor, A. 2000. Constraints and Mechanisms in the Theories of Anaphor Processing. *Proceedings of Architectures and Mechanisms for Language Processing 2000*, ed. M. J. Pickering, C. Clifton Jr., & M. Crocker, 1–15. Cambridge, UK: Cambridge University Press.

Almor, A., & P. D. Eimas. 2008. Focus and Noun Phrase Anaphors in Spoken Language Comprehension. *Language and Cognitive Processes 23* (2): 201–25.

Belletti, A., & L. Rizzi. 1988. Psych-verbs and θ-theory. *Natural Language & Linguistic Theory 6* (3): 291–352.

Bond, T. G., & C. M. Fox. 2007. *Applying the Rasch Model: Fundamental Measurement in the Human Sciences* (2nd ed.). New York: Routledge.

Carminati, M. N. 2002. The Processing of Italian Subject Pronouns. Doctoral dissertation, University of Massachusetts, Amherst, MA.

Dowty, D. 1991. Thematic Proto-roles and Argument Selection. *Language 67* (3): 547–619.

Gordon, P. C., B. J. Grosz, & L. A. Gillom. 1993. Pronouns, Names and the Centering of Attention in Discourse. *Cognitive Science 17*: 311–47.

Gundel, J. K., N. Hedberg, & R. Zacharski. 1993. Cognitive Status and the Form of Referring Expressions in Discourse. *Language 69* (2): 274–307.

Landau, I. 2010. *The Locative Syntax of Experiencers*. Cambridge: MIT Press.

Lee-Ellis, S. 2009. The Development and Validation of a Korean C-Test Using Rasch Analysis. *Language Testing 26* (2): 245–74.

Montrul, S. 2009. How Similar Are Adult Second Language Learners and Spanish Heritage Speakers? Spanish Clitics and Word Order. *Applied Psycholinguistics 31* (1): 167–207.

Slabakova, R., & I. Ivanov. 2011. A More Careful Look at the Syntax–Discourse Interface. *Lingua 121* (4): 637–51.

Sorace, A. 2011. Pinning Down the Concept of 'Interface' in Bilingualism. *Linguistic Approaches to Bilingualism 1* (1): 1–33.

Sorace, A., & F. Filliaci. 2006. Anaphora Resolution in Near-native Speakers of Italian. *Second Language Research 22* (3): 339–68.

Ueno, M., & A. Kehler. 2010. The Interpretation of Null and Overt Pronouns in Japanese: Grammatical and Pragmatic Factors. *Proceedings of the 32nd Annual Meeting of the Cognitive Science Society*, ed. S. Ohlsson & R. Catrambone, 2057–62. Austin, TX: Cognitive Science Society.

White, L. 2011. Second Language Acquisition at the Interfaces. *Lingua 121* (4): 577–90.

Yang, D. 1999. Case Features and Case Particles. *Proceedings of the 18th West Coast Conference on Formal Linguistics*, ed. S. Bird, A. Carnie, J. Haugen, & P. Norquest, 626–39. Sommerville, MA: Cascadilla Press.

Part VI

Poster Session Abstracts

Poster Session Abstracts

For this edition of the Japanese/Korean Linguistics proceedings volume, presenters from both the talk and poster sessions of the conference were invited to contribute a paper for their work. The abstracts by authors from the poster session appear below. Their full papers are available on the volume's supplementary webpage at

https://cslipublications.stanford.edu/ja-ko-contents/JK23/

Deconstructing Clause Noun Modifying Constructions

ANNA BUGAEVA
National Institute for Japanese Language and Linguistics
JOHN WHITMAN
National Institute for Japanese Language and Linguistics / Cornell

Comrie (1996) and Matsumoto (1997) argue that in languages such as Japanese and Korean, relative clauses (RCs) and clausal noun complements (NCs) have the same structure. RCs in these and similar prehead relative languages are claimed not to obey island constraints, and to allow a very wide range of relations between the clause and head noun. We demonstrate that prehead RCs and NCs in Japanese, Korean, Ainu, Tundra Nenets, Turkic, and Sakha are systematically distinguished by phenomena such as agreement and N' pronominalization. The apparent violability of islands in these languages is due to independent phenomena, such as the existence of major subject constructions.

Two Types of Accusative Subjects in Japanese

SAYAKA GOTO
University of Maryland

In this paper, I show that Accusative subjects (AS) in Accusative subject constructions in Japanese behave differently depending on the predicate that takes the complement clause. The different behavior can be explained by the present proposal that there are two types of predicates, "think"-type predicates and "conclude"-type predicates, and an AS is base-generated in the embedded clause when the clause is selected by the former, whereas it is base-generated in the matrix clause when the clause is selected by the latter.

The Evolution of /r/ Final Verbs in Korean
TAEWOO KIM
Seoul National University

The morpho-phonology of a language consists of a number of different layers reflecting the phonology of different periods. Most of the theoretical considerations regarding morpho-phonology attempt to account for the irregularities caused by this layering. In this paper I reject such theoretical approaches, and instead return to a historical approach in order to give a substantive explanation. The irregularity of Korean /r/-final verbs are analyzed in terms of a "timing gap" between the sound change and the morphological change.

When Months Are Numbered While Days Are Not: Korean Children's Acquisition of Time Words
NIAN LIU
University of Oklahoma
YU KYOUNG SHIN
Sogang University

In this study we show that Korean-speaking children acquire the numerical naming system of the months of the year (MOY) at an earlier stage than their mastering of the arbitrary naming system of the days of the week (DOW), despite the fact that MOY is of lower daily-use frequency. The result indicates that the use of pre-acquired simple numeric sequence in time words facilitates the early mastery of time concepts, providing support for the hypothesis that symbolic system (such as language) has an effect on children's acquisition of concept systems (such as time), even within a single language system.

Doubly-Oriented Secondary Predicates in Japanese
MIKINARI MATSUOKA
University of Yamanashi

The paper studies adjectival secondary predicates in Japanese that describe a personal taste of the referent of the object argument from the perspective of the subject argument, focusing on the question of how they are associated with the two arguments. By providing data indicating that these secondary predicates are generated in the complement domain of V, it is argued that they are construed with the object by forming a complex predicate with V. On the other hand, the secondary predicates are claimed to be connected to the subject by having a control relation via thematic roles.

Prosodic Focus and Nominative/Accusative Alternation in Japanese

SATOSHI NAMBU
National Institute for Japanese Language and Linguistics
HYUN KYUNG HWANG
National Institute for Japanese Language and Linguistics

This paper discusses a case alternation between nominative and accusative on objects in Japanese, particularly focusing on a relationship between adjacency and prosodic focus. After confirming the effect of adjacency between an object and its predicate, we conducted a perception experiment using varied prosodic contours that represent different focus positions. The results suggest that nominative objects were rated high when it receives prosodic focus. On the contrary, accusative objects were rated high when prosodic focus was on a preverbal element due to the default focus assignment.

Korean ECM Constructions and Cyclic Linearization

DONGWOO PARK
University of Maryland, College Park

In this paper, I suggest that, under Fox and Pesetsky's (2005) Cyclic Linearization (CL), a FP must exist between vP and VP, and that FP provides a place for the shifted object, the accusative-marked ECM subject, and some manner adverbs. I also propose that the ECM subject moving out of embedded CP to an A-position in the matrix clause, must not pass through the embedded Spec, CP, which is explained by adopting CL, while rejecting the PIC. This circumvents improper movement that would be induced if the ECM subject moved to the matrix clause through the embedded Spec, CP.

Scope and Disjunction Feed an Even More Argument for Argument Ellipsis in Japanese

YUTA SAKAMOTO
University of Connecticut

In this paper, I provide novel data on null arguments in Japanese, and argue that they can only be handled by Oku's (1998) argument ellipsis. Specifically, I show that the interpretation produced by the interaction of null arguments with scope and disjunction favors the argument ellipsis analysis over the major alternative analyses such as Kuroda's (1965) empty pronoun analysis and Otani and Whitman's (1991) V-stranding VP-ellipsis, which seems to necessitate the availability of argument ellipsis in Japanese. Although null elements are difficult to investigate due to their emptiness, I provide some tools to investigate the nature of them.

A Feature Inheritance Approach Towards Head-Final Languages

Ji Young Shim
Université de Genève

The present study develops Chomsky's feature inheritance into a full-fledged system to account for language variation, and proposes that feature inheritance is regulated by two principles and governed by three operational rules, which are at play both in the C-T and the v-Asp domains. It will be shown that languages differ from one another with respect to EPP-specifications on the features on C and v, and feature valuation on C and v via feature inheritance accounts for the word order contrast between the head-final structure of Japanese and Korean and the head-initial structure of English.

How Differing Phonetic Realizations Influence Perception of Personal Characteristics: Speech Perception and Vowel Variations in Seoul Korean

So Young Yi
University of Hawai'i at Mānoa

The current study aims to examine how people perceive speaker's personal cahracteristics depending on vowel variations in Seoul Korean. Thirty Seoul Korean speakers participated in the matched-guise test to evaluate 12 characteristics of each stimuli speaker. The results show that the raised variant [u] influences the way participants perceive some of the speaker's characteristics including sincerity, conservativeness, outgoingness, economic class, masculinity and cuteness. The different vowel variations also interact with speaker's age or listener's age. Moreoever, in addition to the vowel raising, speaker's age appears to be another crucial factor that affects listener's judgment.